Ayu Watanabe

L♥DK

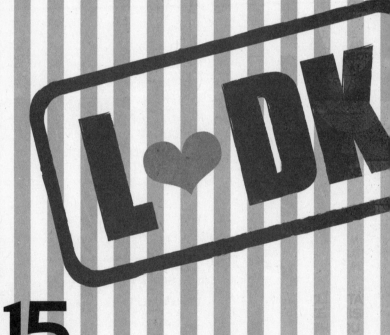

15

L♥DK

Ayu Watanabe

15

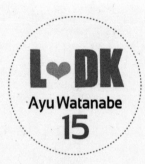

contents

L♥DK

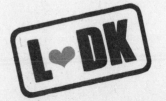

#57 Wall Fantasista

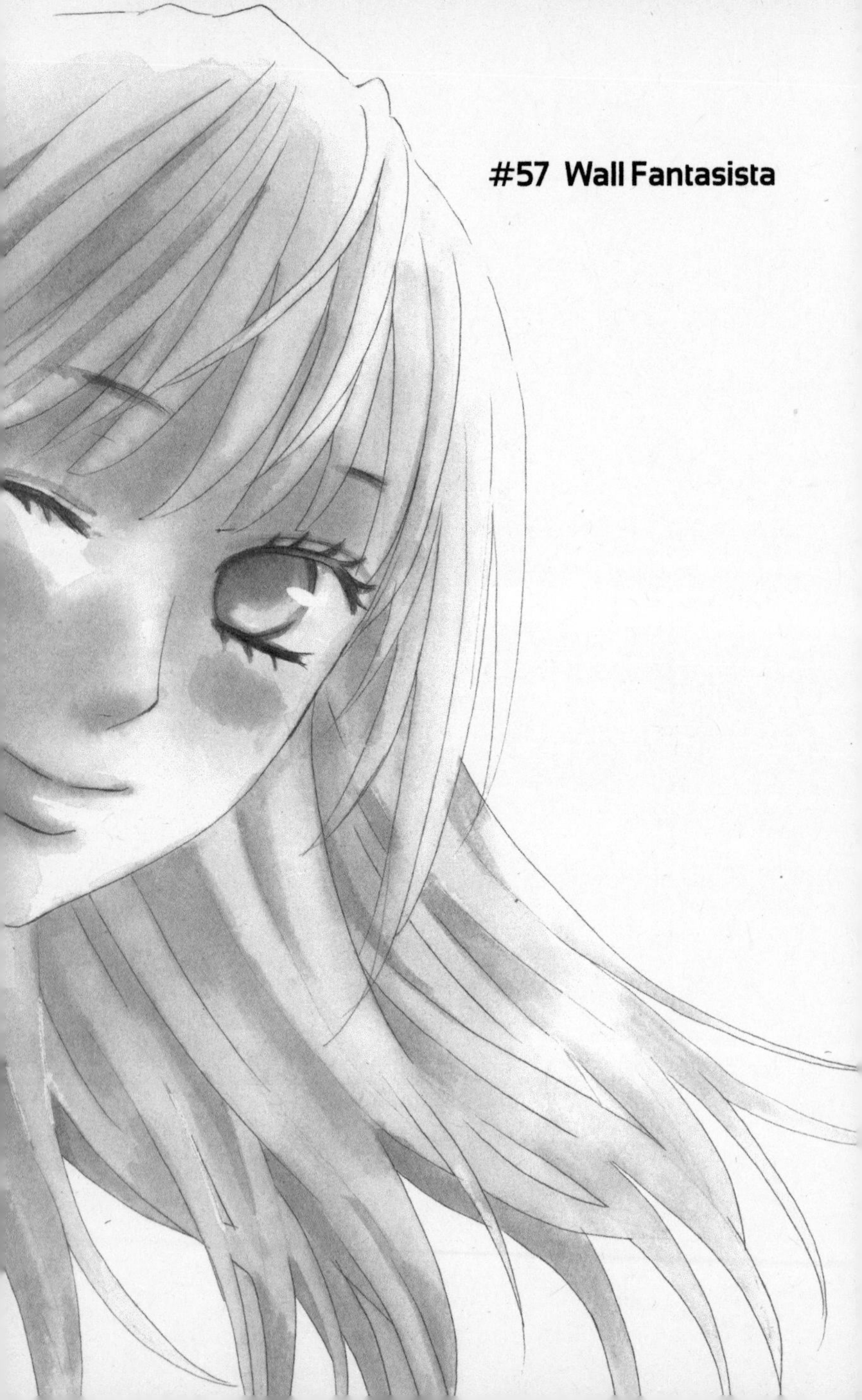

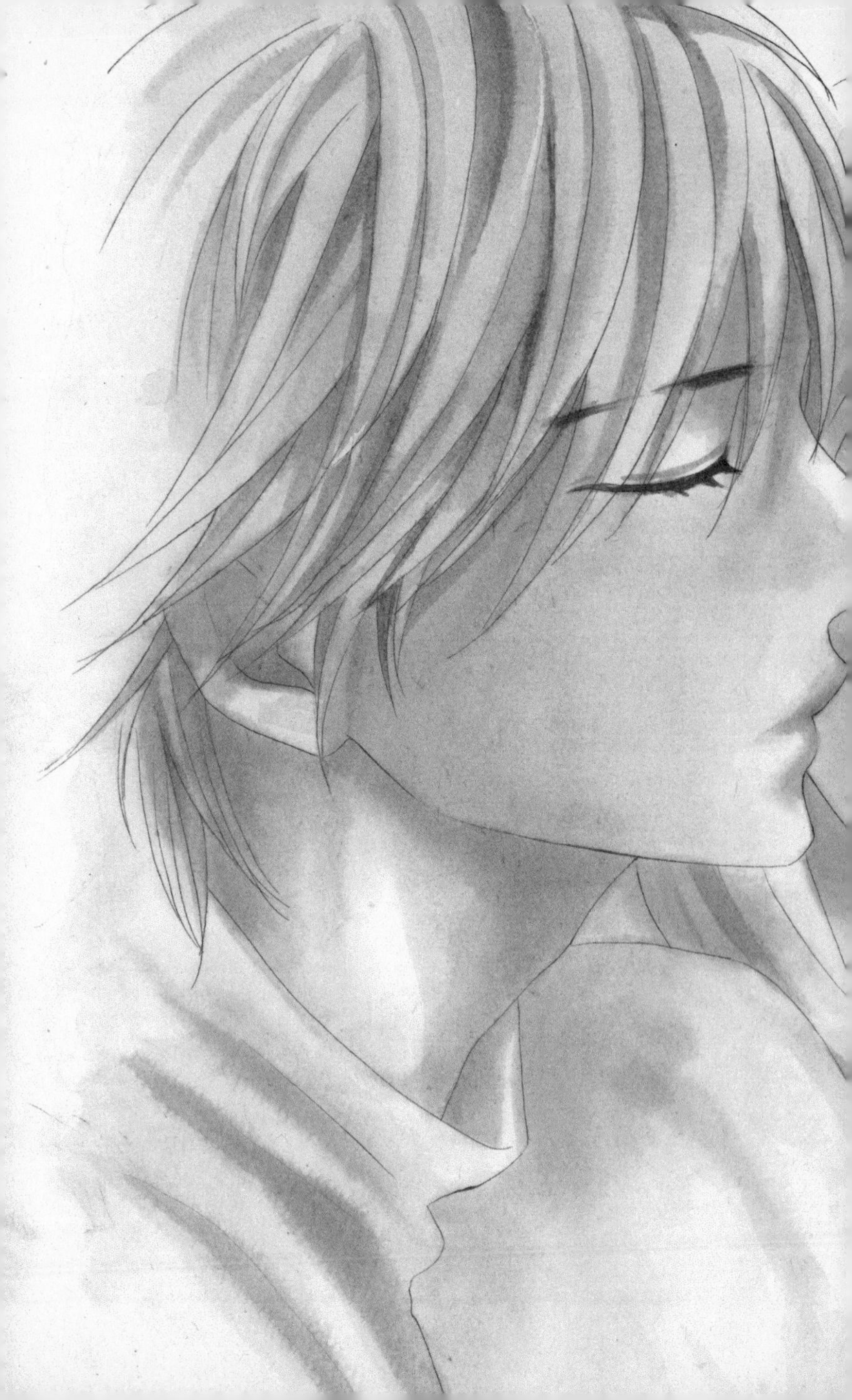

STREET POLICE-SAMA!

Street Police-sama!
An "otome" game that Aoi is obsessed with. The player acts the part of Nadeshiko, a rookie cop who helps tackle an unsolved mystery with her commanding officers, including the handsome Takuya.

Story So Far

L♥DK

Story

Since her parents had to move for work, Aoi has lived on her own while she finishes high school. But before long, she finds herself sharing her apartment with the school hottie: Shusei! While Shusei gives her a hard time, knowing he has her wrapped around his finger, Aoi comes to know his gentler side and his tragic past. At long last, the two become a proper couple. But when her father finds out about their living situation, he declares he'll only allow it to continue under the condition that they don't engage in any sexual relations until graduation. But will they be able to hold up their end of the bargain...?!

Cast

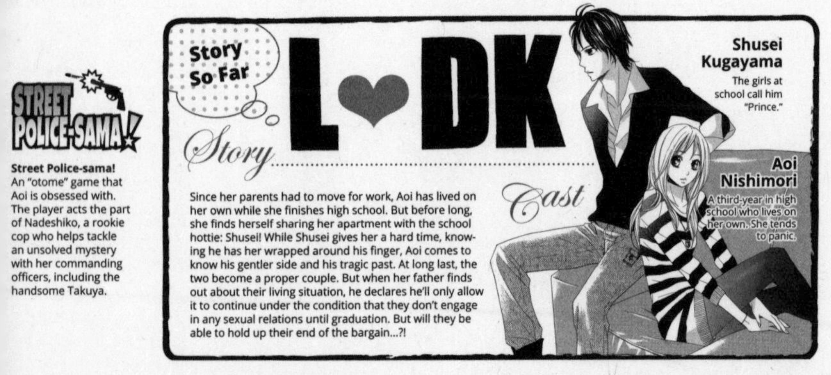

Shusei Kugayama
The girls at school call him "Prince."

Aoi Nishimori
A third-year in high school who lives on her own. She tends to panic.

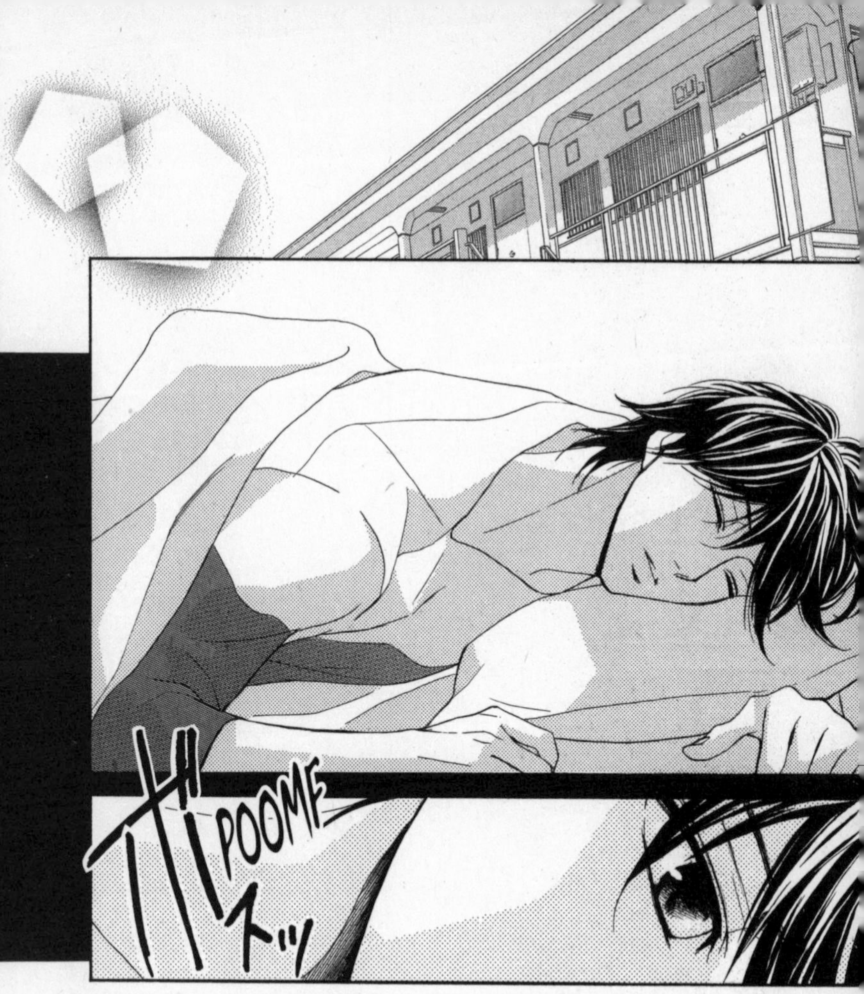
POOME

L♥DK

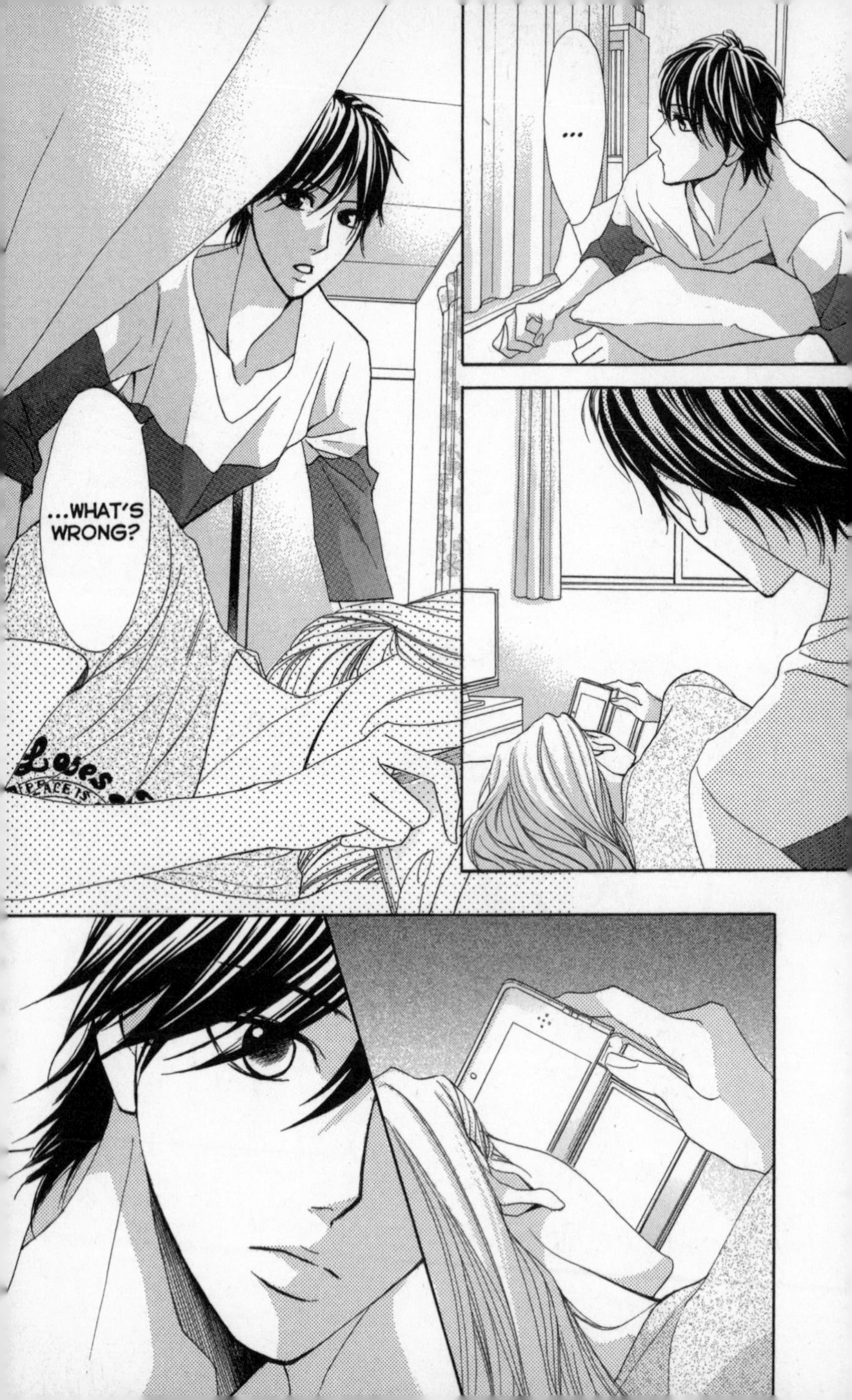
...
...WHAT'S WRONG?

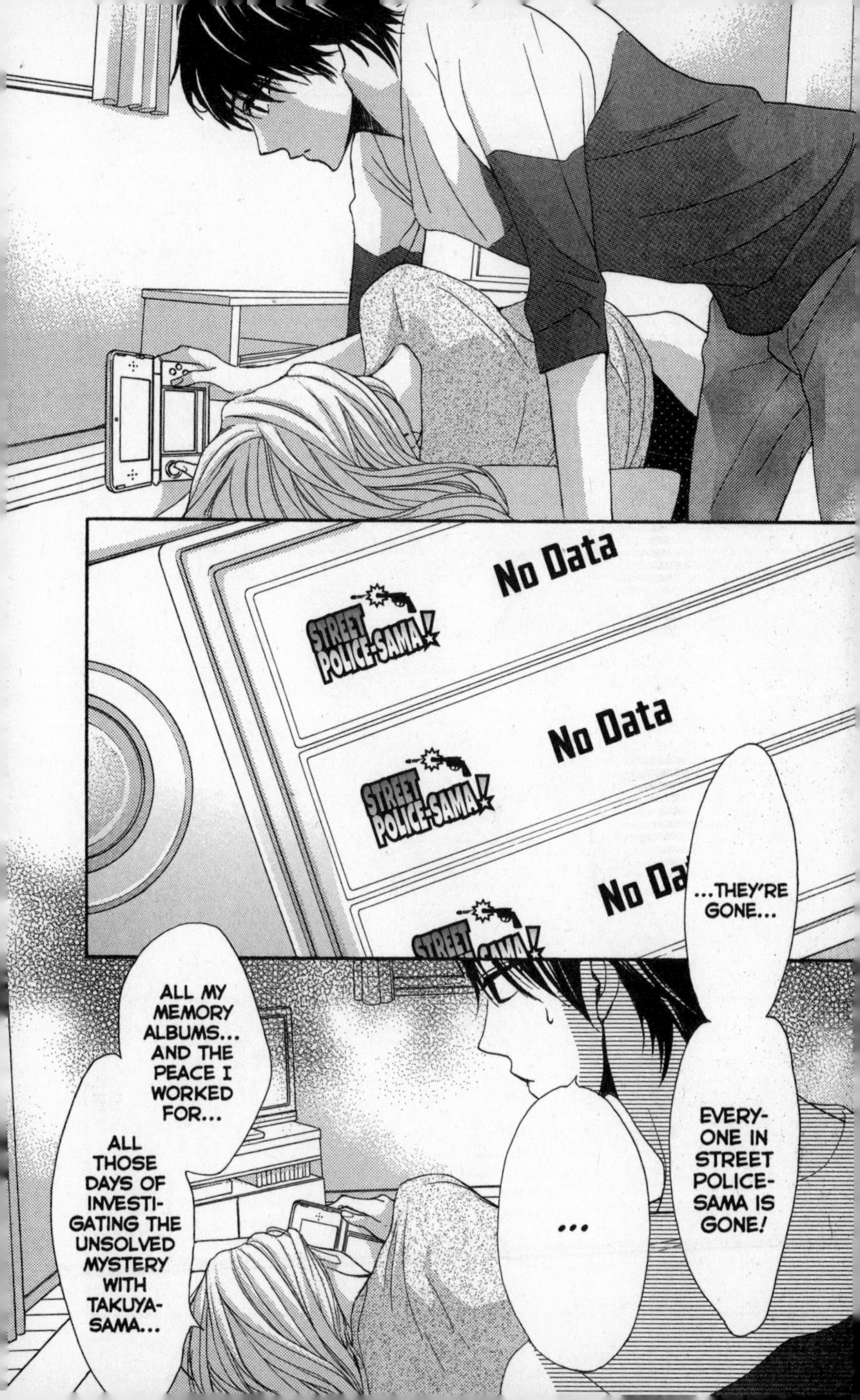
No Data
STREET POLICE-SAMA!
No Data
STREET POLICE-SAMA!
...THEY'RE GONE...
EVERYONE IN STREET POLICE-SAMA IS GONE!
...
ALL MY MEMORY ALBUMS... AND THE PEACE I WORKED FOR...
ALL THOSE DAYS OF INVESTIGATING THE UNSOLVED MYSTERY WITH TAKUYA-SAMA...

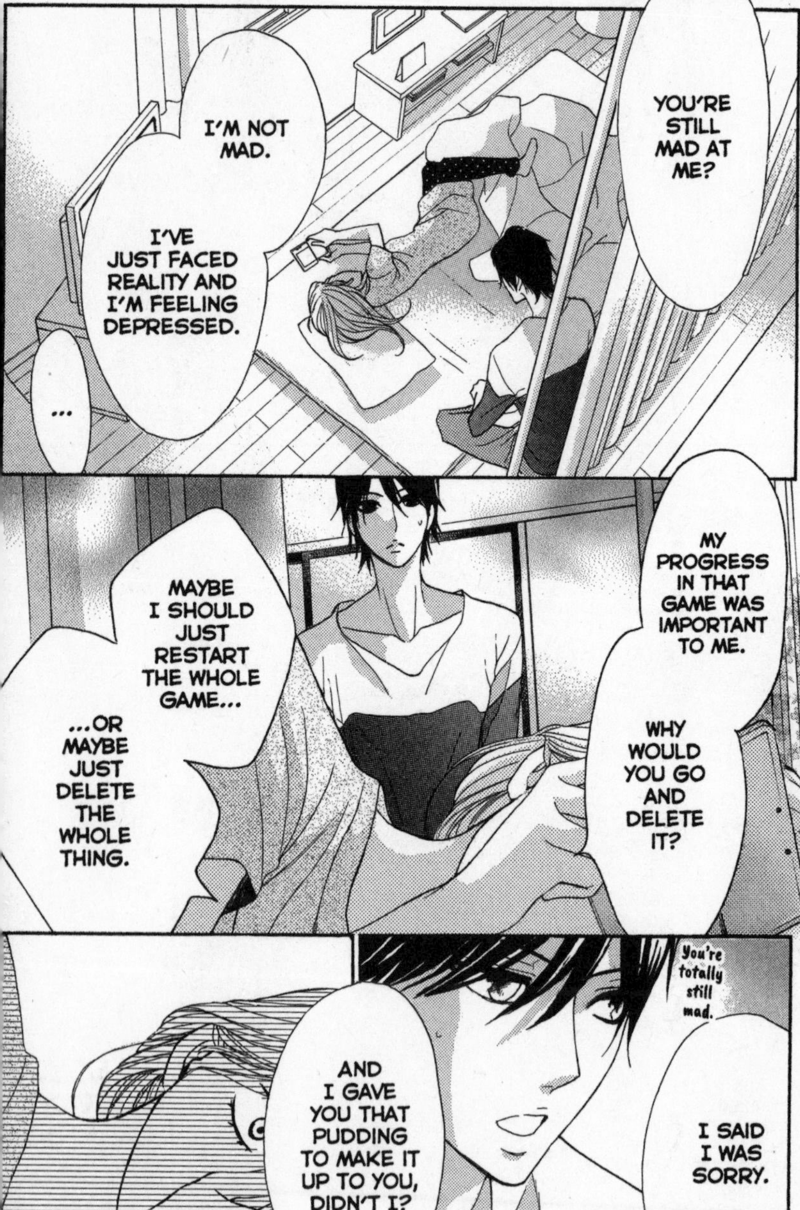

YOU'RE STILL MAD AT ME?
I'M NOT MAD.
I'VE JUST FACED REALITY AND I'M FEELING DEPRESSED.
...
MY PROGRESS IN THAT GAME WAS IMPORTANT TO ME.
WHY WOULD YOU GO AND DELETE IT?
MAYBE I SHOULD JUST RESTART THE WHOLE GAME...
...OR MAYBE JUST DELETE THE WHOLE THING.
You're totally still mad.
I SAID I WAS SORRY.
AND I GAVE YOU THAT PUDDING TO MAKE IT UP TO YOU, DIDN'T I?

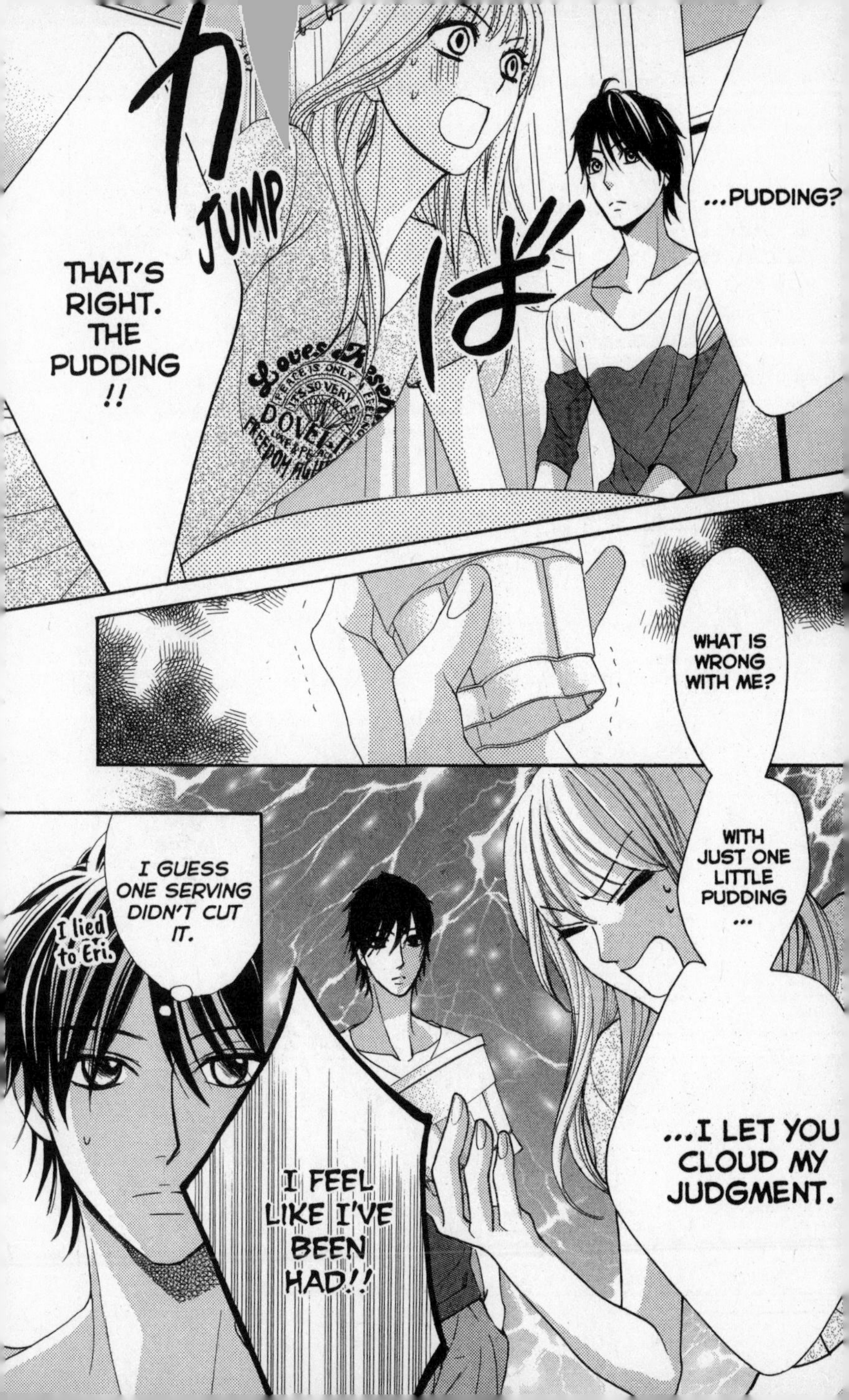
...PUDDING?
JUMP
THAT'S RIGHT. THE PUDDING!!
WHAT IS WRONG WITH ME?
WITH JUST ONE LITTLE PUDDING...
...I LET YOU CLOUD MY JUDGMENT.
I FEEL LIKE I'VE BEEN HAD!!
I GUESS ONE SERVING DIDN'T CUT IT.
I lied to Eri.

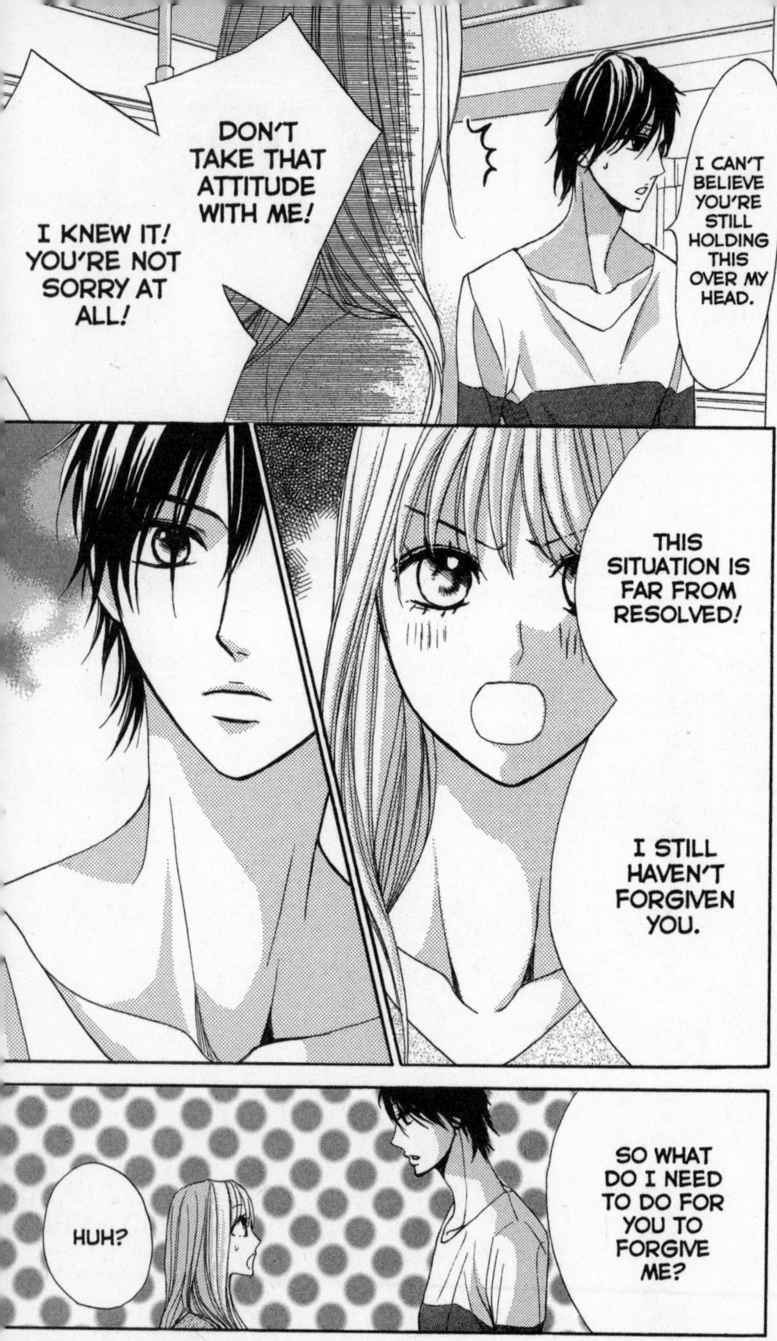
I CAN'T BELIEVE YOU'RE STILL HOLDING THIS OVER MY HEAD.
DON'T TAKE THAT ATTITUDE WITH ME!
I KNEW IT! YOU'RE NOT SORRY AT ALL!
THIS SITUATION IS FAR FROM RESOLVED!
I STILL HAVEN'T FORGIVEN YOU.
SO WHAT DO I NEED TO DO FOR YOU TO FORGIVE ME?
HUH?

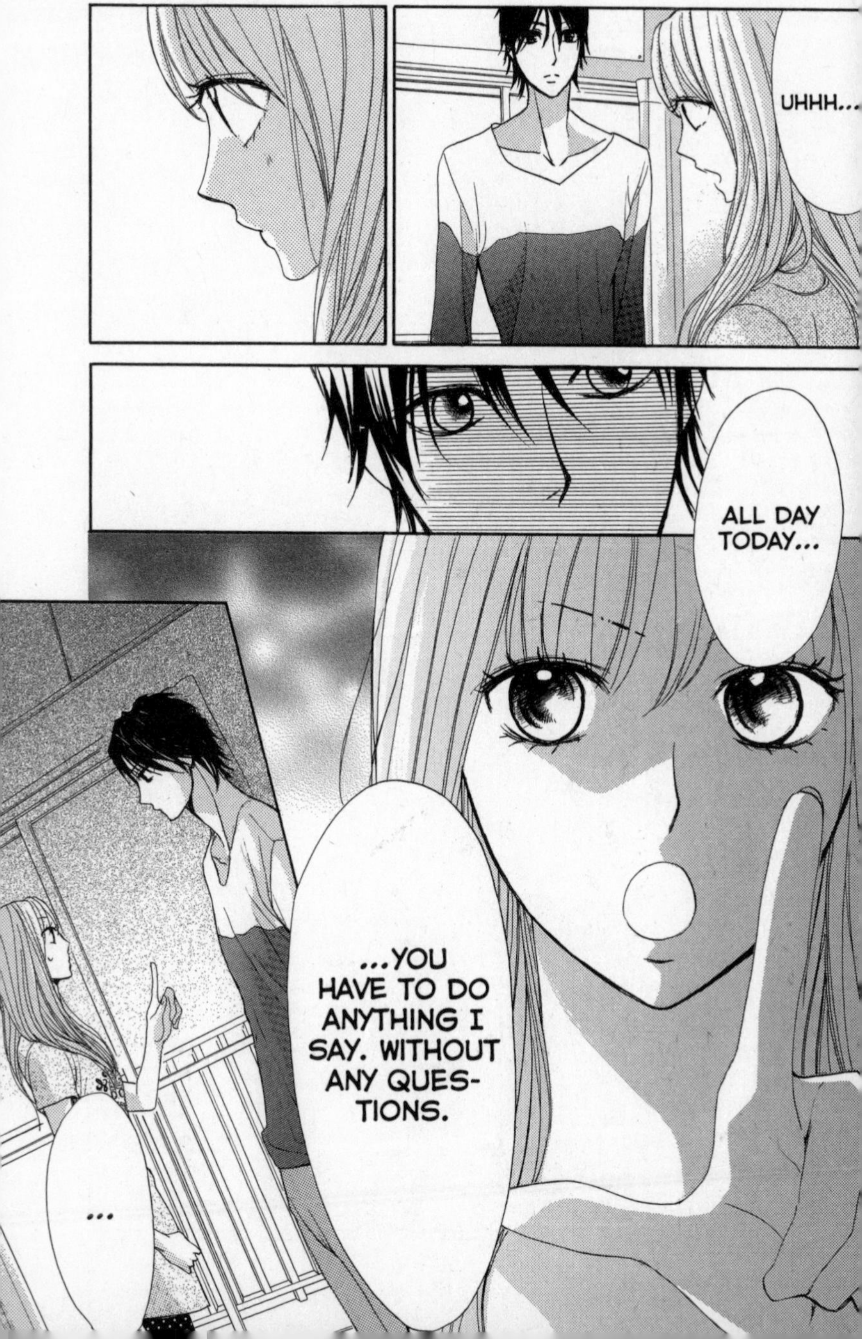
UHHH...
ALL DAY TODAY...
...YOU HAVE TO DO ANYTHING I SAY. WITHOUT ANY QUES-TIONS.
...

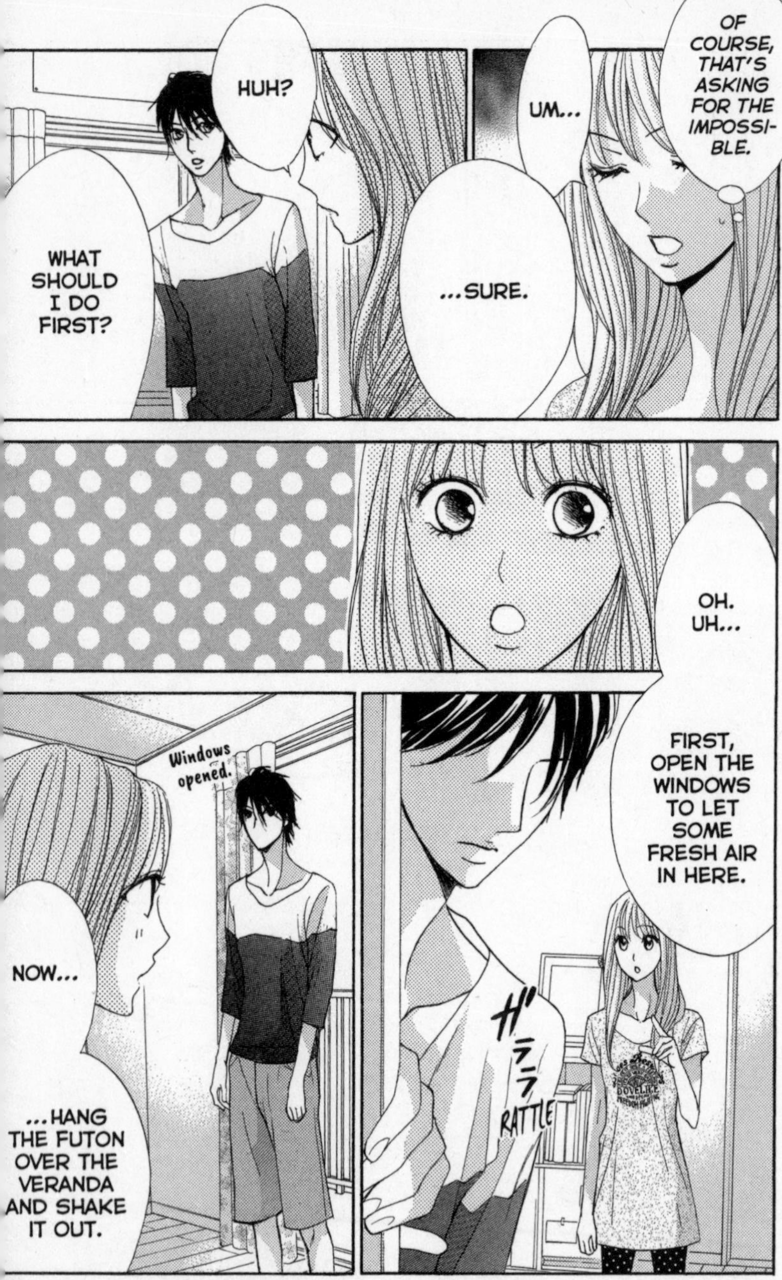
OF COURSE, THAT'S ASKING FOR THE IMPOSSIBLE.
UM...
...SURE.
HUH?
WHAT SHOULD I DO FIRST?
OH. UH...
FIRST, OPEN THE WINDOWS TO LET SOME FRESH AIR IN HERE.
RATTLE
Windows opened.
NOW...
...HANG THE FUTON OVER THE VERANDA AND SHAKE IT OUT.

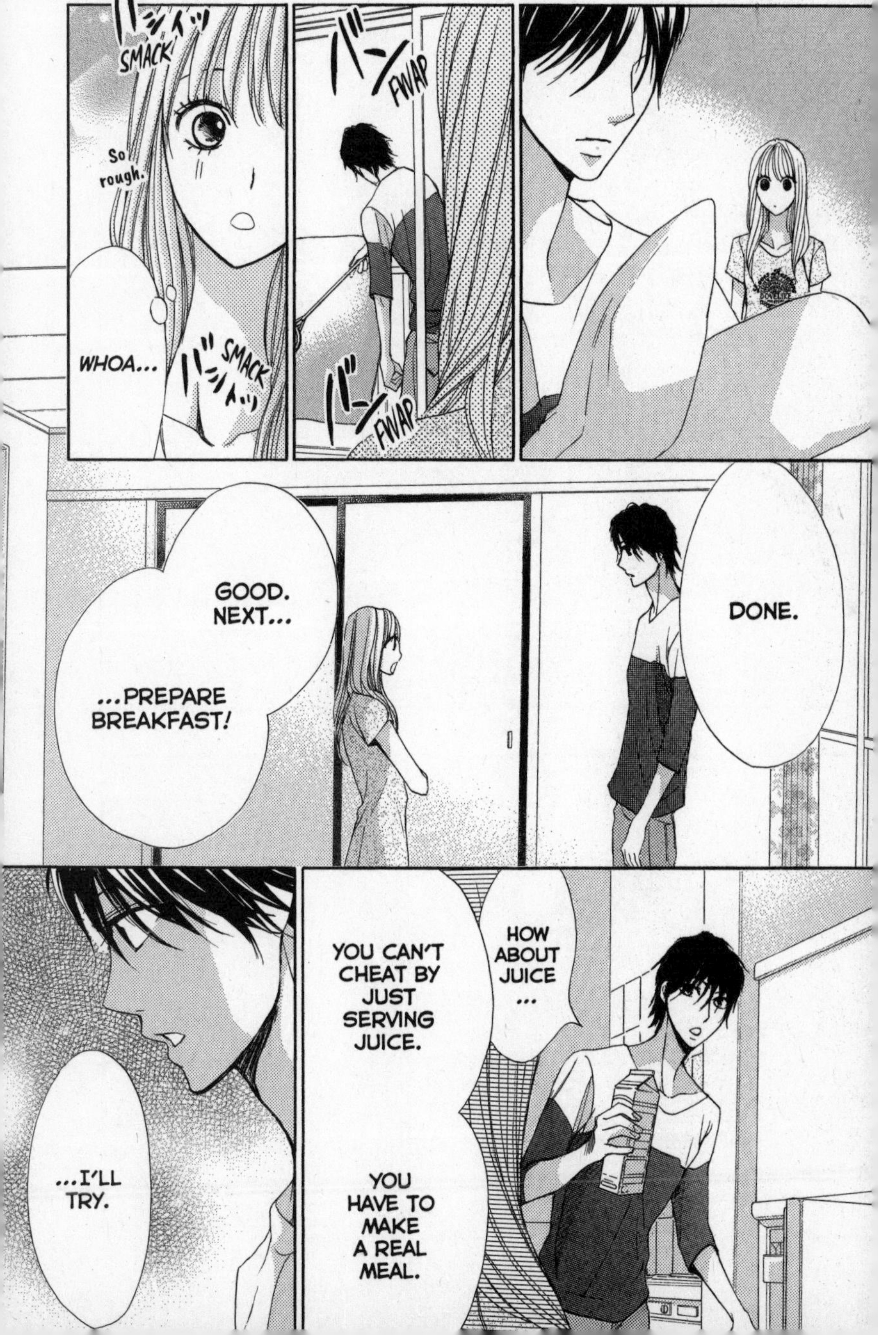
FWAP
FWAP
SMACK
So rough.
WHOA...
SMACK
DONE.
GOOD. NEXT...
...PREPARE BREAKFAST!
HOW ABOUT JUICE...
YOU CAN'T CHEAT BY JUST SERVING JUICE.
YOU HAVE TO MAKE A REAL MEAL.
...I'LL TRY.

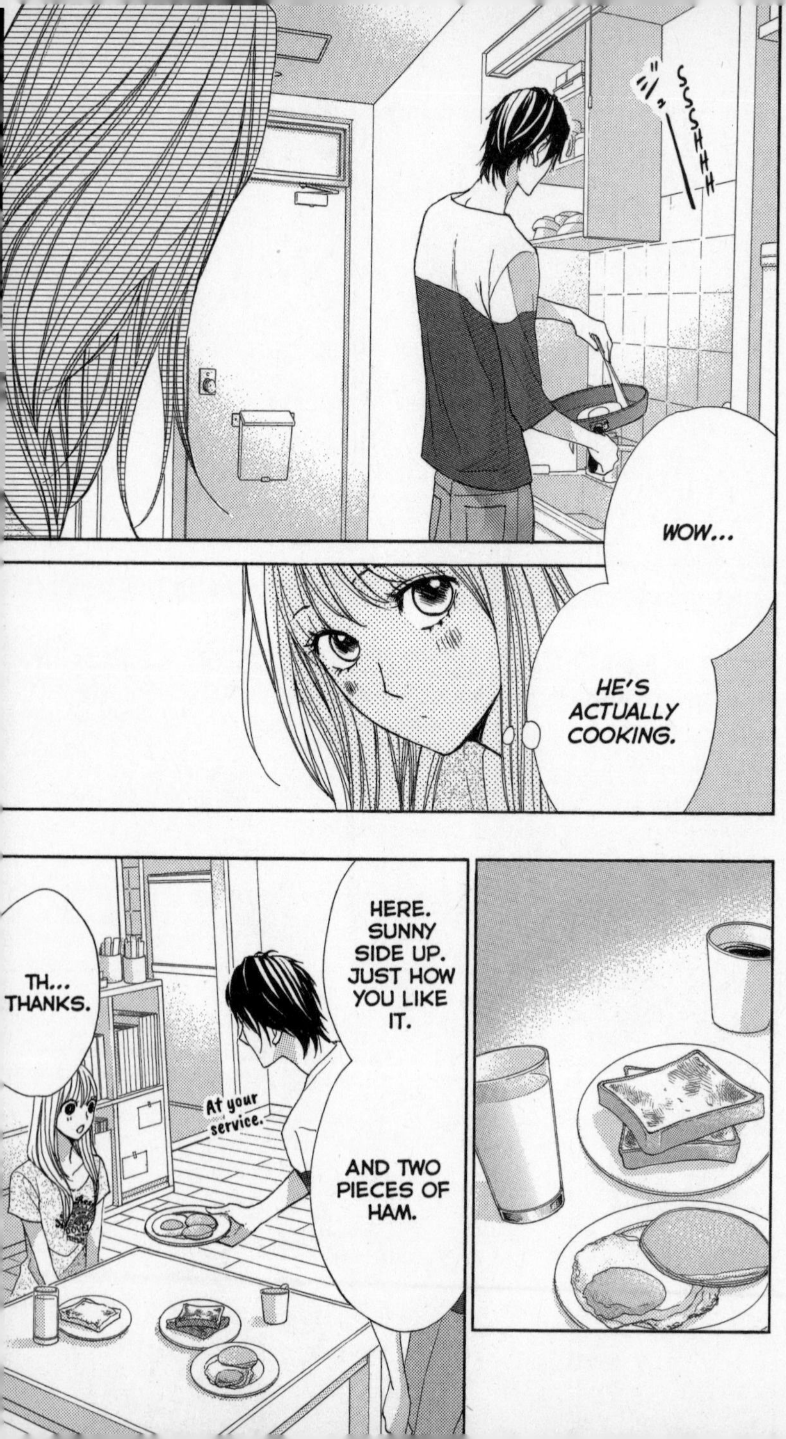
SSSHHH
WOW...
HE'S ACTUALLY COOKING.
HERE. SUNNY SIDE UP. JUST HOW YOU LIKE IT.
AND TWO PIECES OF HAM.
At your service.
TH... THANKS.

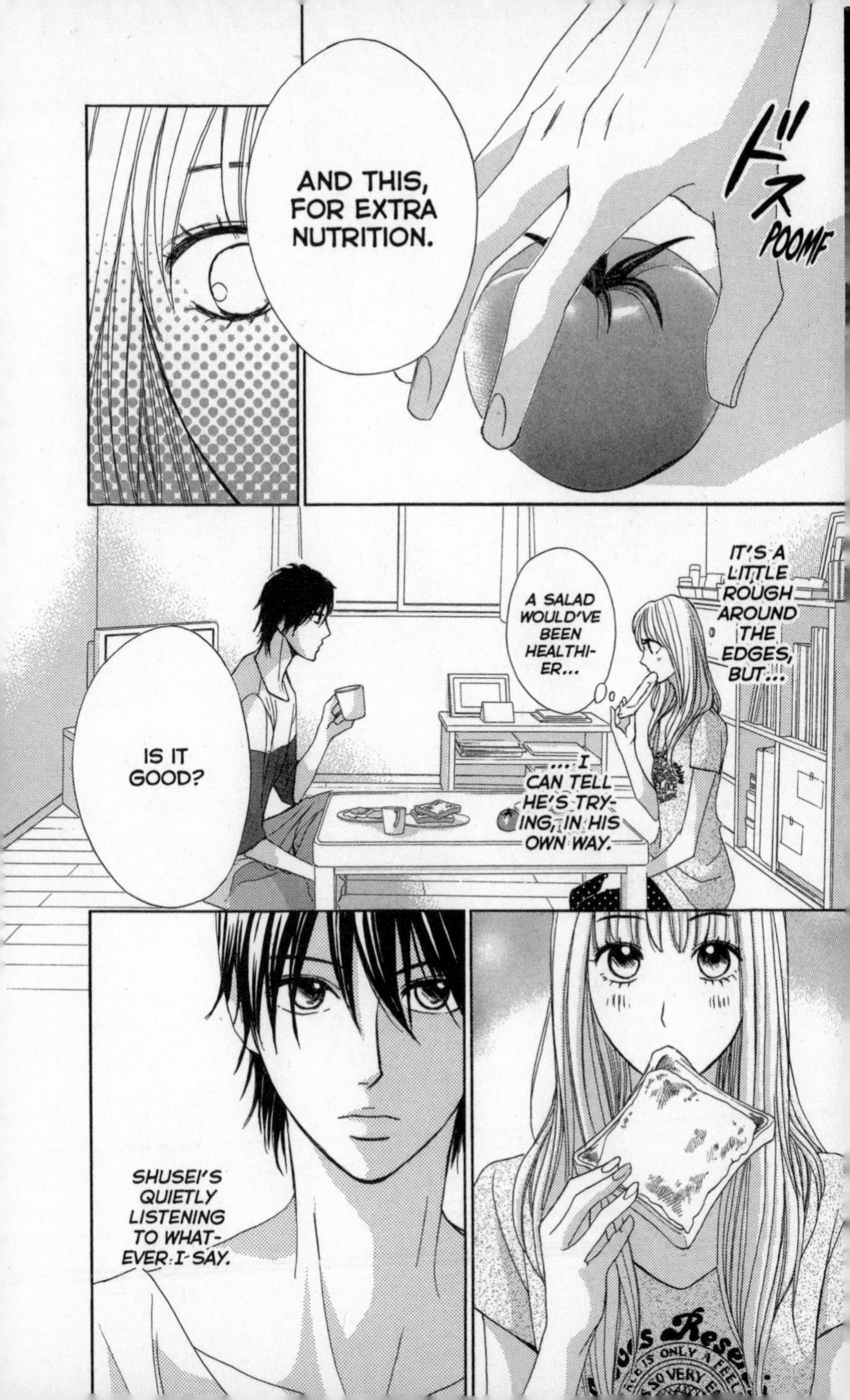
ドス
POOMF
AND THIS, FOR EXTRA NUTRITION.
IT'S A LITTLE ROUGH AROUND THE EDGES, BUT...
A SALAD WOULD'VE BEEN HEALTHI-ER...
...I CAN TELL HE'S TRY-ING, IN HIS OWN WAY.
IS IT GOOD?
SHUSEI'S QUIETLY LISTENING TO WHAT-EVER I SAY.

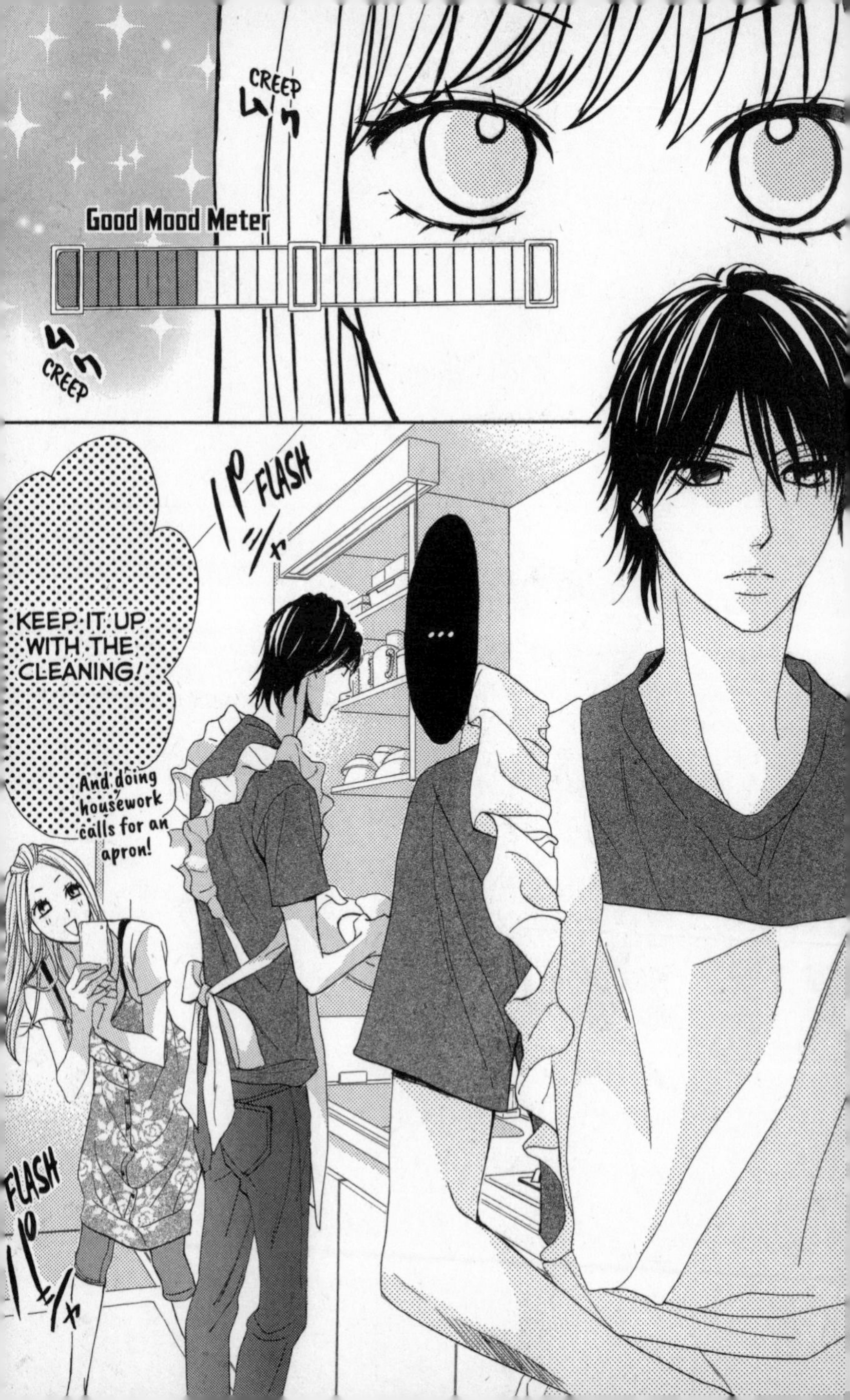
CREEP
Good Mood Meter
CREEP
...
FLASH
KEEP IT UP WITH THE CLEANING!
And doing housework calls for an apron!
FLASH

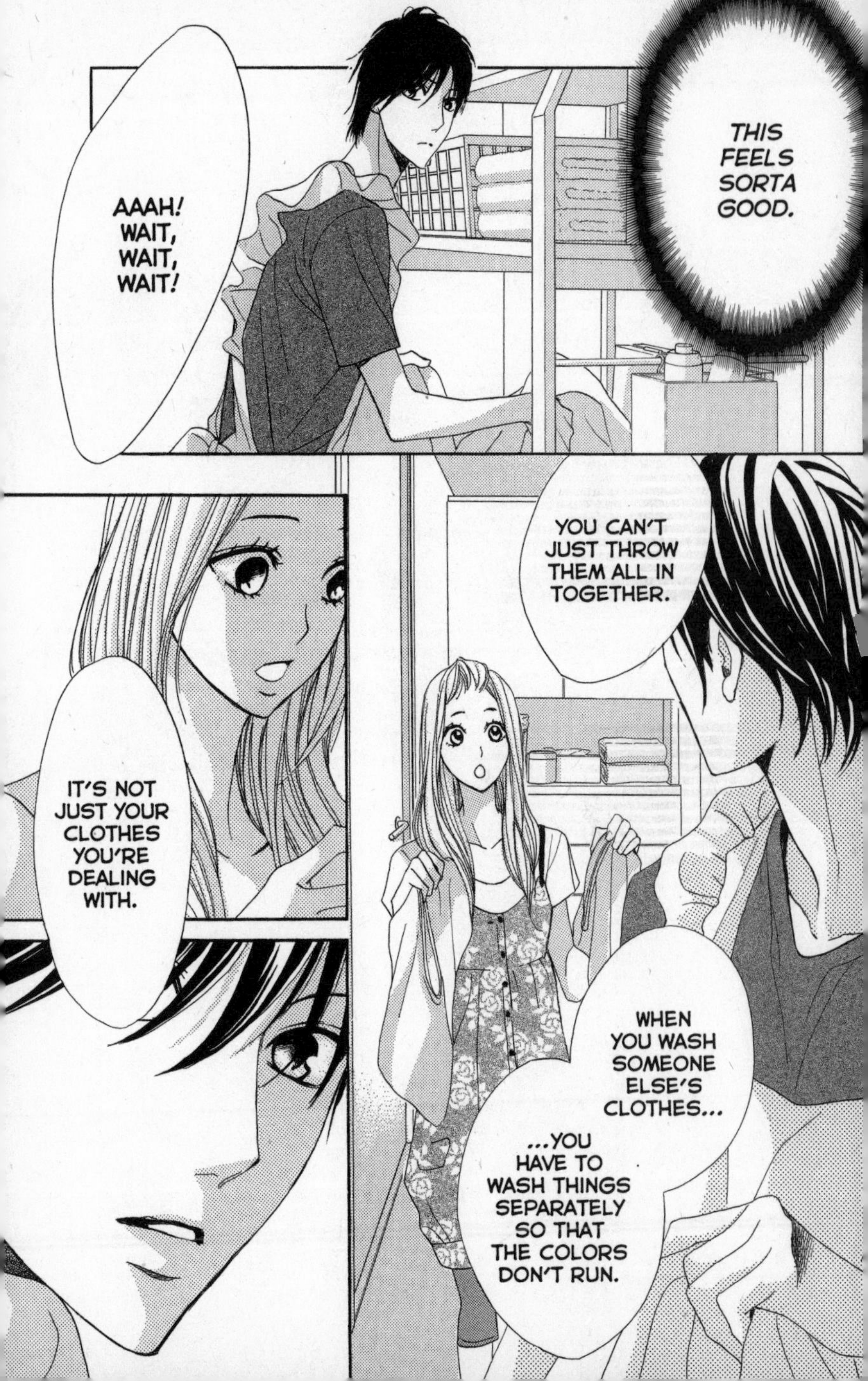
THIS FEELS SORTA GOOD.
AAAH! WAIT, WAIT, WAIT!
YOU CAN'T JUST THROW THEM ALL IN TOGETHER.
WHEN YOU WASH SOMEONE ELSE'S CLOTHES...
...YOU HAVE TO WASH THINGS SEPARATELY SO THAT THE COLORS DON'T RUN.
IT'S NOT JUST YOUR CLOTHES YOU'RE DEALING WITH.

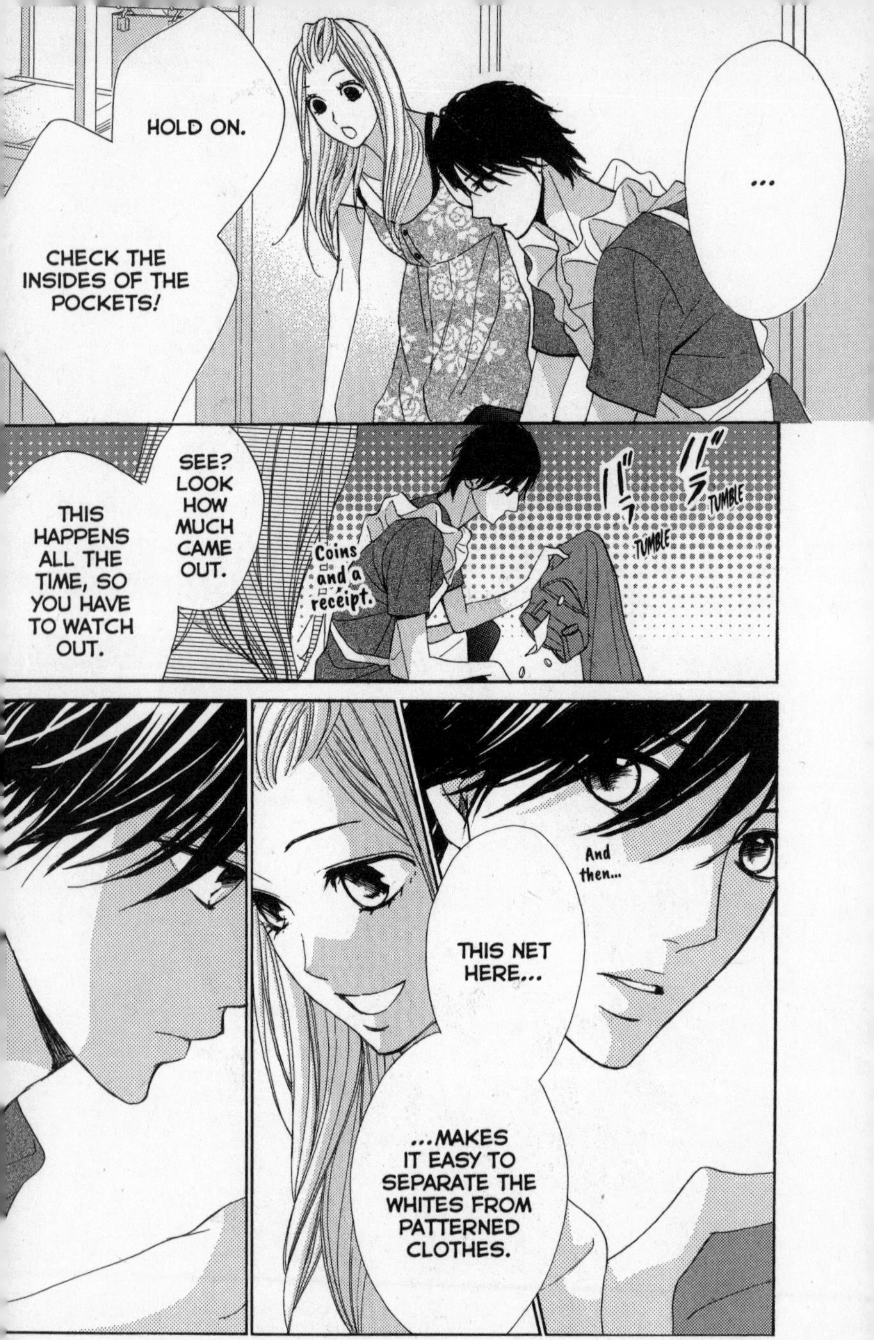
...
HOLD ON.
CHECK THE INSIDES OF THE POCKETS!
TUMBLE
TUMBLE
Coins and a receipt.
SEE? LOOK HOW MUCH CAME OUT.
THIS HAPPENS ALL THE TIME, SO YOU HAVE TO WATCH OUT.
And then...
THIS NET HERE...
...MAKES IT EASY TO SEPARATE THE WHITES FROM PATTERNED CLOTHES.

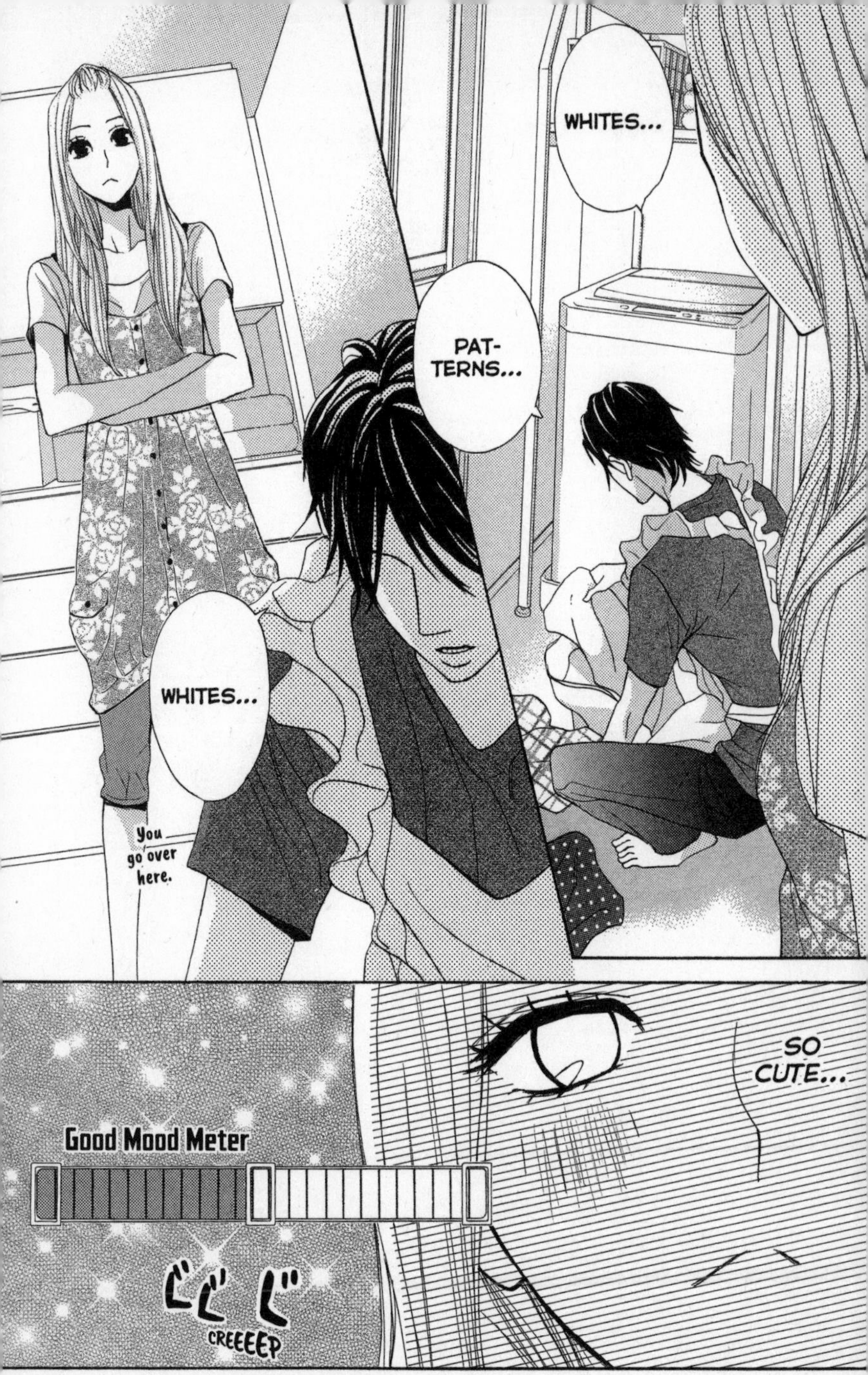
WHITES...
PAT-
TERNS...
WHITES...
You go over here.
SO CUTE...
Good Mood Meter
ぐぐぐ
CREEEEP

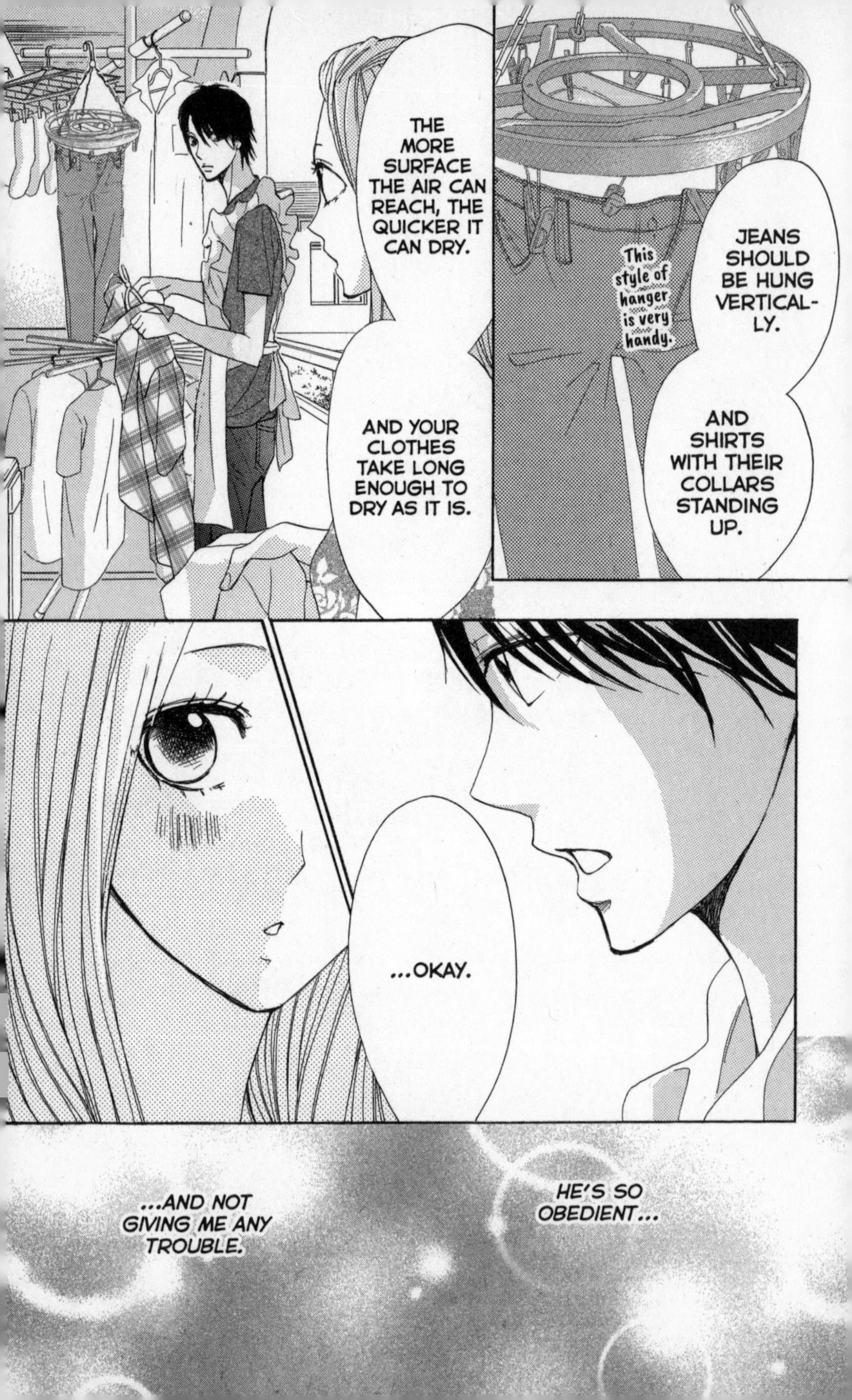
JEANS SHOULD BE HUNG VERTICAL-LY.
AND SHIRTS WITH THEIR COLLARS STANDING UP.
This style of hanger is very handy.
THE MORE SURFACE THE AIR CAN REACH, THE QUICKER IT CAN DRY.
AND YOUR CLOTHES TAKE LONG ENOUGH TO DRY AS IT IS.
...OKAY.
HE'S SO OBEDIENT...
...AND NOT GIVING ME ANY TROUBLE.

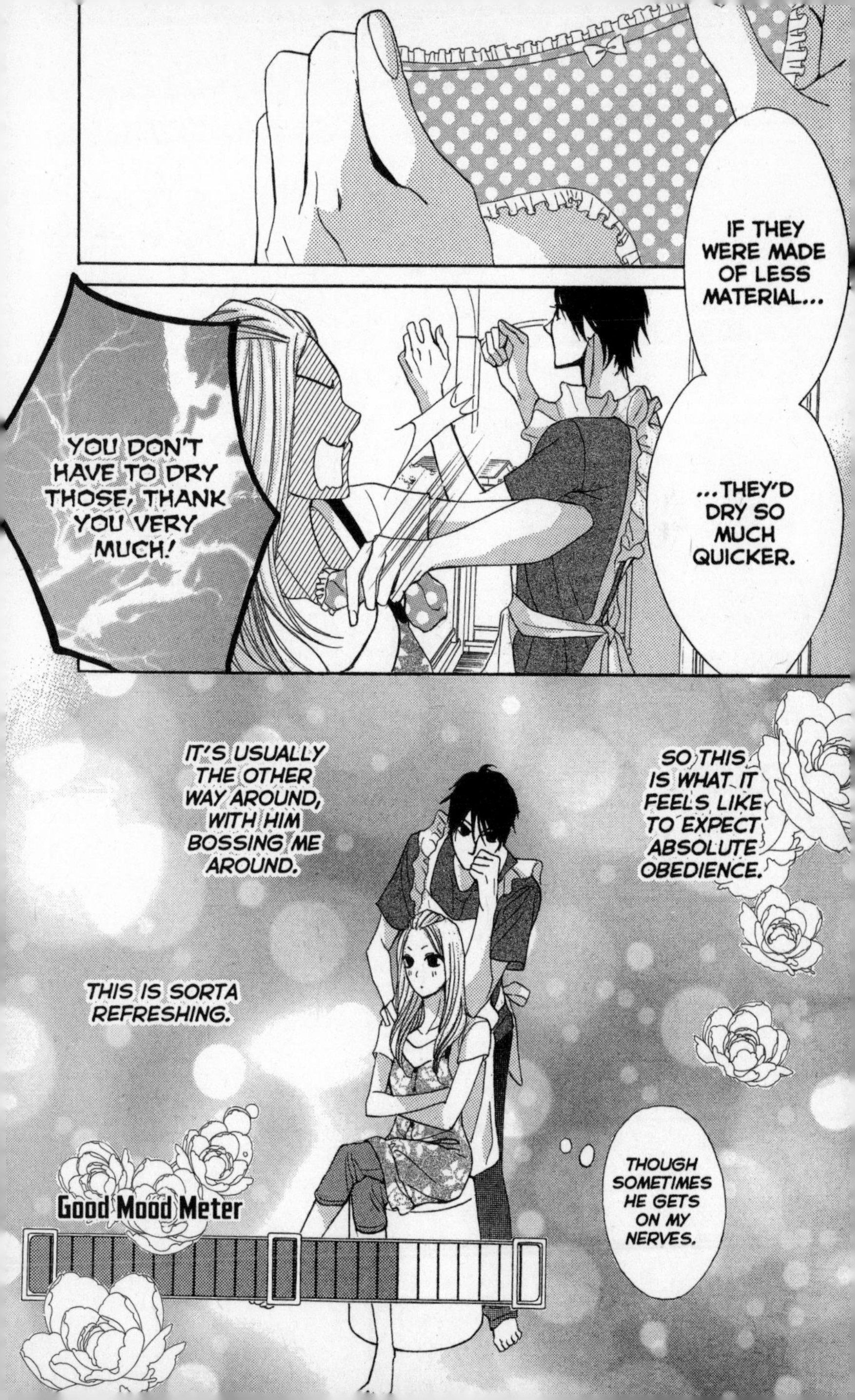
IF THEY WERE MADE OF LESS MATERIAL...
...THEY'D DRY SO MUCH QUICKER.
YOU DON'T HAVE TO DRY THOSE, THANK YOU VERY MUCH!
SO THIS IS WHAT IT FEELS LIKE TO EXPECT ABSOLUTE OBEDIENCE.
IT'S USUALLY THE OTHER WAY AROUND, WITH HIM BOSSING ME AROUND.
THIS IS SORTA REFRESHING.
THOUGH SOMETIMES HE GETS ON MY NERVES.
Good Mood Meter

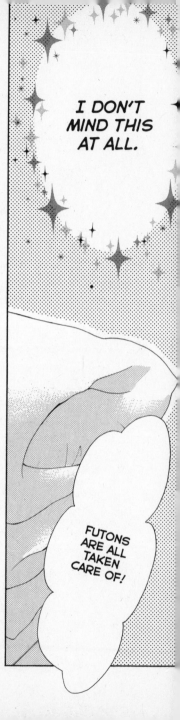

I DON'T MIND THIS AT ALL.

FUTONS ARE ALL TAKEN CARE OF!

NOW, WHAT TO DO NEXT...

HOLD ON. LET ME TAKE A BREATH-ER.

AAAAW!

YOU'RE GOING TO FALL ASLEEP IF YOU STAY THERE.

Ah!

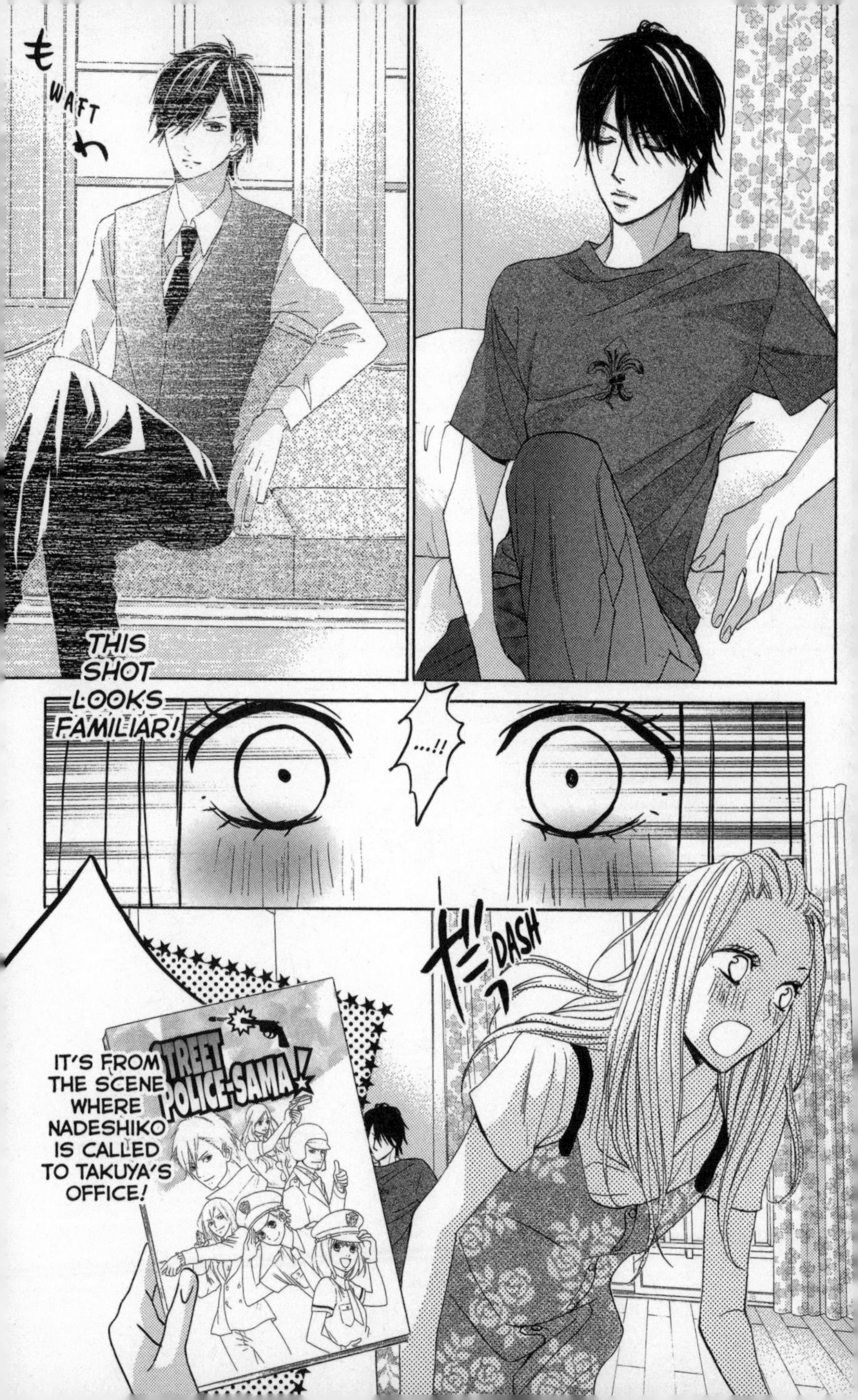

もわ
WAFT
THIS SHOT LOOKS FAMILIAR!
...!!
ダッ
DASH
IT'S FROM THE SCENE WHERE NADESHIKO IS CALLED TO TAKUYA'S OFFICE!
TREET POLICE-SAMA!

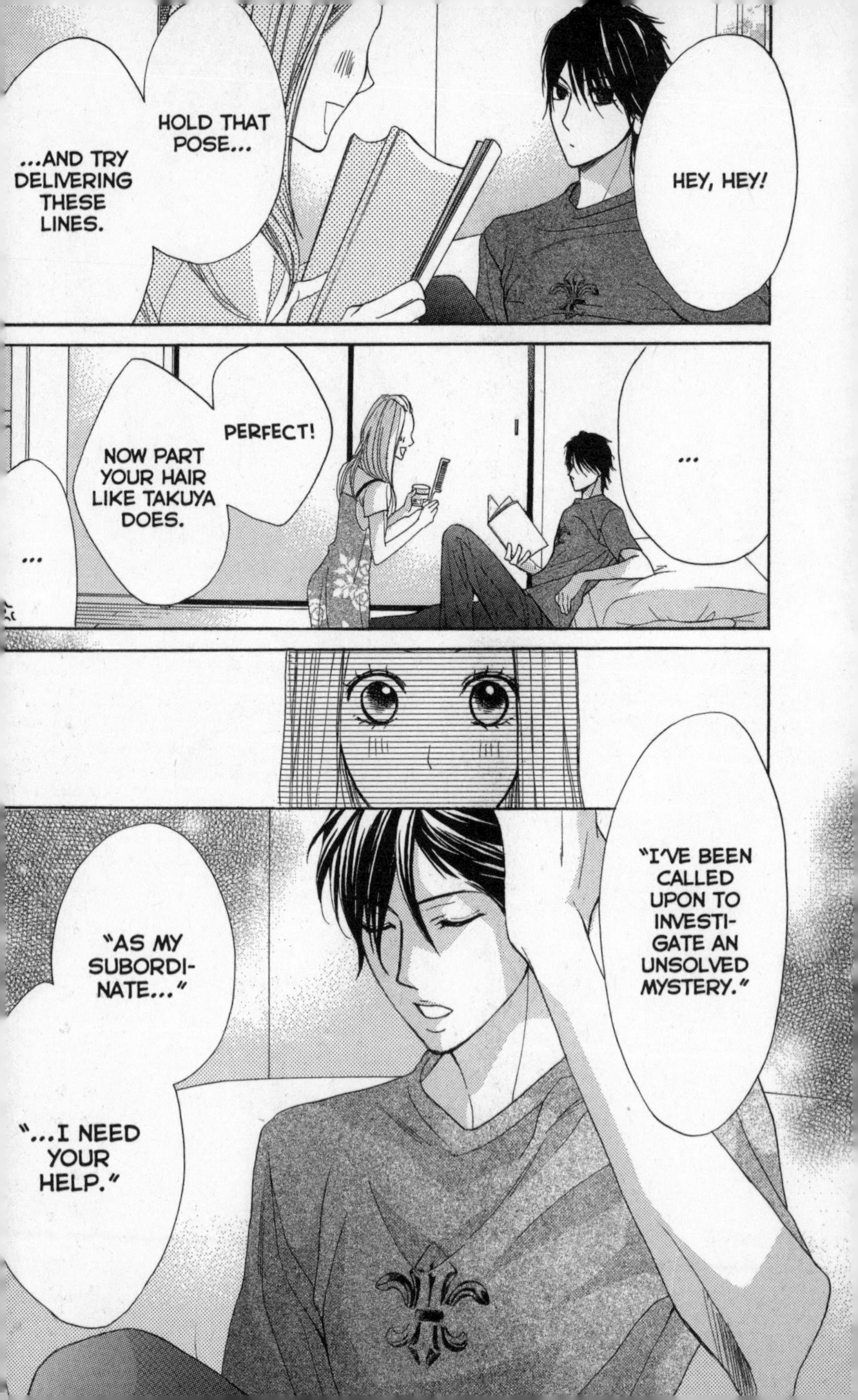
HEY, HEY!
HOLD THAT POSE...
...AND TRY DELIVERING THESE LINES.
...
PERFECT!
NOW PART YOUR HAIR LIKE TAKUYA DOES.
...
"I'VE BEEN CALLED UPON TO INVESTI-GATE AN UNSOLVED MYSTERY."
"AS MY SUBORDI-NATE..."
"...I NEED YOUR HELP."

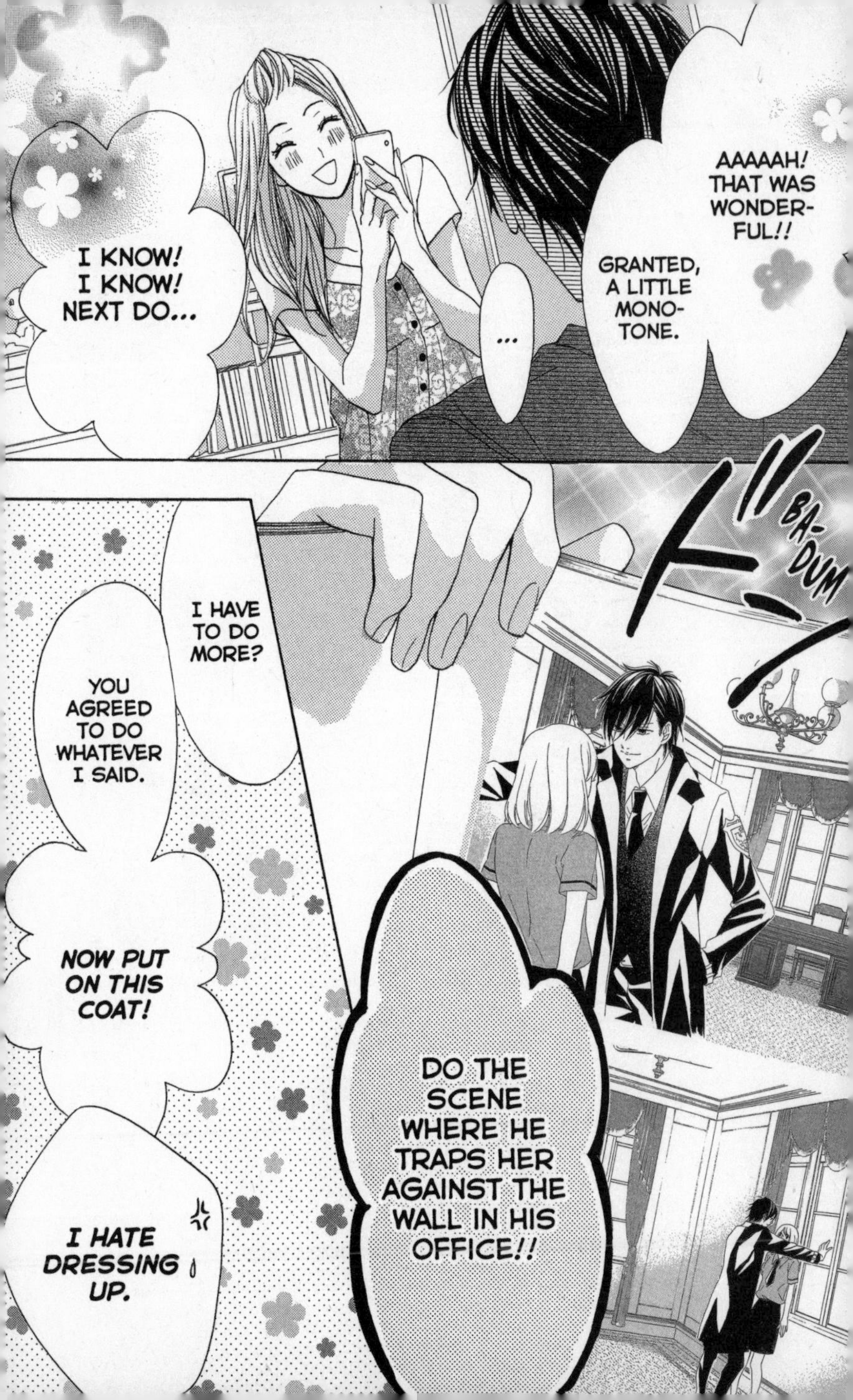
AAAAAH! THAT WAS WONDER-FUL!!
GRANTED, A LITTLE MONO-TONE.
...
I KNOW! I KNOW! NEXT DO...
BA-DUM
DO THE SCENE WHERE HE TRAPS HER AGAINST THE WALL IN HIS OFFICE!!
I HAVE TO DO MORE?
YOU AGREED TO DO WHATEVER I SAID.
NOW PUT ON THIS COAT!
I HATE DRESSING UP.

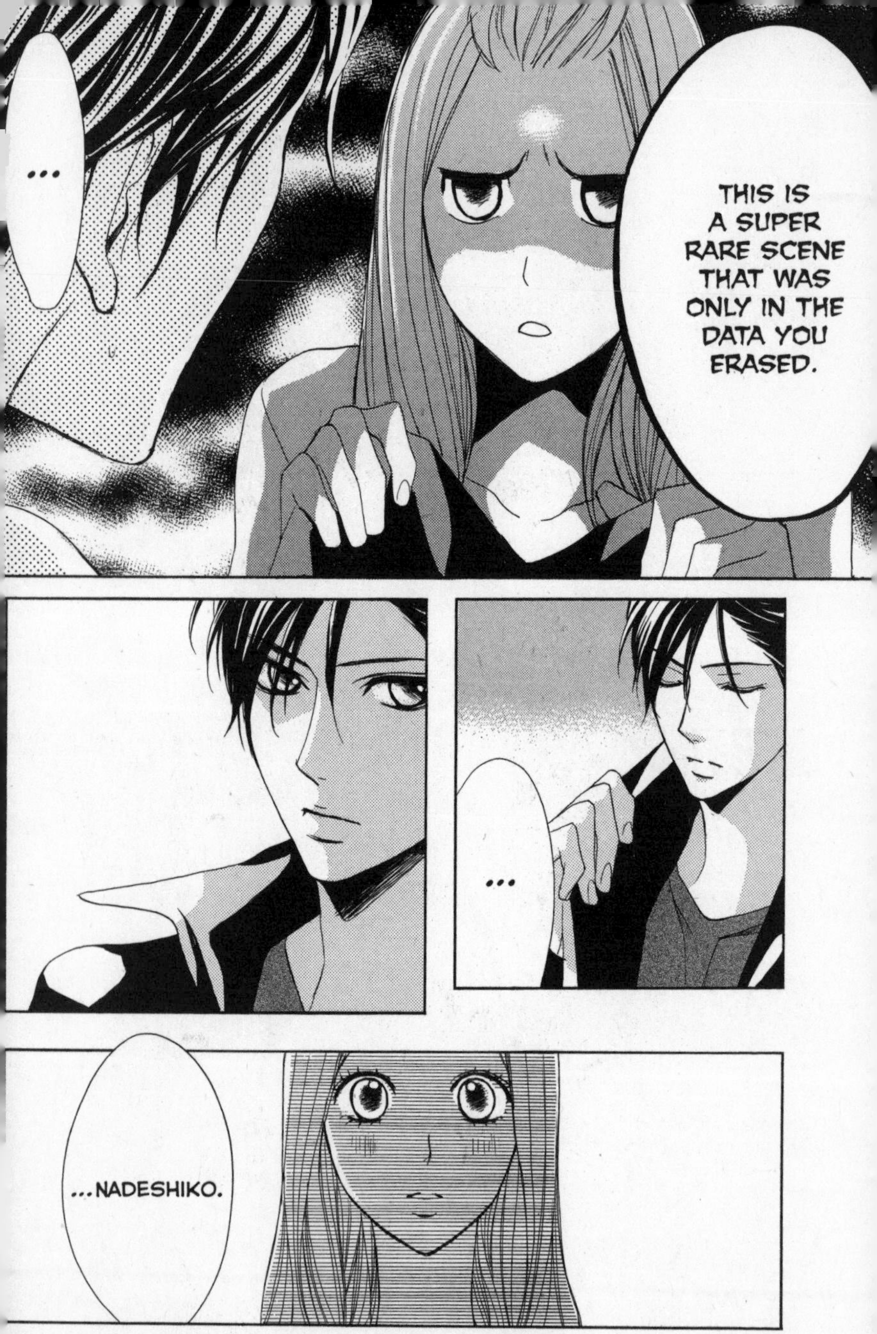
THIS IS A SUPER RARE SCENE THAT WAS ONLY IN THE DATA YOU ERASED.
...
...
...NADESHIKO.

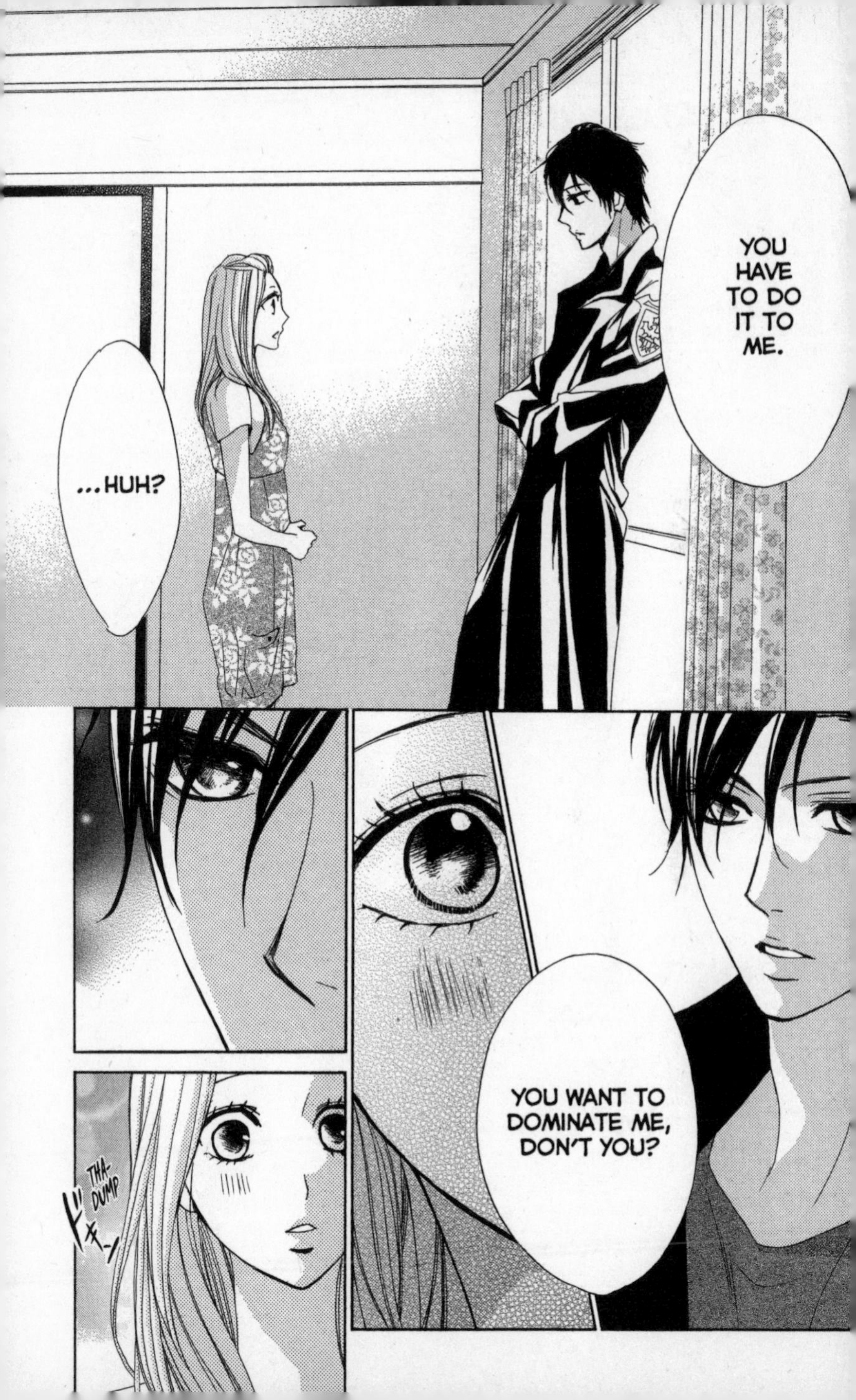
YOU HAVE TO DO IT TO ME.
...HUH?
YOU WANT TO DOMINATE ME, DON'T YOU?
THA-DUMP

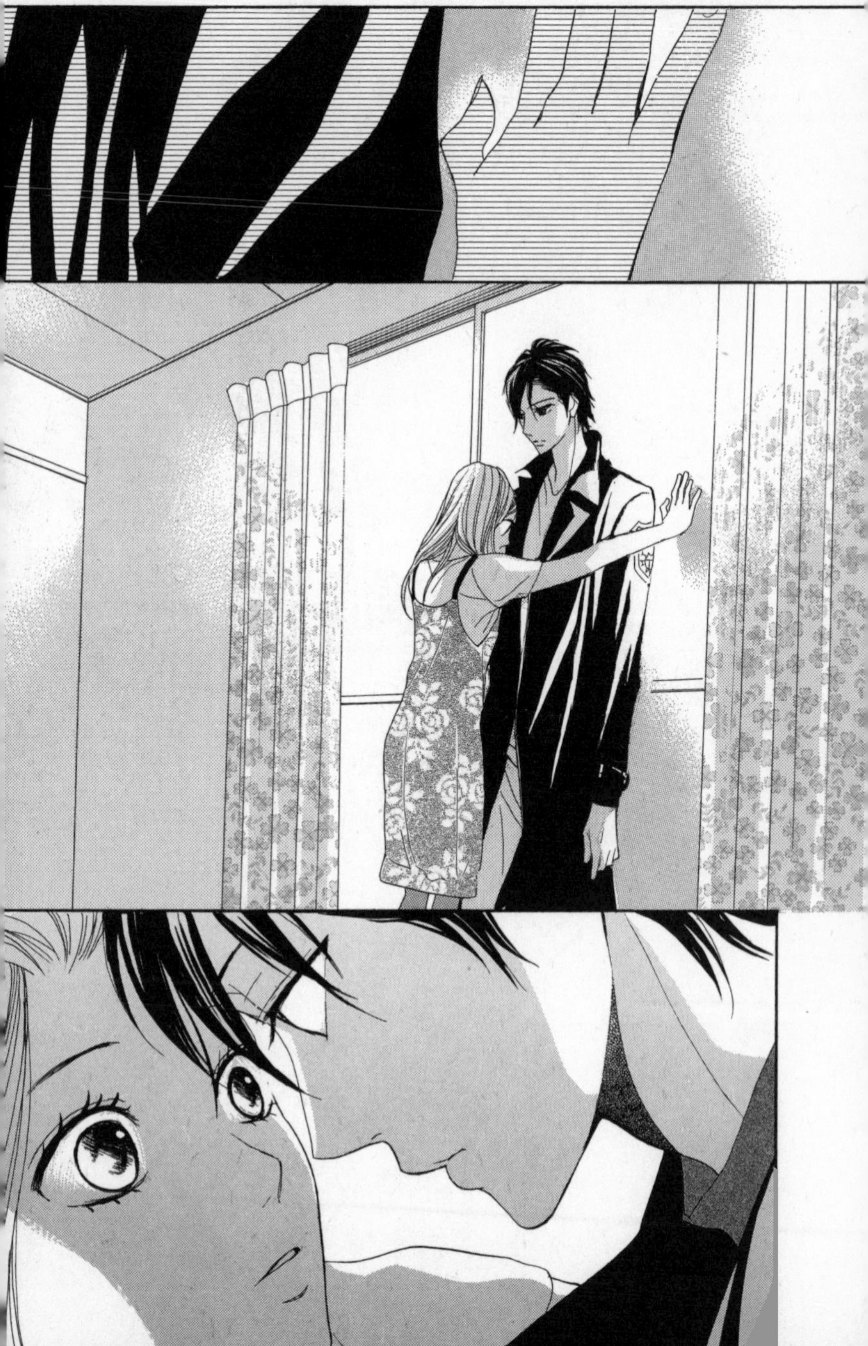

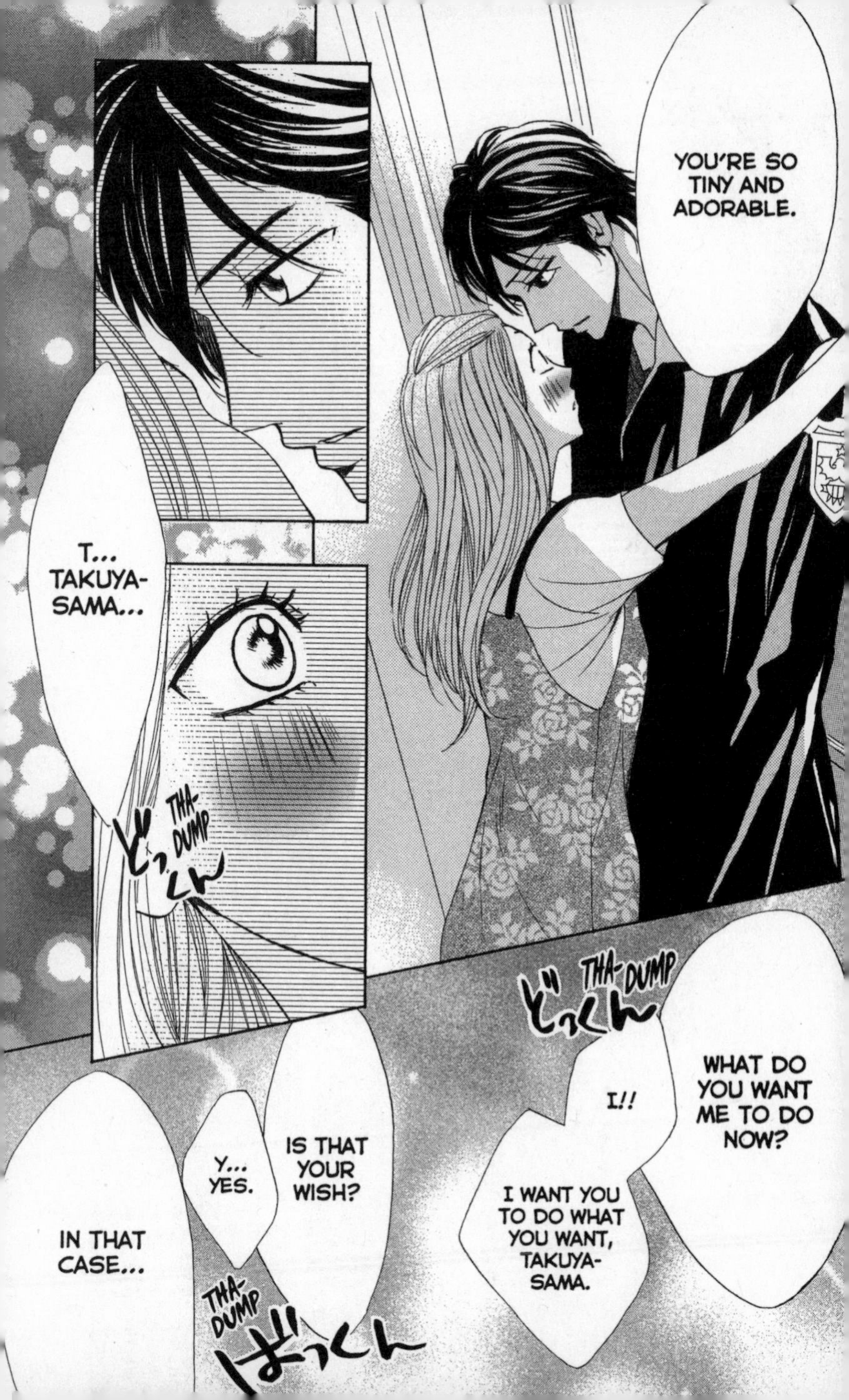
YOU'RE SO TINY AND ADORABLE.
T... TAKUYA-SAMA...
THA-DUMP
WHAT DO YOU WANT ME TO DO NOW?
THA-DUMP
I!!
I WANT YOU TO DO WHAT YOU WANT, TAKUYA-SAMA.
IS THAT YOUR WISH?
Y... YES.
THA-DUMP
IN THAT CASE...

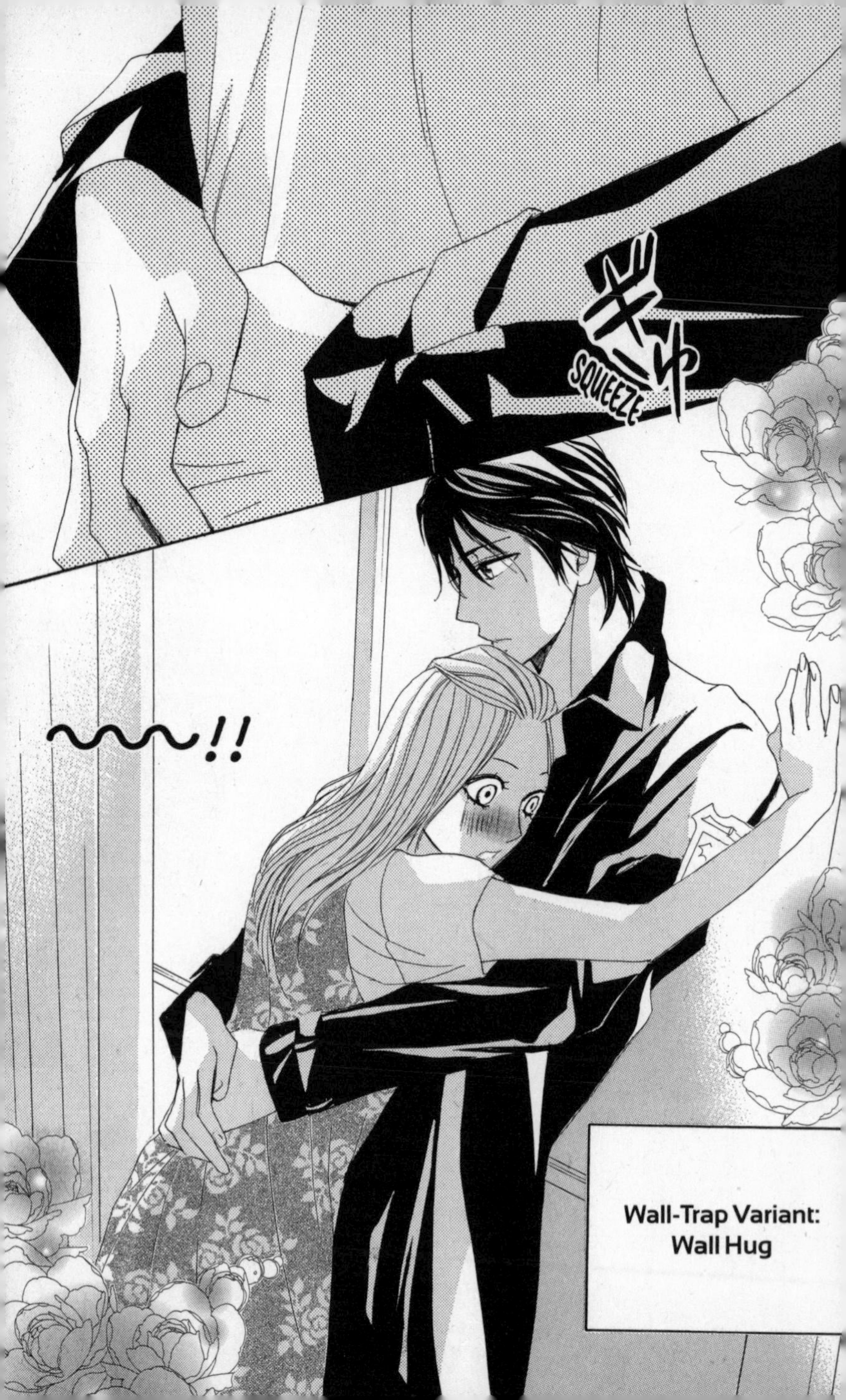
ギュ
SQUEEZE
〜〜〜!!
Wall-Trap Variant:
Wall Hug

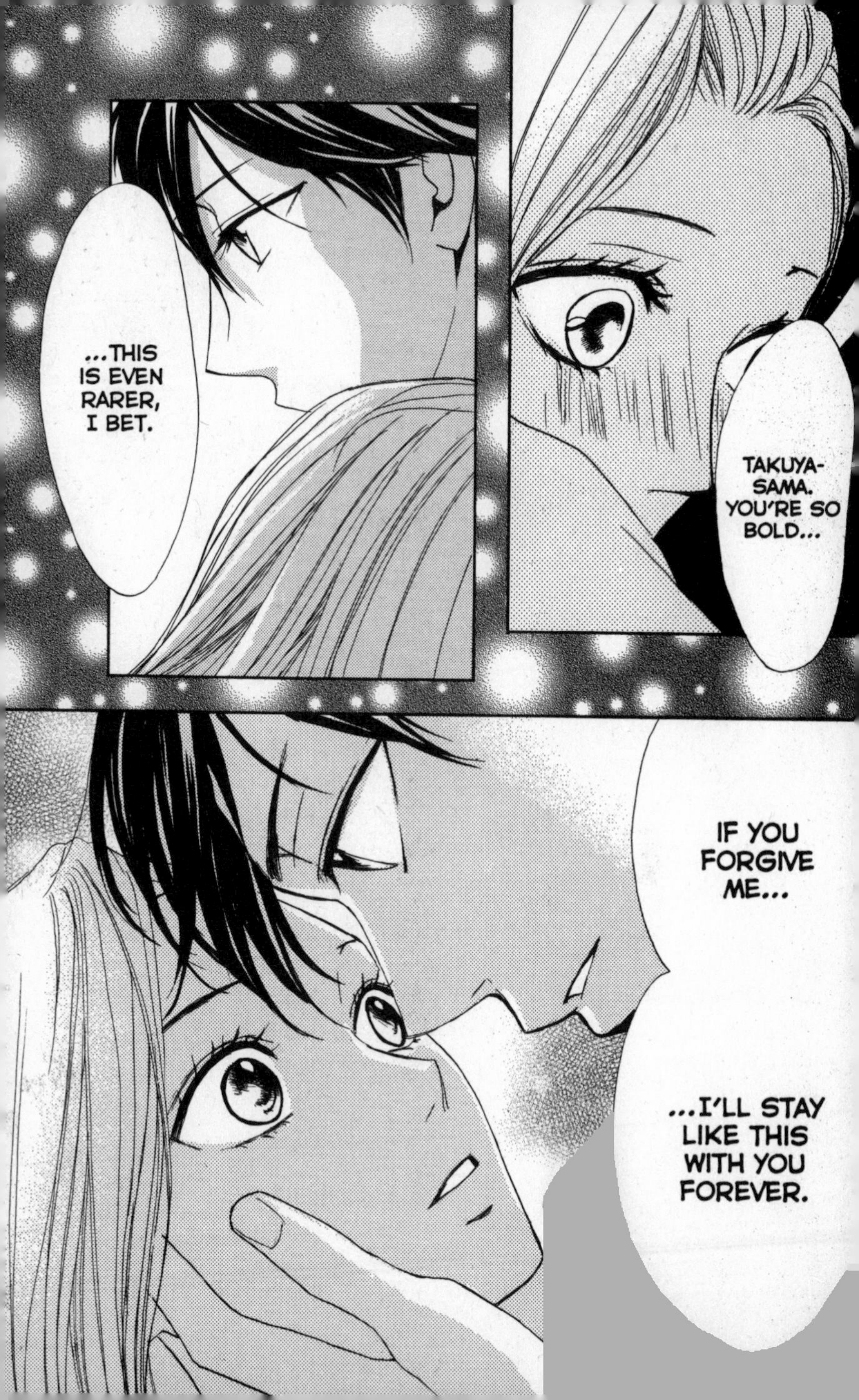
TAKUYA-SAMA. YOU'RE SO BOLD...
...THIS IS EVEN RARER, I BET.
IF YOU FORGIVE ME...
...I'LL STAY LIKE THIS WITH YOU FOREVER.

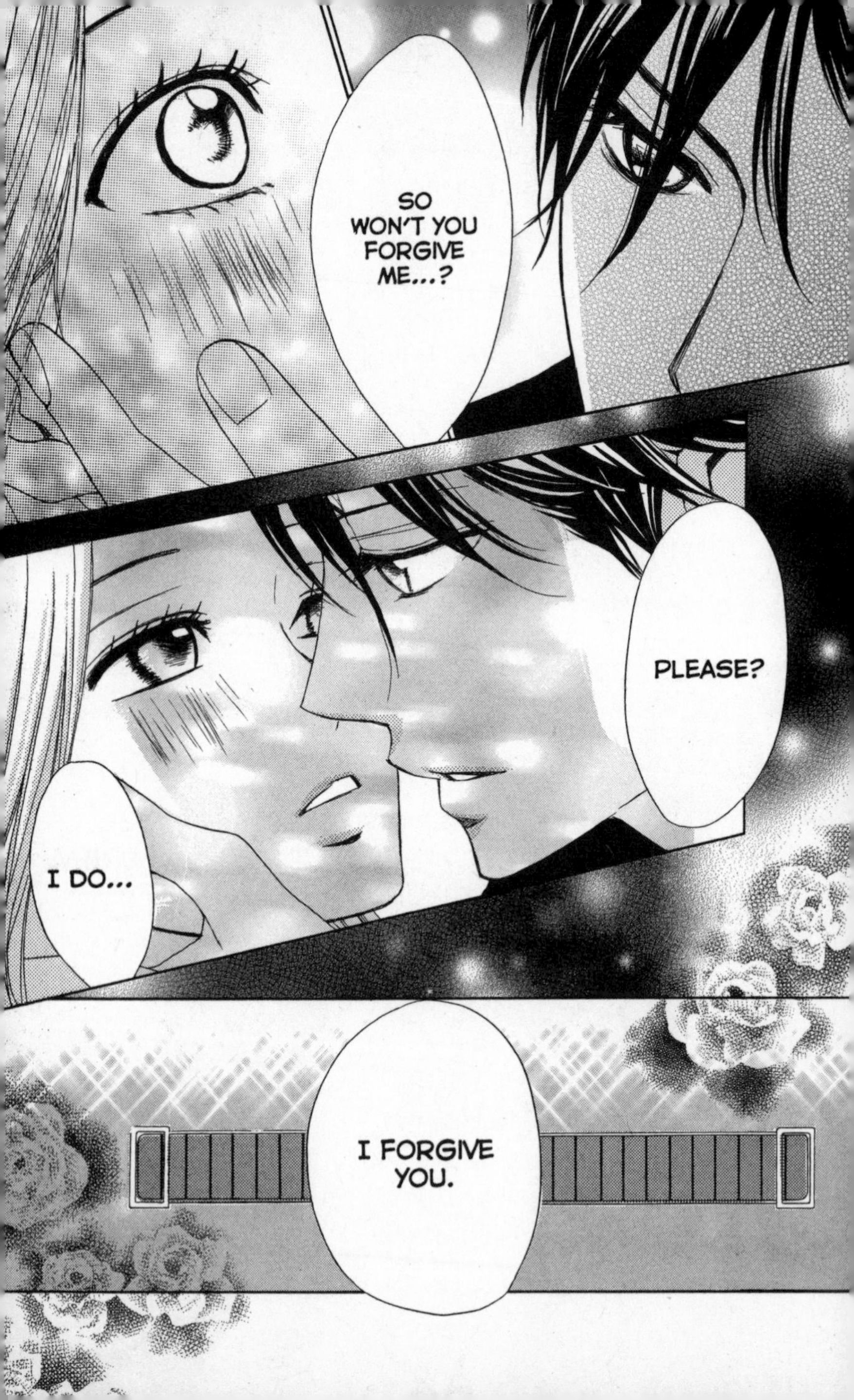
SO WON'T YOU FORGIVE ME...?
PLEASE?
I DO...
I FORGIVE YOU.

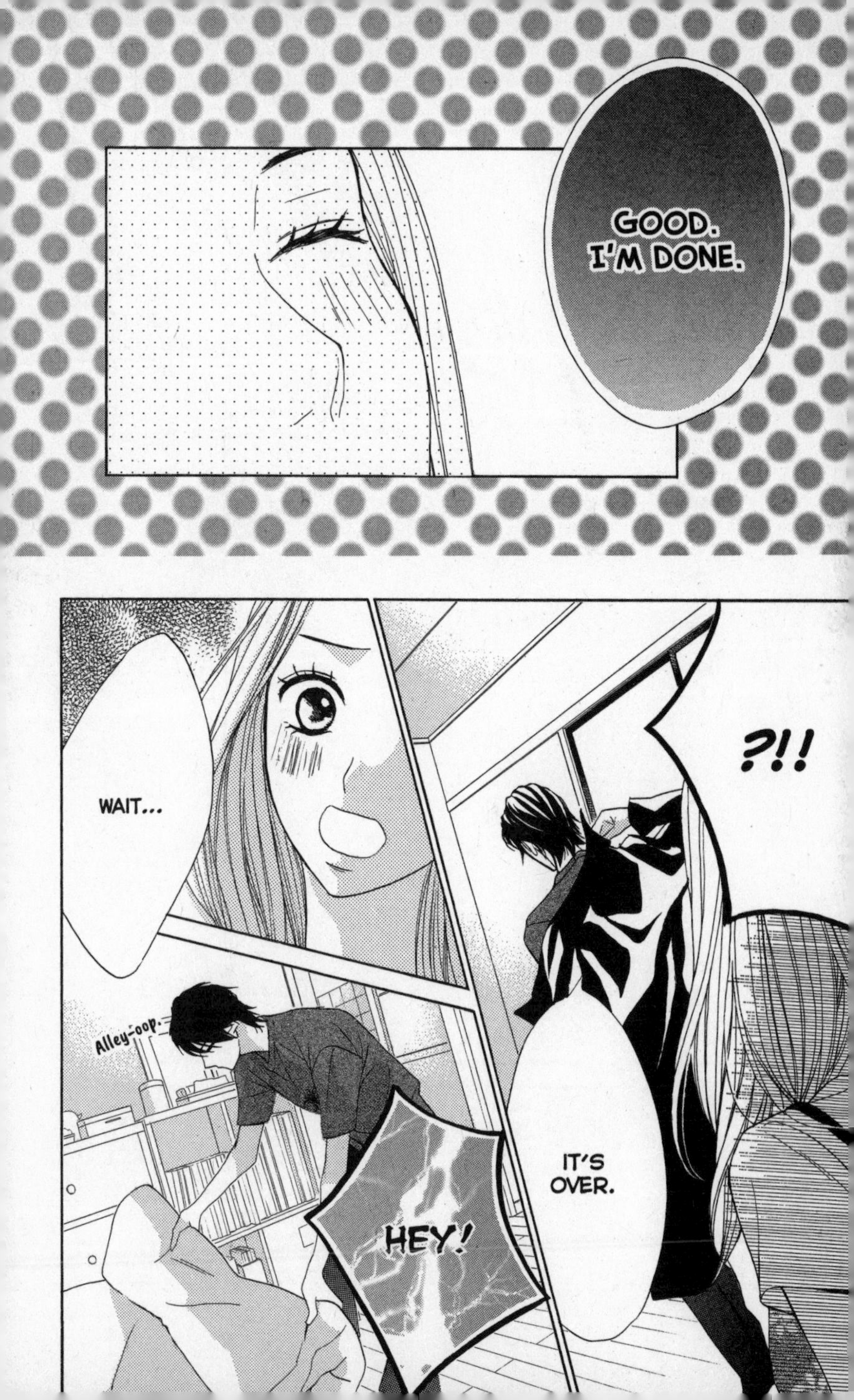
GOOD. I'M DONE.
?!!
IT'S OVER.
WAIT...
Alley-oop.
HEY!

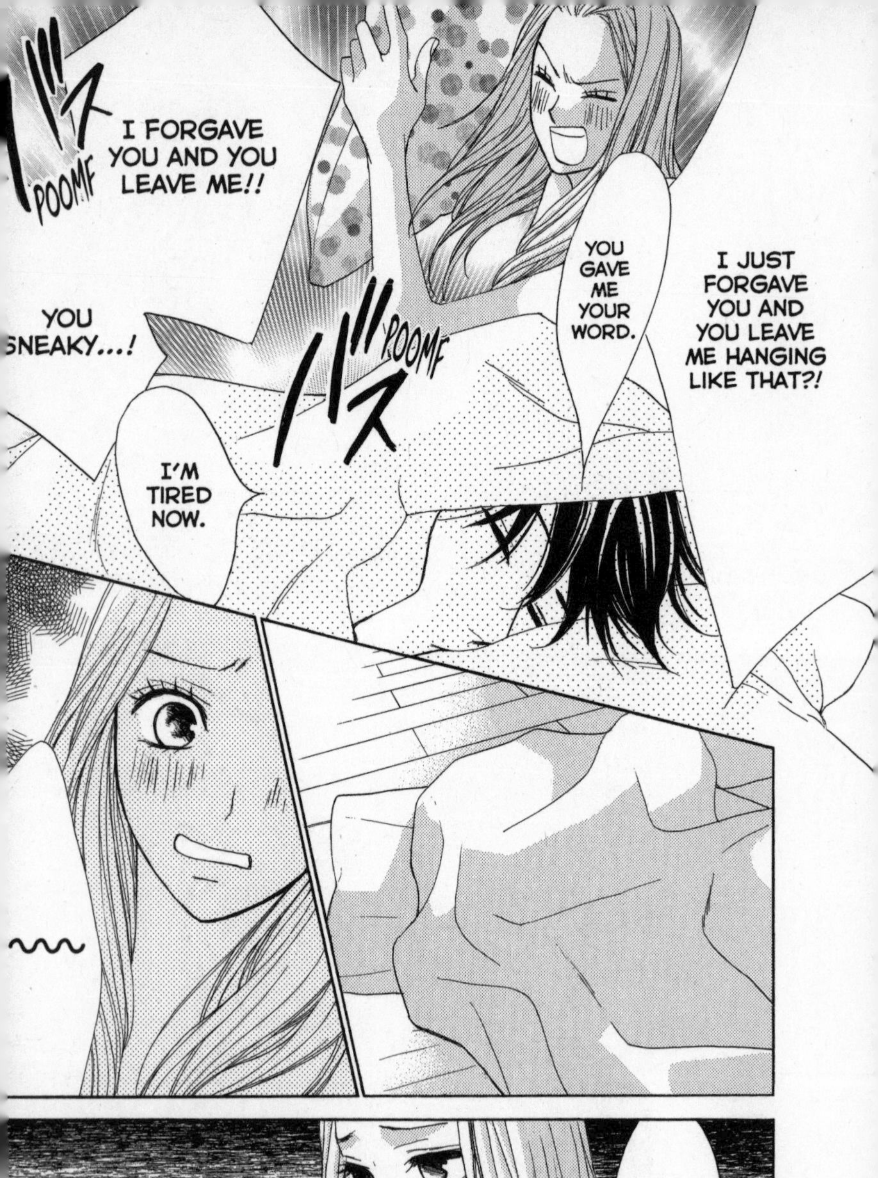
POOMF
I FORGAVE YOU AND YOU LEAVE ME!!
I JUST FORGAVE YOU AND YOU LEAVE ME HANGING LIKE THAT?!
YOU GAVE ME YOUR WORD.
POOMF
YOU SNEAKY...!
I'M TIRED NOW.
...

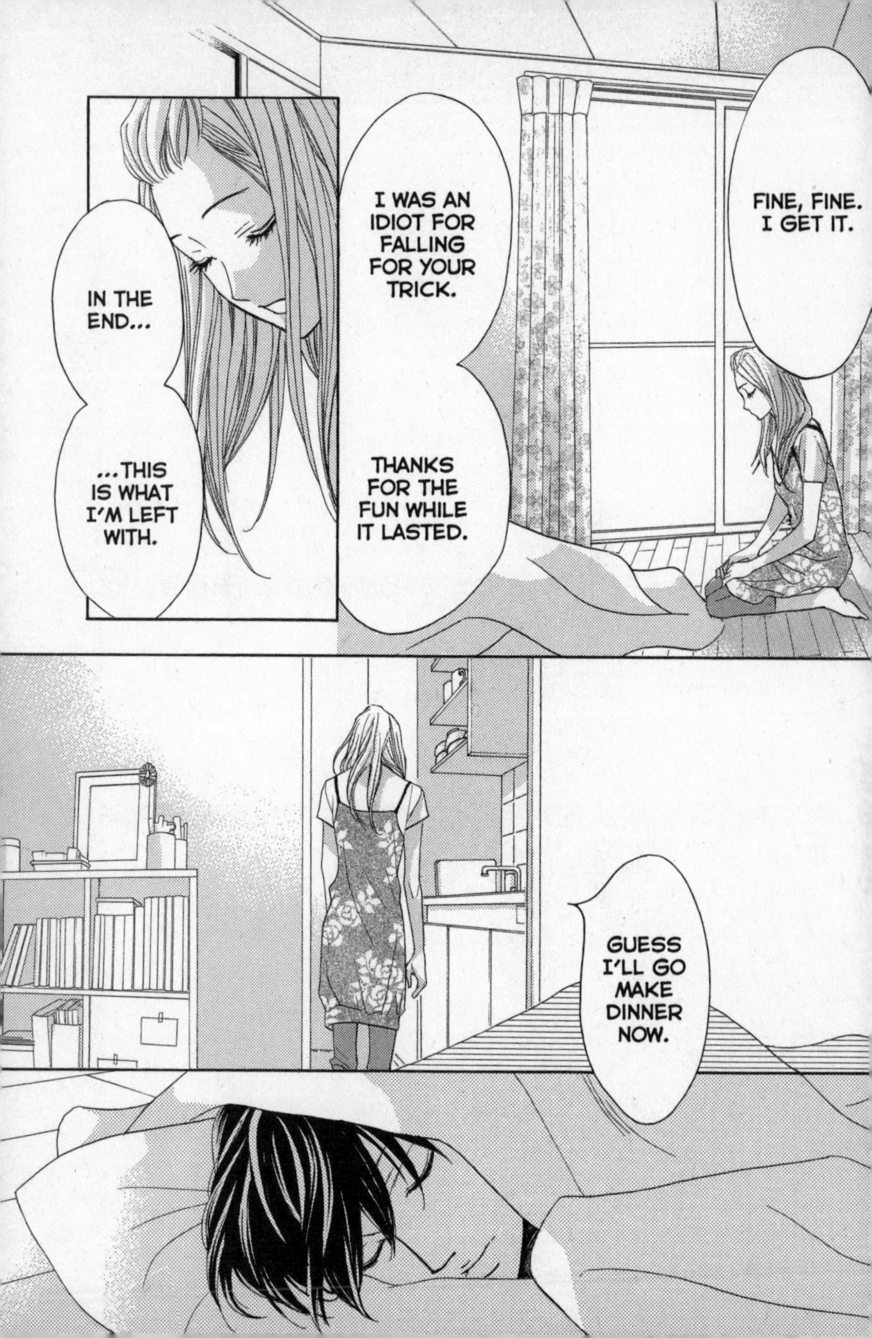
FINE, FINE. I GET IT.
I WAS AN IDIOT FOR FALLING FOR YOUR TRICK.
THANKS FOR THE FUN WHILE IT LASTED.
IN THE END...
...THIS IS WHAT I'M LEFT WITH.
GUESS I'LL GO MAKE DINNER NOW.

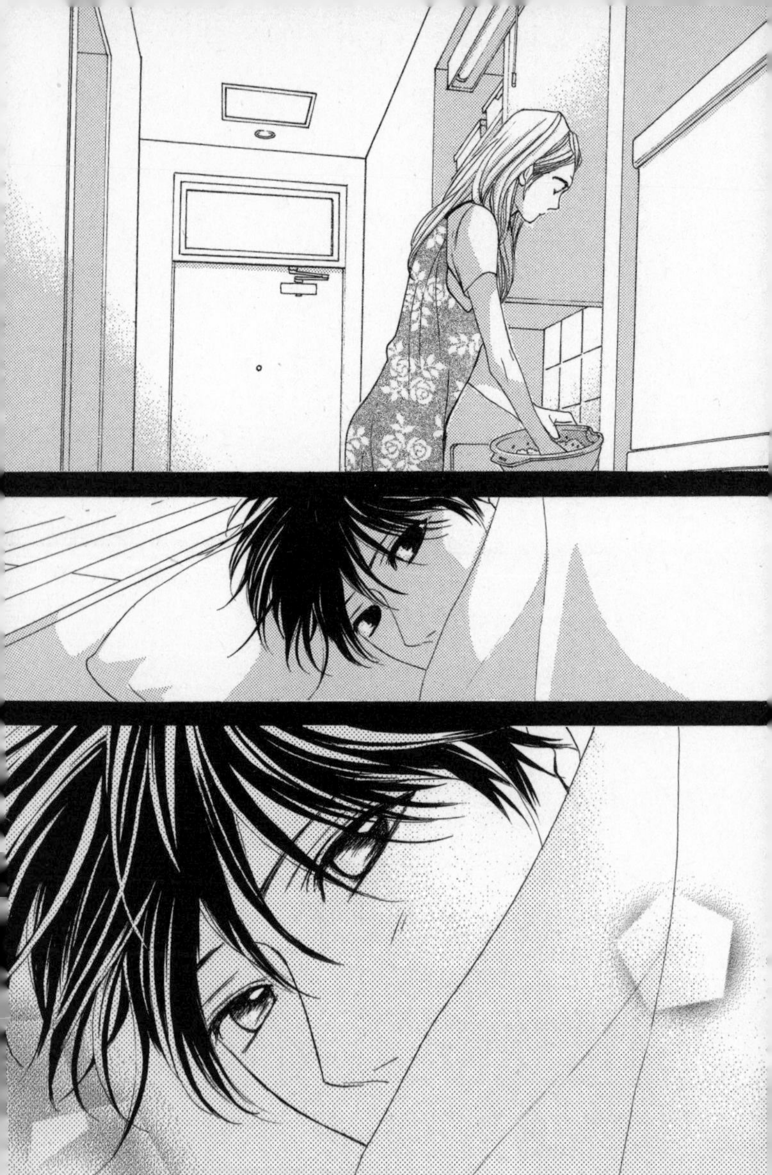

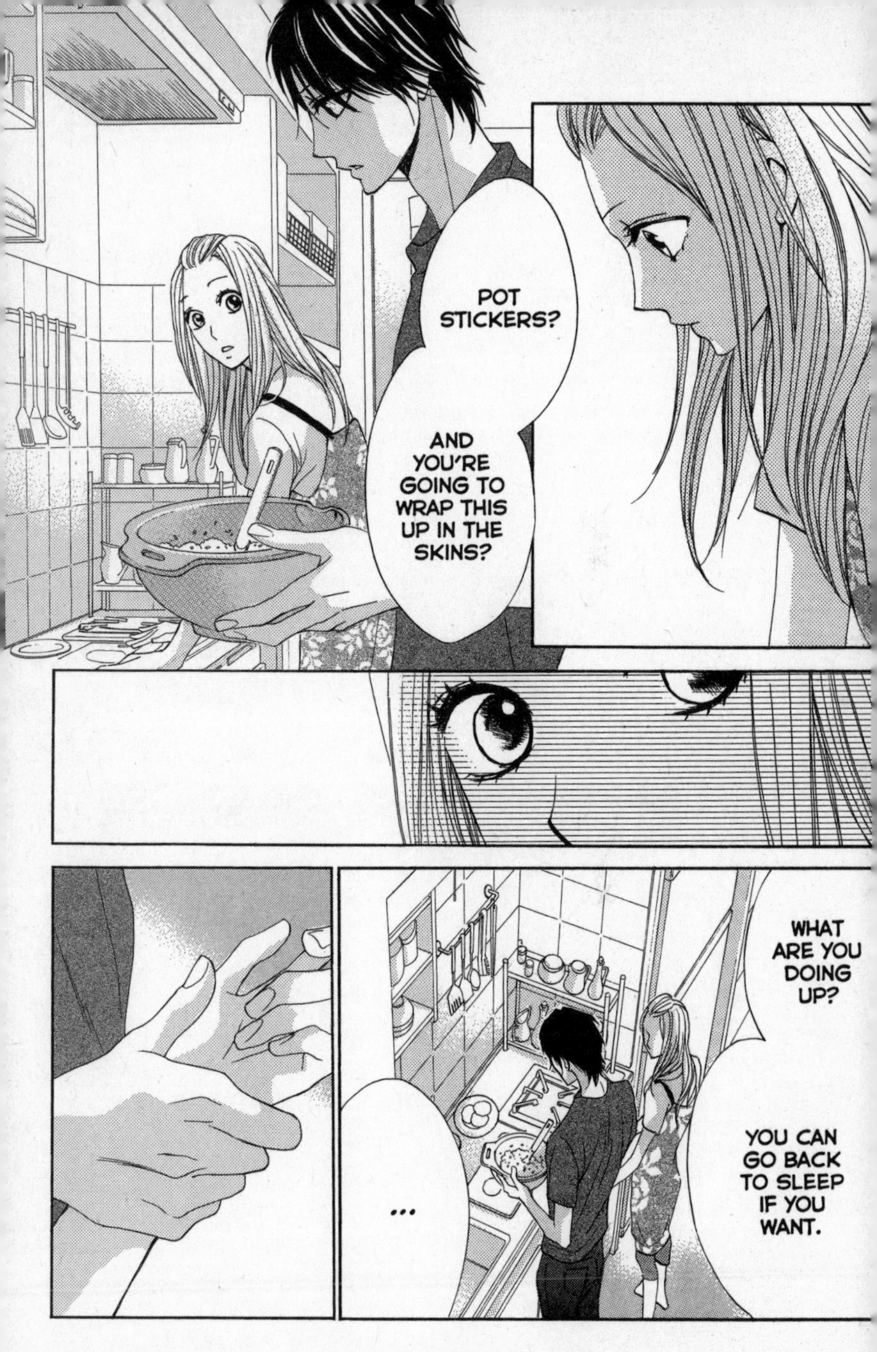
POT STICKERS?
AND YOU'RE GOING TO WRAP THIS UP IN THE SKINS?
WHAT ARE YOU DOING UP?
YOU CAN GO BACK TO SLEEP IF YOU WANT.
...

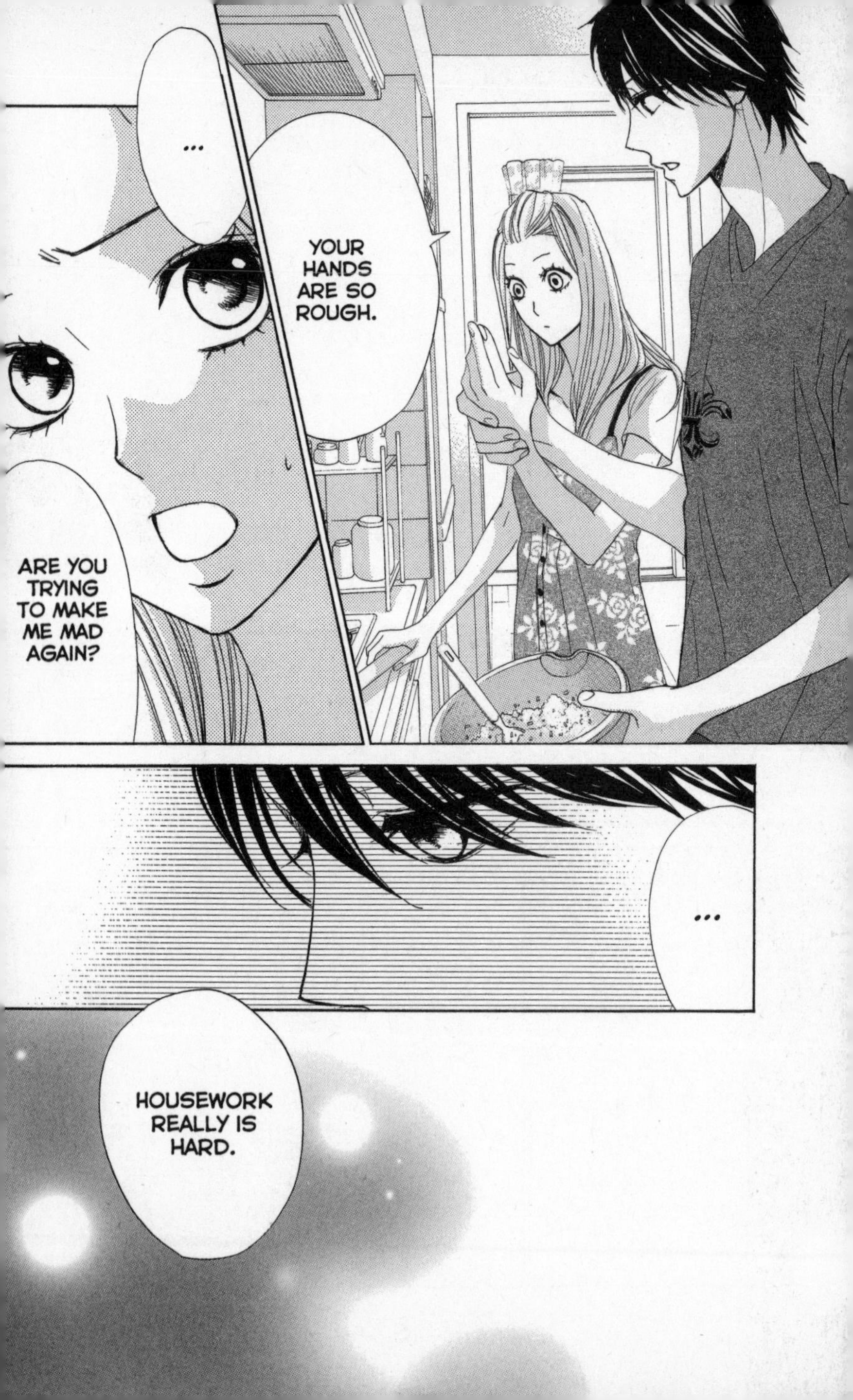
YOUR HANDS ARE SO ROUGH.
...
ARE YOU TRYING TO MAKE ME MAD AGAIN?
...
HOUSEWORK REALLY IS HARD.

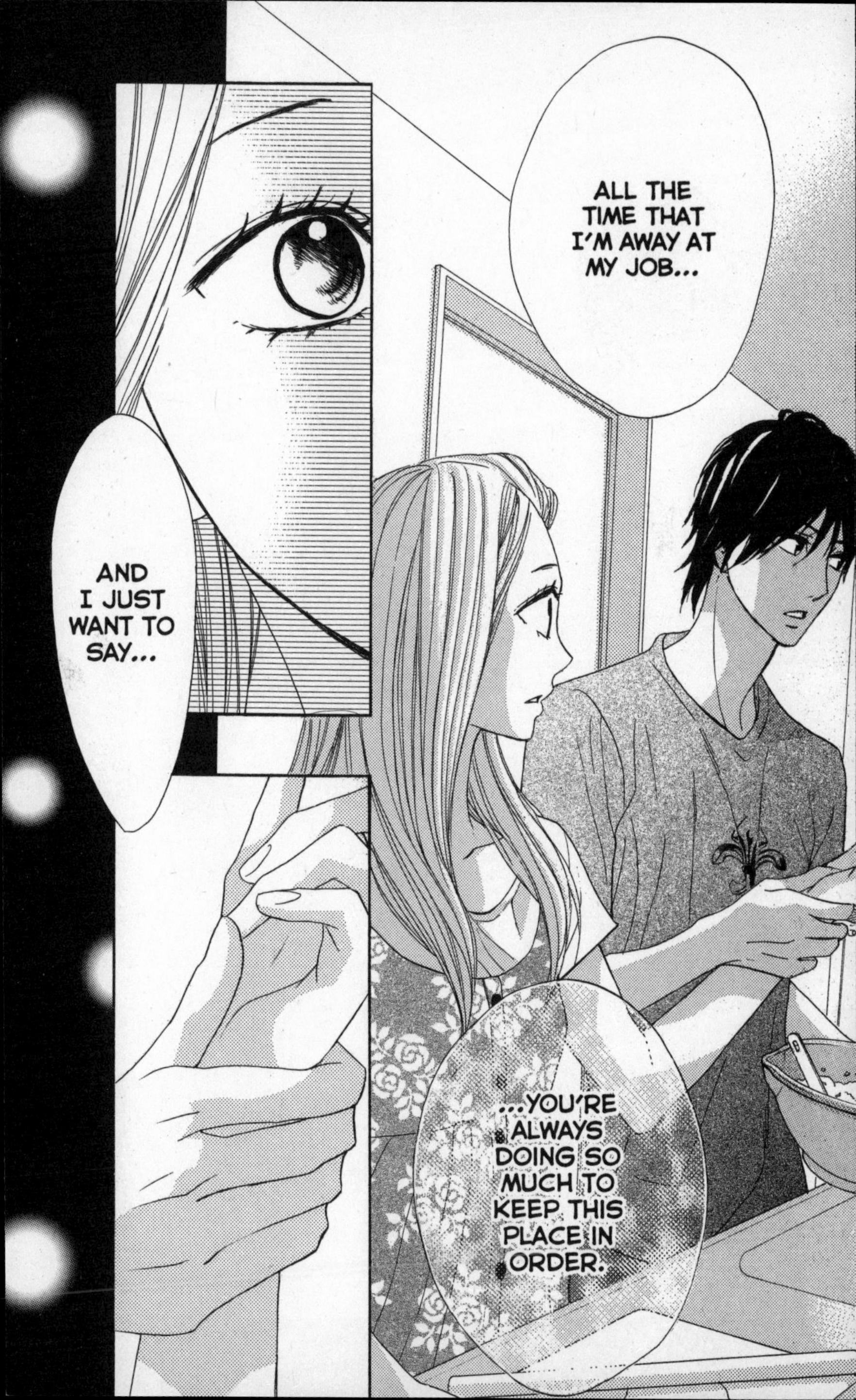
ALL THE TIME THAT I'M AWAY AT MY JOB...
...YOU'RE ALWAYS DOING SO MUCH TO KEEP THIS PLACE IN ORDER.
AND I JUST WANT TO SAY...

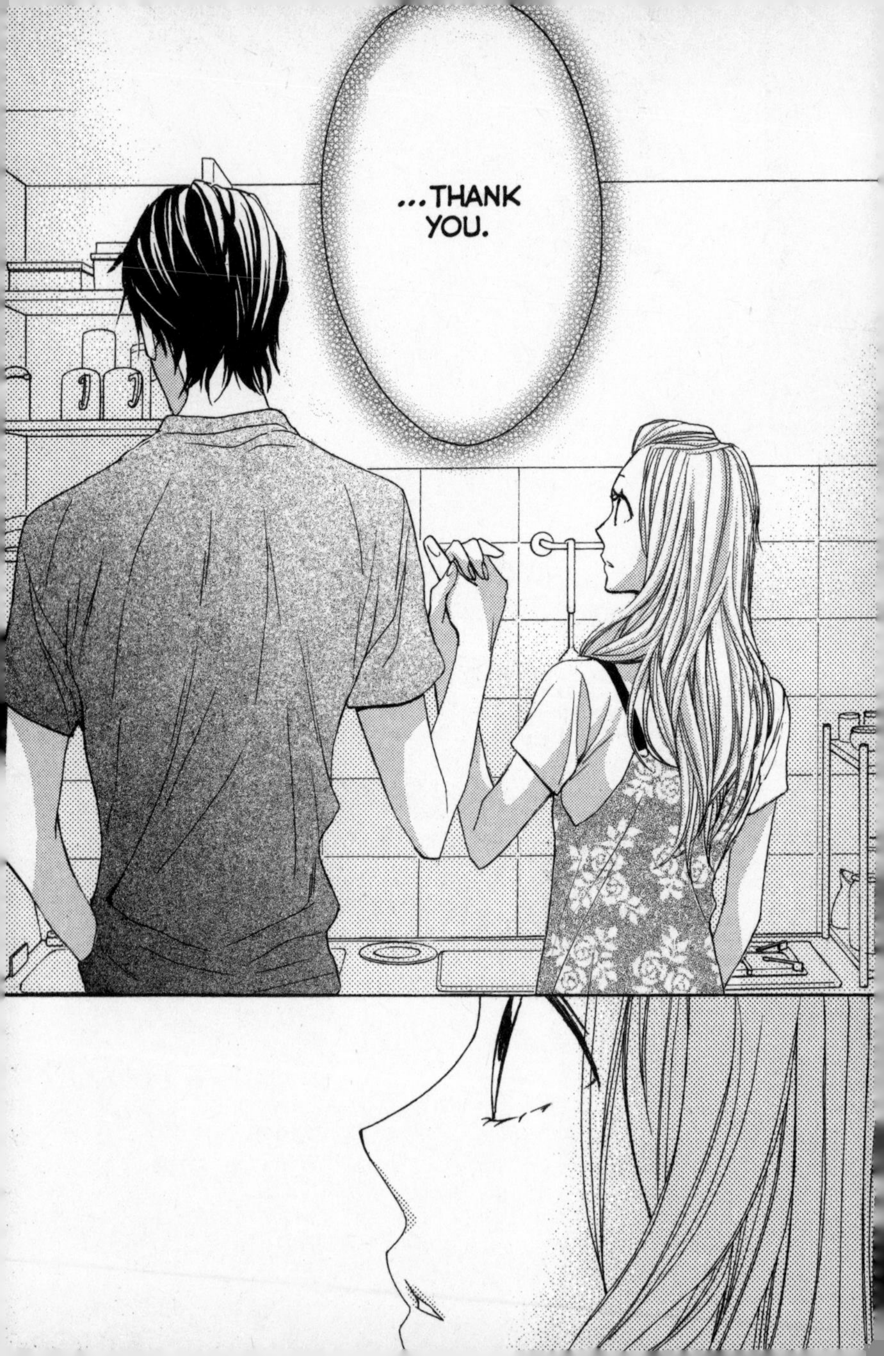
...THANK YOU.

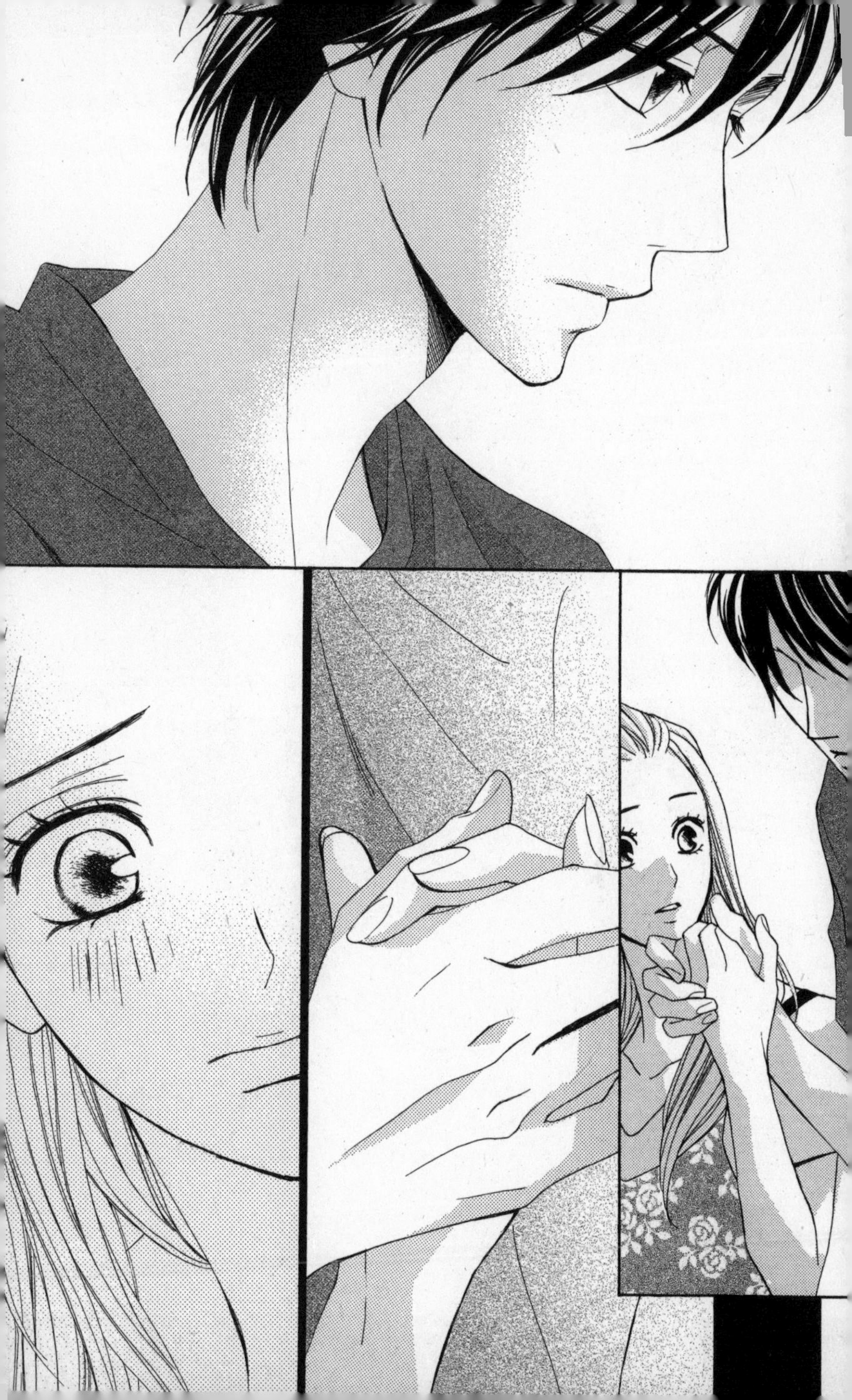

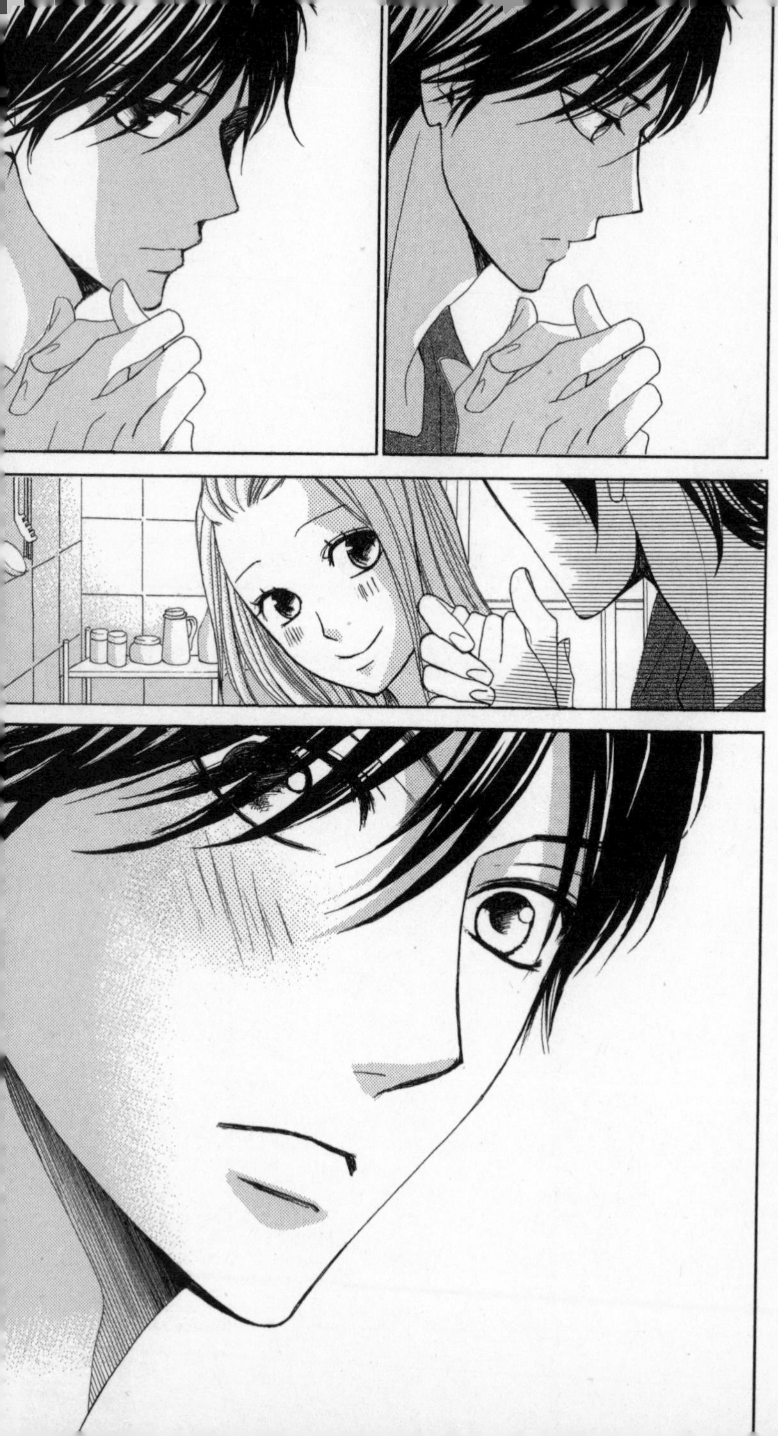

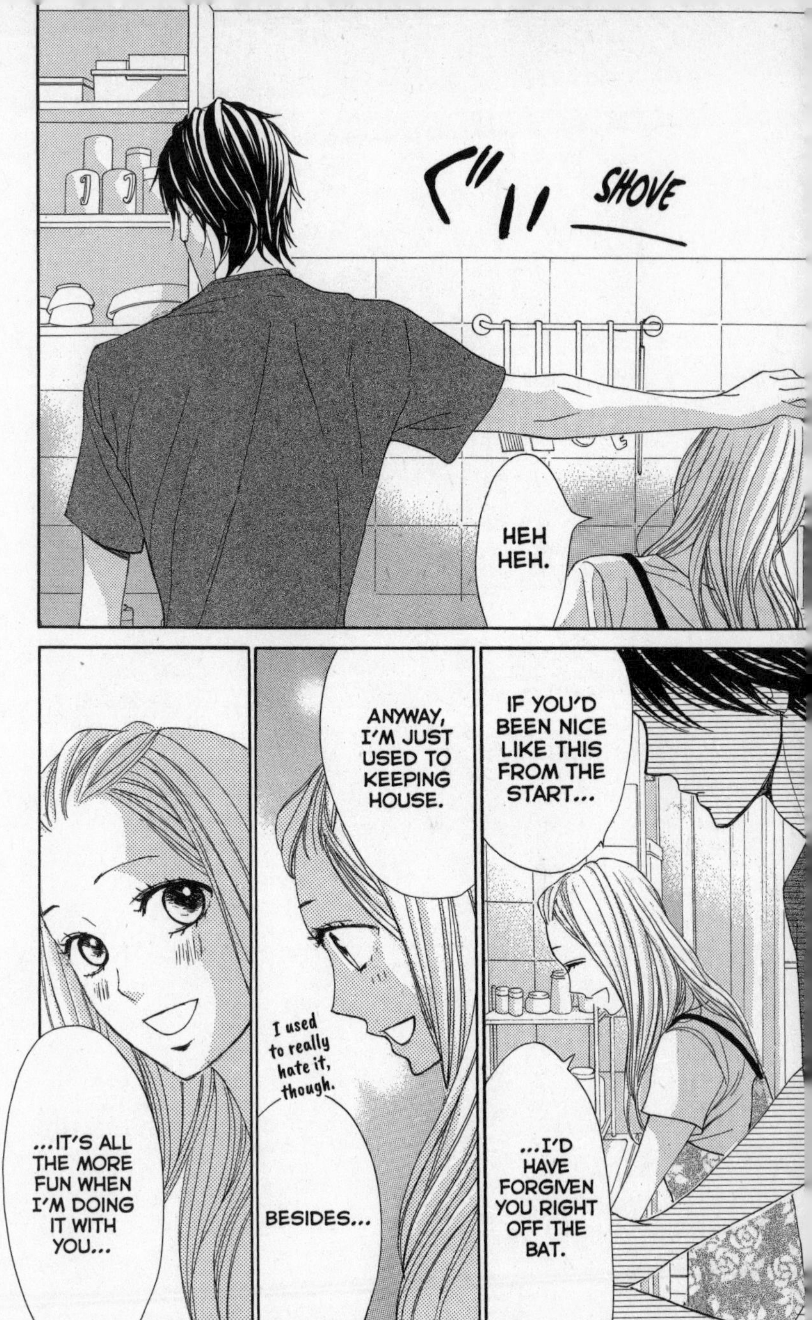
SHOVE
HEH HEH.
IF YOU'D BEEN NICE LIKE THIS FROM THE START...
...I'D HAVE FORGIVEN YOU RIGHT OFF THE BAT.
ANYWAY, I'M JUST USED TO KEEPING HOUSE.
I used to really hate it, though.
BESIDES...
...IT'S ALL THE MORE FUN WHEN I'M DOING IT WITH YOU...

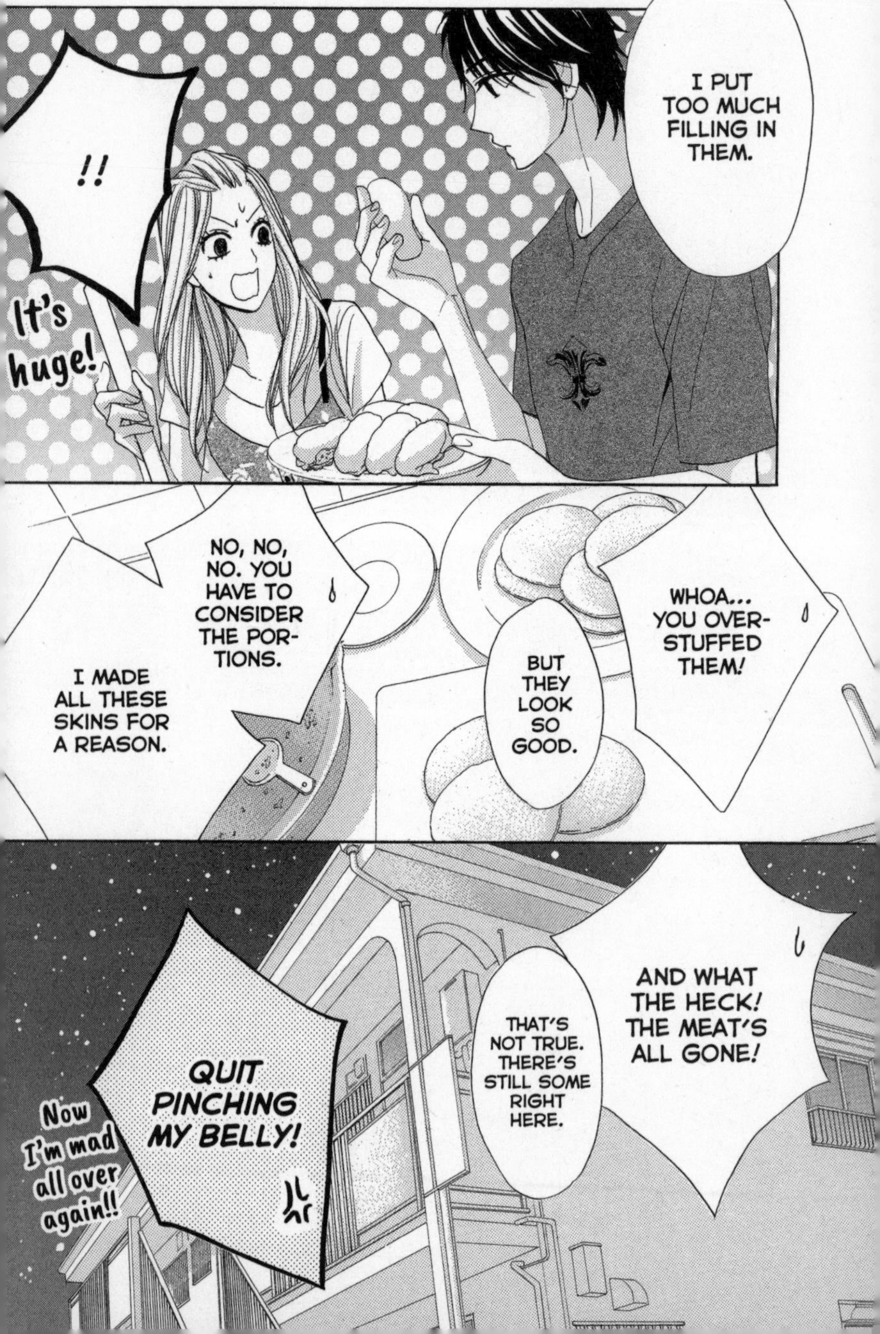
I PUT TOO MUCH FILLING IN THEM.
!!
It's huge!
WHOA... YOU OVER-STUFFED THEM!
BUT THEY LOOK SO GOOD.
NO, NO, NO. YOU HAVE TO CONSIDER THE POR-TIONS.
I MADE ALL THESE SKINS FOR A REASON.
AND WHAT THE HECK! THE MEAT'S ALL GONE!
THAT'S NOT TRUE. THERE'S STILL SOME RIGHT HERE.
QUIT PINCHING MY BELLY!
Now I'm mad all over again!!

L♥DK

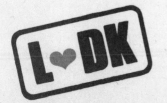

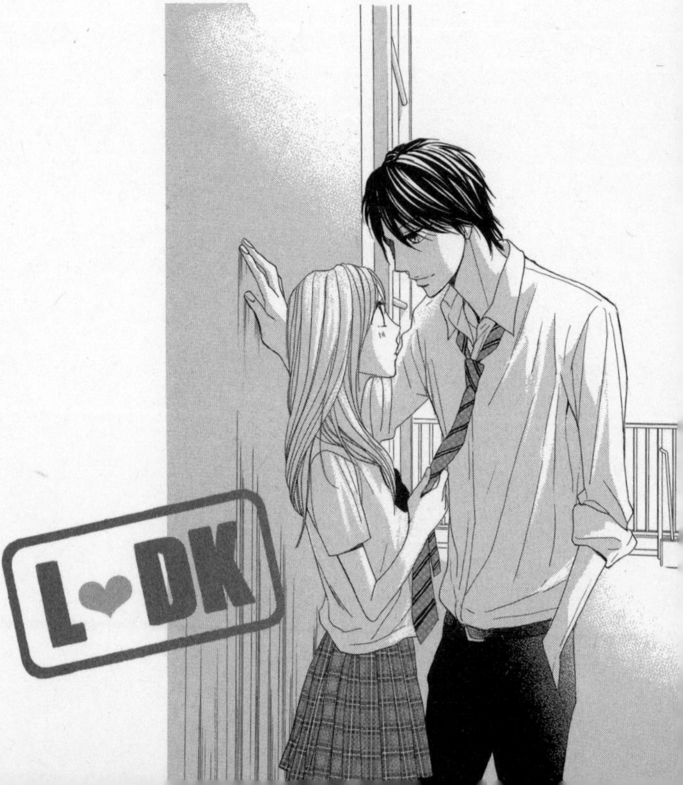
L♥DK

#58 Double Date

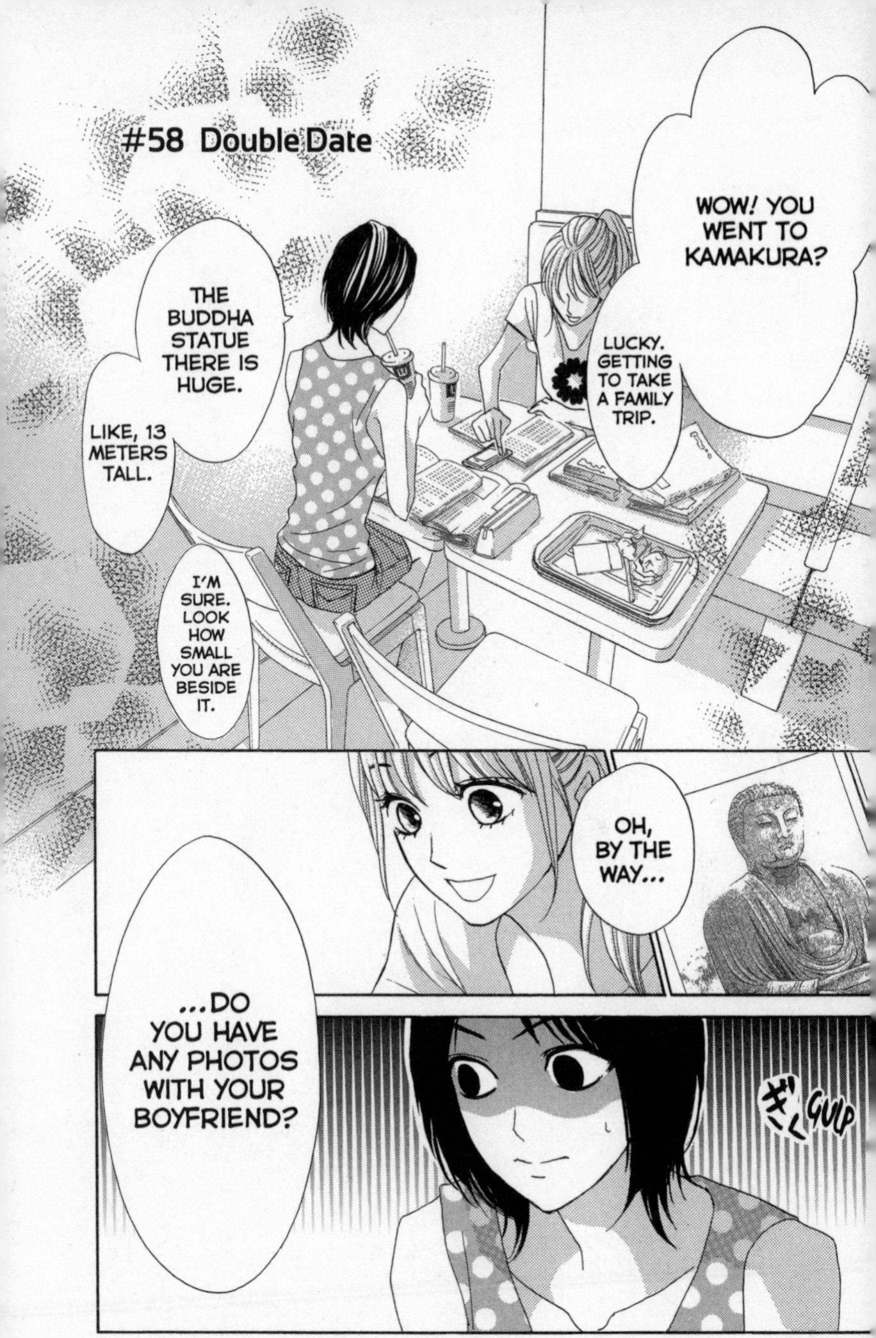
WOW! YOU WENT TO KAMAKURA?
LUCKY. GETTING TO TAKE A FAMILY TRIP.
THE BUDDHA STATUE THERE IS HUGE.
LIKE, 13 METERS TALL.
I'M SURE. LOOK HOW SMALL YOU ARE BESIDE IT.
OH, BY THE WAY...
...DO YOU HAVE ANY PHOTOS WITH YOUR BOYFRIEND?
ぎく GULP

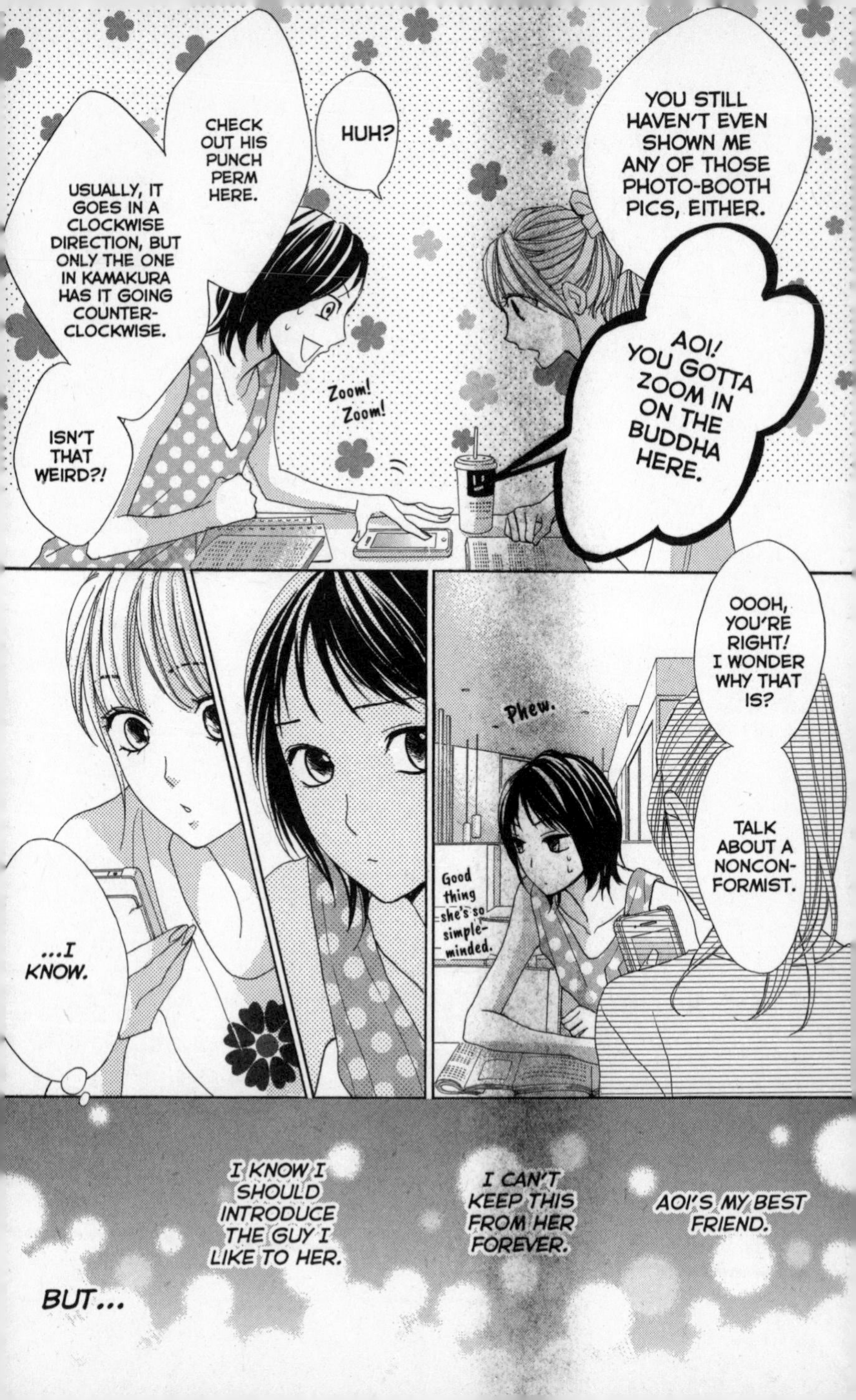
YOU STILL HAVEN'T EVEN SHOWN ME ANY OF THOSE PHOTO-BOOTH PICS, EITHER.
AOI! YOU GOTTA ZOOM IN ON THE BUDDHA HERE.
HUH?
CHECK OUT HIS PUNCH PERM HERE.
Zoom! Zoom!
USUALLY, IT GOES IN A CLOCKWISE DIRECTION, BUT ONLY THE ONE IN KAMAKURA HAS IT GOING COUNTER-CLOCKWISE.
ISN'T THAT WEIRD?!
OOOH, YOU'RE RIGHT! I WONDER WHY THAT IS?
TALK ABOUT A NONCON-FORMIST.
Phew.
Good thing she's so simple-minded.
...I KNOW.
AOI'S MY BEST FRIEND.
I CAN'T KEEP THIS FROM HER FOREVER.
I KNOW I SHOULD INTRODUCE THE GUY I LIKE TO HER.
BUT...

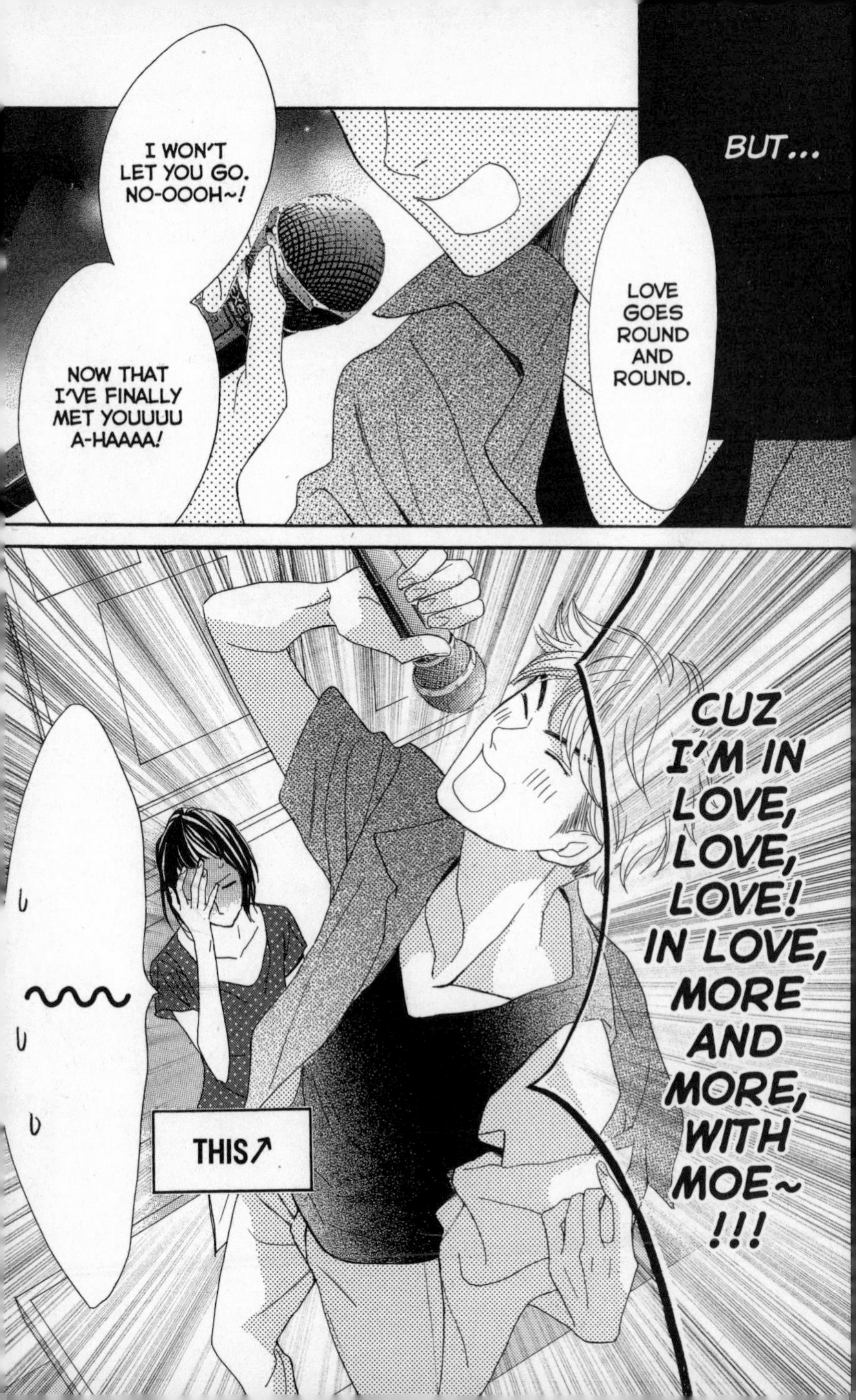
BUT...
LOVE GOES ROUND AND ROUND.
I WON'T LET YOU GO. NO-OOOH~!
NOW THAT I'VE FINALLY MET YOUUUU A-HAAAA!
CUZ I'M IN LOVE, LOVE, LOVE! IN LOVE, MORE AND MORE, WITH MOE~ !!!
THIS↗

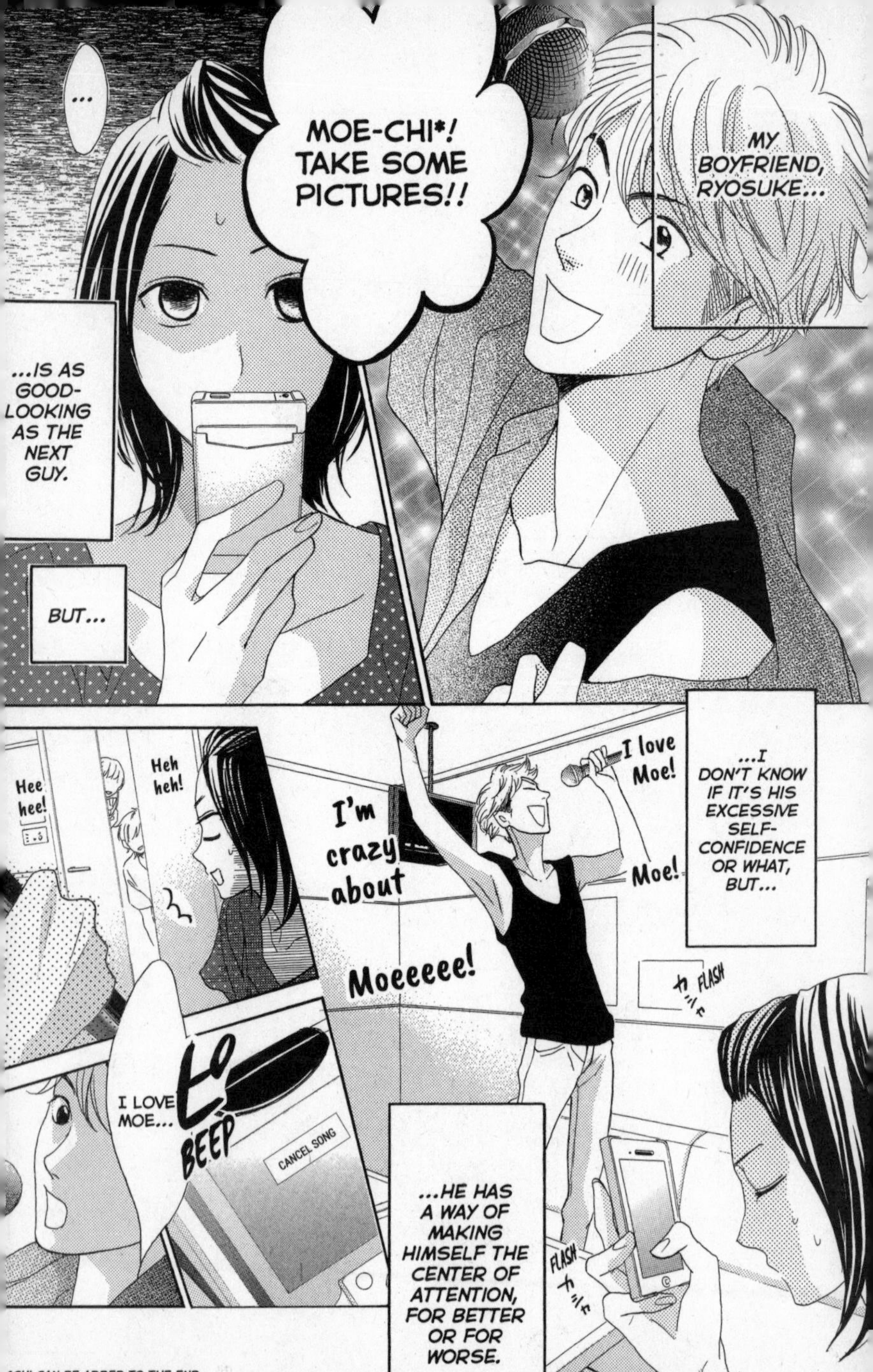
MY BOYFRIEND, RYOSUKE...
MOE-CHI*! TAKE SOME PICTURES!!
...
...IS AS GOOD-LOOKING AS THE NEXT GUY.
BUT...
...I DON'T KNOW IF IT'S HIS EXCESSIVE SELF-CONFIDENCE OR WHAT, BUT...
I love Moe!
Moe!
I'm crazy about
Moeeeee!
FLASH
Heh heh!
Hee hee!
I LOVE MOE...
BEEP
CANCEL SONG
...HE HAS A WAY OF MAKING HIMSELF THE CENTER OF ATTENTION, FOR BETTER OR FOR WORSE.
FLASH

*CHI CAN BE ADDED TO THE END OF A NAME TO BE CUTE OR INDICATE CLOSENESS TO SOMEONE.

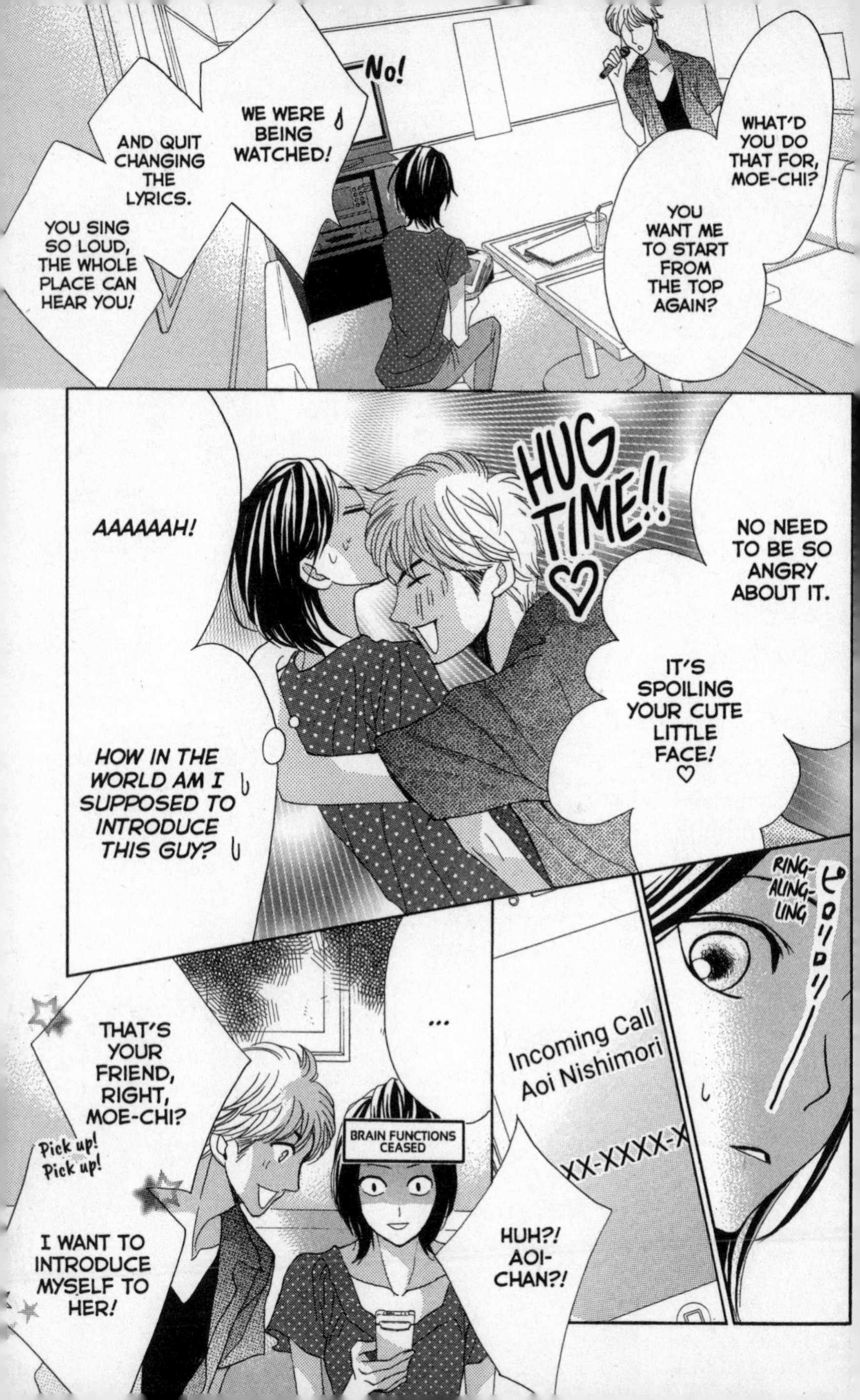
WHAT'D YOU DO THAT FOR, MOE-CHI?
YOU WANT ME TO START FROM THE TOP AGAIN?
No!
WE WERE BEING WATCHED!
AND QUIT CHANGING THE LYRICS.
YOU SING SO LOUD, THE WHOLE PLACE CAN HEAR YOU!
HUG TIME!! ♡
NO NEED TO BE SO ANGRY ABOUT IT.
IT'S SPOILING YOUR CUTE LITTLE FACE! ♡
AAAAAAH!
HOW IN THE WORLD AM I SUPPOSED TO INTRODUCE THIS GUY?
RING-ALING-LING
ピロリロリ
Incoming Call Aoi Nishimori
XX-XXXX-X
...
HUH?! AOI-CHAN?!
BRAIN FUNCTIONS CEASED
THAT'S YOUR FRIEND, RIGHT, MOE-CHI?
Pick up! Pick up!
I WANT TO INTRODUCE MYSELF TO HER!

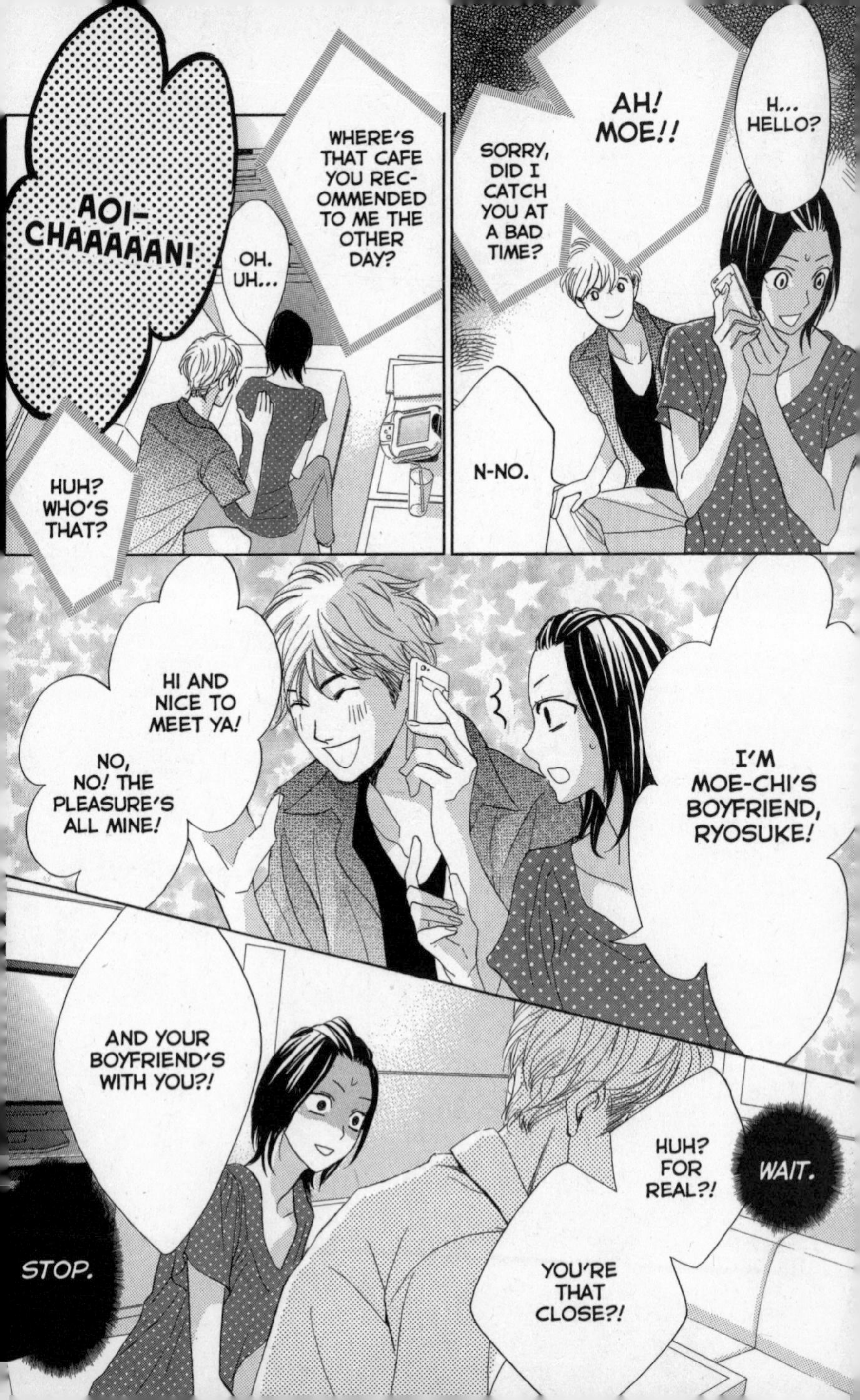
H... HELLO?
AH! MOE!!
SORRY, DID I CATCH YOU AT A BAD TIME?
N-NO.
WHERE'S THAT CAFE YOU REC-OMMENDED TO ME THE OTHER DAY?
OH. UH...
AOI-CHAAAAAN!
HUH? WHO'S THAT?
I'M MOE-CHI'S BOYFRIEND, RYOSUKE!
HI AND NICE TO MEET YA!
NO, NO! THE PLEASURE'S ALL MINE!
WAIT.
HUH? FOR REAL?!
YOU'RE THAT CLOSE?!
AND YOUR BOYFRIEND'S WITH YOU?!
STOP.

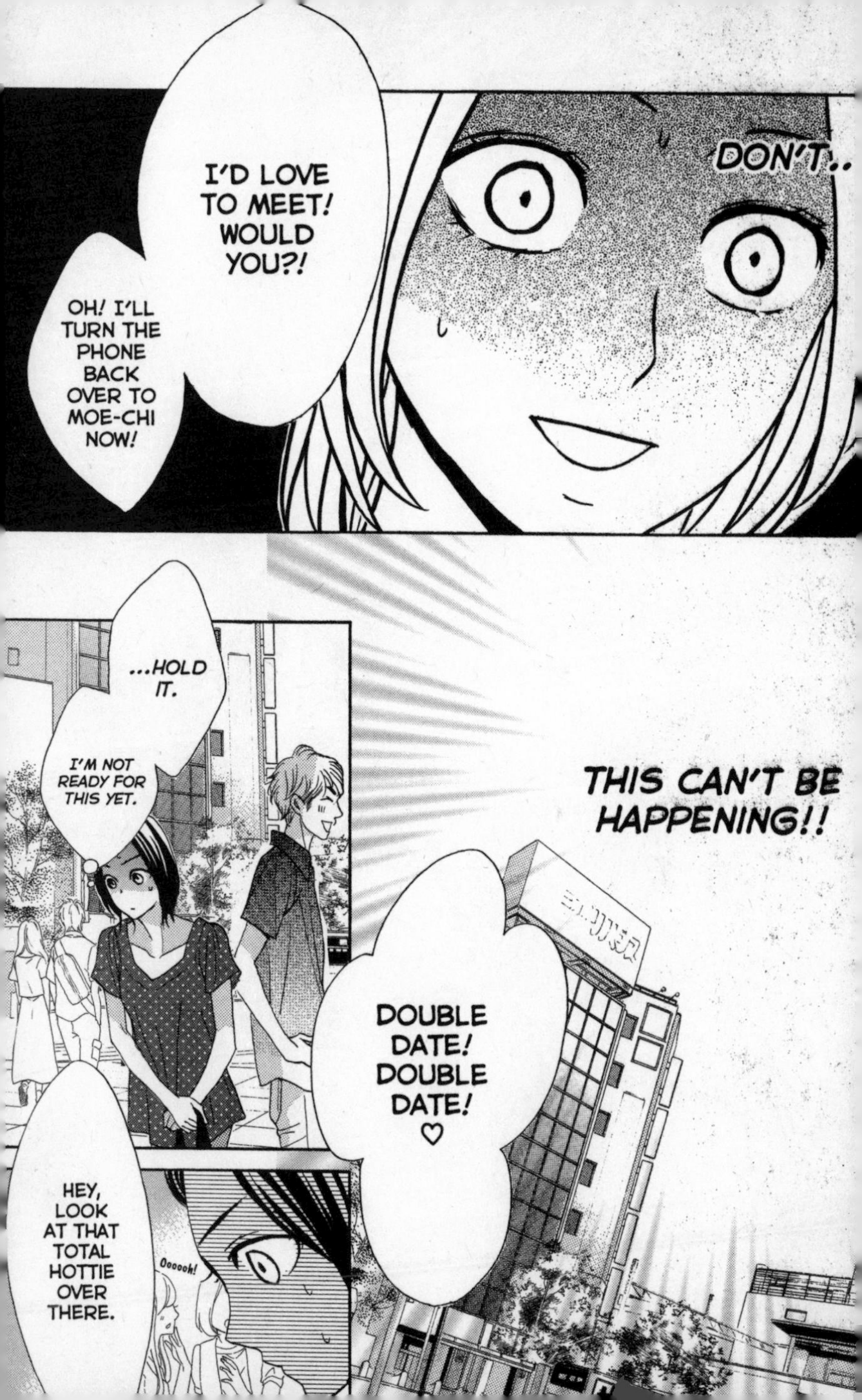
DON'T...
I'D LOVE TO MEET! WOULD YOU?!
OH! I'LL TURN THE PHONE BACK OVER TO MOE-CHI NOW!
THIS CAN'T BE HAPPENING!!
DOUBLE DATE! DOUBLE DATE! ♡
...HOLD IT.
I'M NOT READY FOR THIS YET.
HEY, LOOK AT THAT TOTAL HOTTIE OVER THERE.
Oooooh!

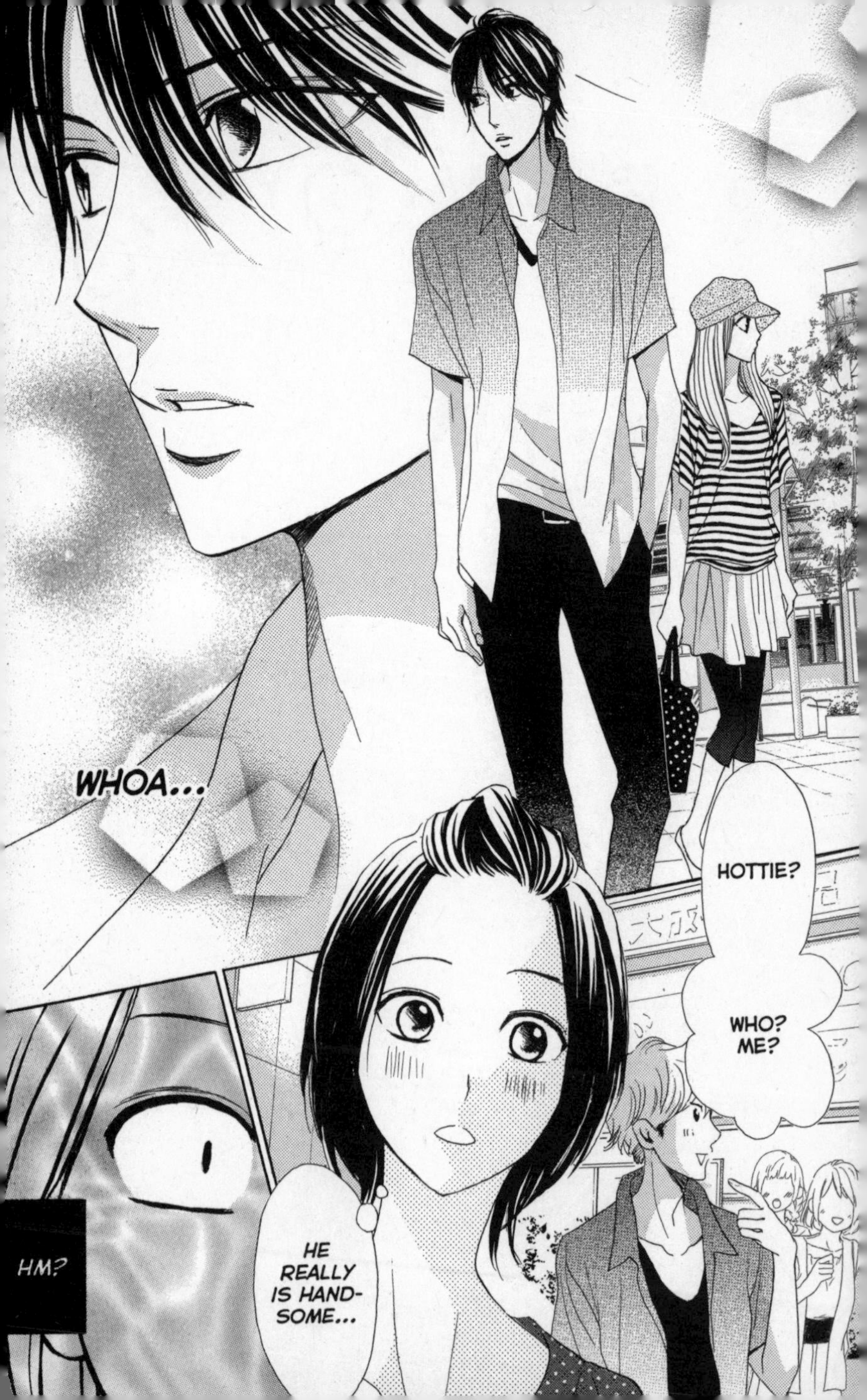
WHOA...
HOTTIE?
WHO? ME?
HE REALLY IS HAND-SOME...
HM?

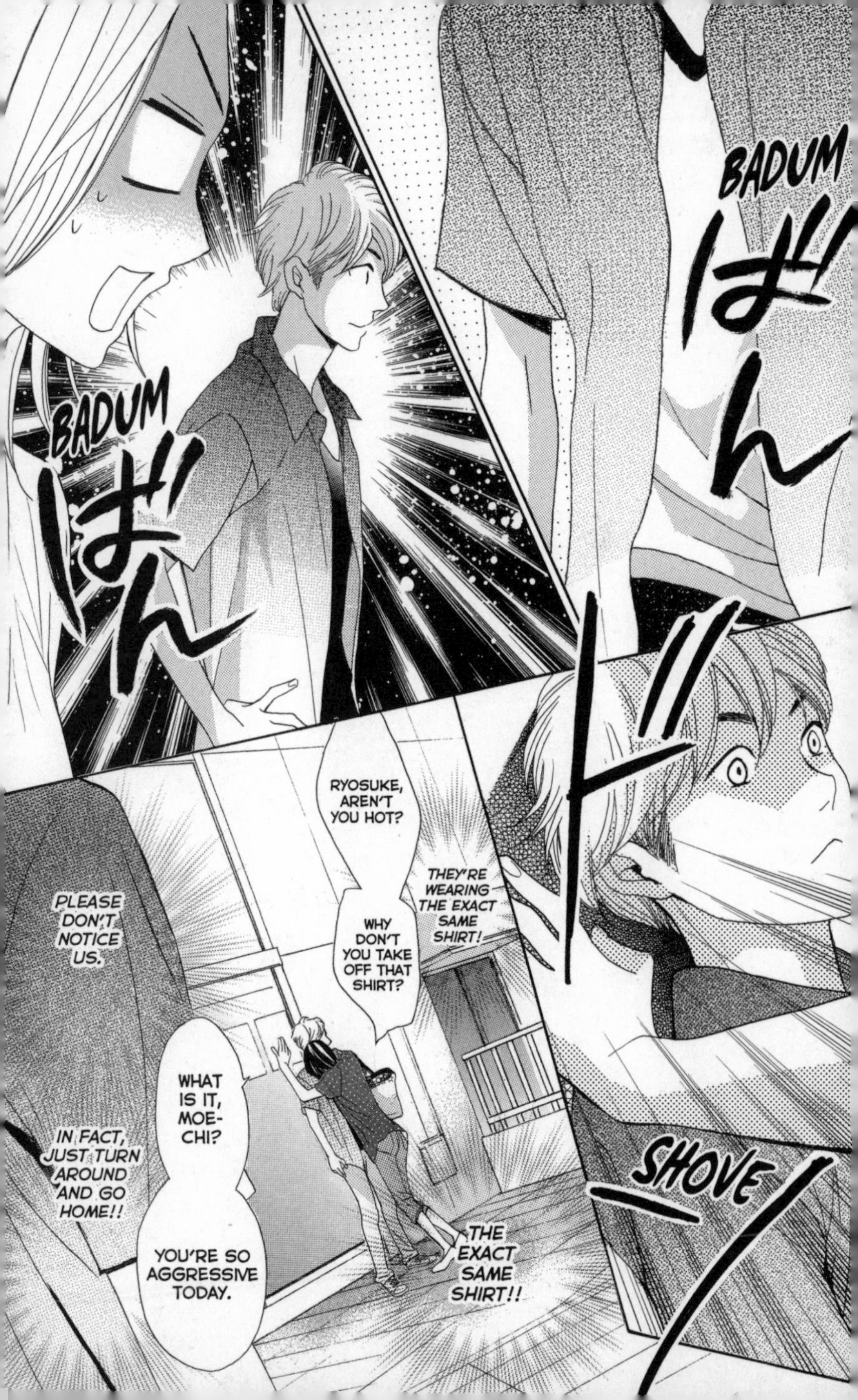
BADUM
ばん
BADUM
ばん
SHOVE
RYOSUKE, AREN'T YOU HOT?
THEY'RE WEARING THE EXACT SAME SHIRT!
WHY DON'T YOU TAKE OFF THAT SHIRT?
PLEASE DON'T NOTICE US.
WHAT IS IT, MOE-CHI?
THE EXACT SAME SHIRT!!
IN FACT, JUST TURN AROUND AND GO HOME!!
YOU'RE SO AGGRESSIVE TODAY.

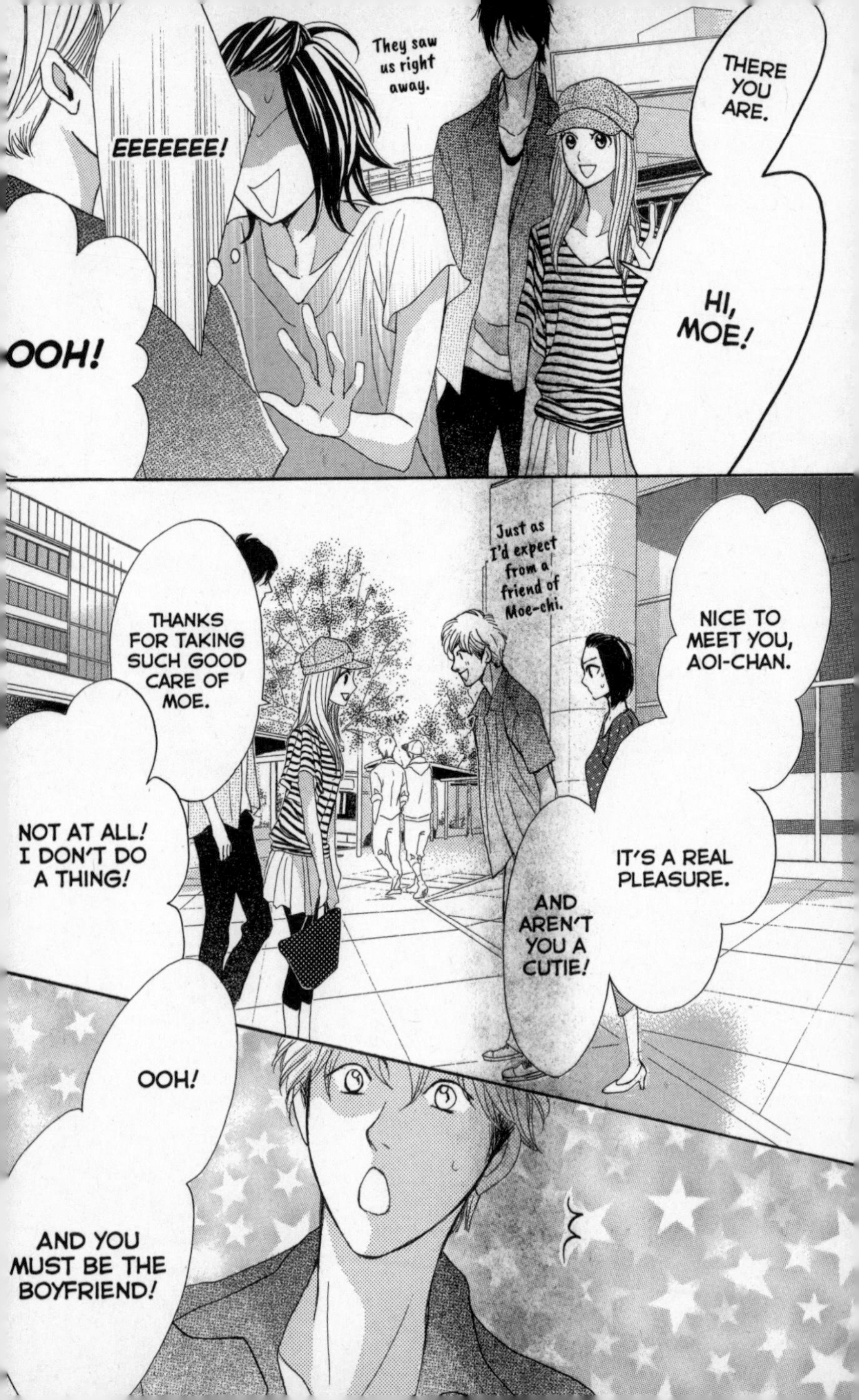
THERE YOU ARE.
HI, MOE!
They saw us right away.
EEEEEEE!
OOH!
NICE TO MEET YOU, AOI-CHAN.
IT'S A REAL PLEASURE.
AND AREN'T YOU A CUTIE!
Just as I'd expect from a friend of Moe-chi.
THANKS FOR TAKING SUCH GOOD CARE OF MOE.
NOT AT ALL! I DON'T DO A THING!
OOH!
AND YOU MUST BE THE BOYFRIEND!

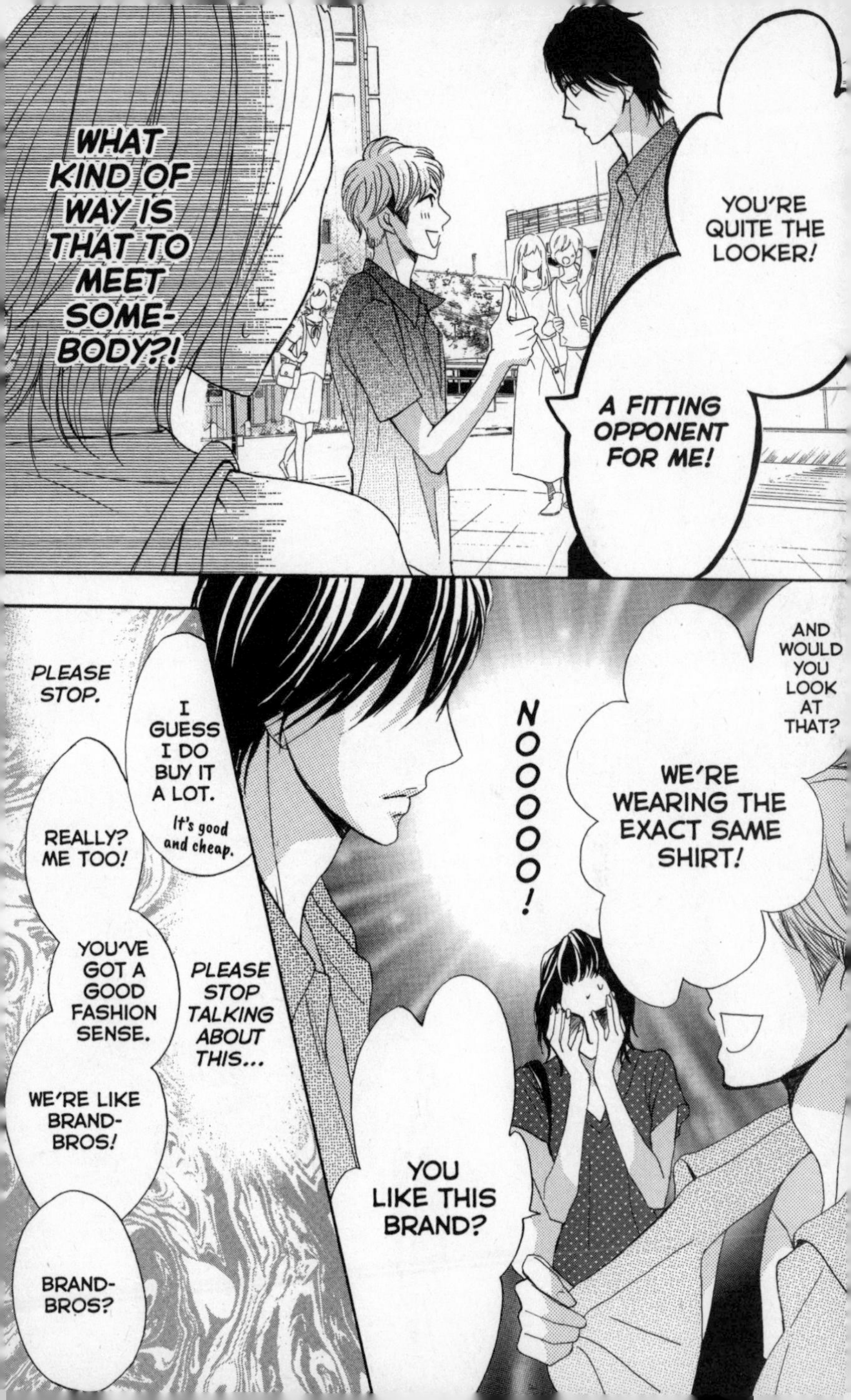
YOU'RE QUITE THE LOOKER!
A FITTING OPPONENT FOR ME!
WHAT KIND OF WAY IS THAT TO MEET SOME-BODY?!
AND WOULD YOU LOOK AT THAT?
WE'RE WEARING THE EXACT SAME SHIRT!
NOOOOOO!
YOU LIKE THIS BRAND?
I GUESS I DO BUY IT A LOT.
It's good and cheap.
PLEASE STOP.
REALLY? ME TOO!
YOU'VE GOT A GOOD FASHION SENSE.
PLEASE STOP TALKING ABOUT THIS...
WE'RE LIKE BRAND-BROS!
BRAND-BROS?

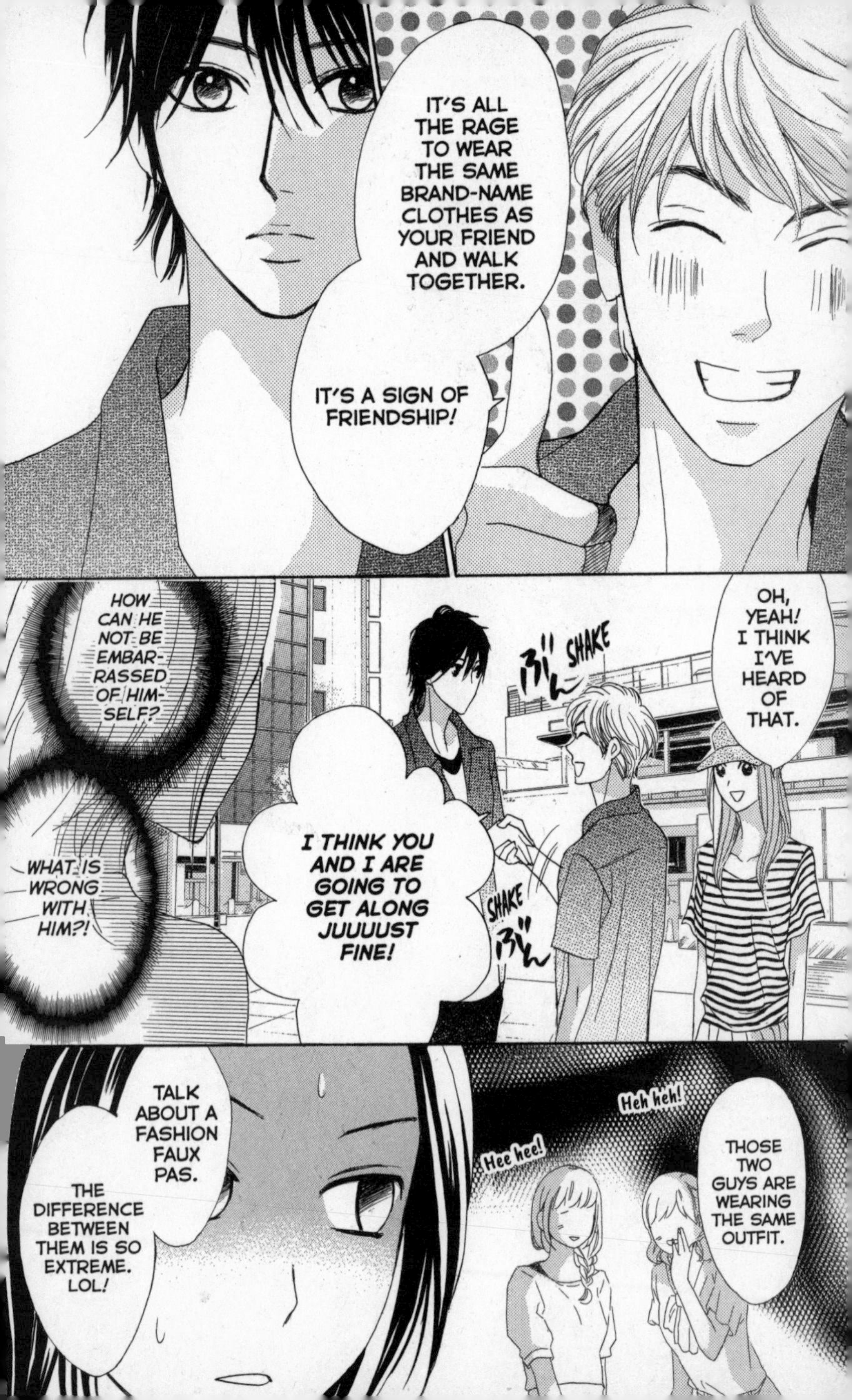
IT'S ALL THE RAGE TO WEAR THE SAME BRAND-NAME CLOTHES AS YOUR FRIEND AND WALK TOGETHER.
IT'S A SIGN OF FRIENDSHIP!
OH, YEAH! I THINK I'VE HEARD OF THAT.
ぶん SHAKE
I THINK YOU AND I ARE GOING TO GET ALONG JUUUUST FINE!
SHAKE ぶん
HOW CAN HE NOT BE EMBAR-RASSED OF HIM-SELF?
WHAT IS WRONG WITH HIM?!
THOSE TWO GUYS ARE WEARING THE SAME OUTFIT.
Heh heh!
Hee hee!
TALK ABOUT A FASHION FAUX PAS.
THE DIFFERENCE BETWEEN THEM IS SO EXTREME. LOL!

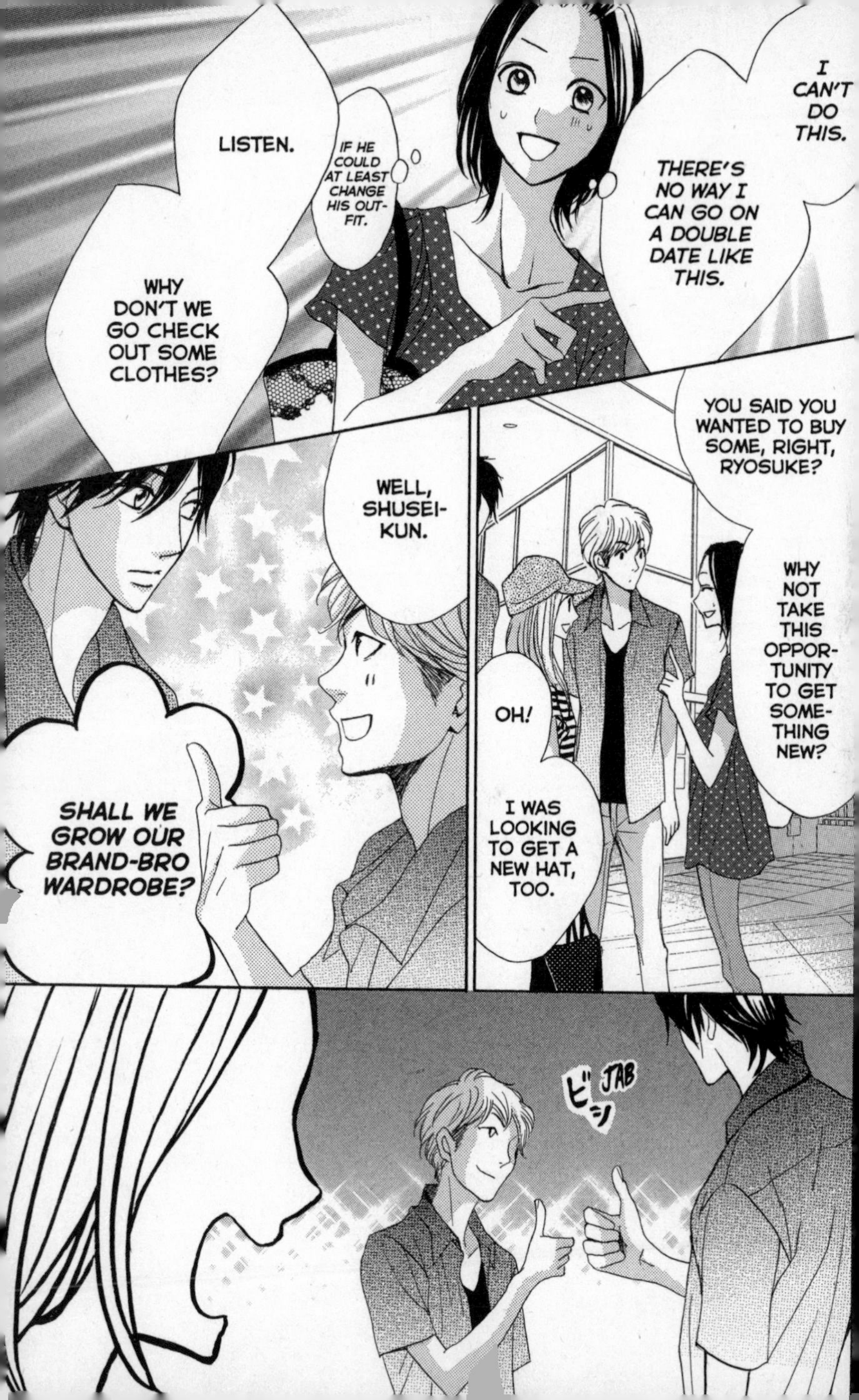
I CAN'T DO THIS.
THERE'S NO WAY I CAN GO ON A DOUBLE DATE LIKE THIS.
IF HE COULD AT LEAST CHANGE HIS OUT-FIT.
LISTEN.
WHY DON'T WE GO CHECK OUT SOME CLOTHES?
YOU SAID YOU WANTED TO BUY SOME, RIGHT, RYOSUKE?
WHY NOT TAKE THIS OPPOR-TUNITY TO GET SOME-THING NEW?
OH!
I WAS LOOKING TO GET A NEW HAT, TOO.
WELL, SHUSEI-KUN.
SHALL WE GROW OUR BRAND-BRO WARDROBE?
ビシ
JAB

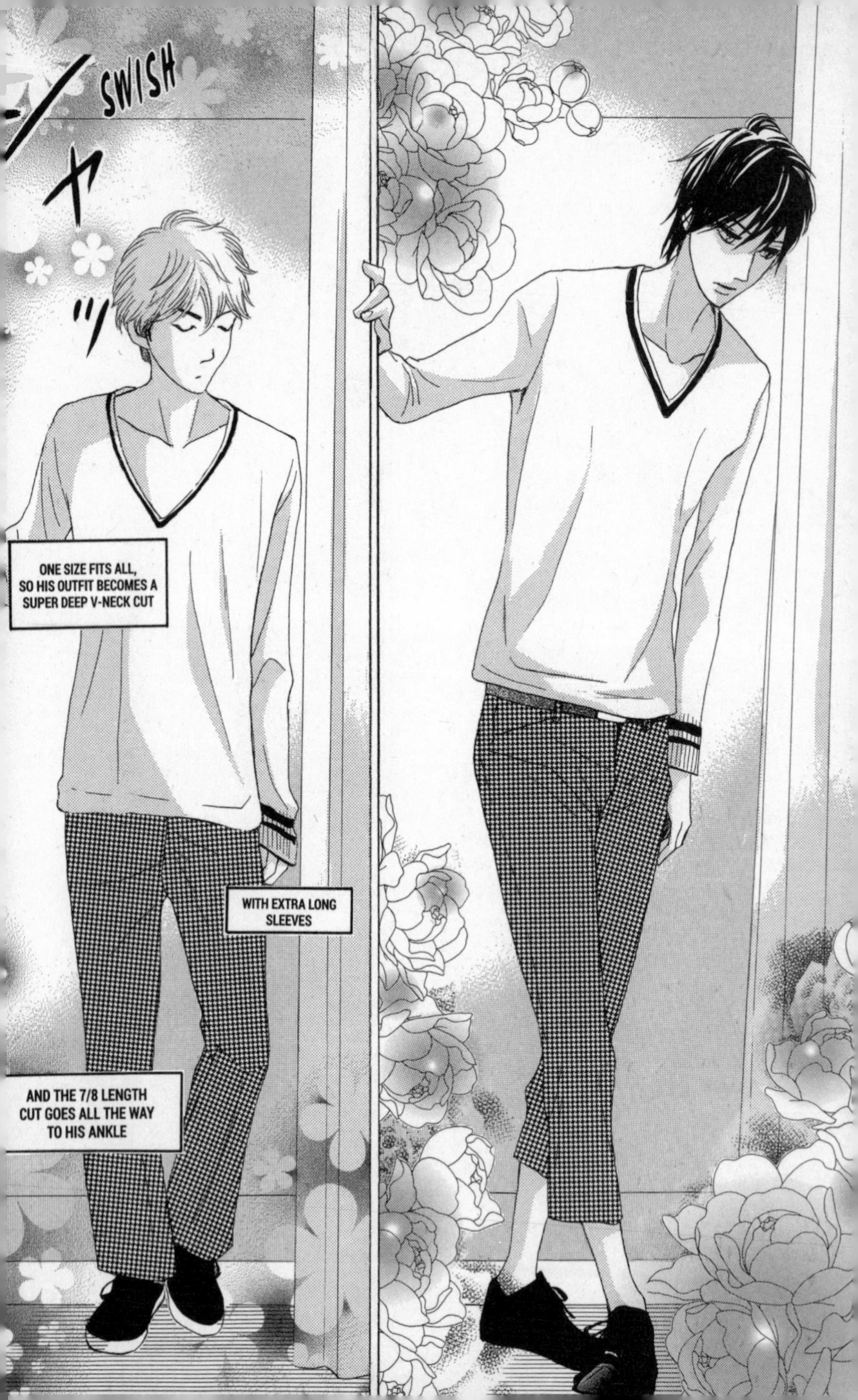
SWISH
ONE SIZE FITS ALL, SO HIS OUTFIT BECOMES A SUPER DEEP V-NECK CUT
WITH EXTRA LONG SLEEVES
AND THE 7/8 LENGTH CUT GOES ALL THE WAY TO HIS ANKLE

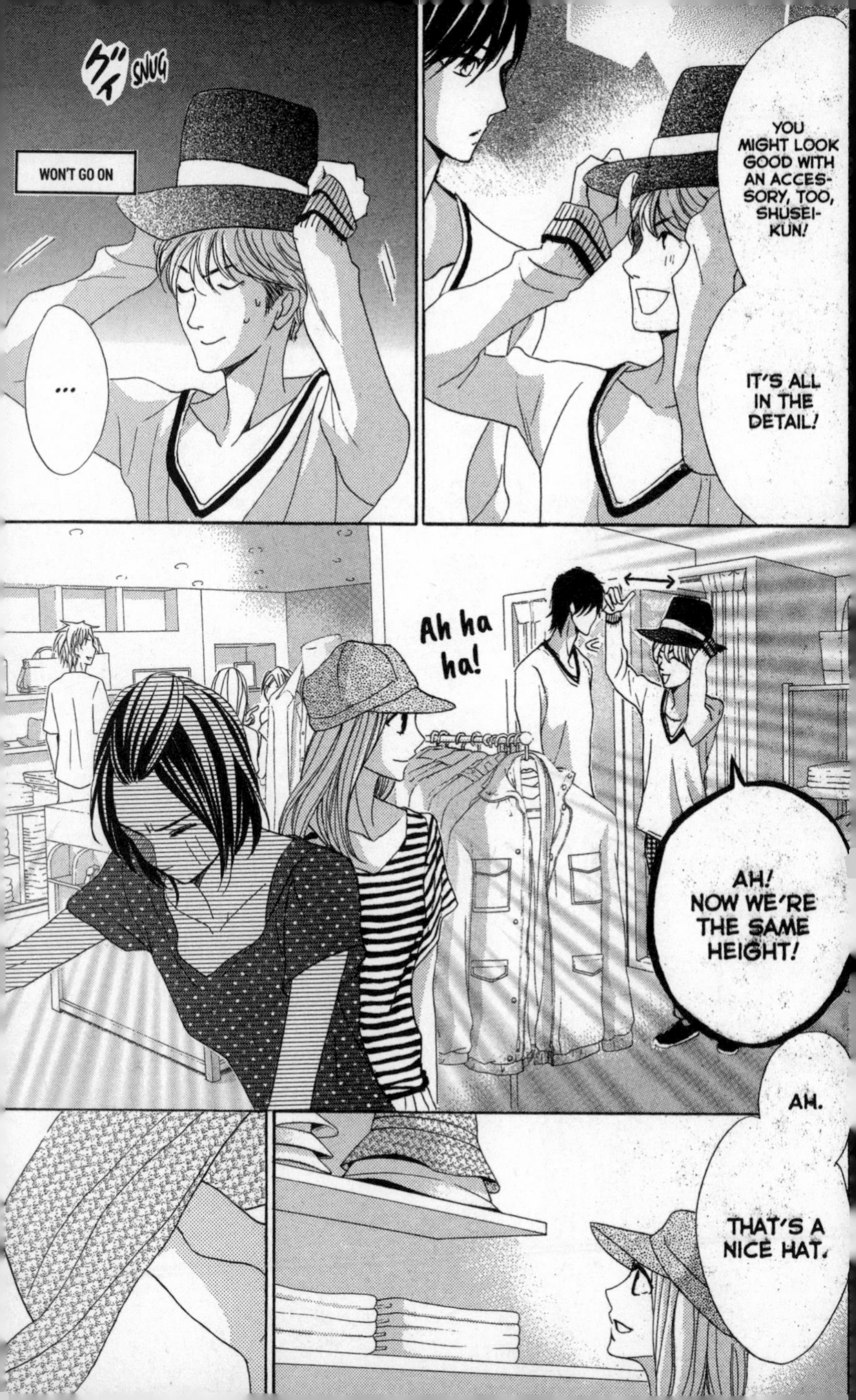
YOU MIGHT LOOK GOOD WITH AN ACCESSORY, TOO, SHUSEI-KUN!
IT'S ALL IN THE DETAIL!
グイ SNUG
WON'T GO ON
...
AH! NOW WE'RE THE SAME HEIGHT!
Ah ha ha!
AH.
THAT'S A NICE HAT.

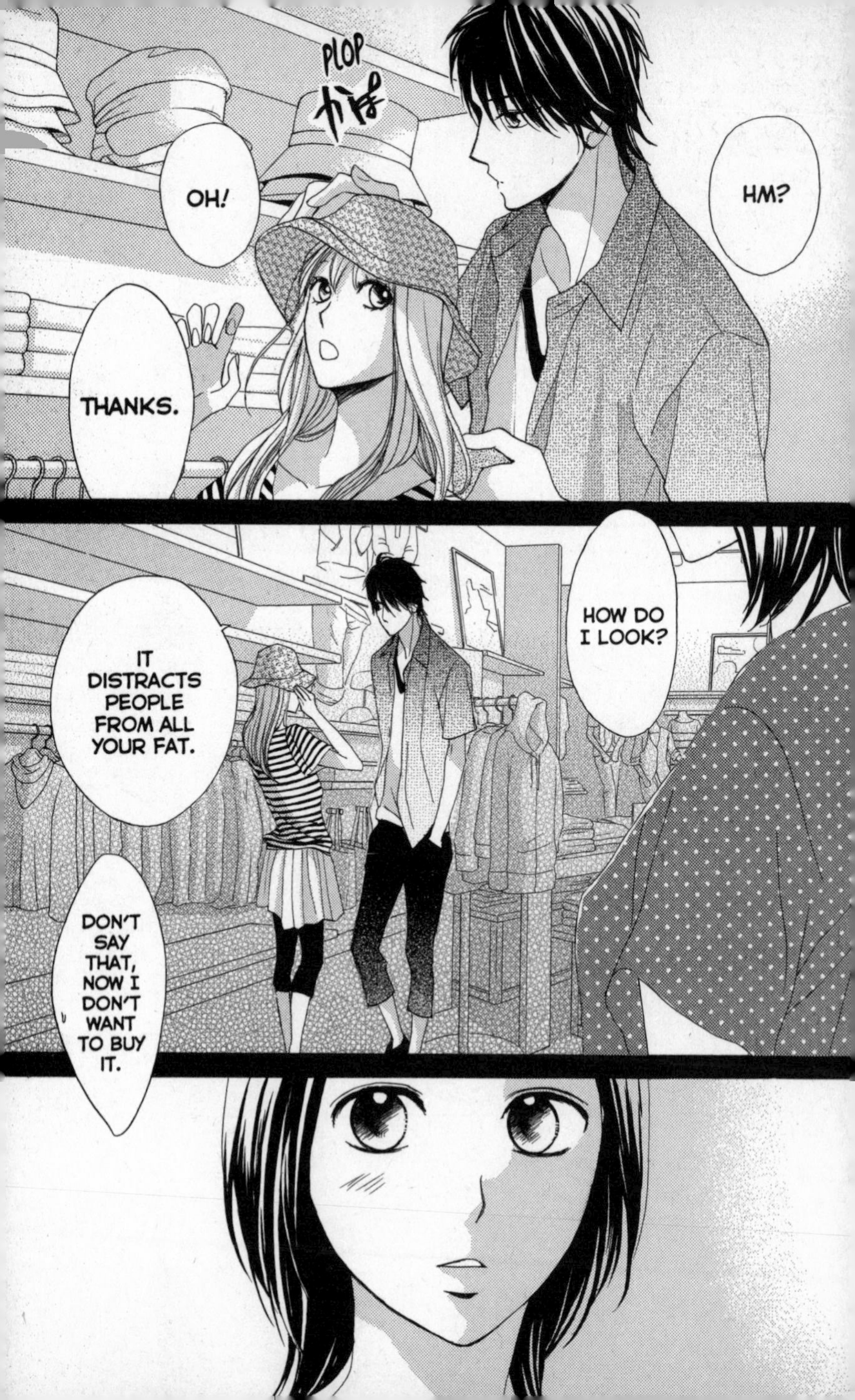
PLOP
かぽ
HM?
OH!
THANKS.
HOW DO I LOOK?
IT DISTRACTS PEOPLE FROM ALL YOUR FAT.
DON'T SAY THAT, NOW I DON'T WANT TO BUY IT.

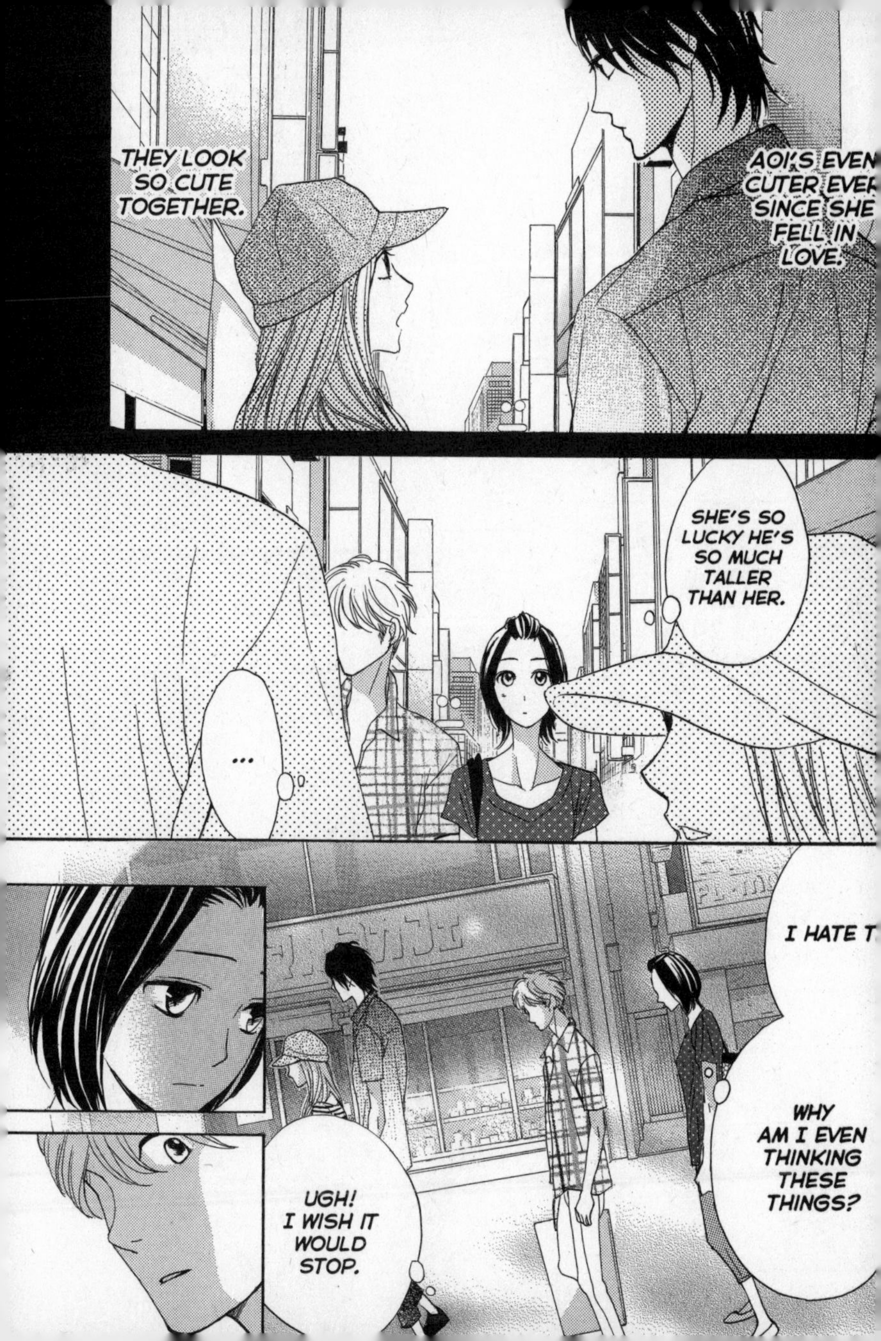
AOI'S EVEN CUTER EVER SINCE SHE FELL IN LOVE.
THEY LOOK SO CUTE TOGETHER.
SHE'S SO LUCKY HE'S SO MUCH TALLER THAN HER.
...
I HATE T
WHY AM I EVEN THINKING THESE THINGS?
UGH! I WISH IT WOULD STOP.

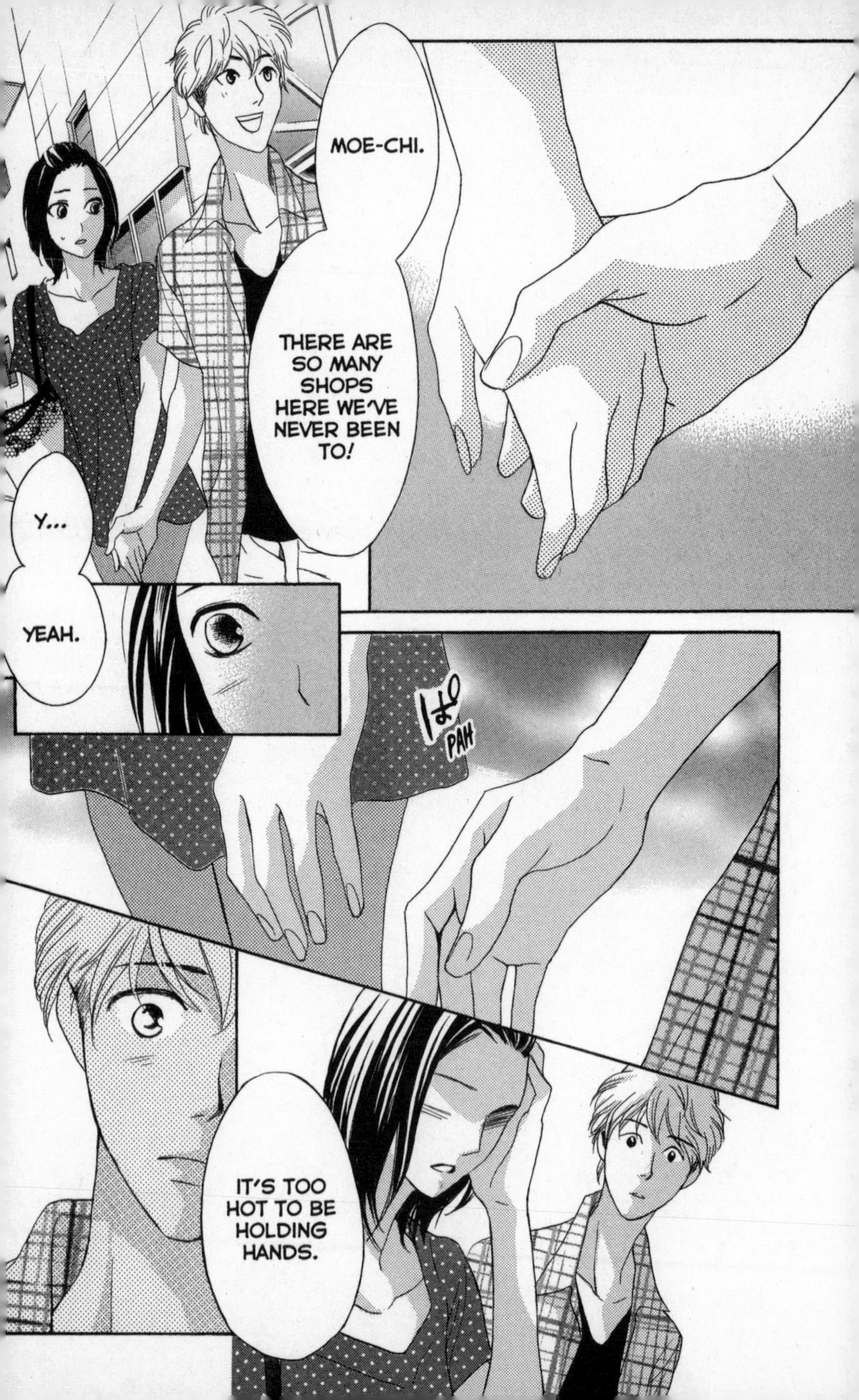
MOE-CHI.
THERE ARE SO MANY SHOPS HERE WE'VE NEVER BEEN TO!
Y...
YEAH.
ぱ
PAH
IT'S TOO HOT TO BE HOLDING HANDS.

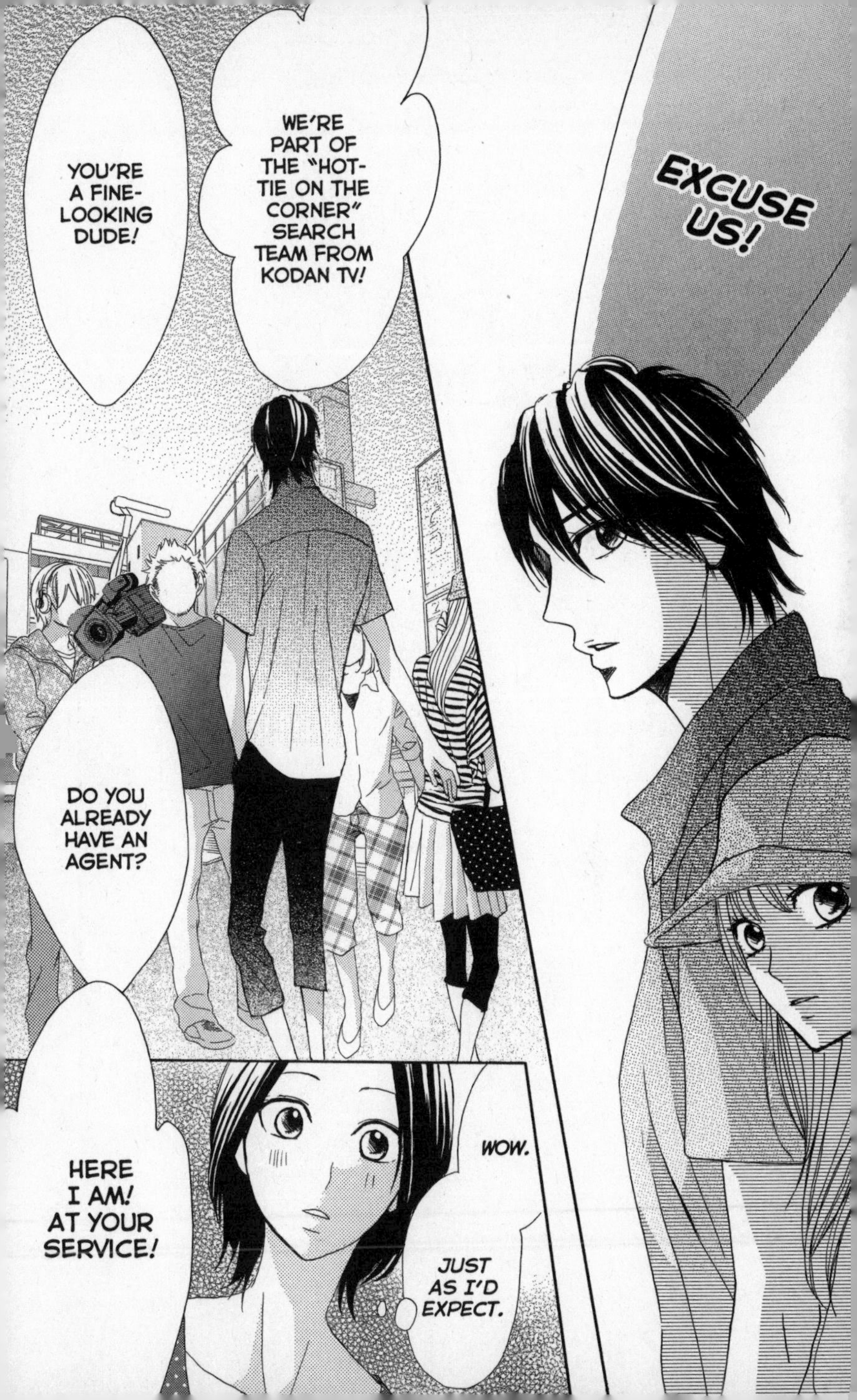
EXCUSE US!
WE'RE PART OF THE "HOT-TIE ON THE CORNER" SEARCH TEAM FROM KODAN TV!
YOU'RE A FINE-LOOKING DUDE!
DO YOU ALREADY HAVE AN AGENT?
WOW.
JUST AS I'D EXPECT.
HERE I AM! AT YOUR SERVICE!

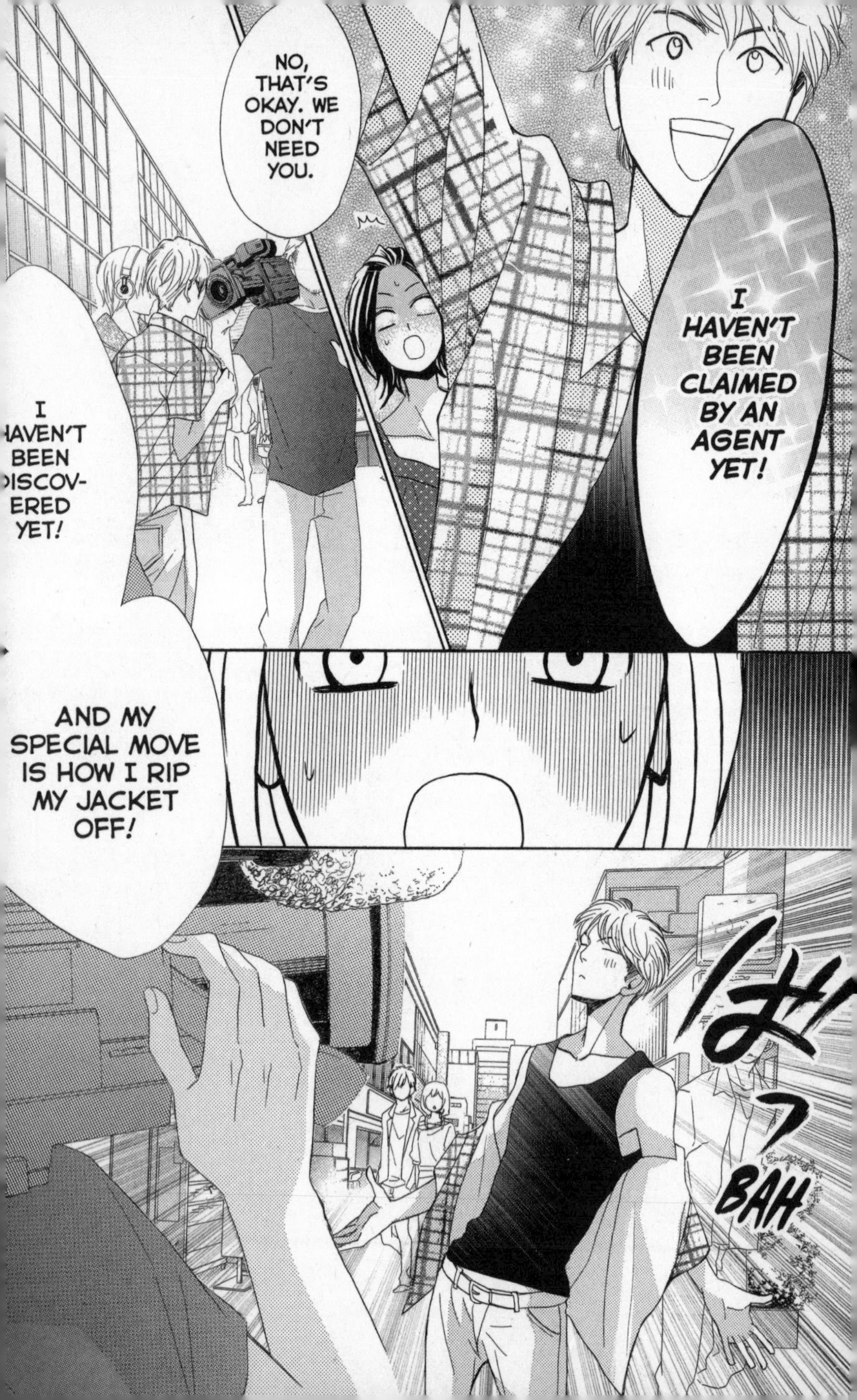
I HAVEN'T BEEN CLAIMED BY AN AGENT YET!
NO, THAT'S OKAY. WE DON'T NEED YOU.
I HAVEN'T BEEN DISCOV-ERED YET!
AND MY SPECIAL MOVE IS HOW I RIP MY JACKET OFF!
ばっ
BAH

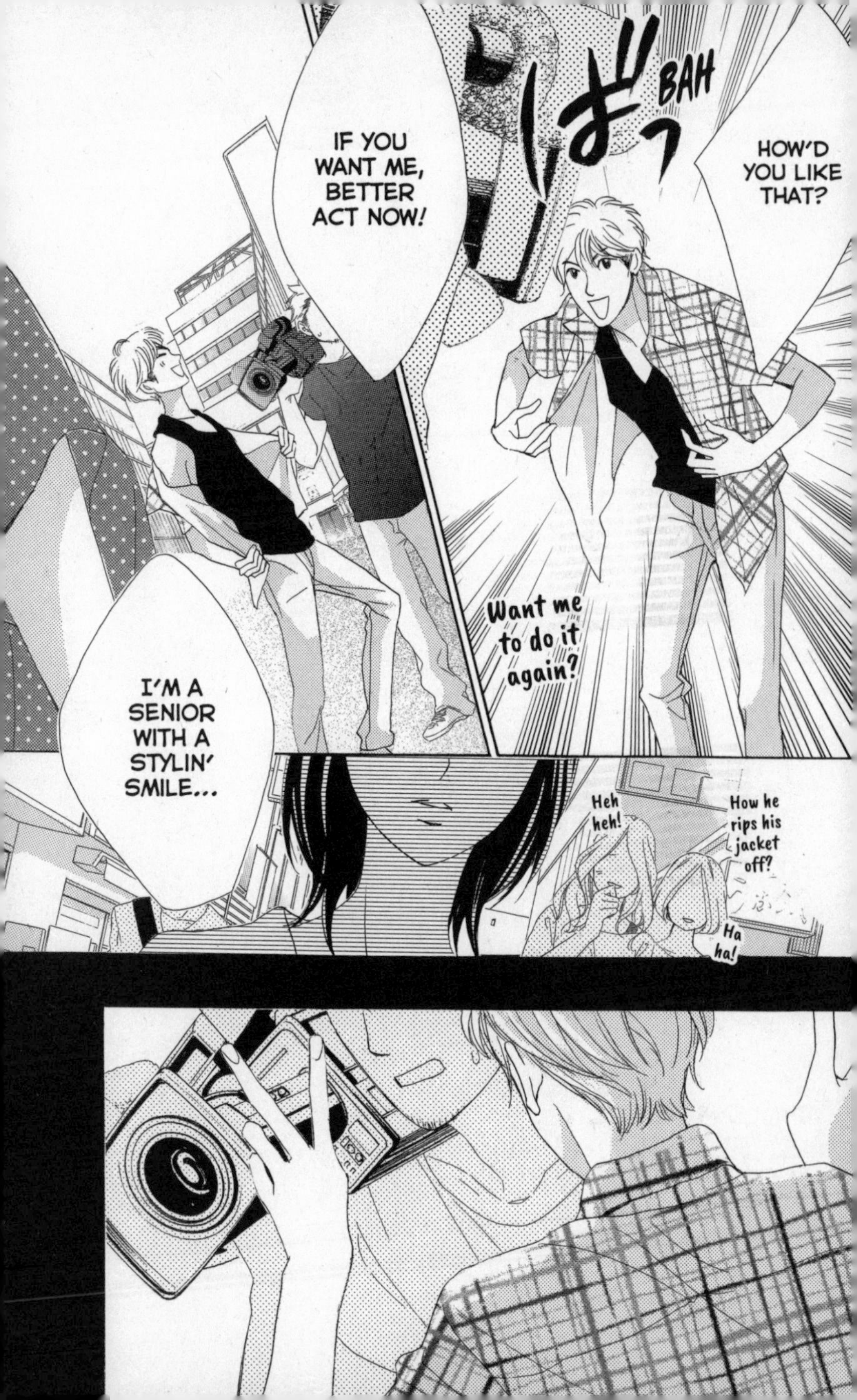
ばっ
BAH
HOW'D YOU LIKE THAT?
Want me to do it again?
IF YOU WANT ME, BETTER ACT NOW!
I'M A SENIOR WITH A STYLIN' SMILE...
How he rips his jacket off?
Heh heh!
Ha ha!

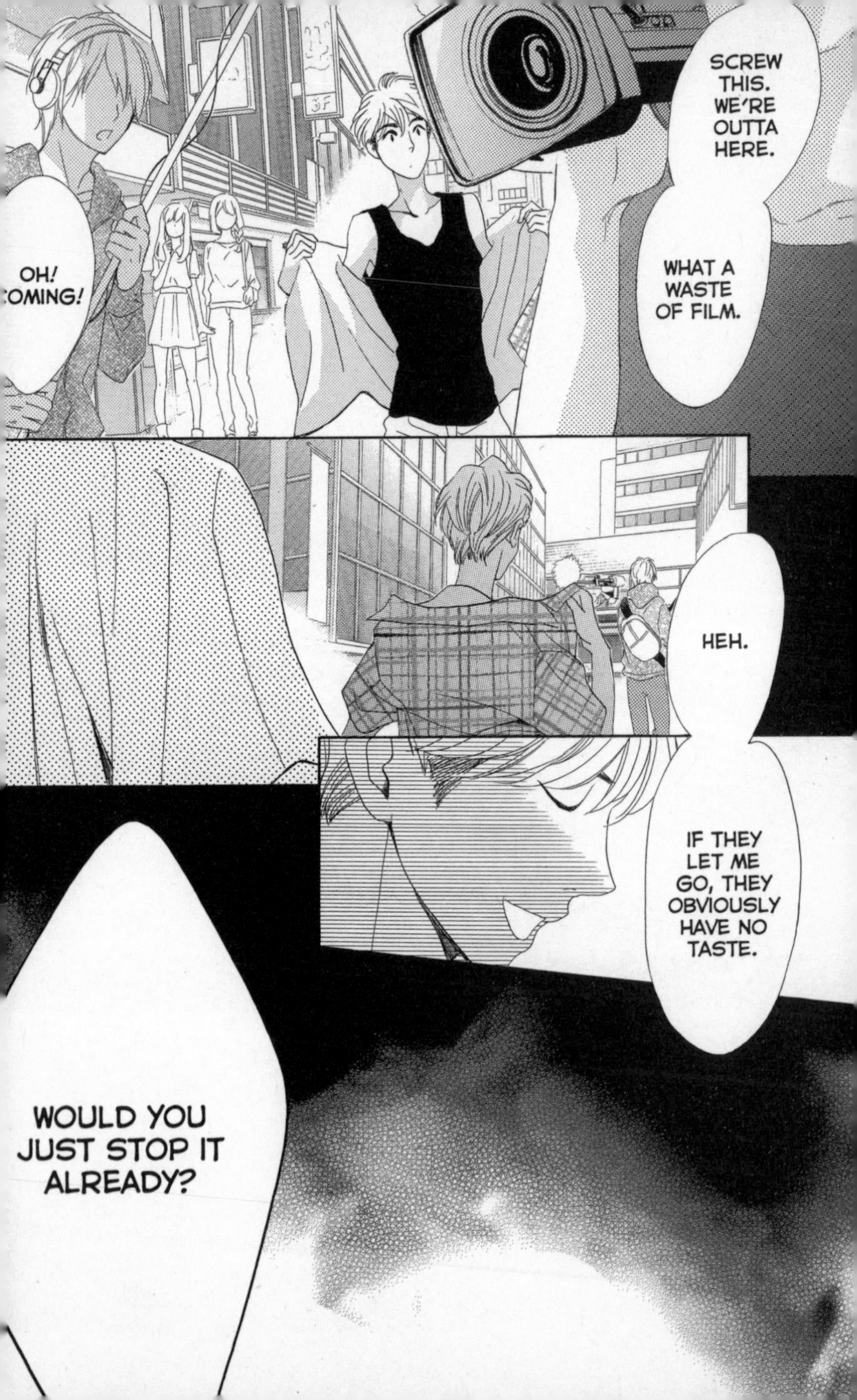
SCREW THIS. WE'RE OUTTA HERE.
WHAT A WASTE OF FILM.
OH! OMING!
HEH.
IF THEY LET ME GO, THEY OBVIOUSLY HAVE NO TASTE.
WOULD YOU JUST STOP IT ALREADY?

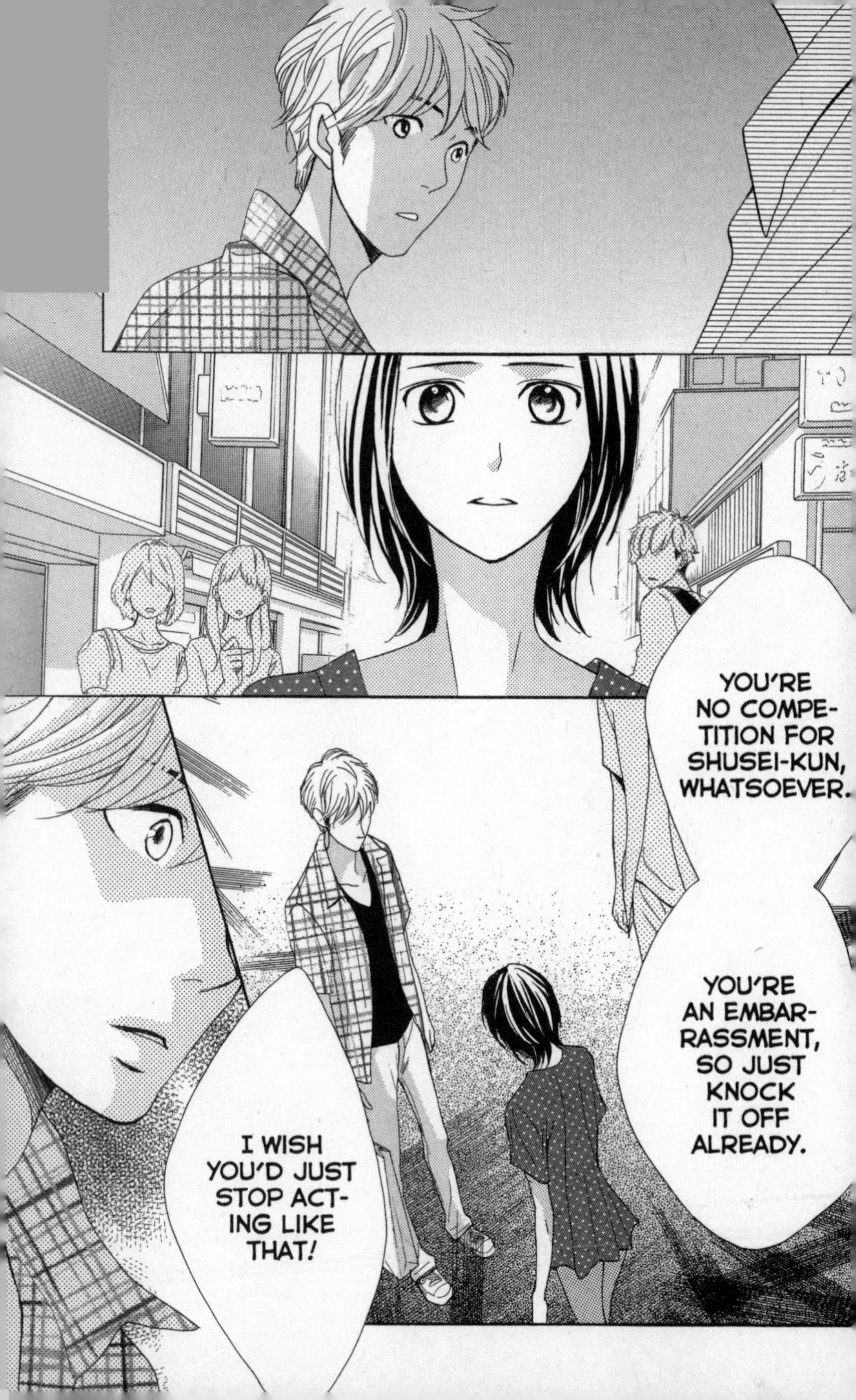
YOU'RE NO COMPETITION FOR SHUSEI-KUN, WHATSOEVER.
YOU'RE AN EMBARRASSMENT, SO JUST KNOCK IT OFF ALREADY.
I WISH YOU'D JUST STOP ACTING LIKE THAT!

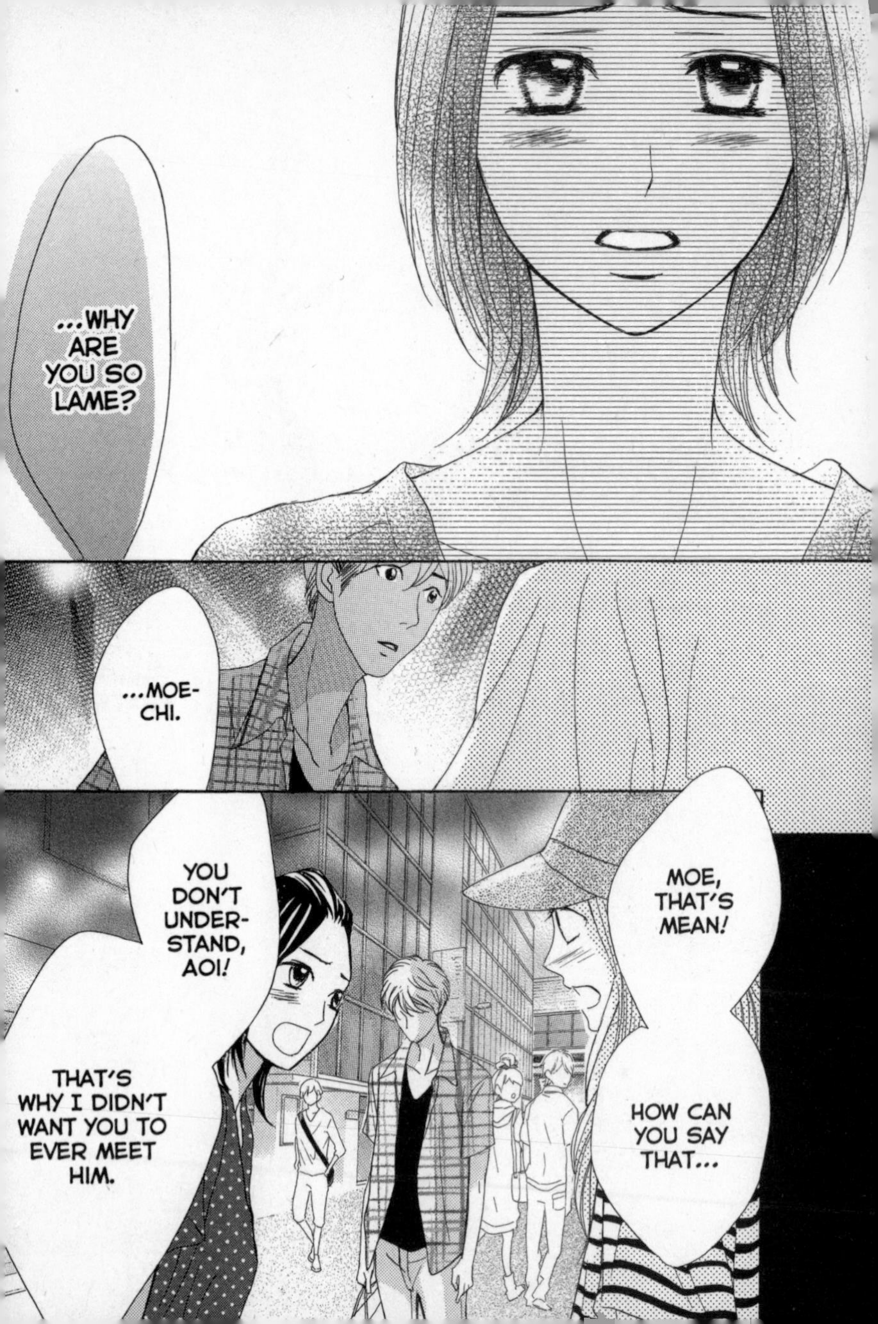
...WHY ARE YOU SO LAME?
...MOE-CHI.
MOE, THAT'S MEAN!
HOW CAN YOU SAY THAT...
YOU DON'T UNDERSTAND, AOI!
THAT'S WHY I DIDN'T WANT YOU TO EVER MEET HIM.

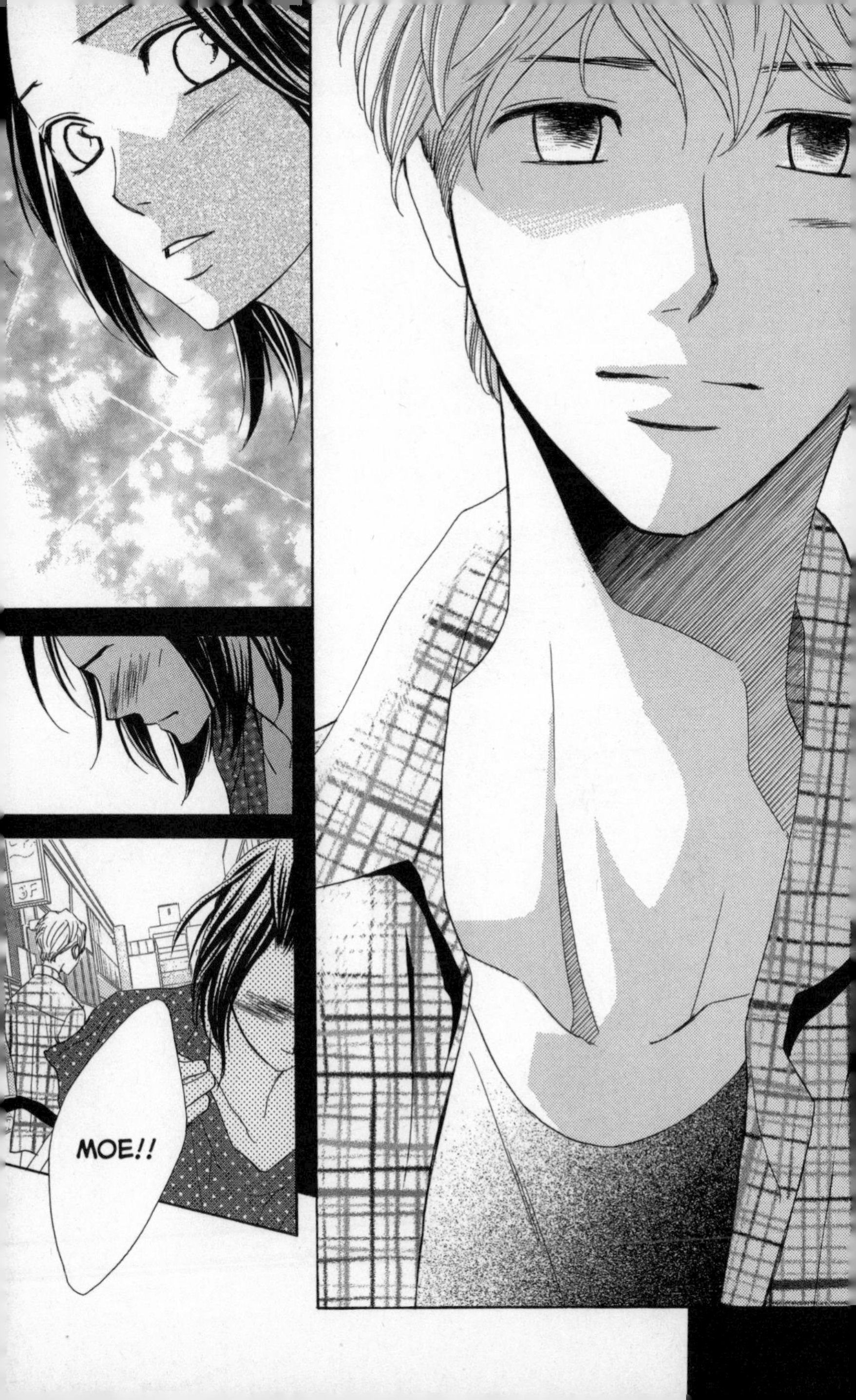
MOE!!

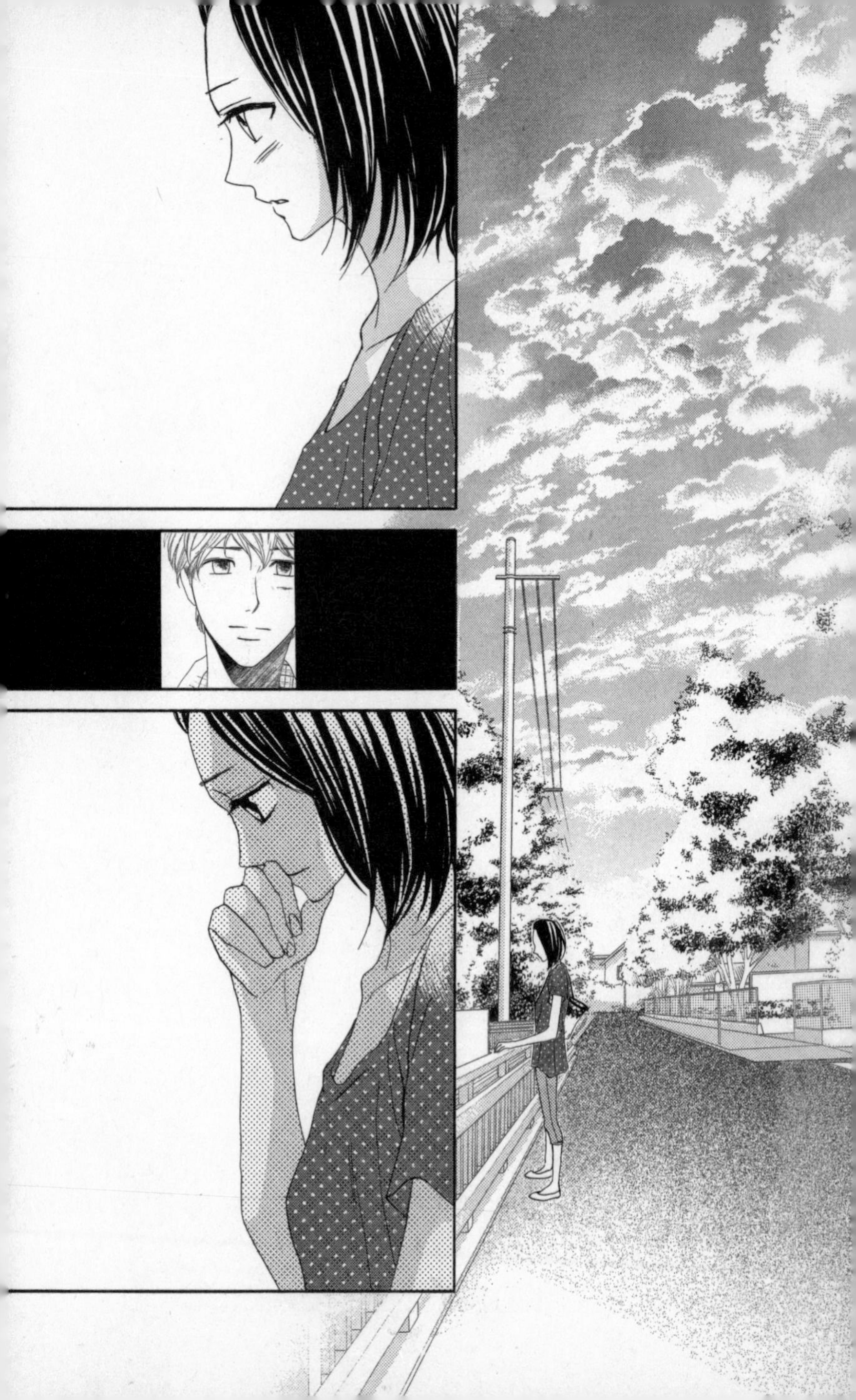

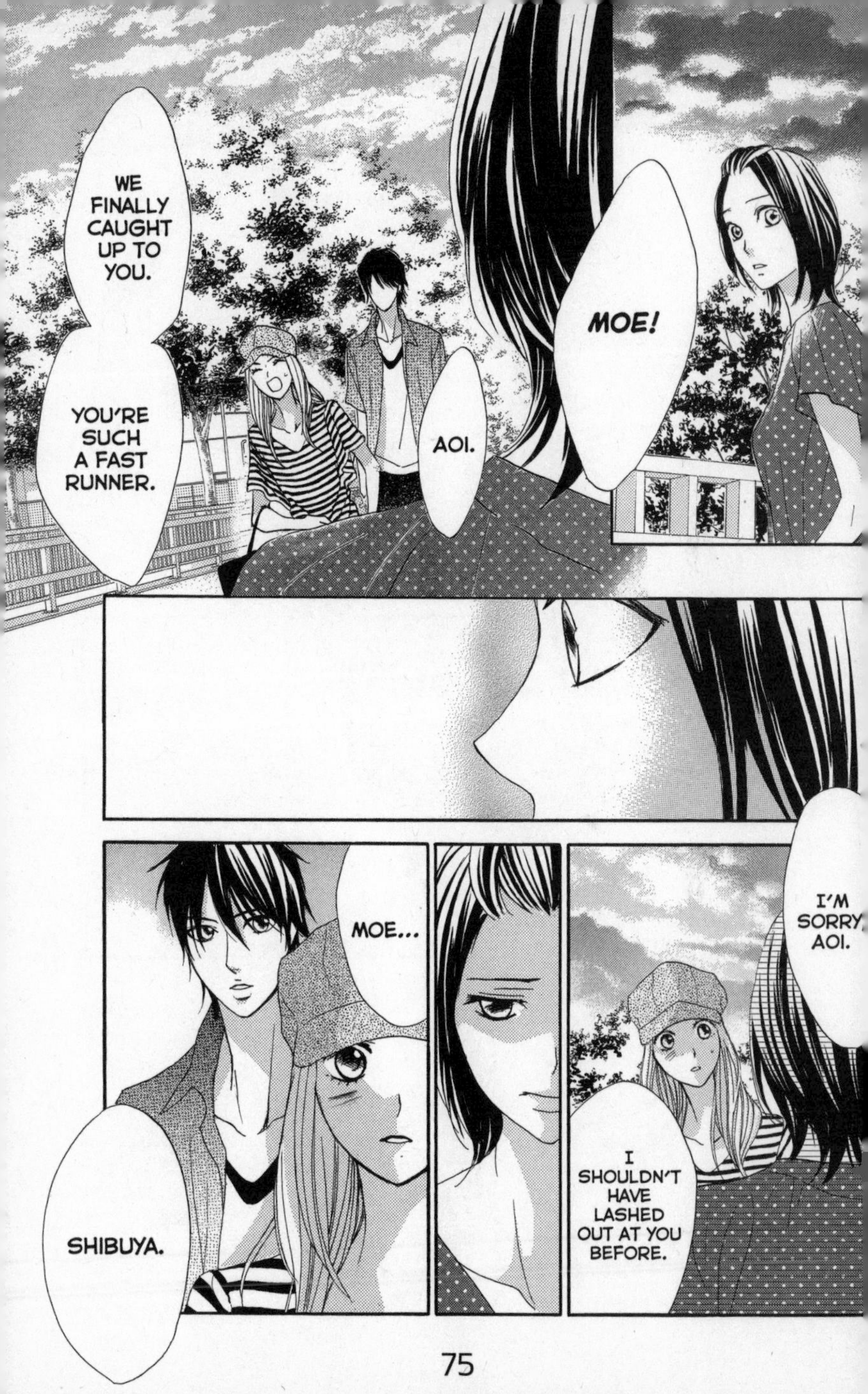
MOE!
AOI.
WE FINALLY CAUGHT UP TO YOU.
YOU'RE SUCH A FAST RUNNER.
I'M SORRY, AOI.
I SHOULDN'T HAVE LASHED OUT AT YOU BEFORE.
MOE...
SHIBUYA.

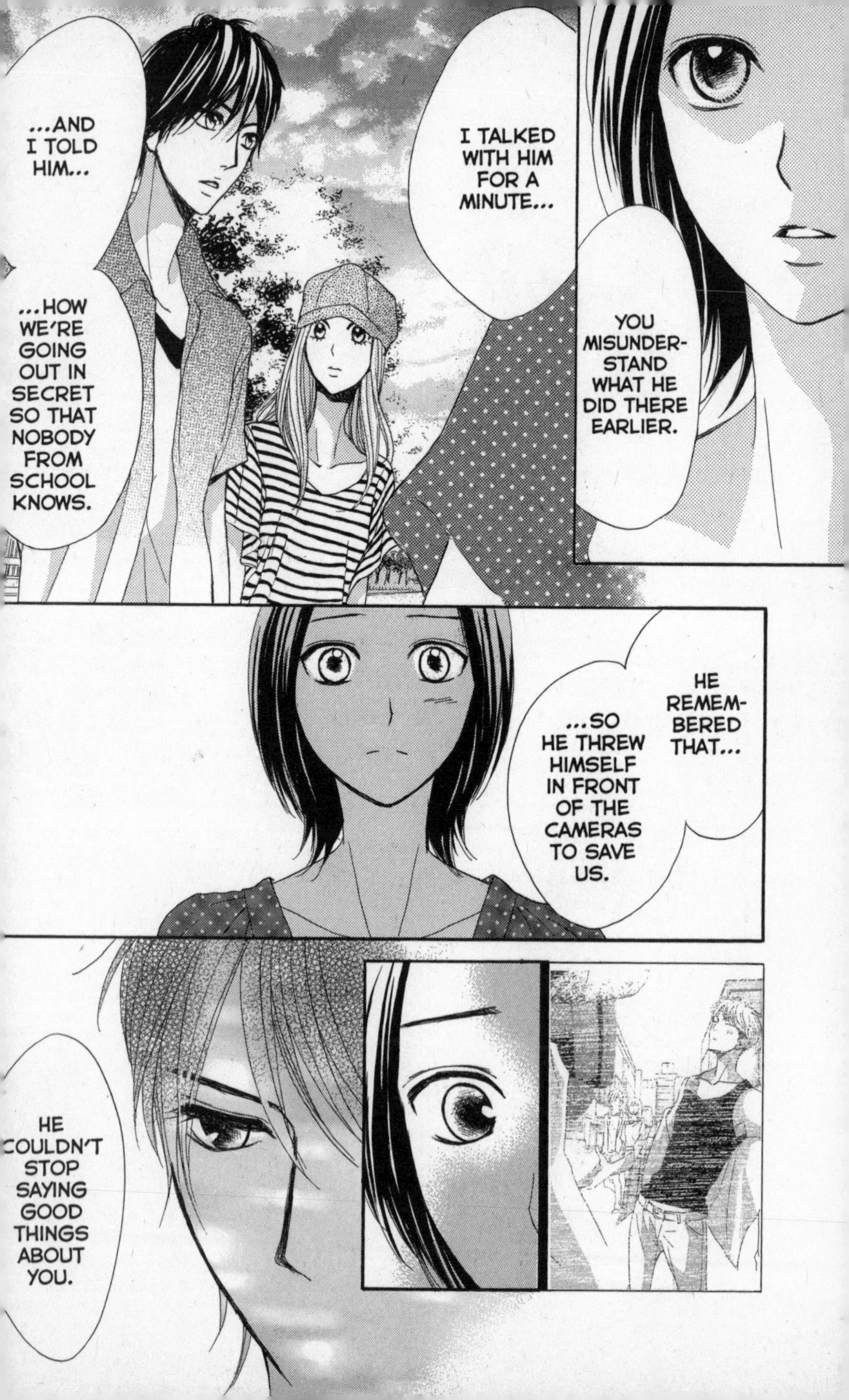
YOU MISUNDERSTAND WHAT HE DID THERE EARLIER.
I TALKED WITH HIM FOR A MINUTE...
...AND I TOLD HIM...
...HOW WE'RE GOING OUT IN SECRET SO THAT NOBODY FROM SCHOOL KNOWS.
HE REMEMBERED THAT...
...SO HE THREW HIMSELF IN FRONT OF THE CAMERAS TO SAVE US.
HE COULDN'T STOP SAYING GOOD THINGS ABOUT YOU.

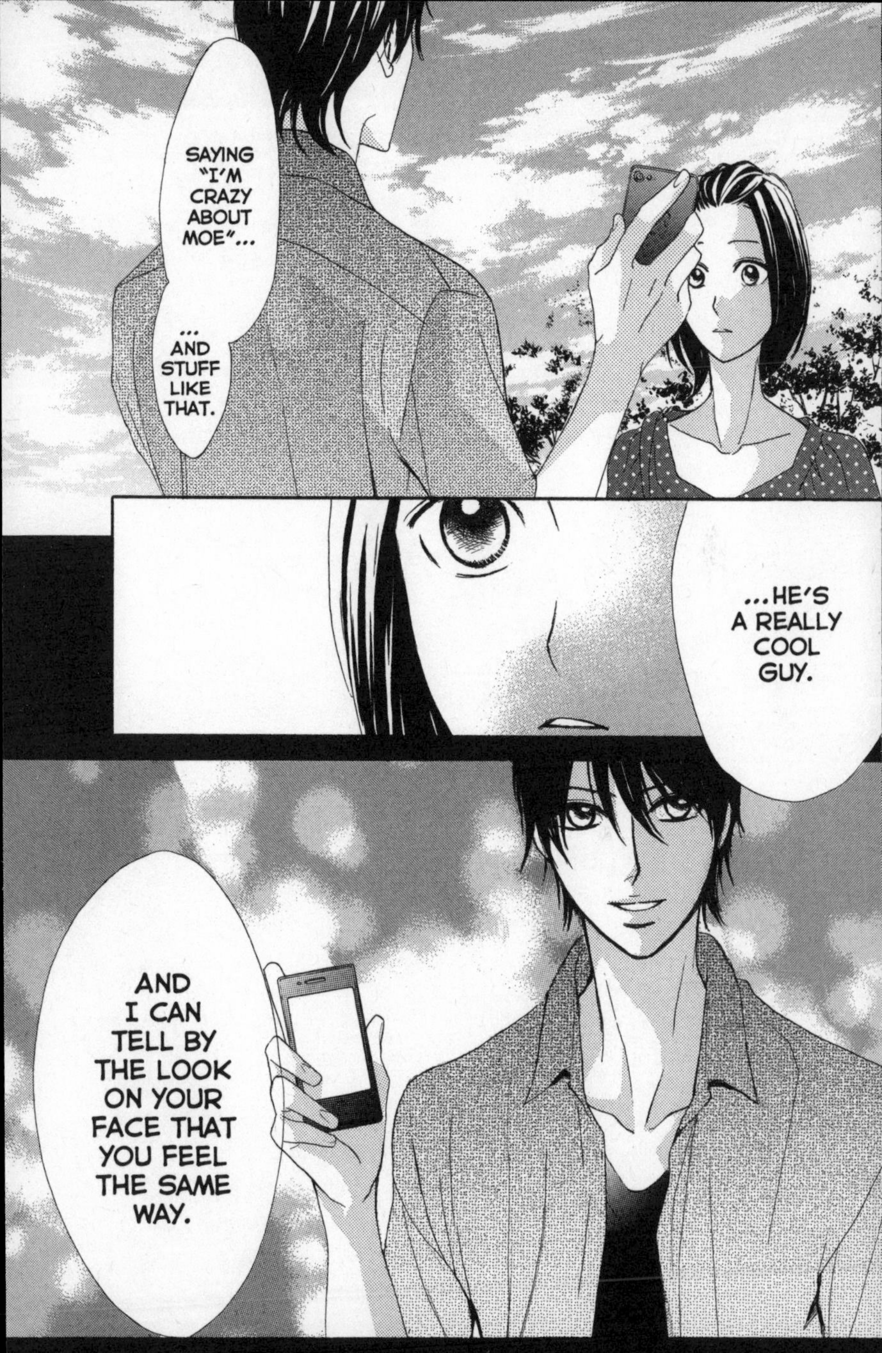
SAYING "I'M CRAZY ABOUT MOE"...
... AND STUFF LIKE THAT.
...HE'S A REALLY COOL GUY.
AND I CAN TELL BY THE LOOK ON YOUR FACE THAT YOU FEEL THE SAME WAY.

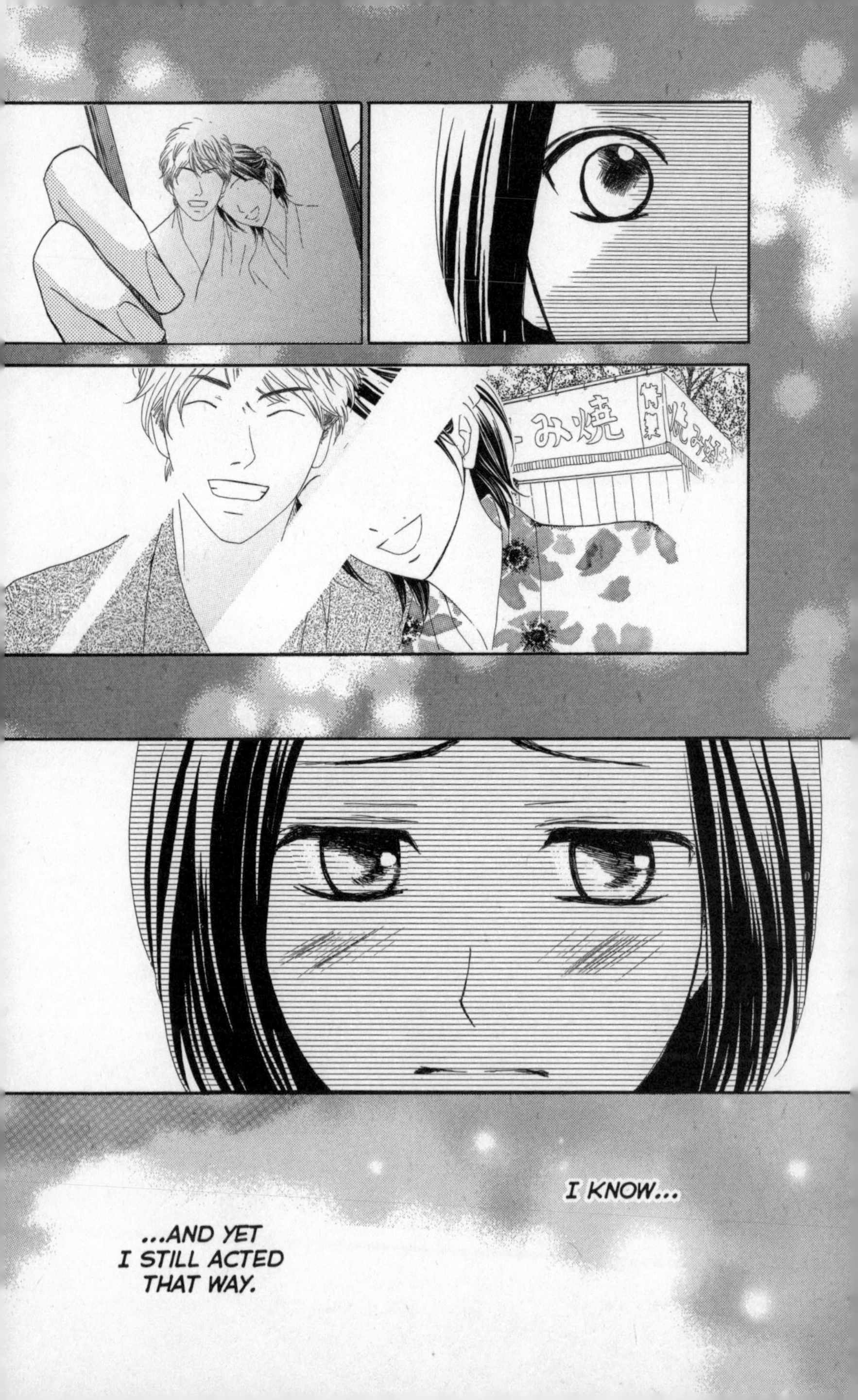
I KNOW...
...AND YET I STILL ACTED THAT WAY.

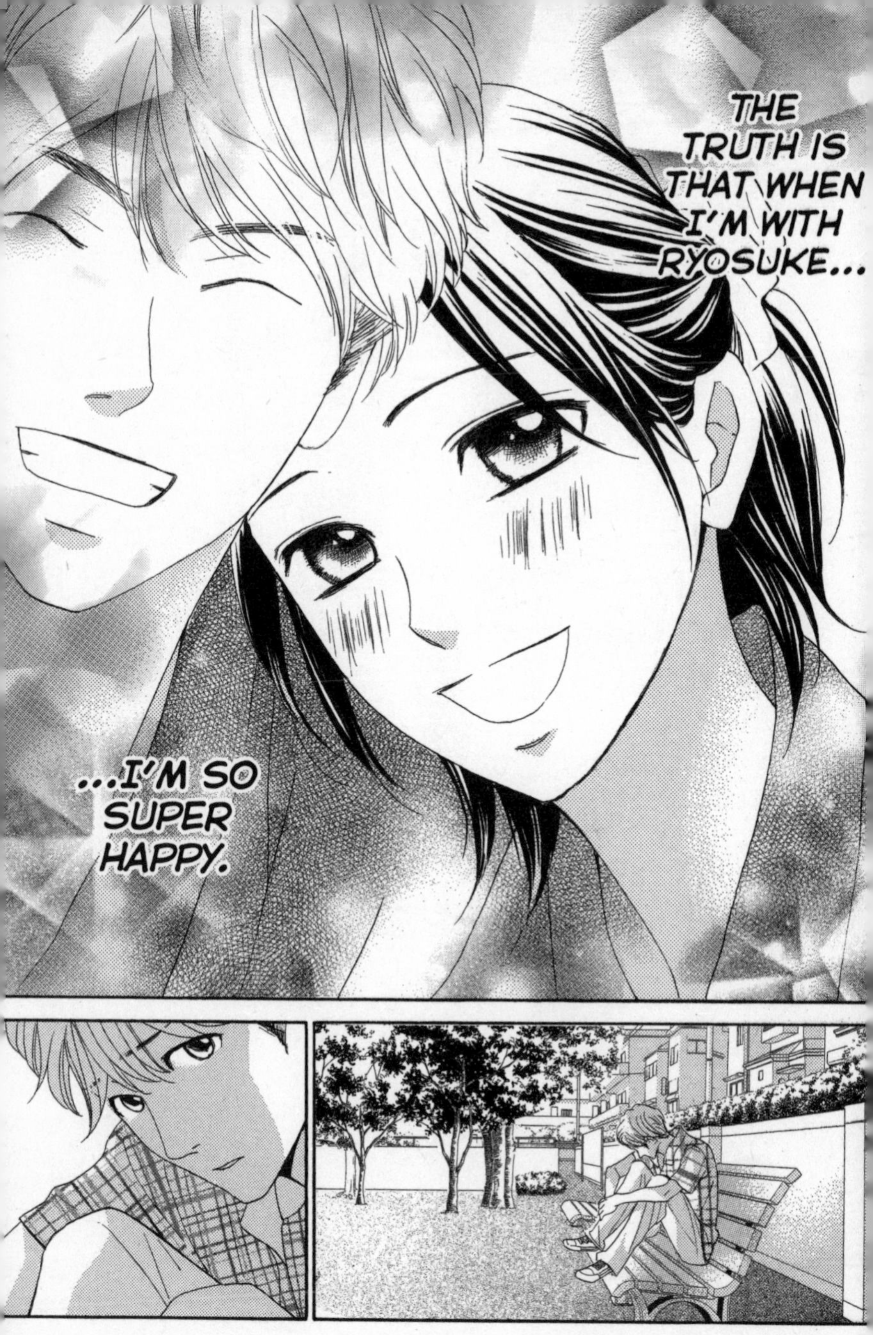
THE TRUTH IS THAT WHEN I'M WITH RYOSUKE...
...I'M SO SUPER HAPPY.

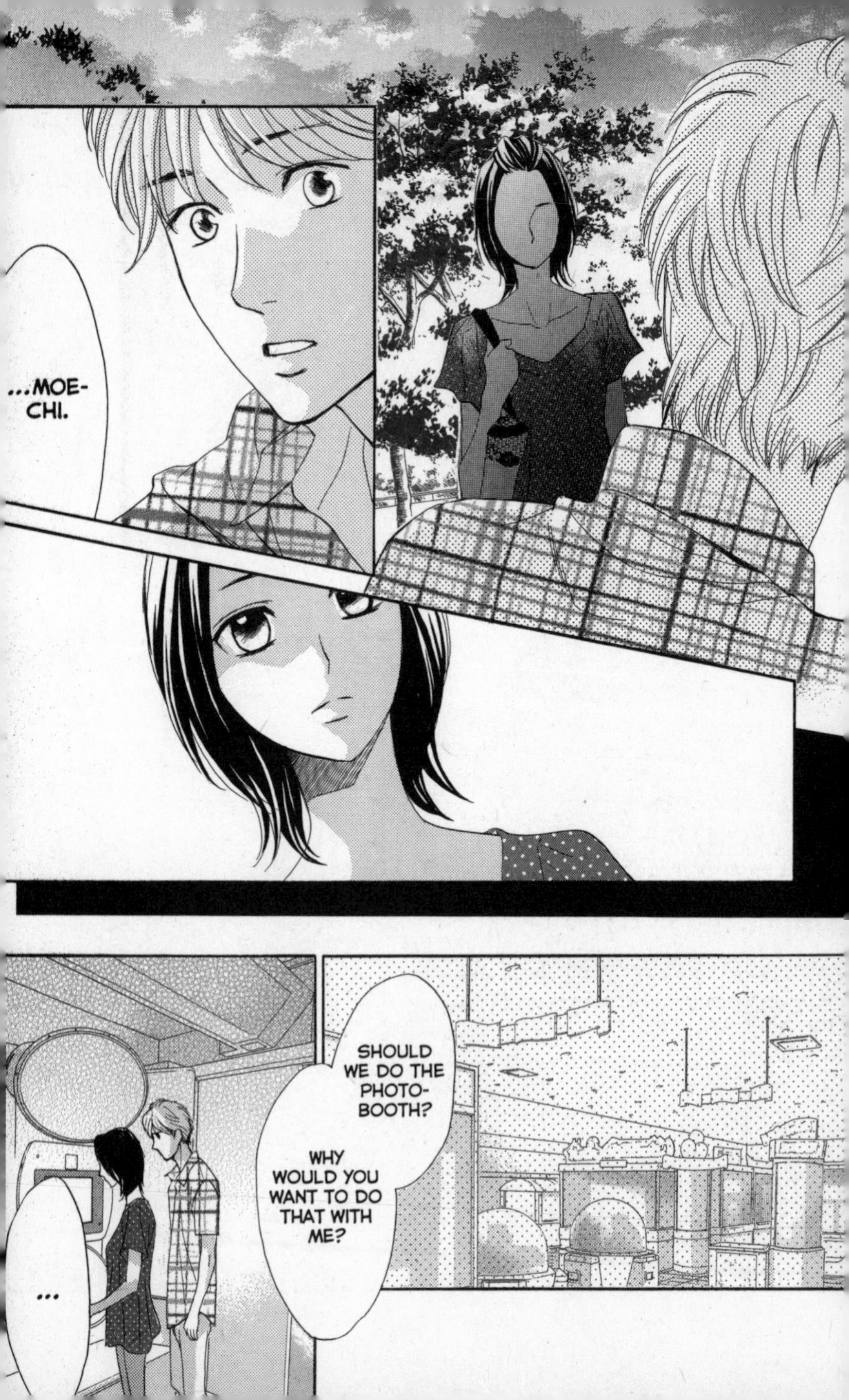
...MOE-CHI.
SHOULD WE DO THE PHOTO-BOOTH?
WHY WOULD YOU WANT TO DO THAT WITH ME?
...

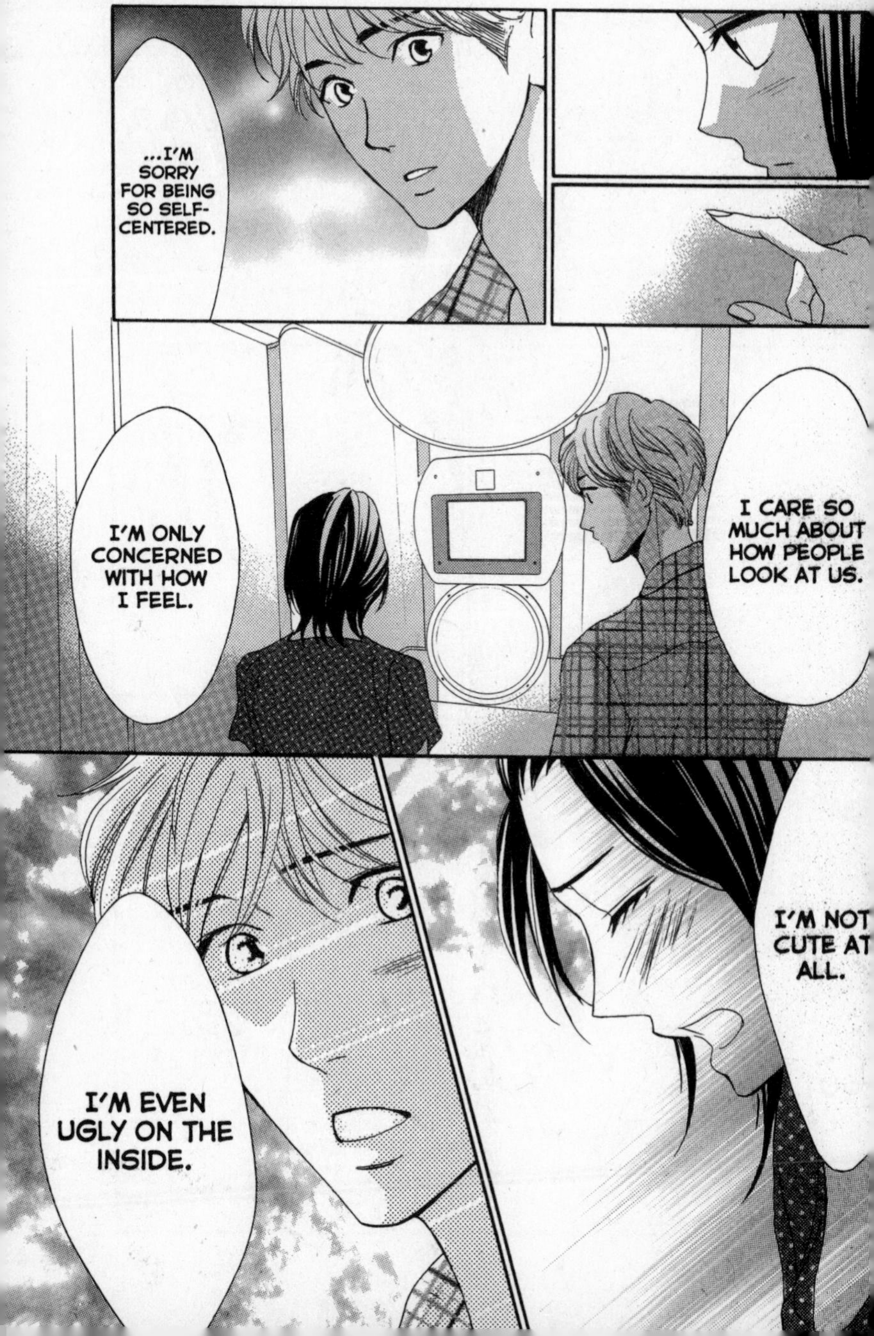
...I'M SORRY FOR BEING SO SELF-CENTERED.
I CARE SO MUCH ABOUT HOW PEOPLE LOOK AT US.
I'M ONLY CONCERNED WITH HOW I FEEL.
I'M NOT CUTE AT ALL.
I'M EVEN UGLY ON THE INSIDE.

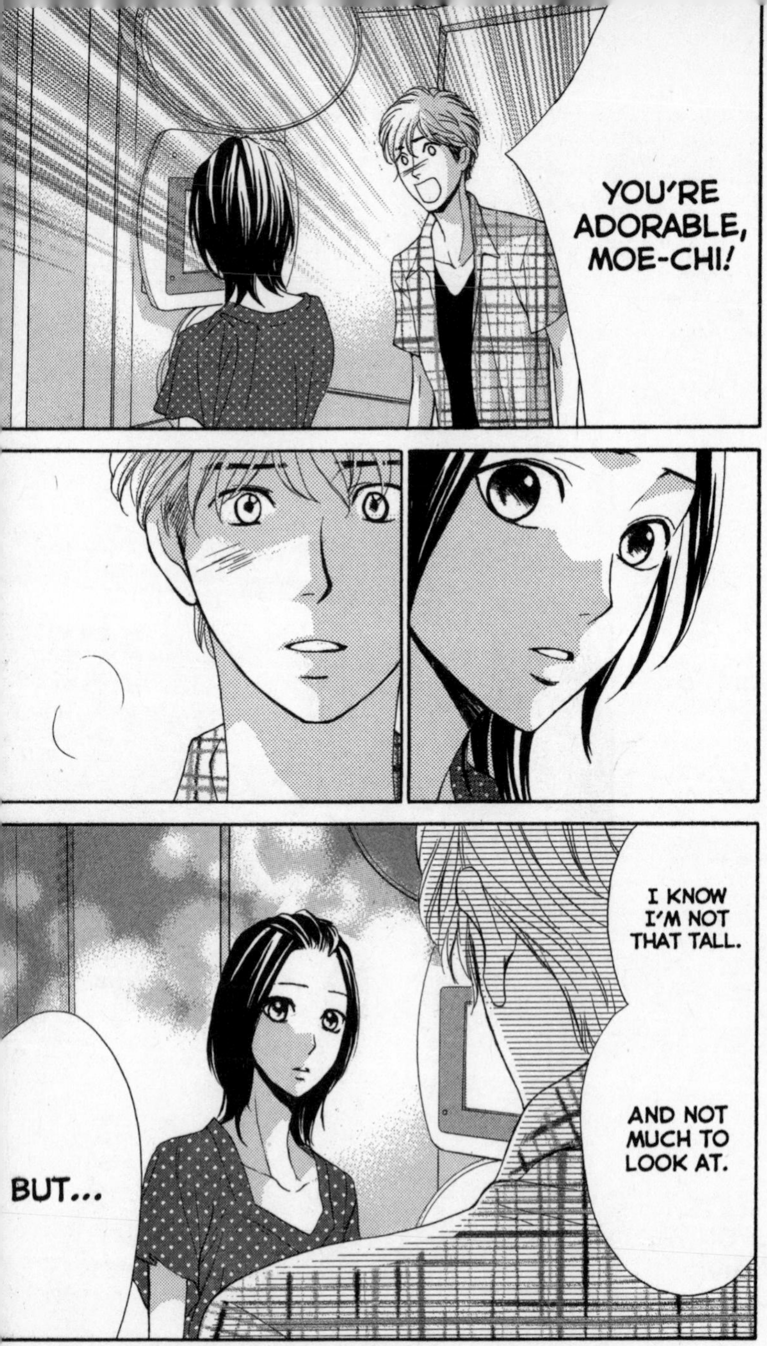
YOU'RE ADORABLE, MOE-CHI!
I KNOW I'M NOT THAT TALL.
AND NOT MUCH TO LOOK AT.
BUT...

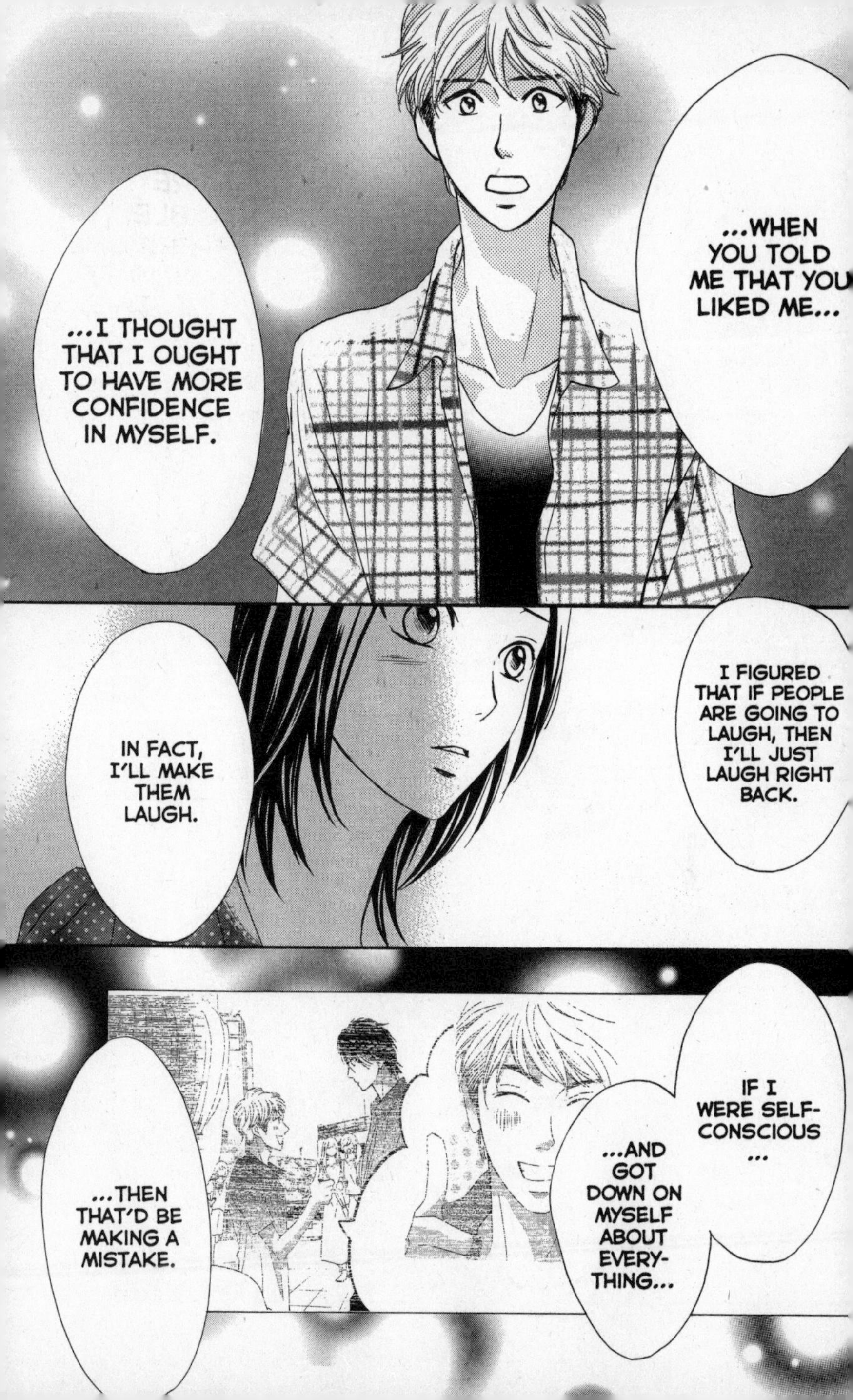
...WHEN YOU TOLD ME THAT YOU LIKED ME...
...I THOUGHT THAT I OUGHT TO HAVE MORE CONFIDENCE IN MYSELF.
I FIGURED THAT IF PEOPLE ARE GOING TO LAUGH, THEN I'LL JUST LAUGH RIGHT BACK.
IN FACT, I'LL MAKE THEM LAUGH.
IF I WERE SELF-CONSCIOUS ...
...AND GOT DOWN ON MYSELF ABOUT EVERY-THING...
...THEN THAT'D BE MAKING A MISTAKE.

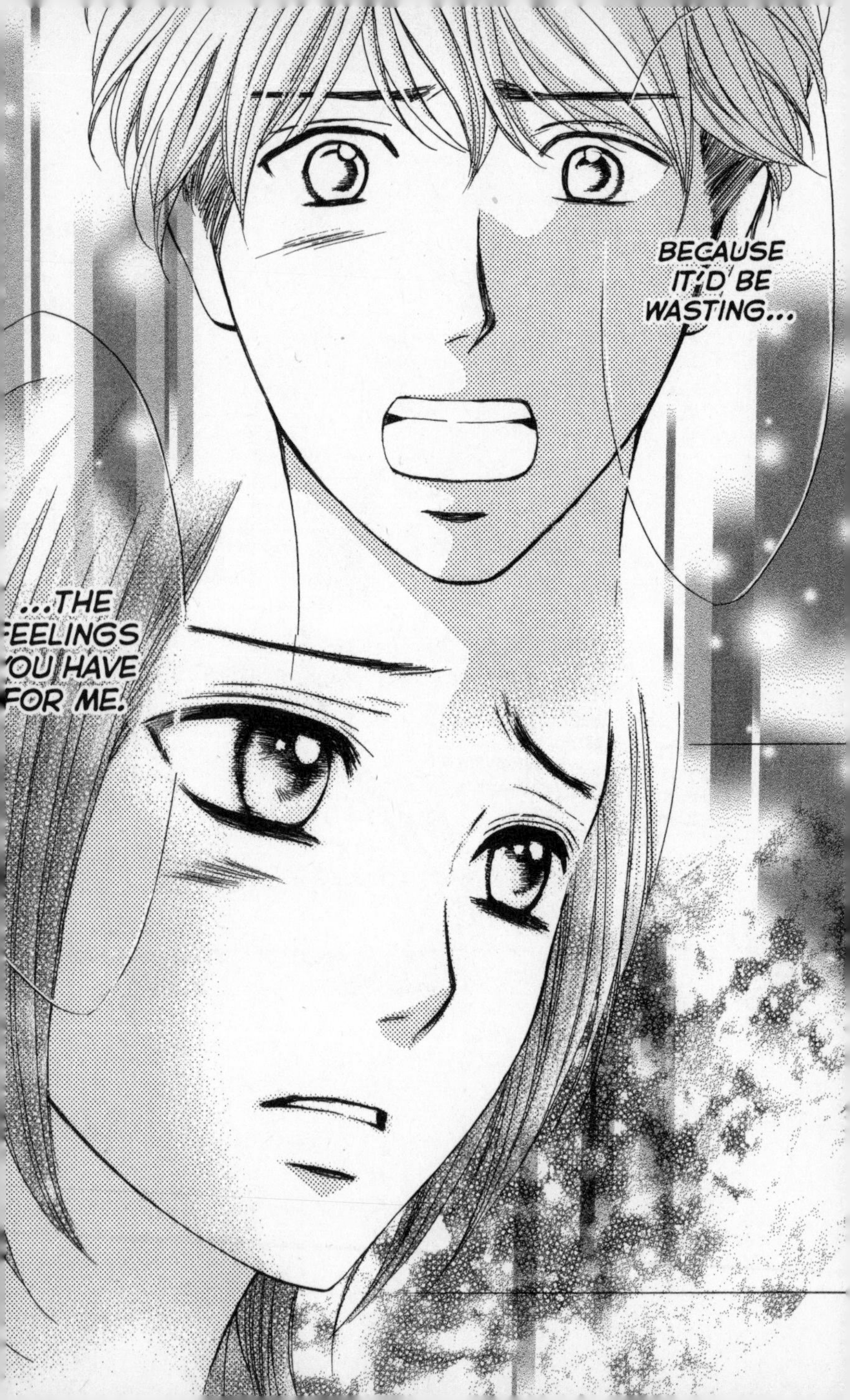

BECAUSE IT'D BE WASTING...
...THE FEELINGS YOU HAVE FOR ME.

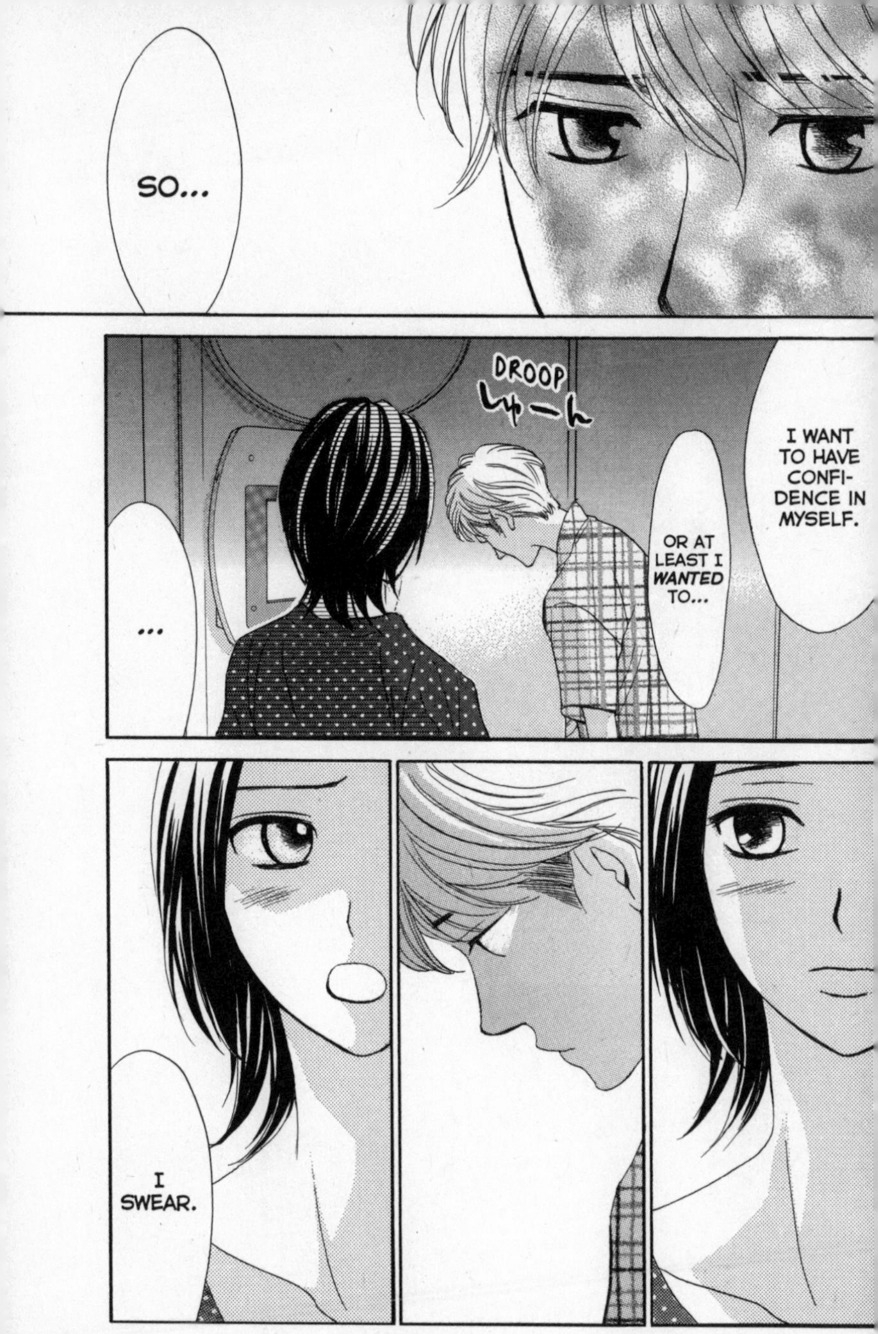
SO...
I WANT TO HAVE CONFI-DENCE IN MYSELF.
OR AT LEAST I *WANTED* TO...
DROOP
しゅーん
...
I SWEAR.

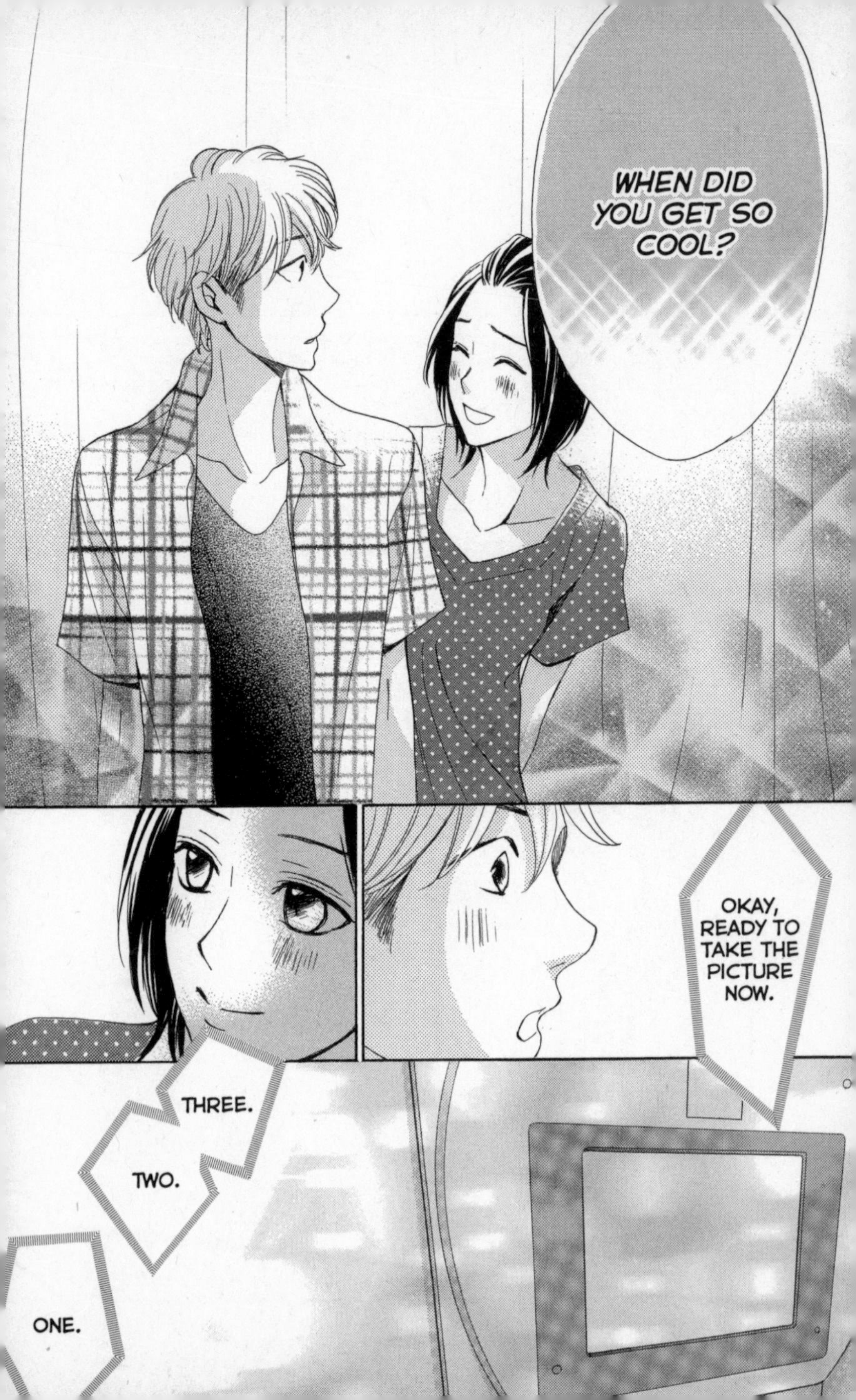
WHEN DID YOU GET SO COOL?
OKAY, READY TO TAKE THE PICTURE NOW.
THREE.
TWO.
ONE.

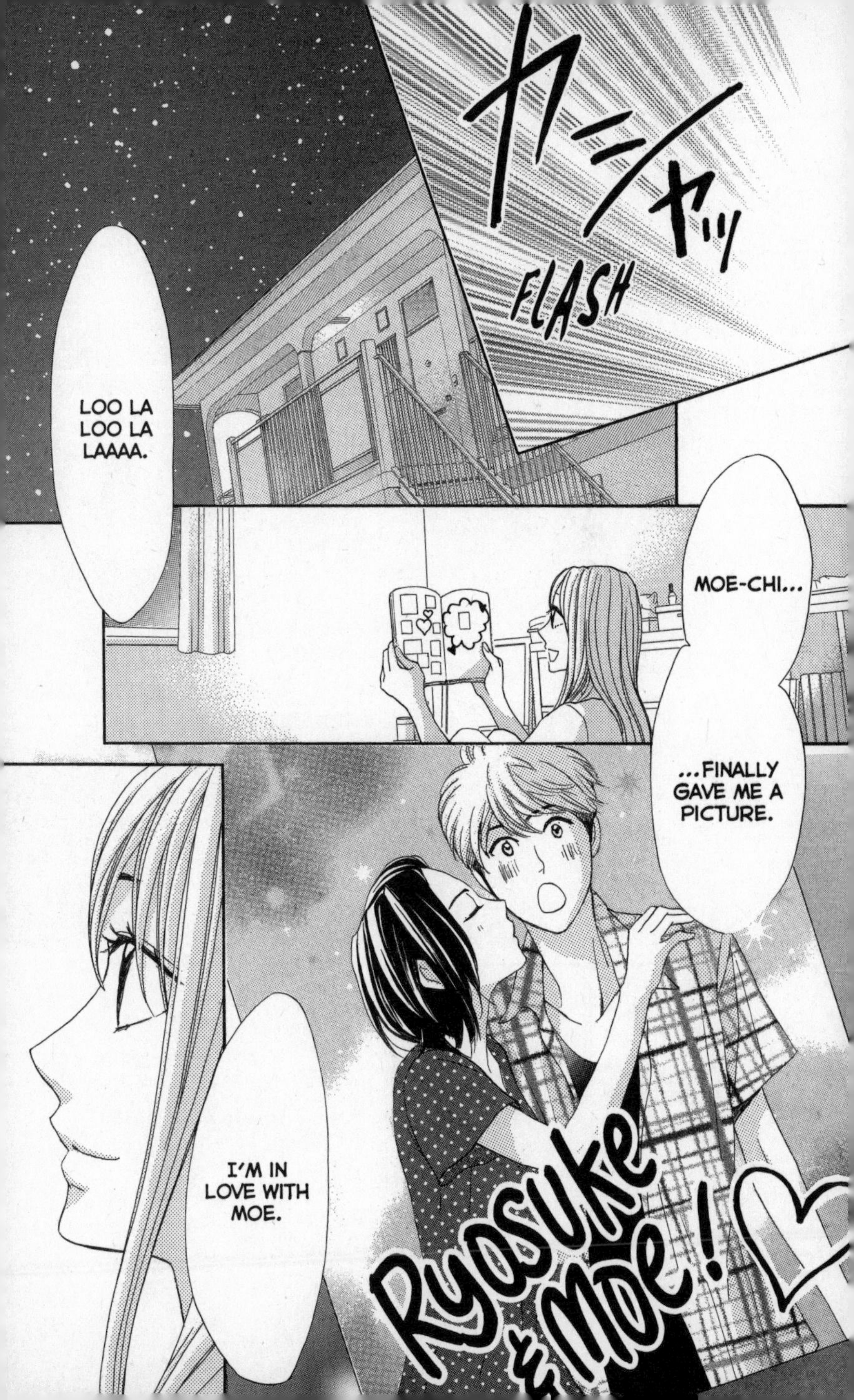
カシャッ
FLASH
LOO LA LOO LA LAAAA.
MOE-CHI...
...FINALLY GAVE ME A PICTURE.
Ryosuke & Moe!
I'M IN LOVE WITH MOE.

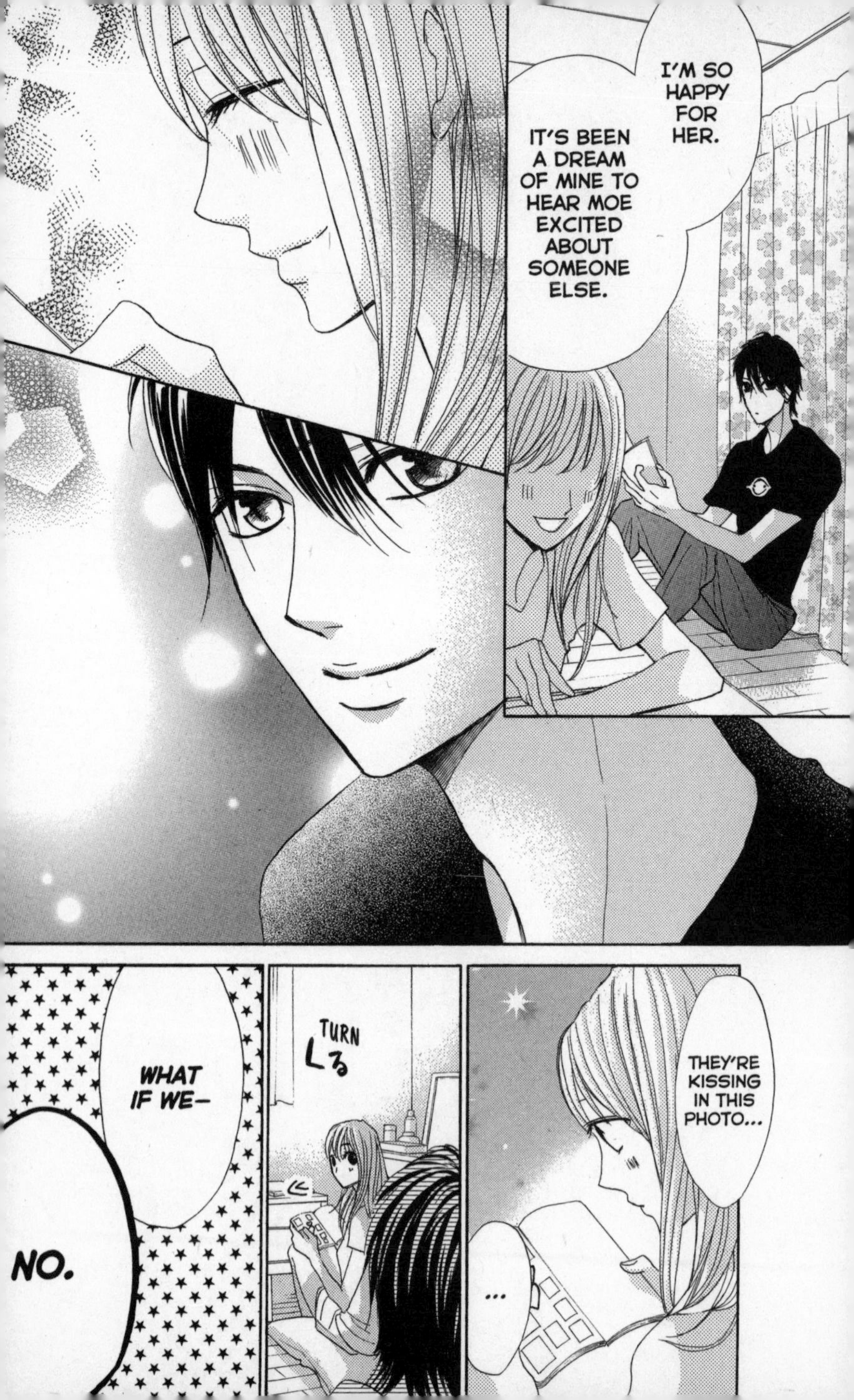
I'M SO HAPPY FOR HER.
IT'S BEEN A DREAM OF MINE TO HEAR MOE EXCITED ABOUT SOMEONE ELSE.
THEY'RE KISSING IN THIS PHOTO...
...
TURN
WHAT IF WE–
NO.

L♥DK

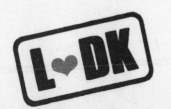

#59 Wonderfall!

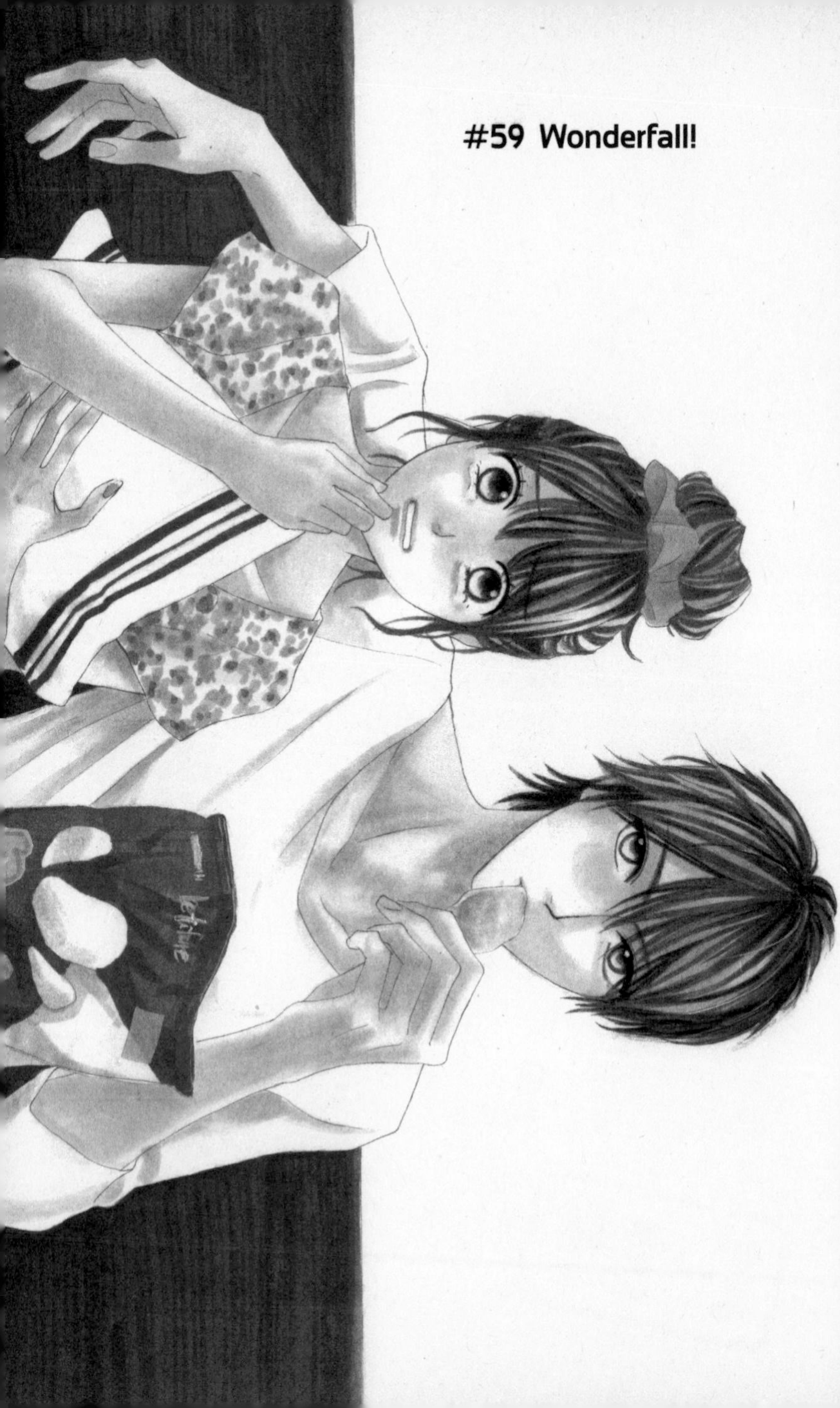

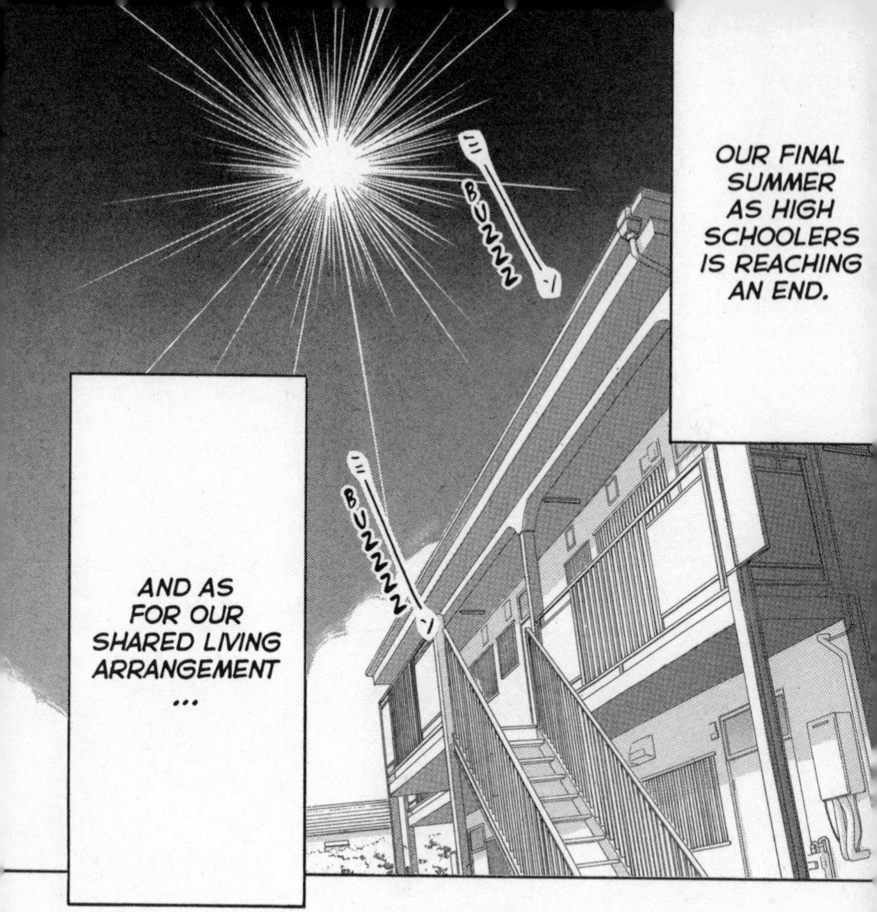
OUR FINAL SUMMER AS HIGH SCHOOLERS IS REACHING AN END.
BUZZZ
BUZZZZZ
AND AS FOR OUR SHARED LIVING ARRANGEMENT...

L♥DK

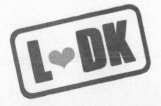

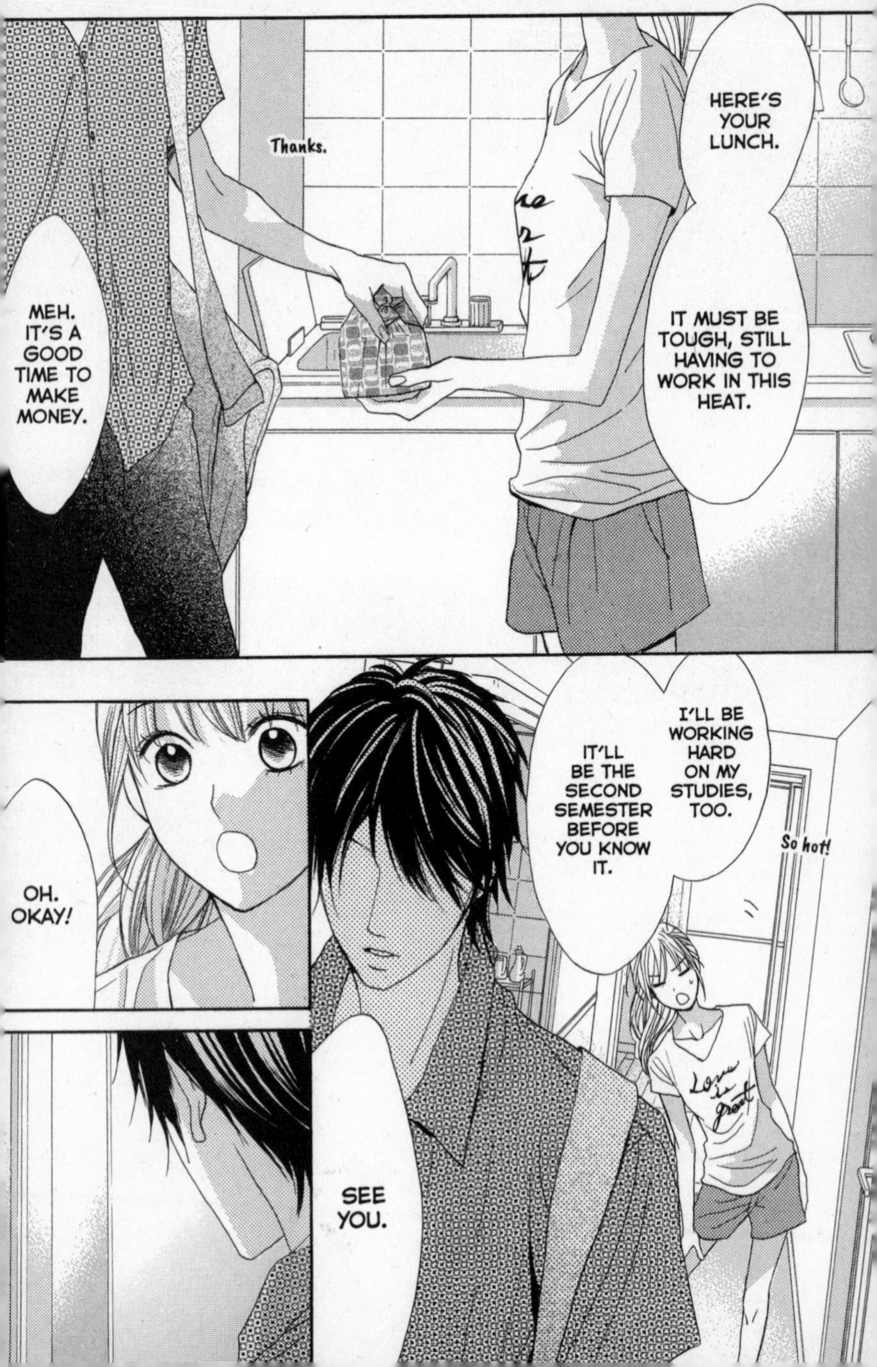
HERE'S YOUR LUNCH.
IT MUST BE TOUGH, STILL HAVING TO WORK IN THIS HEAT.
Thanks.
MEH. IT'S A GOOD TIME TO MAKE MONEY.
I'LL BE WORKING HARD ON MY STUDIES, TOO.
IT'LL BE THE SECOND SEMESTER BEFORE YOU KNOW IT.
So hot!
SEE YOU.
OH. OKAY!

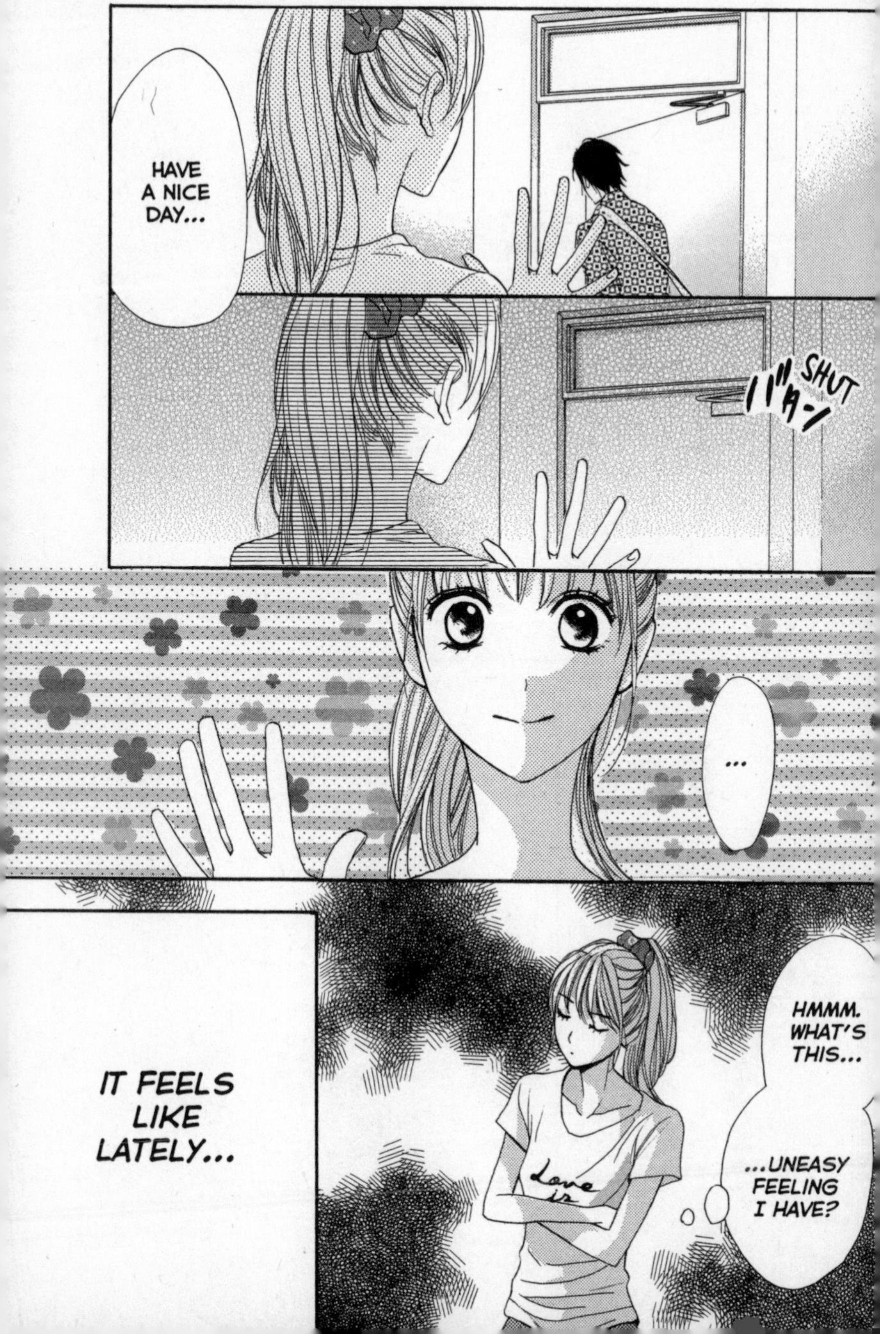
HAVE A NICE DAY...
SHUT
...
HMMM. WHAT'S THIS...
...UNEASY FEELING I HAVE?
IT FEELS LIKE LATELY...

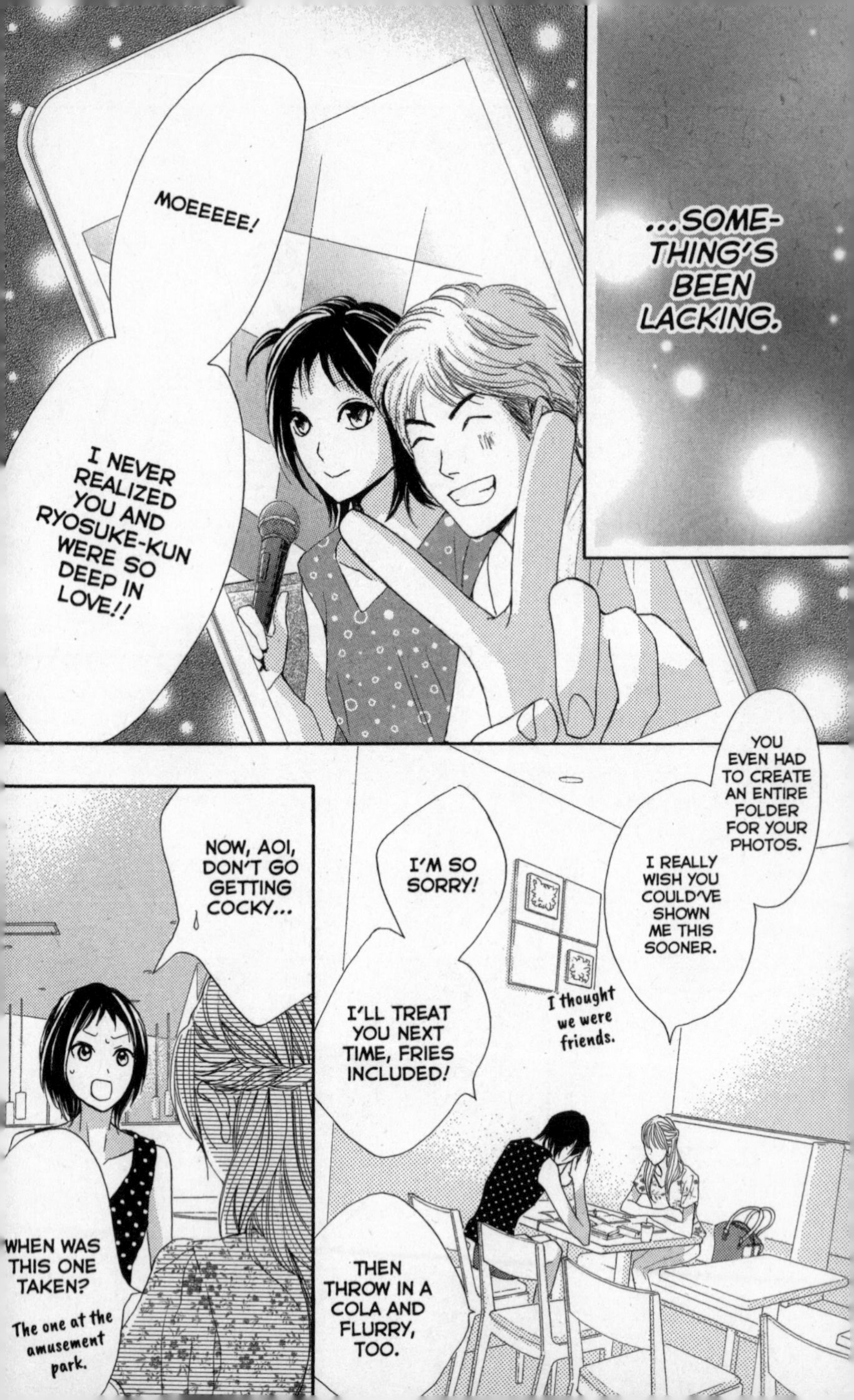
...SOME-THING'S BEEN LACKING.
MOEEEEE!
I NEVER REALIZED YOU AND RYOSUKE-KUN WERE SO DEEP IN LOVE!!
YOU EVEN HAD TO CREATE AN ENTIRE FOLDER FOR YOUR PHOTOS.
I REALLY WISH YOU COULD'VE SHOWN ME THIS SOONER.
I thought we were friends.
I'M SO SORRY!
I'LL TREAT YOU NEXT TIME, FRIES INCLUDED!
THEN THROW IN A COLA AND FLURRY, TOO.
NOW, AOI, DON'T GO GETTING COCKY...
WHEN WAS THIS ONE TAKEN?
The one at the amusement park.

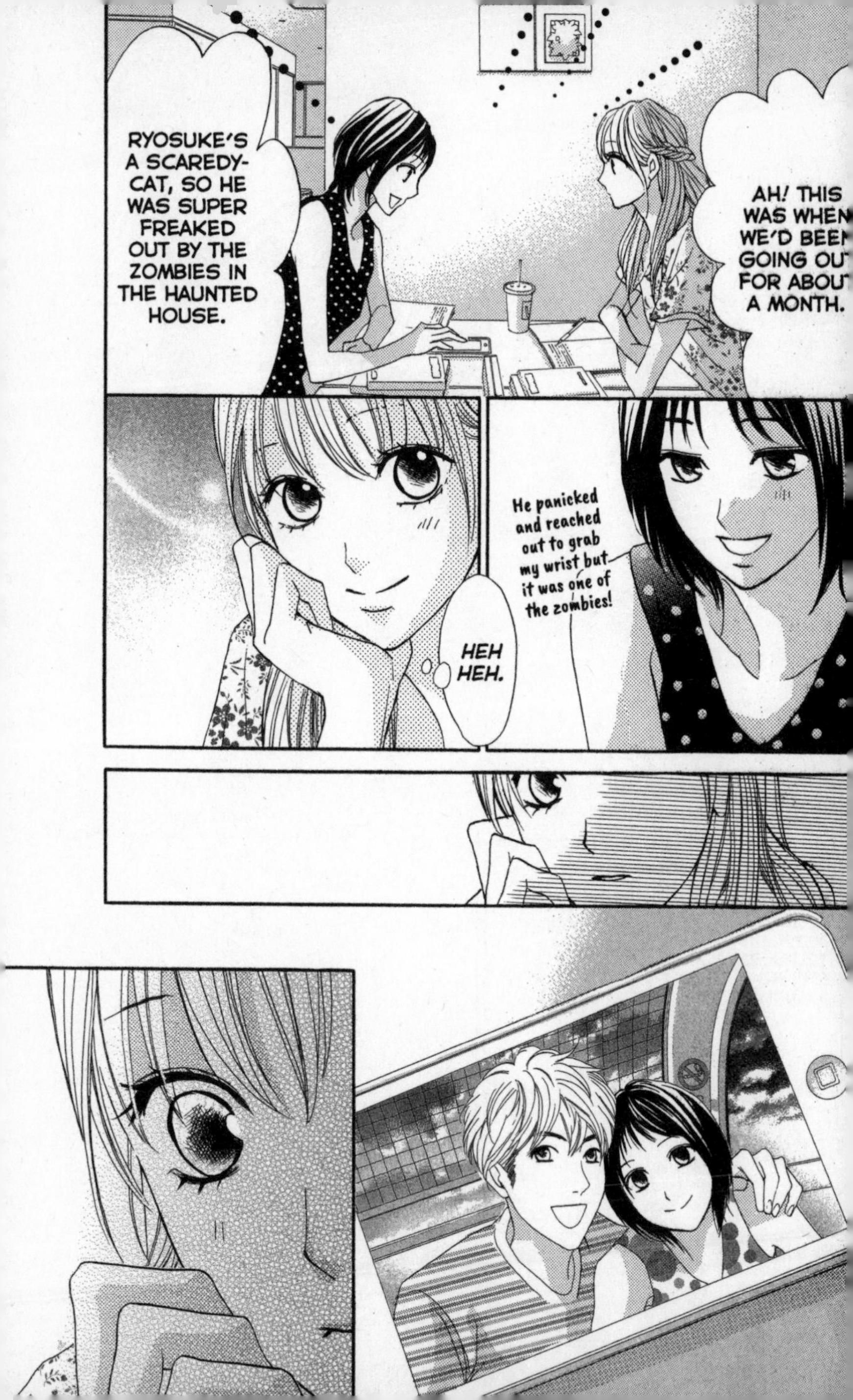
AH! THIS WAS WHEN WE'D BEEN GOING OUT FOR ABOUT A MONTH.
RYOSUKE'S A SCAREDY-CAT, SO HE WAS SUPER FREAKED OUT BY THE ZOMBIES IN THE HAUNTED HOUSE.
He panicked and reached out to grab my wrist but it was one of the zombies!
HEH HEH.

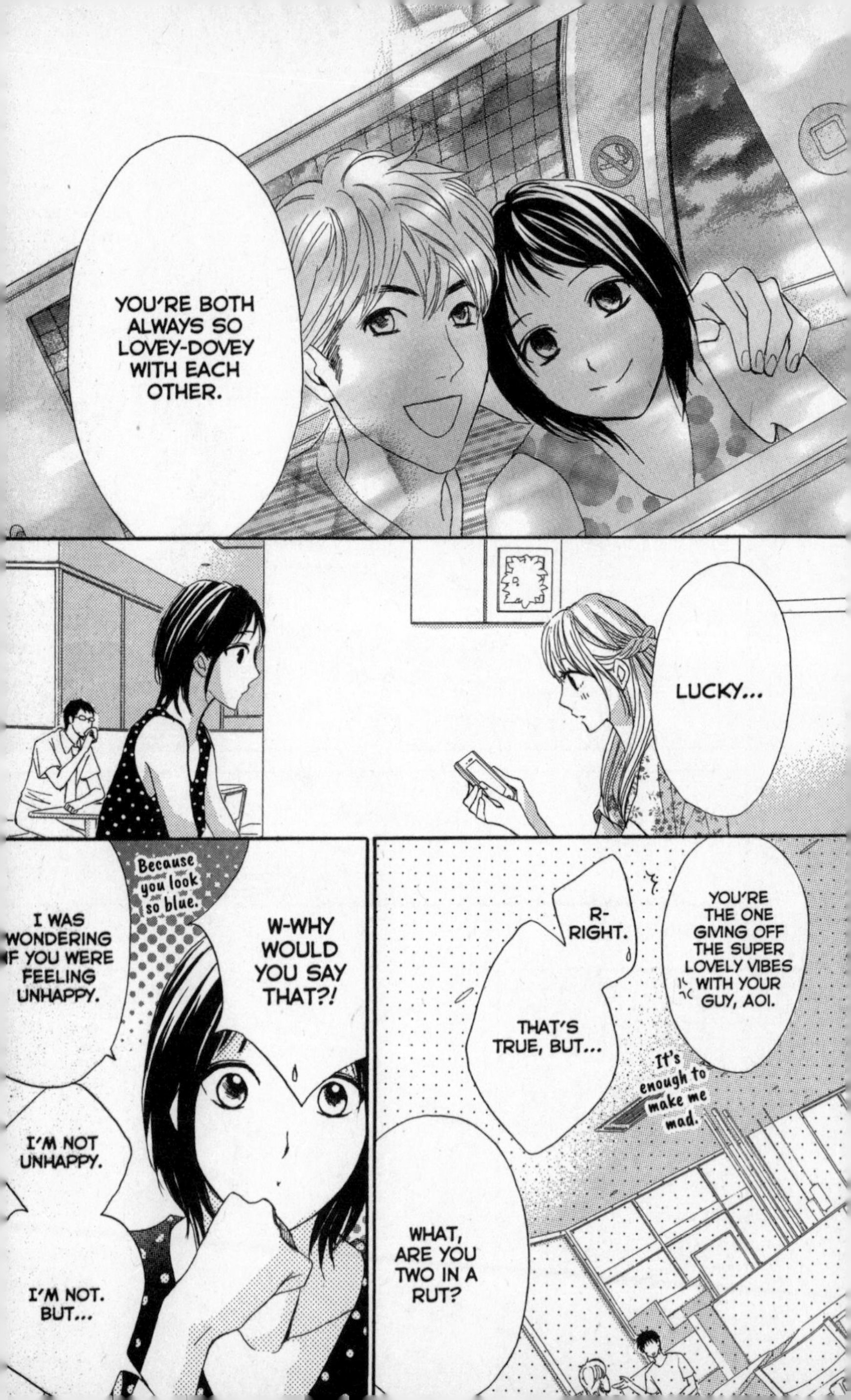
YOU'RE BOTH ALWAYS SO LOVEY-DOVEY WITH EACH OTHER.
LUCKY...
YOU'RE THE ONE GIVING OFF THE SUPER LOVELY VIBES WITH YOUR GUY, AOI.
It's enough to make me mad.
R-RIGHT.
THAT'S TRUE, BUT...
WHAT, ARE YOU TWO IN A RUT?
W-WHY WOULD YOU SAY THAT?!
Because you look so blue.
I WAS WONDERING IF YOU WERE FEELING UNHAPPY.
I'M NOT UNHAPPY.
I'M NOT. BUT...

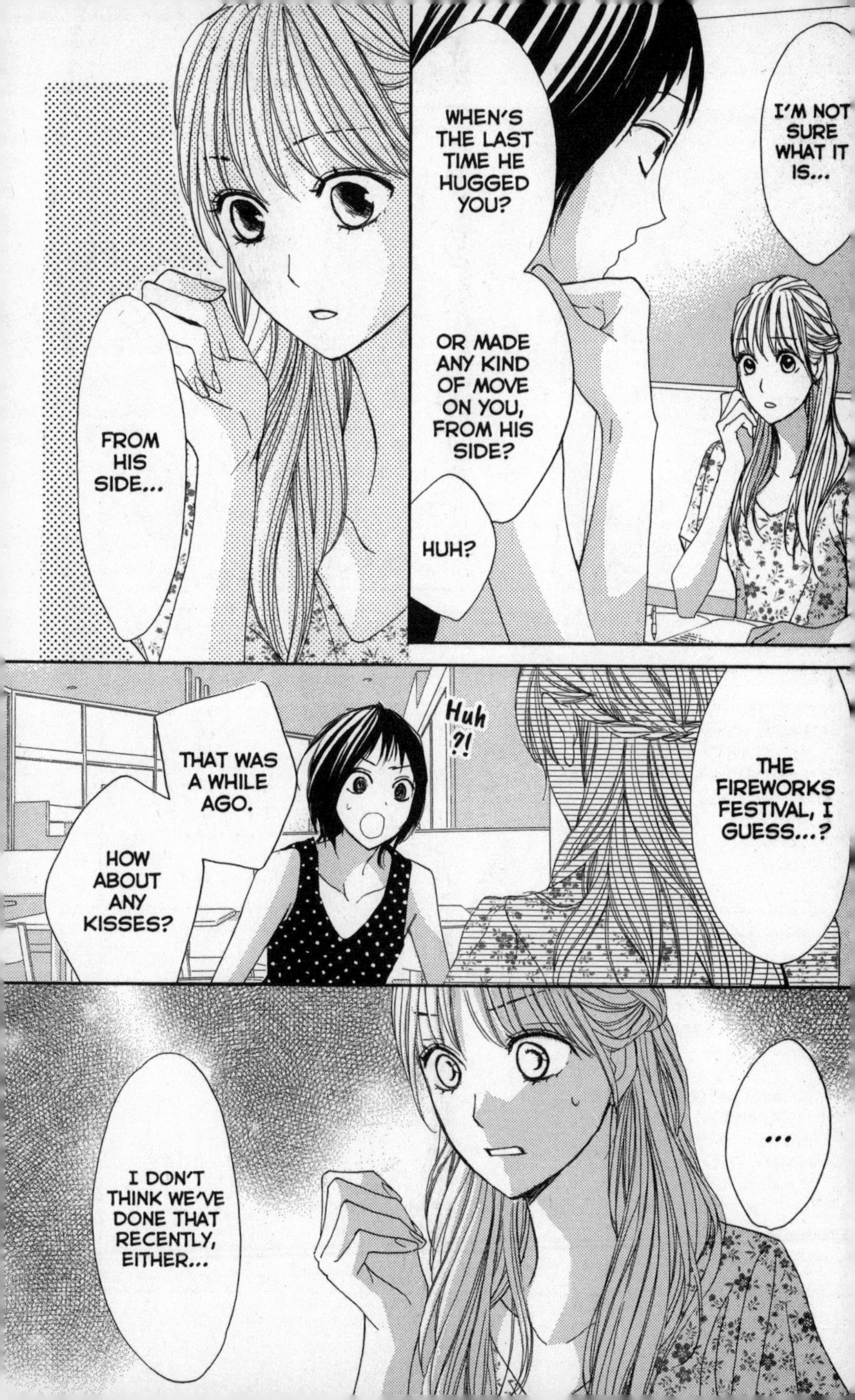
I'M NOT SURE WHAT IT IS...
WHEN'S THE LAST TIME HE HUGGED YOU?
OR MADE ANY KIND OF MOVE ON YOU, FROM HIS SIDE?
HUH?
FROM HIS SIDE...
THE FIREWORKS FESTIVAL, I GUESS...?
Huh ?!
THAT WAS A WHILE AGO.
HOW ABOUT ANY KISSES?
...
I DON'T THINK WE'VE DONE THAT RECENTLY, EITHER...

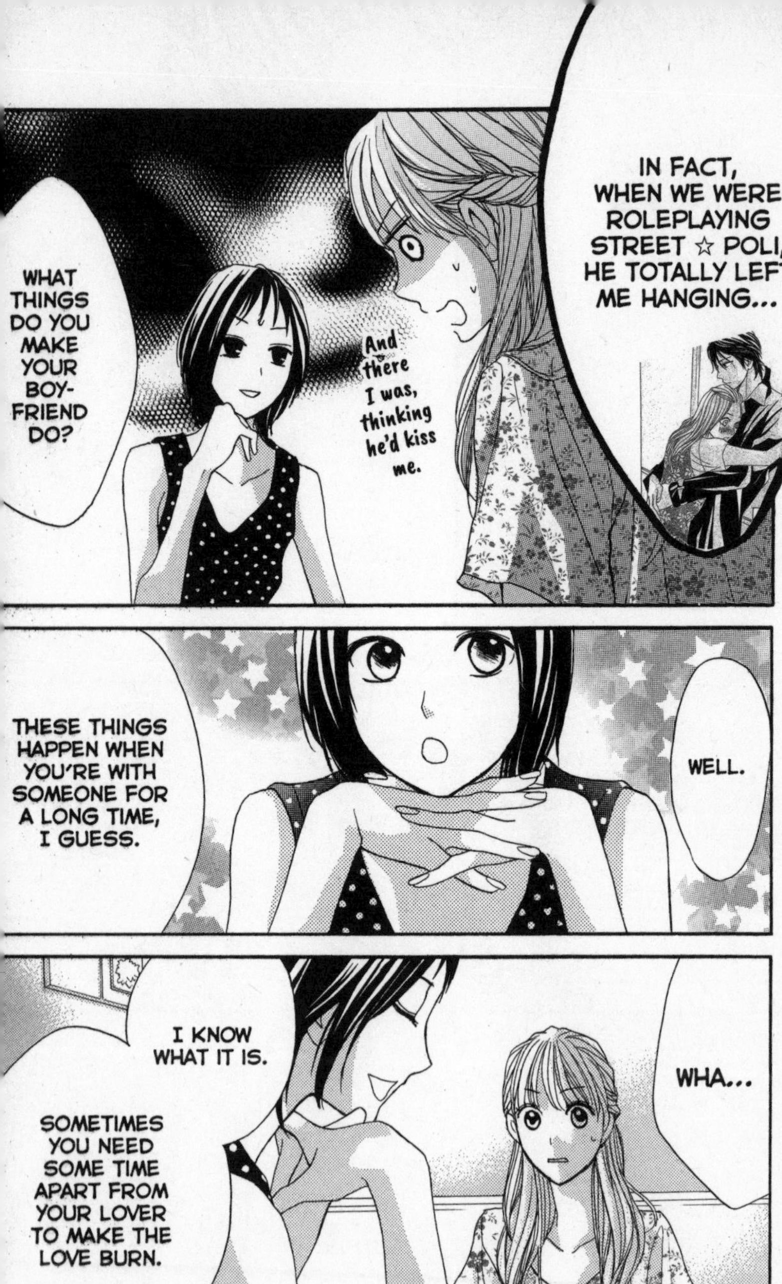
IN FACT, WHEN WE WERE ROLEPLAYING STREET ☆ POLI, HE TOTALLY LEFT ME HANGING...
And there I was, thinking he'd kiss me.
WHAT THINGS DO YOU MAKE YOUR BOY-FRIEND DO?
WELL.
THESE THINGS HAPPEN WHEN YOU'RE WITH SOMEONE FOR A LONG TIME, I GUESS.
WHA...
I KNOW WHAT IT IS.
SOMETIMES YOU NEED SOME TIME APART FROM YOUR LOVER TO MAKE THE LOVE BURN.

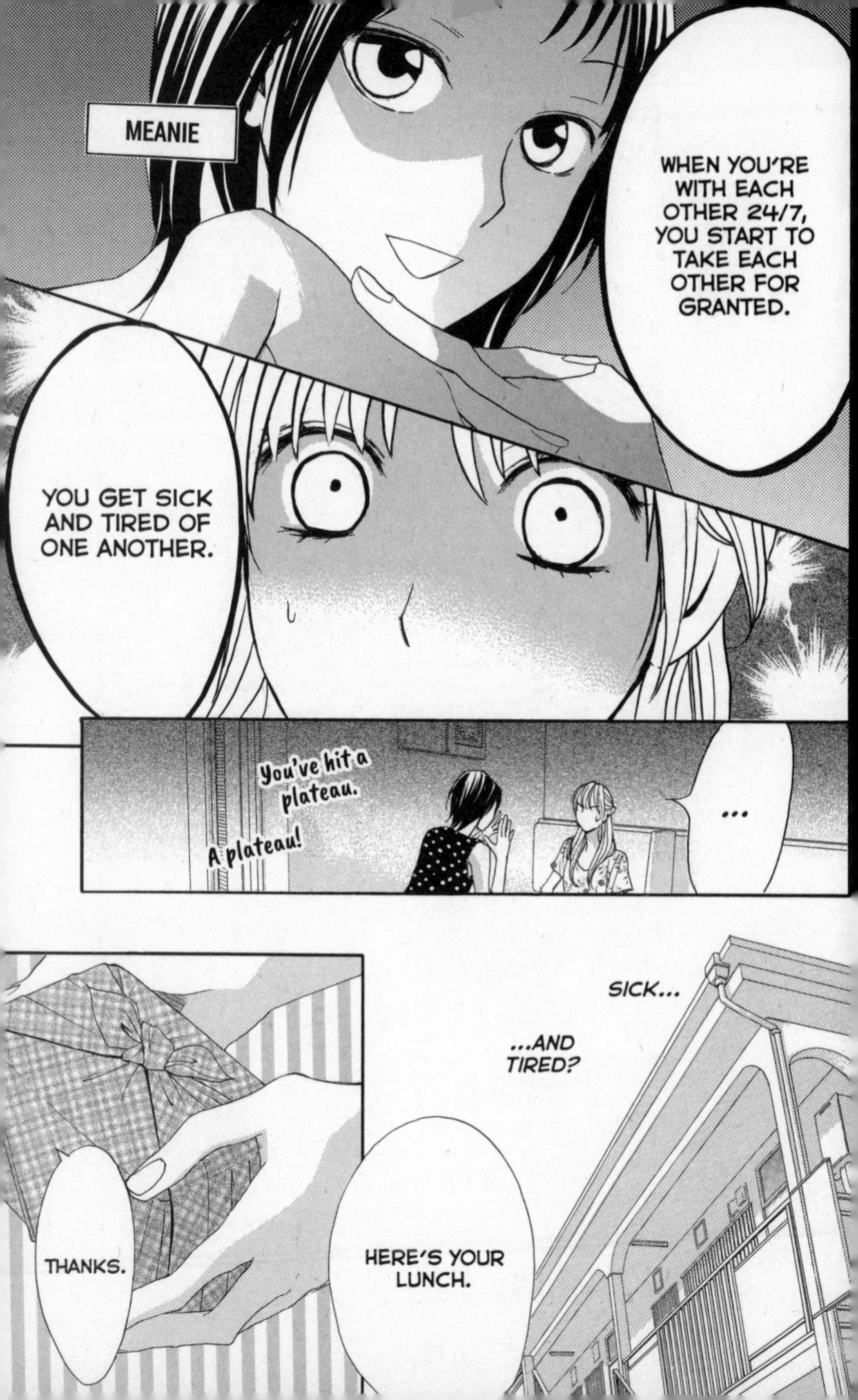
WHEN YOU'RE WITH EACH OTHER 24/7, YOU START TO TAKE EACH OTHER FOR GRANTED.
MEANIE
YOU GET SICK AND TIRED OF ONE ANOTHER.
...
You've hit a plateau.
A plateau!
SICK...
...AND TIRED?
HERE'S YOUR LUNCH.
THANKS.

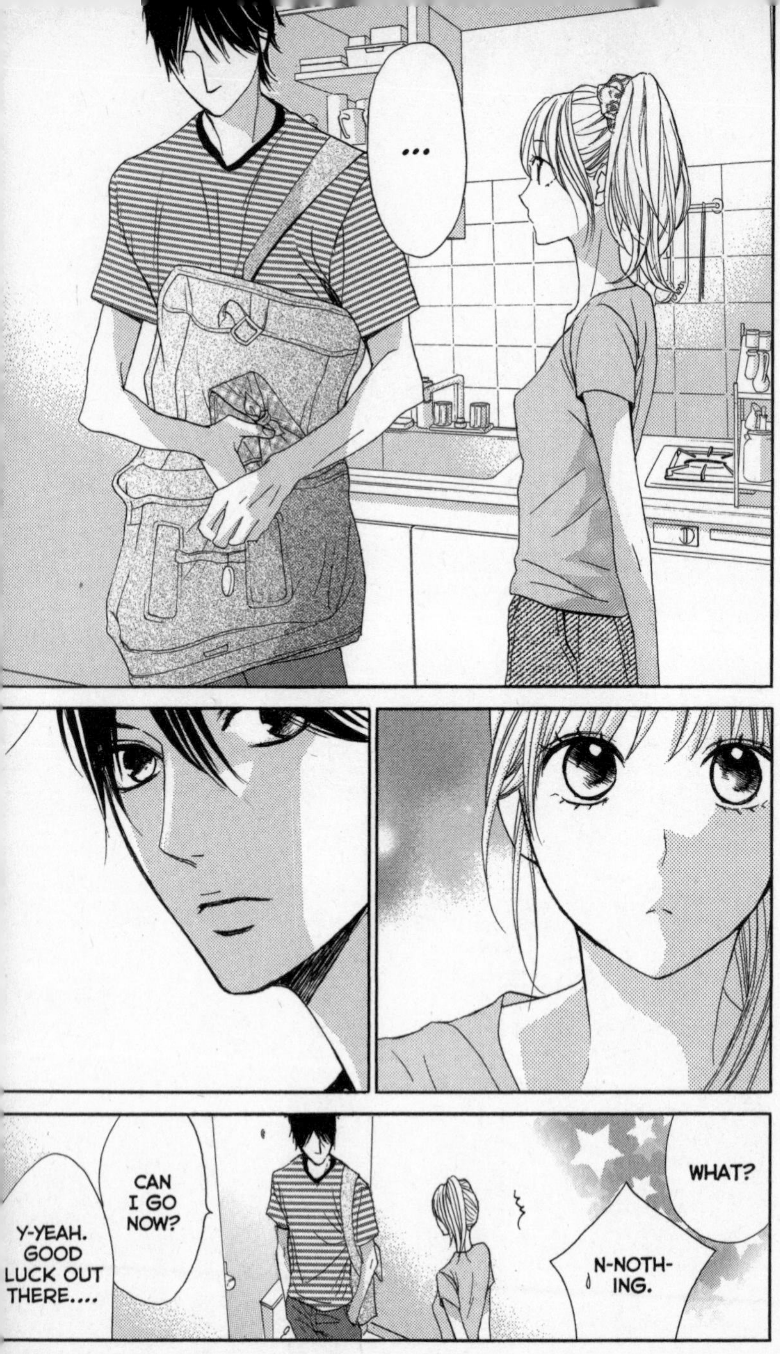
...
WHAT?
N-NOTH-ING.
CAN I GO NOW?
Y-YEAH. GOOD LUCK OUT THERE....

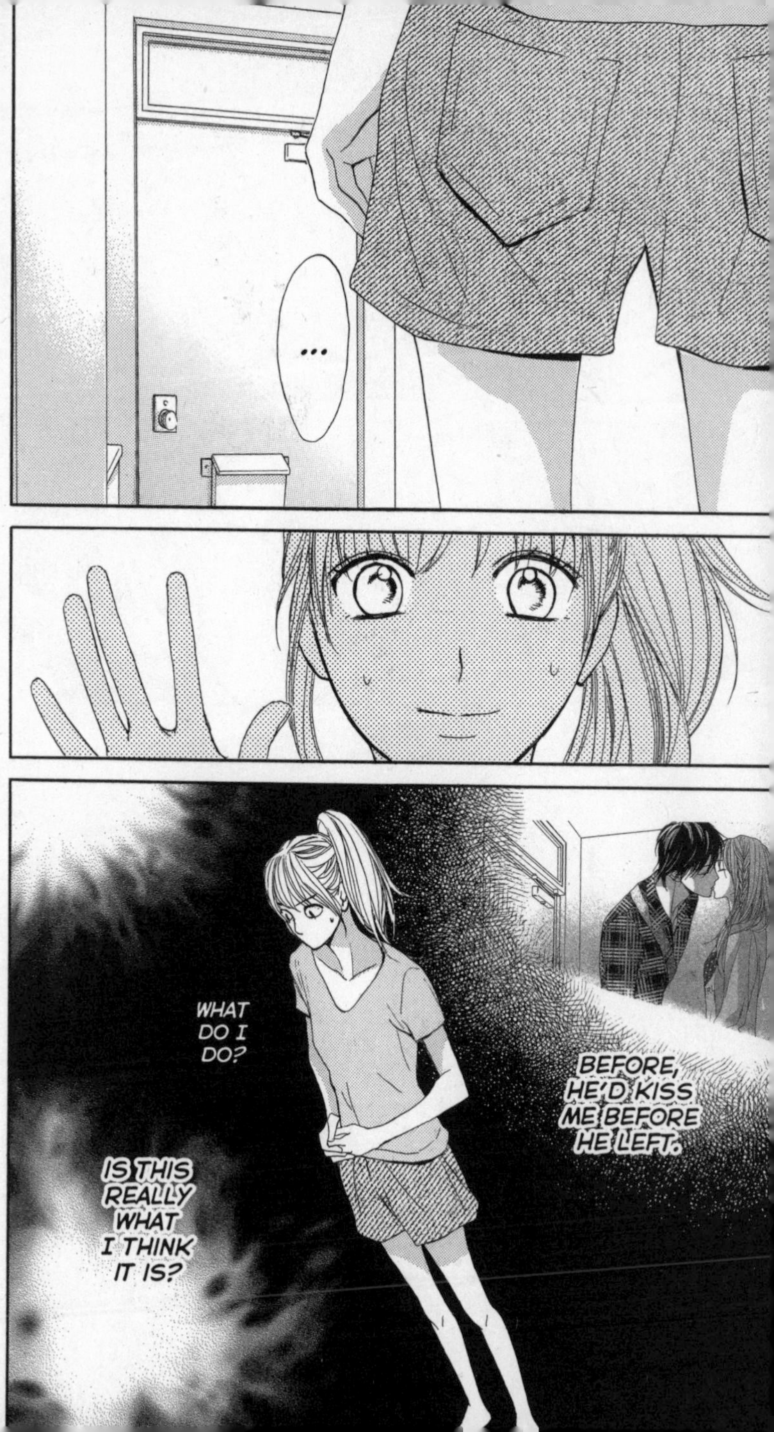
...
BEFORE, HE'D KISS ME BEFORE HE LEFT.
WHAT DO I DO?
IS THIS REALLY WHAT I THINK IT IS?

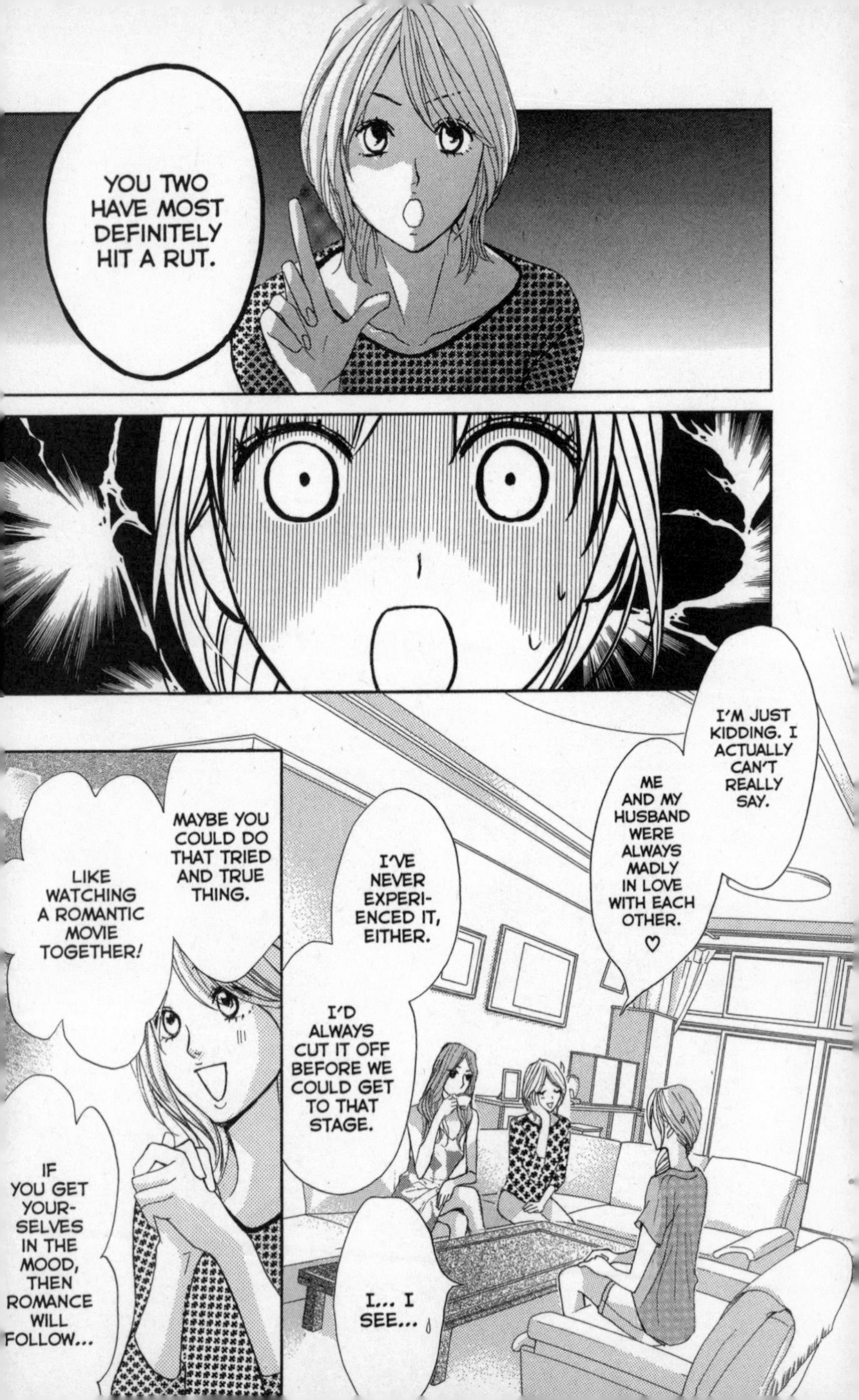
YOU TWO HAVE MOST DEFINITELY HIT A RUT.
I'M JUST KIDDING. I ACTUALLY CAN'T REALLY SAY.
ME AND MY HUSBAND WERE ALWAYS MADLY IN LOVE WITH EACH OTHER. ♡
I'VE NEVER EXPERI-ENCED IT, EITHER.
I'D ALWAYS CUT IT OFF BEFORE WE COULD GET TO THAT STAGE.
I... I SEE...
MAYBE YOU COULD DO THAT TRIED AND TRUE THING.
LIKE WATCHING A ROMANTIC MOVIE TOGETHER!
IF YOU GET YOUR-SELVES IN THE MOOD, THEN ROMANCE WILL FOLLOW...

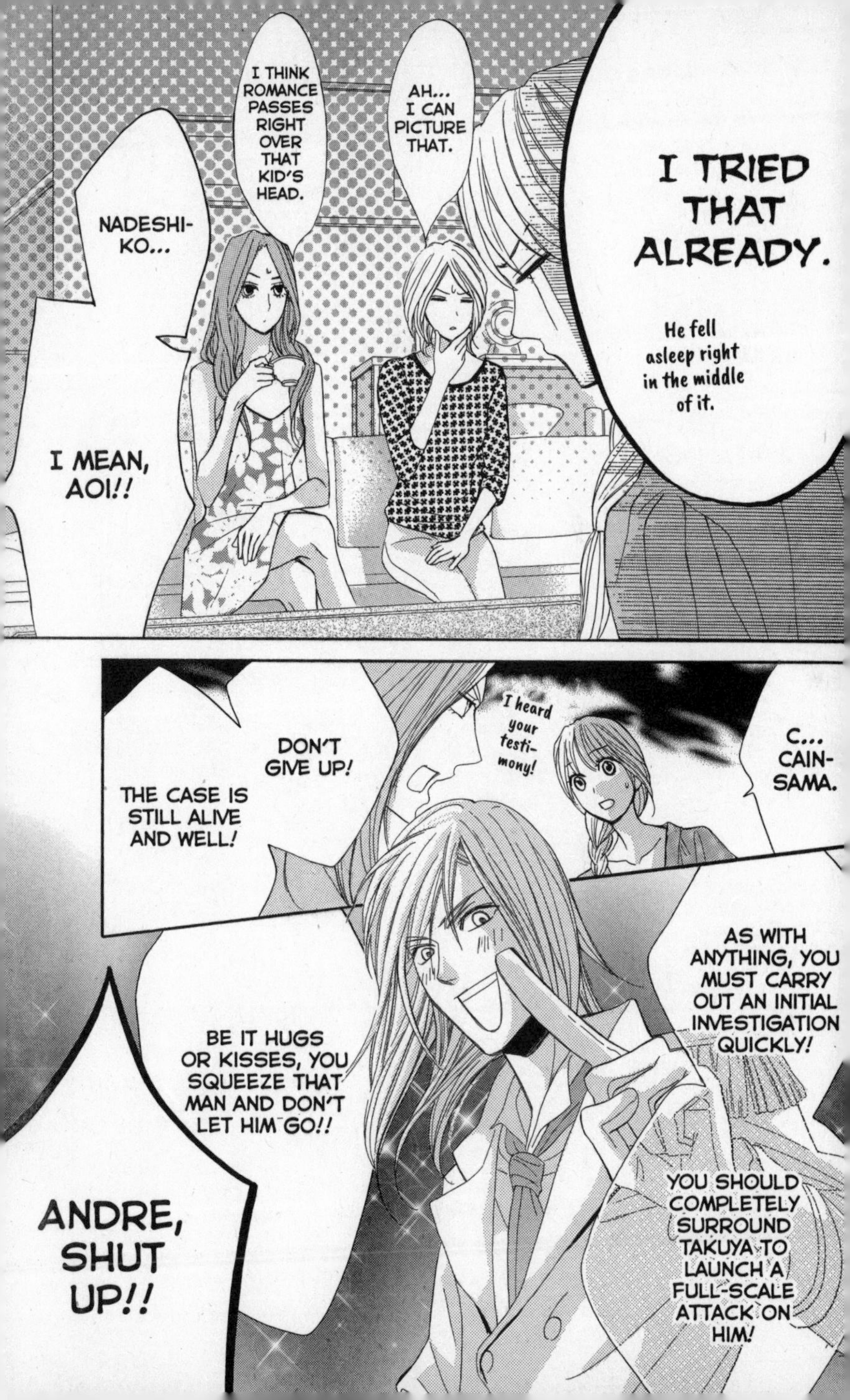
I TRIED THAT ALREADY.
He fell asleep right in the middle of it.
AH... I CAN PICTURE THAT.
I THINK ROMANCE PASSES RIGHT OVER THAT KID'S HEAD.
NADESHIKO... I MEAN, AOI!!
C... CAIN-SAMA.
I heard your testimony!
DON'T GIVE UP! THE CASE IS STILL ALIVE AND WELL!
AS WITH ANYTHING, YOU MUST CARRY OUT AN INITIAL INVESTIGATION QUICKLY!
YOU SHOULD COMPLETELY SURROUND TAKUYA TO LAUNCH A FULL-SCALE ATTACK ON HIM!
BE IT HUGS OR KISSES, YOU SQUEEZE THAT MAN AND DON'T LET HIM GO!!
ANDRE, SHUT UP!!

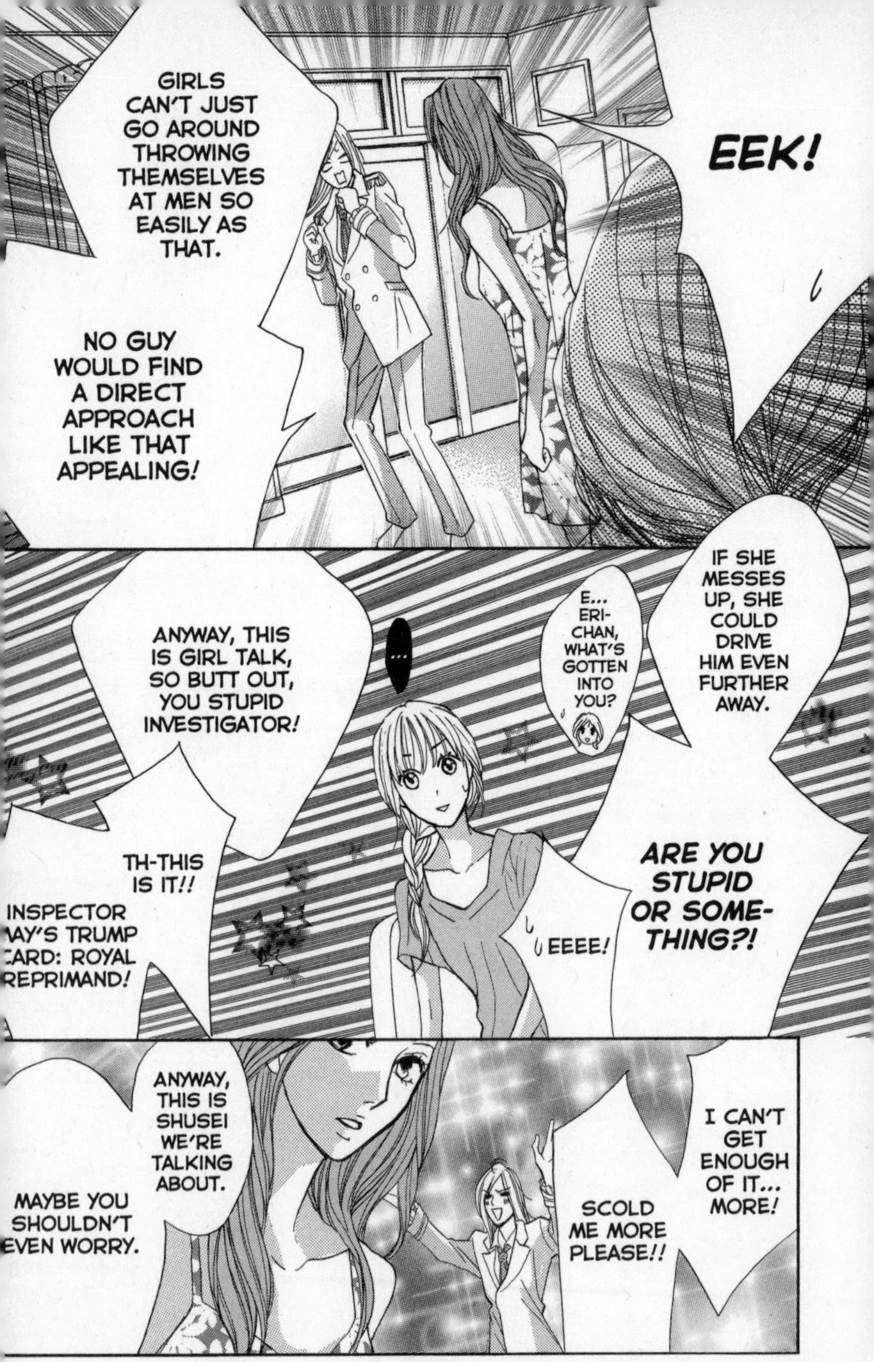
EEK!
GIRLS CAN'T JUST GO AROUND THROWING THEMSELVES AT MEN SO EASILY AS THAT.
NO GUY WOULD FIND A DIRECT APPROACH LIKE THAT APPEALING!
IF SHE MESSES UP, SHE COULD DRIVE HIM EVEN FURTHER AWAY.
ARE YOU STUPID OR SOME-THING?!
E... ERI-CHAN, WHAT'S GOTTEN INTO YOU?
EEEE!
...
ANYWAY, THIS IS GIRL TALK, SO BUTT OUT, YOU STUPID INVESTIGATOR!
TH-THIS IS IT!!
INSPECTOR AY'S TRUMP ARD: ROYAL REPRIMAND!
I CAN'T GET ENOUGH OF IT... MORE!
SCOLD ME MORE PLEASE!!
ANYWAY, THIS IS SHUSEI WE'RE TALKING ABOUT.
MAYBE YOU SHOULDN'T EVEN WORRY.

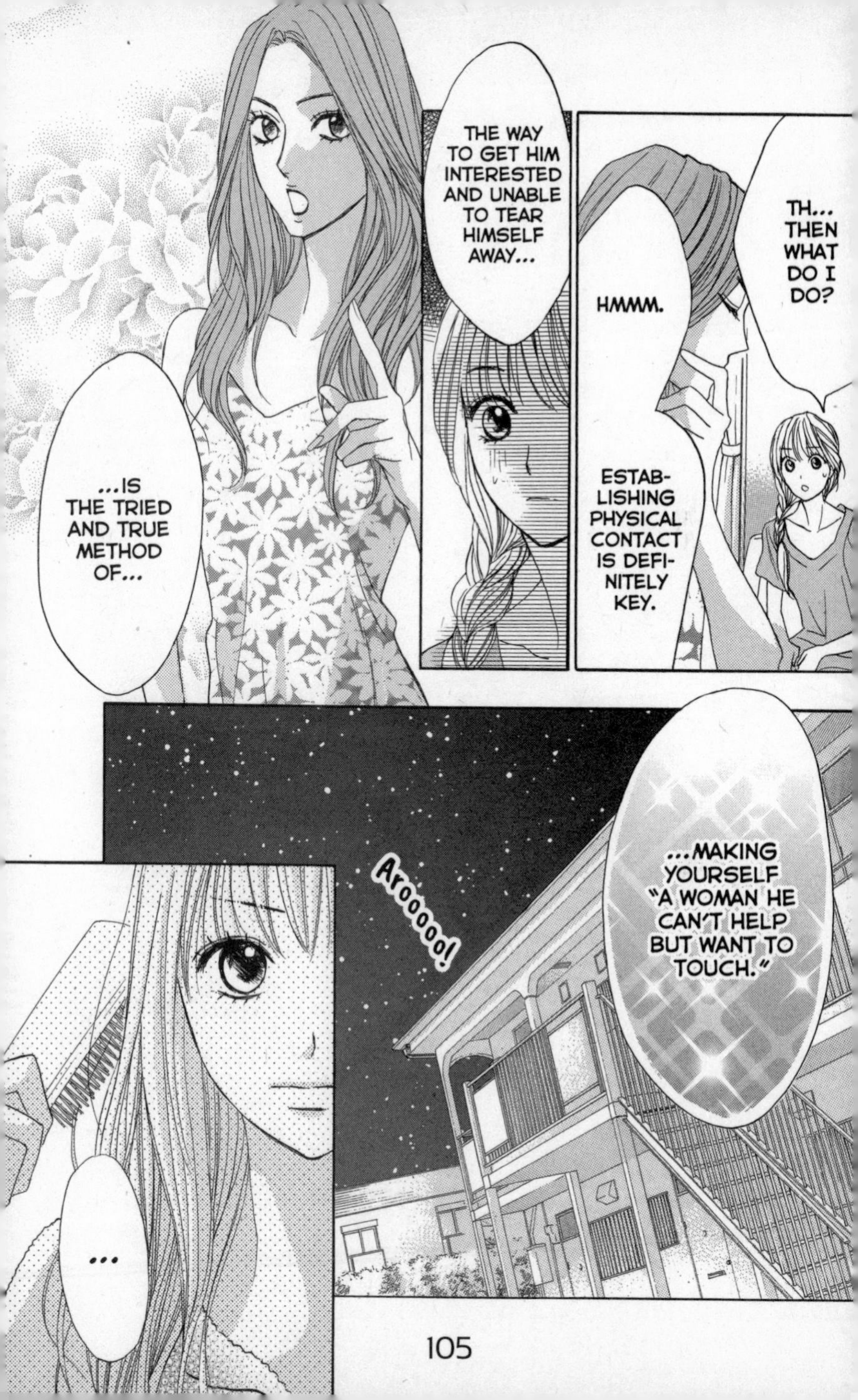
TH... THEN WHAT DO I DO?
HMMM.
ESTAB-LISHING PHYSICAL CONTACT IS DEFI-NITELY KEY.
THE WAY TO GET HIM INTERESTED AND UNABLE TO TEAR HIMSELF AWAY...
...IS THE TRIED AND TRUE METHOD OF...
...MAKING YOURSELF "A WOMAN HE CAN'T HELP BUT WANT TO TOUCH."
Aroooooo!
...

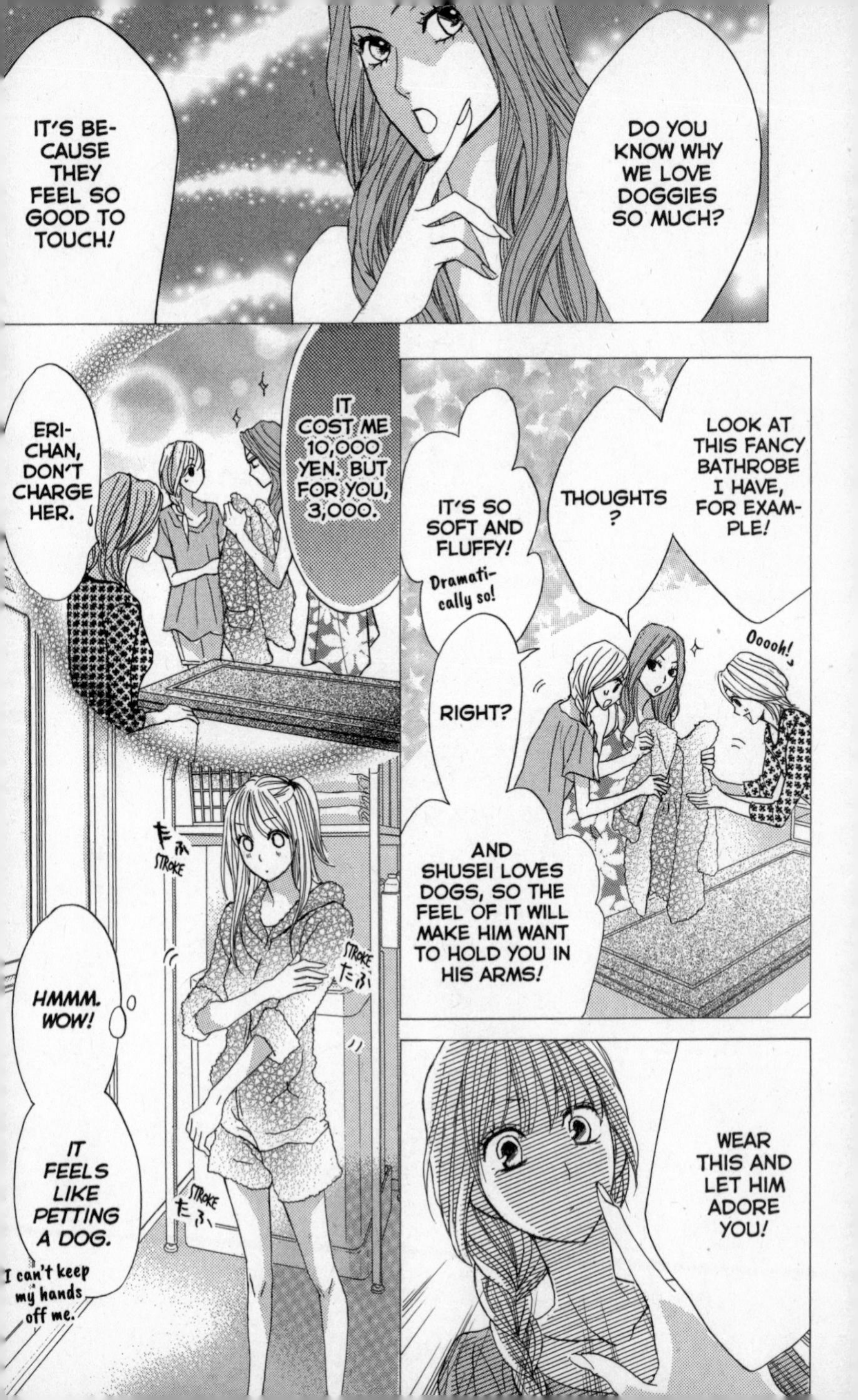
DO YOU KNOW WHY WE LOVE DOGGIES SO MUCH?
IT'S BE-CAUSE THEY FEEL SO GOOD TO TOUCH!
LOOK AT THIS FANCY BATHROBE I HAVE, FOR EXAM-PLE!
THOUGHTS?
Ooooh!
IT'S SO SOFT AND FLUFFY!
Dramati-cally so!
RIGHT?
AND SHUSEI LOVES DOGS, SO THE FEEL OF IT WILL MAKE HIM WANT TO HOLD YOU IN HIS ARMS!
IT COST ME 10,000 YEN. BUT FOR YOU, 3,000.
ERI-CHAN, DON'T CHARGE HER.
WEAR THIS AND LET HIM ADORE YOU!
STROKE
STROKE
STROKE
HMMM. WOW!
IT FEELS LIKE PETTING A DOG.
I can't keep my hands off me.

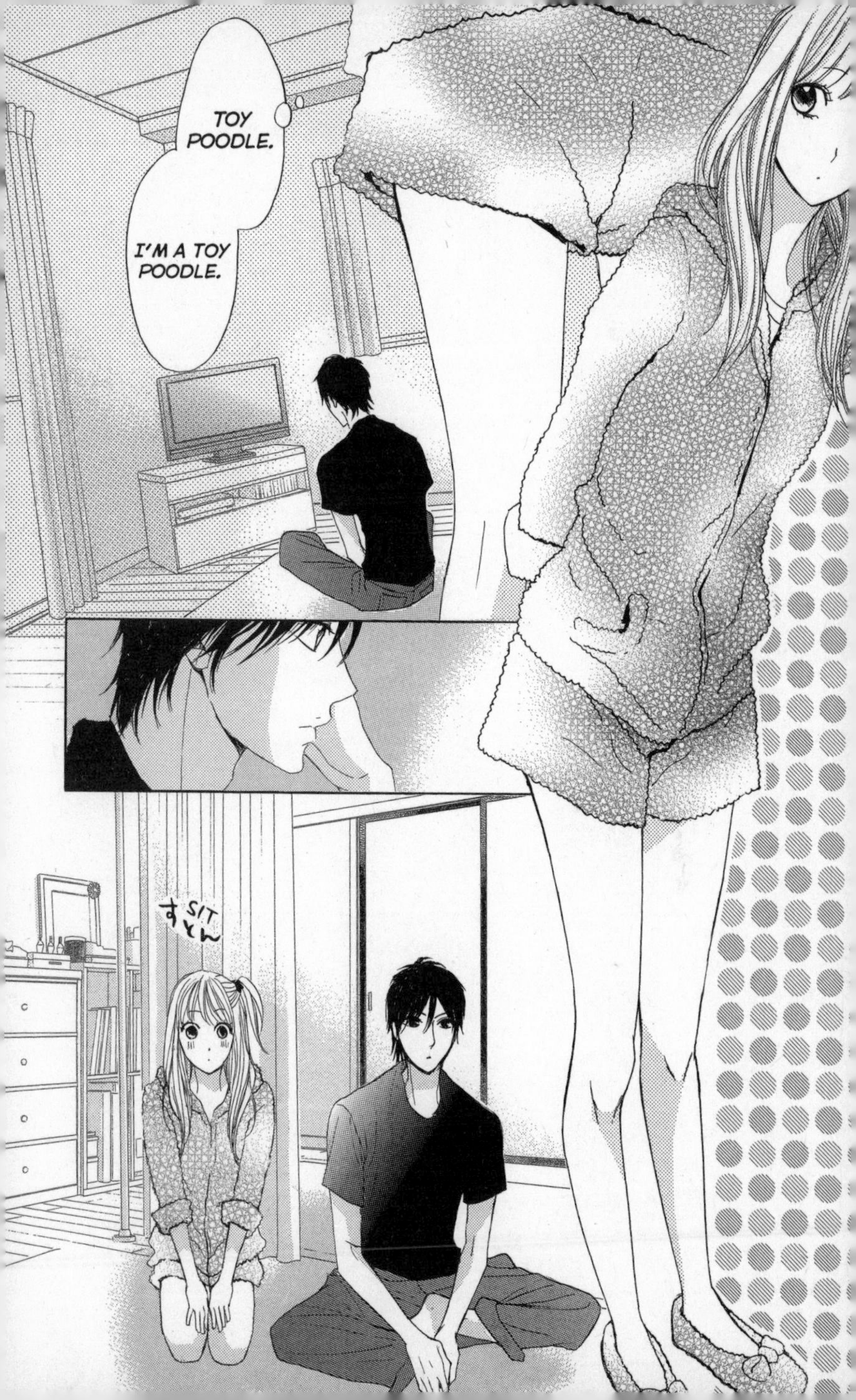

TOY POODLE.
I'M A TOY POODLE.
すとん
SIT

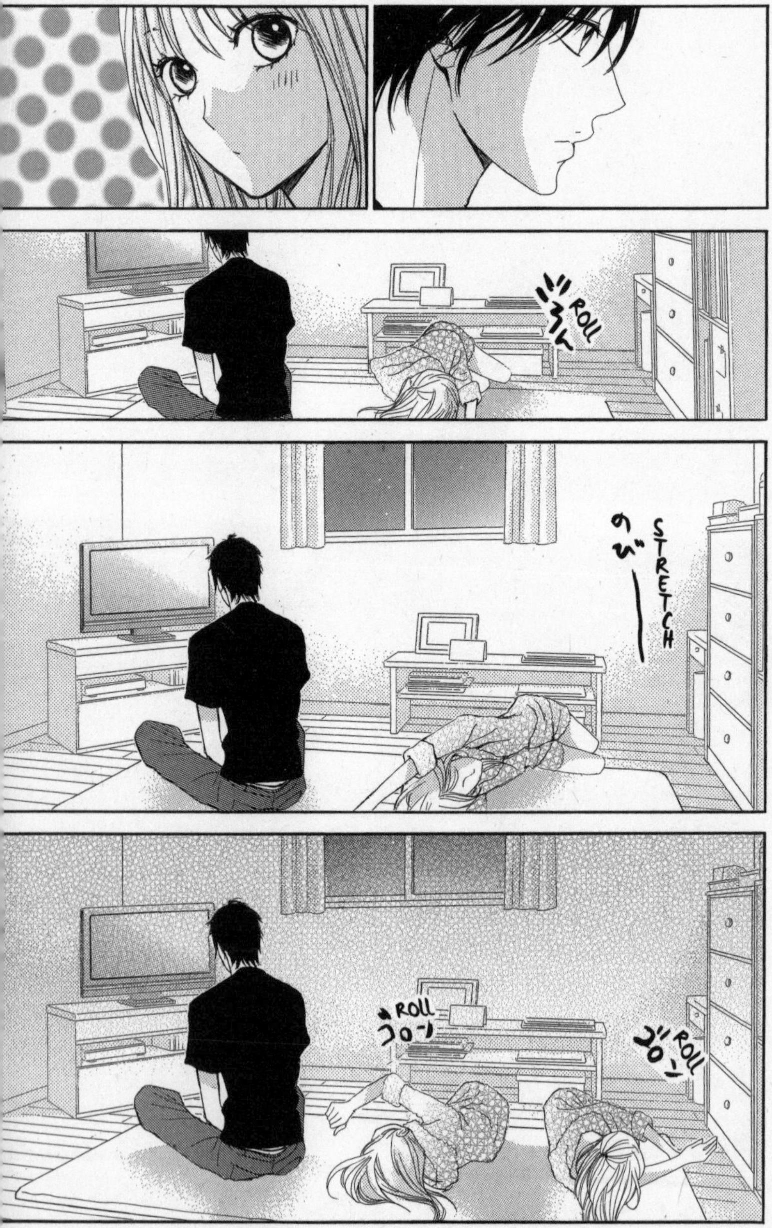
ROLL
STRETCH
ROLL
ROLL

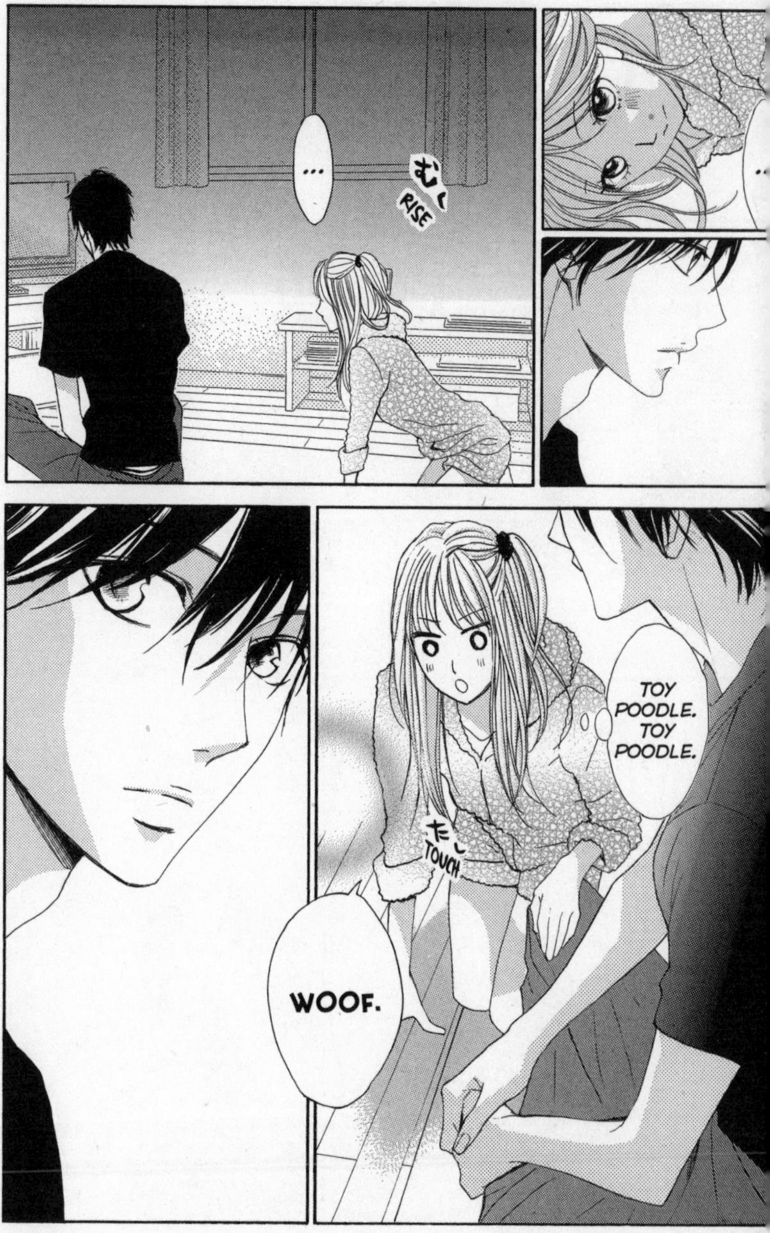
...
...
むく
RISE
TOY POODLE. TOY POODLE.
たし
TOUCH
WOOF.

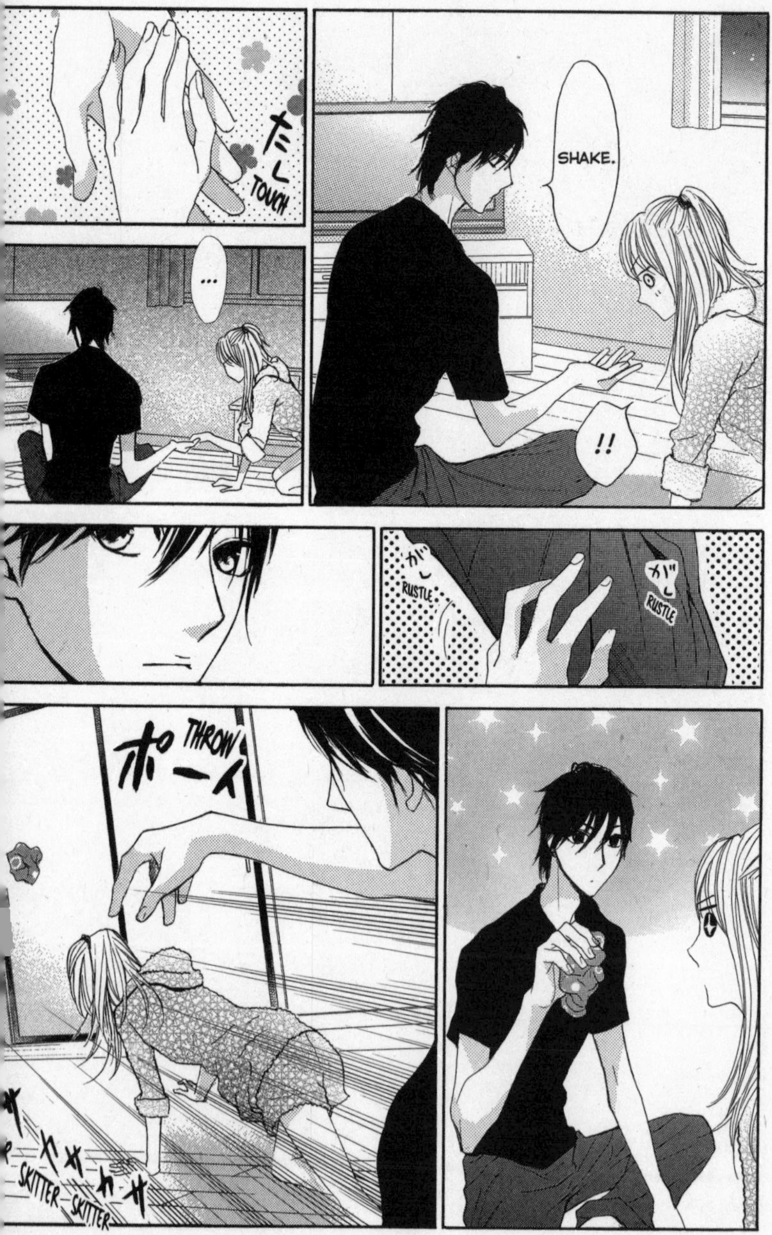
SHAKE.
!!
たし
TOUCH
...
がし
RUSTLE
がし
RUSTLE
ポーイ
THROW
SKITTER SKITTER

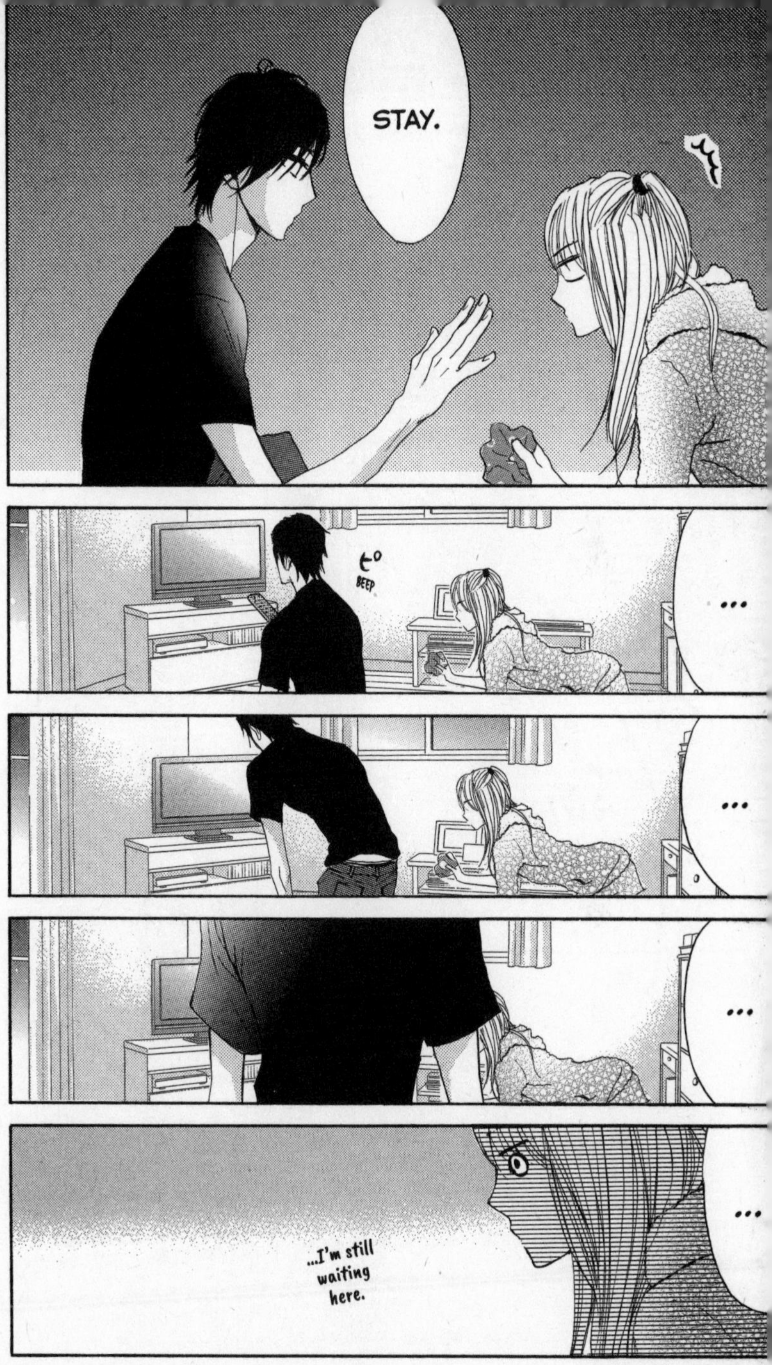
STAY.
...
BEEP
...
...
...
...I'm still waiting here.

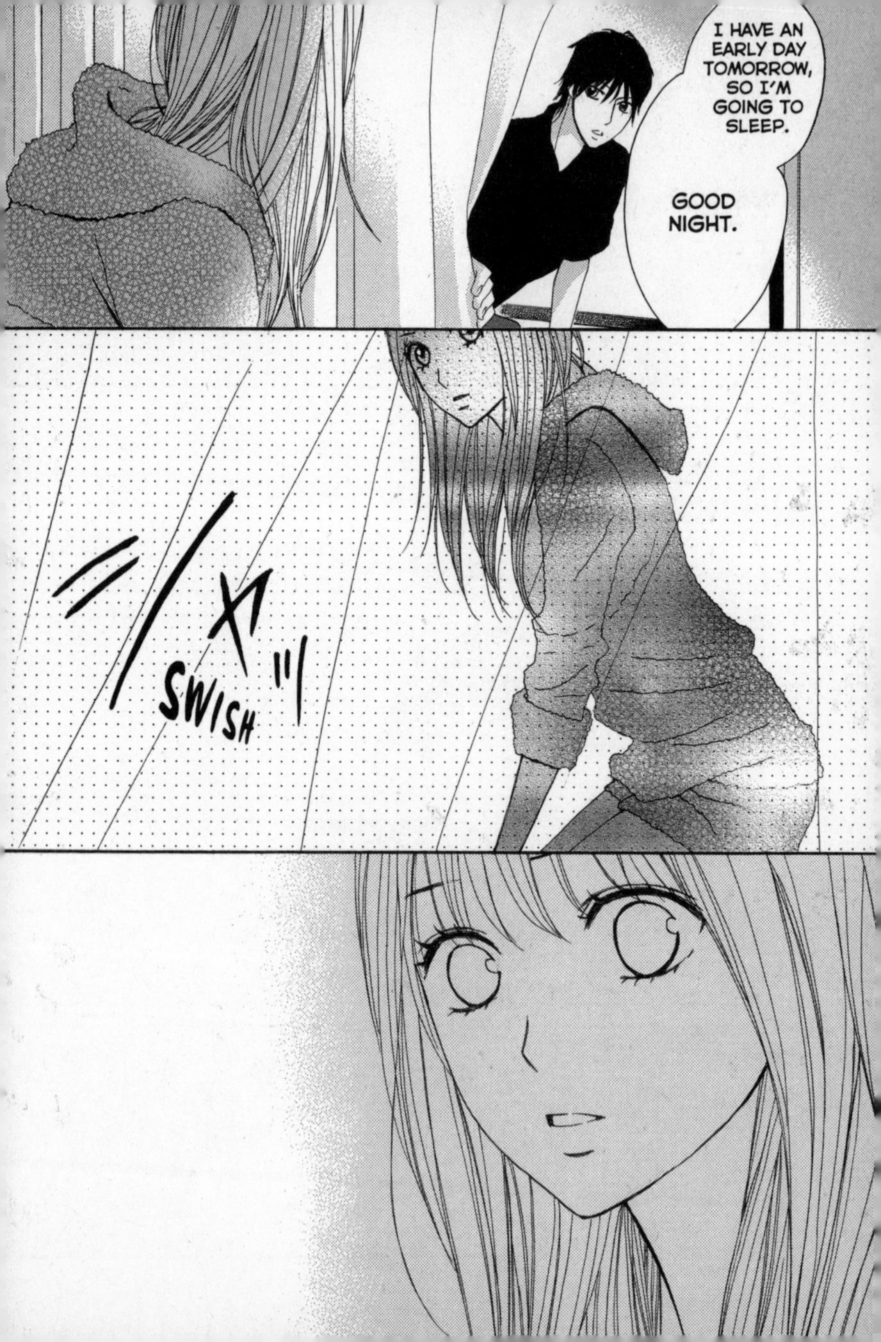
I HAVE AN EARLY DAY TOMORROW, SO I'M GOING TO SLEEP.
GOOD NIGHT.
SWISH

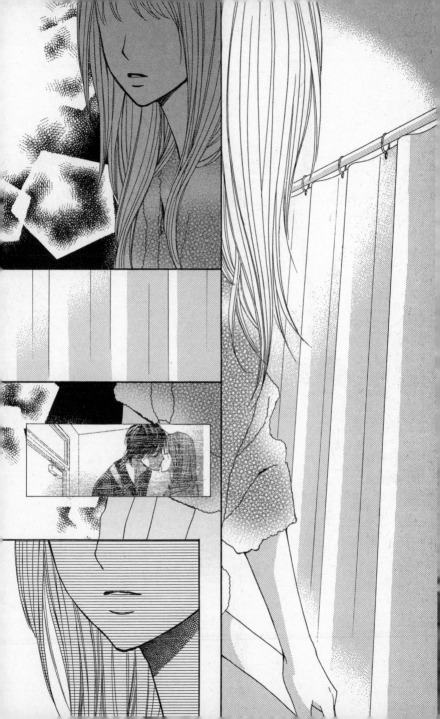

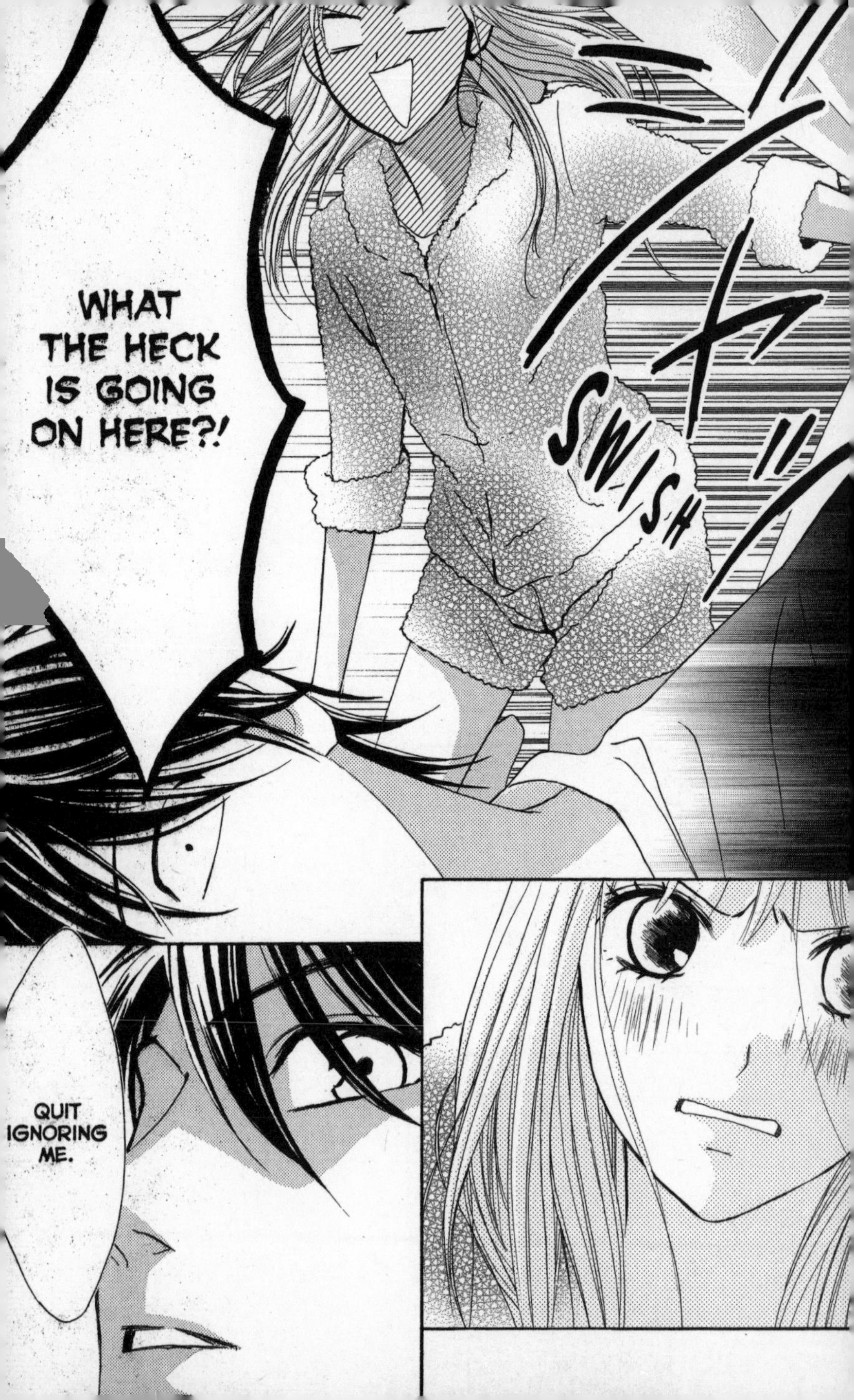
SWISH
WHAT THE HECK IS GOING ON HERE?!
QUIT IGNORING ME.

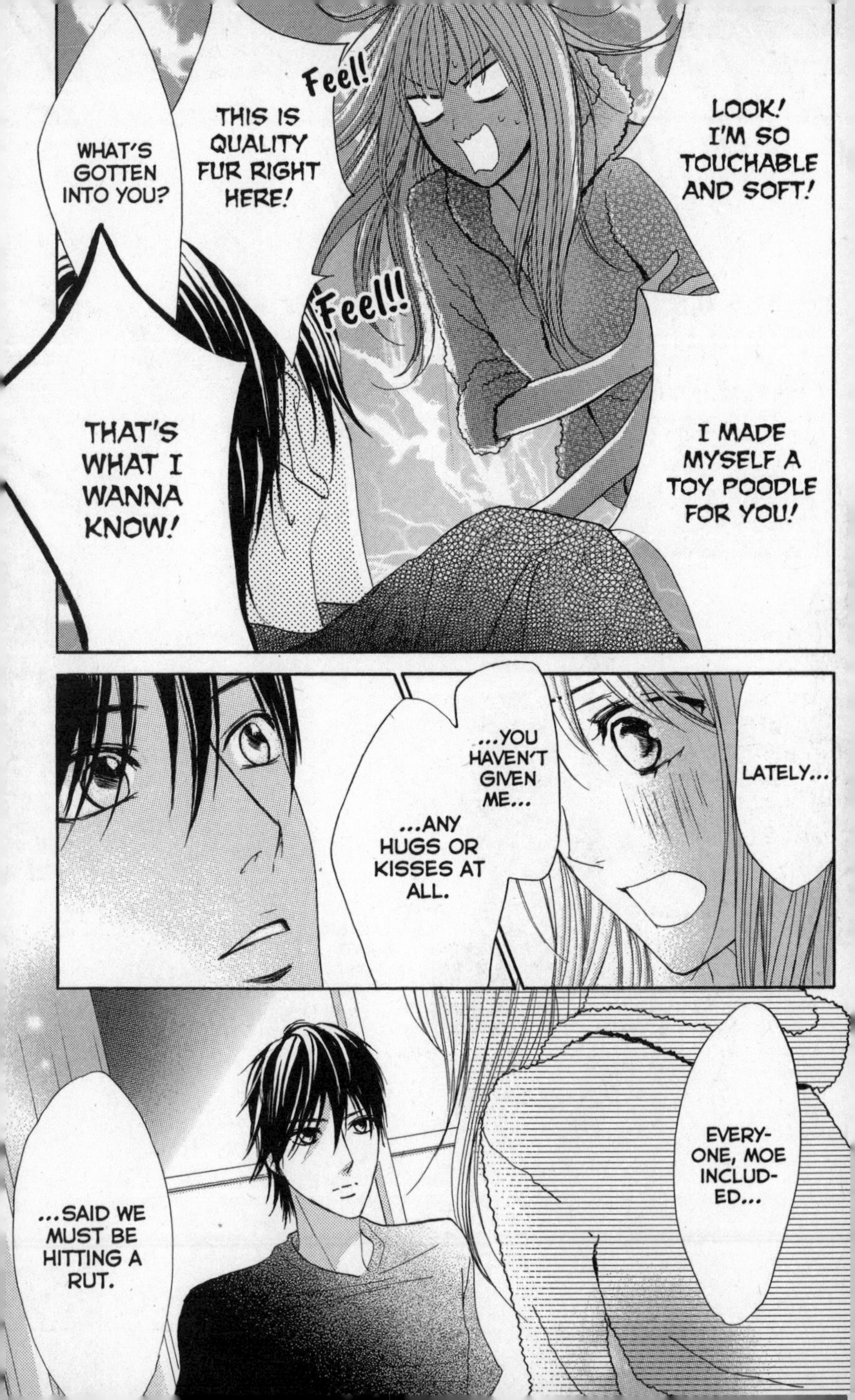
LOOK! I'M SO TOUCHABLE AND SOFT!
Feel!
THIS IS QUALITY FUR RIGHT HERE!
WHAT'S GOTTEN INTO YOU?
I MADE MYSELF A TOY POODLE FOR YOU!
Feel!!
THAT'S WHAT I WANNA KNOW!
LATELY...
...YOU HAVEN'T GIVEN ME...
...ANY HUGS OR KISSES AT ALL.
EVERY-ONE, MOE INCLUD-ED...
...SAID WE MUST BE HITTING A RUT.

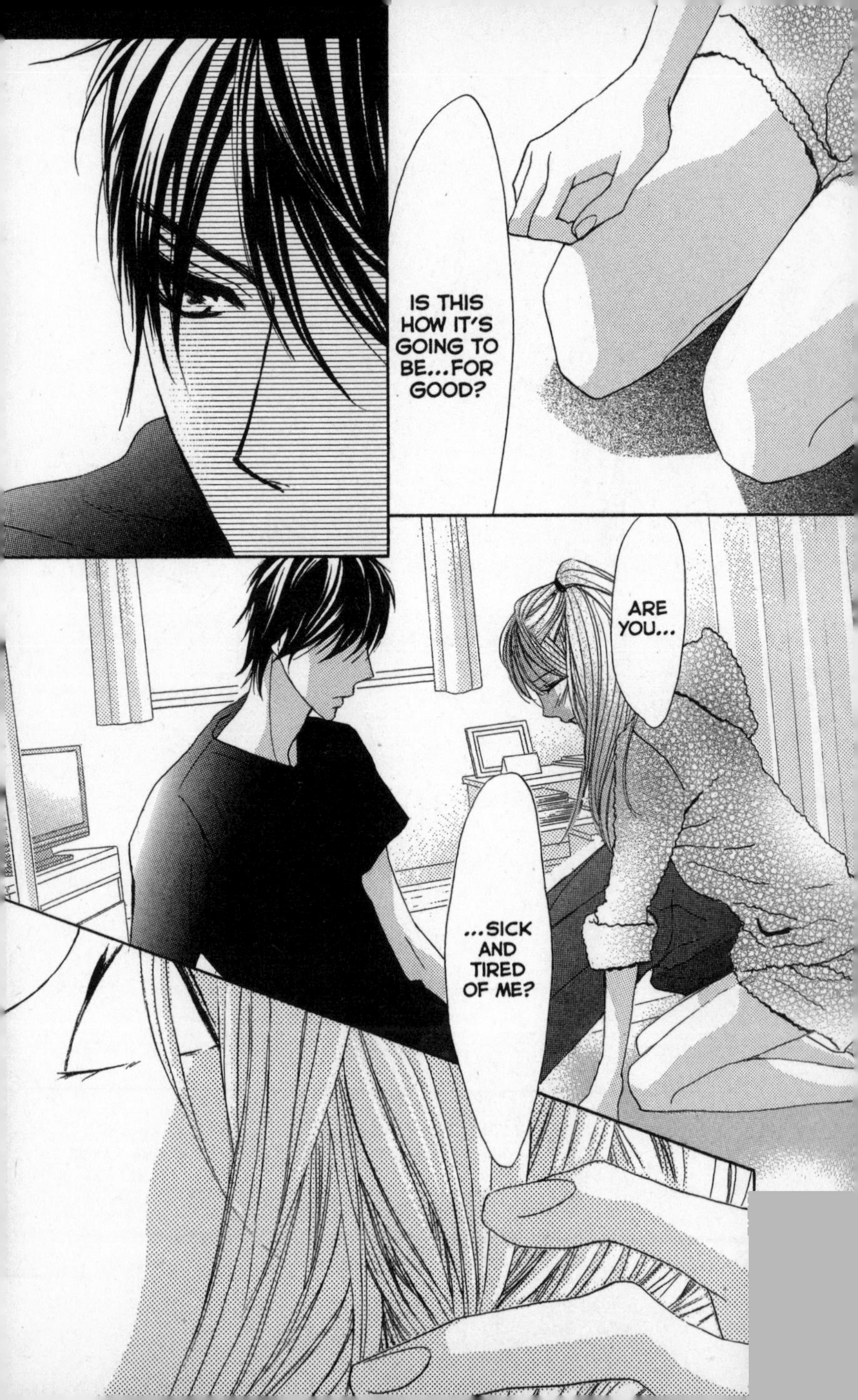
IS THIS HOW IT'S GOING TO BE...FOR GOOD?
ARE YOU...
...SICK AND TIRED OF ME?

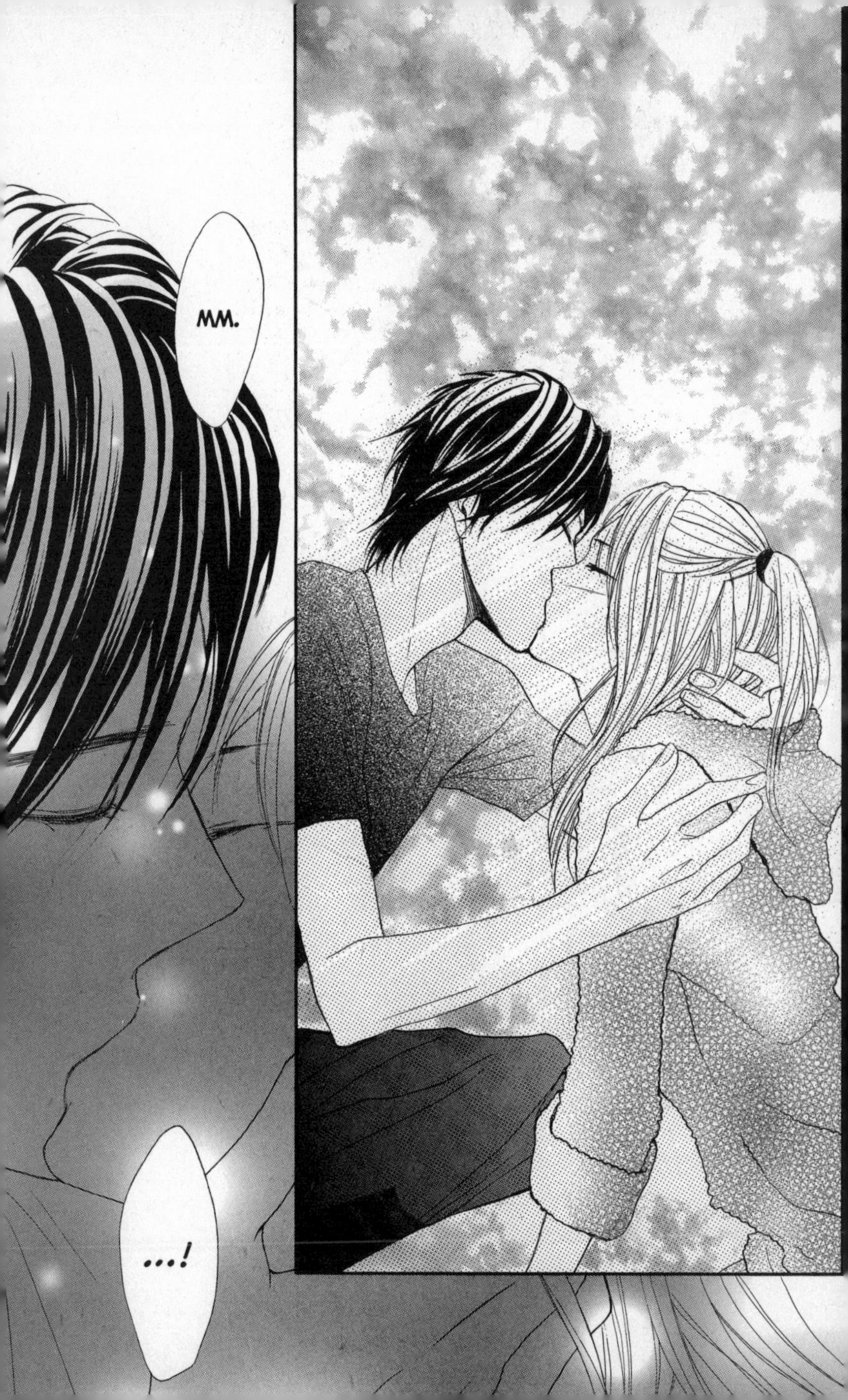
MM.
...!

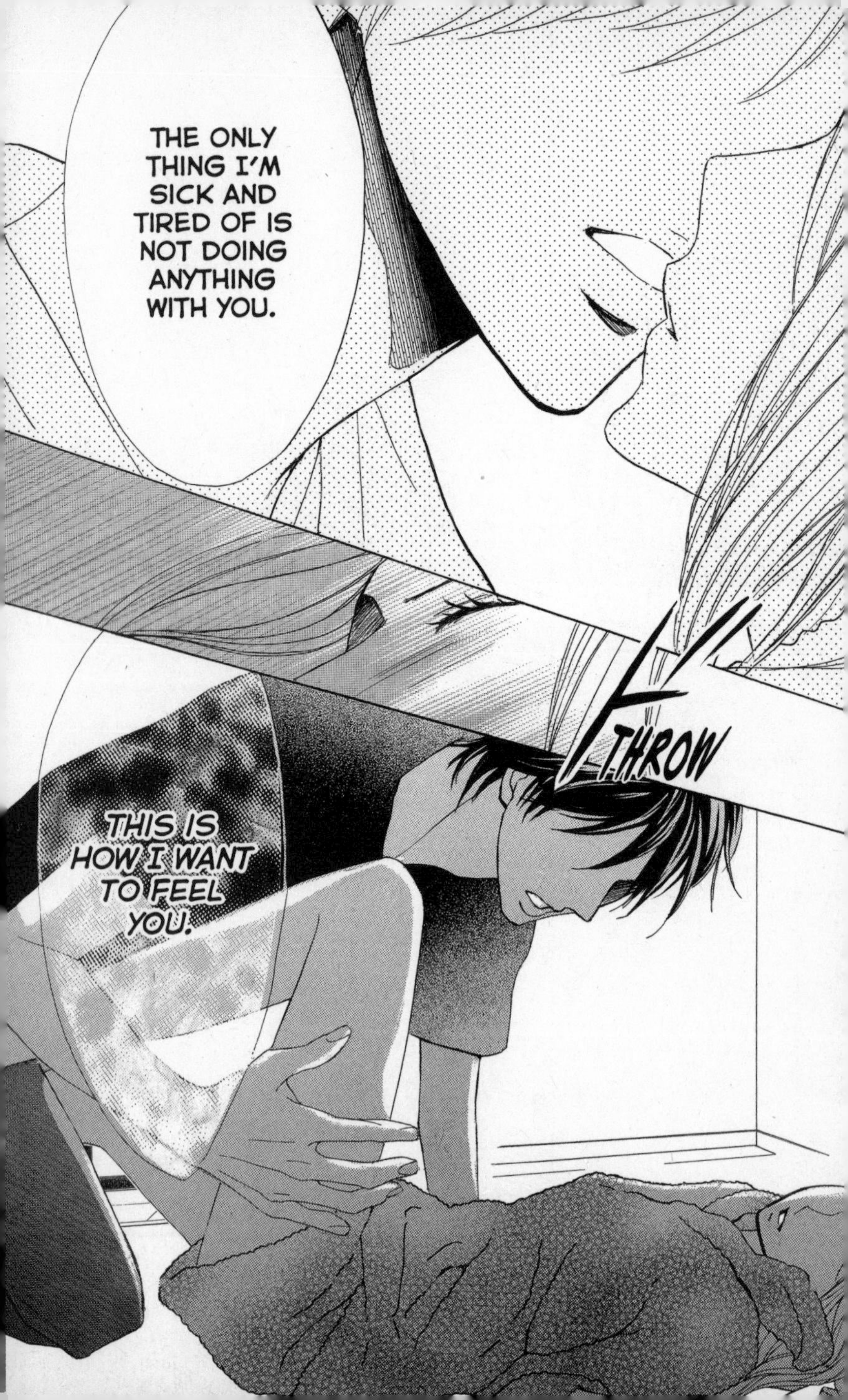
THE ONLY THING I'M SICK AND TIRED OF IS NOT DOING ANYTHING WITH YOU.
THROW
THIS IS HOW I WANT TO FEEL YOU.

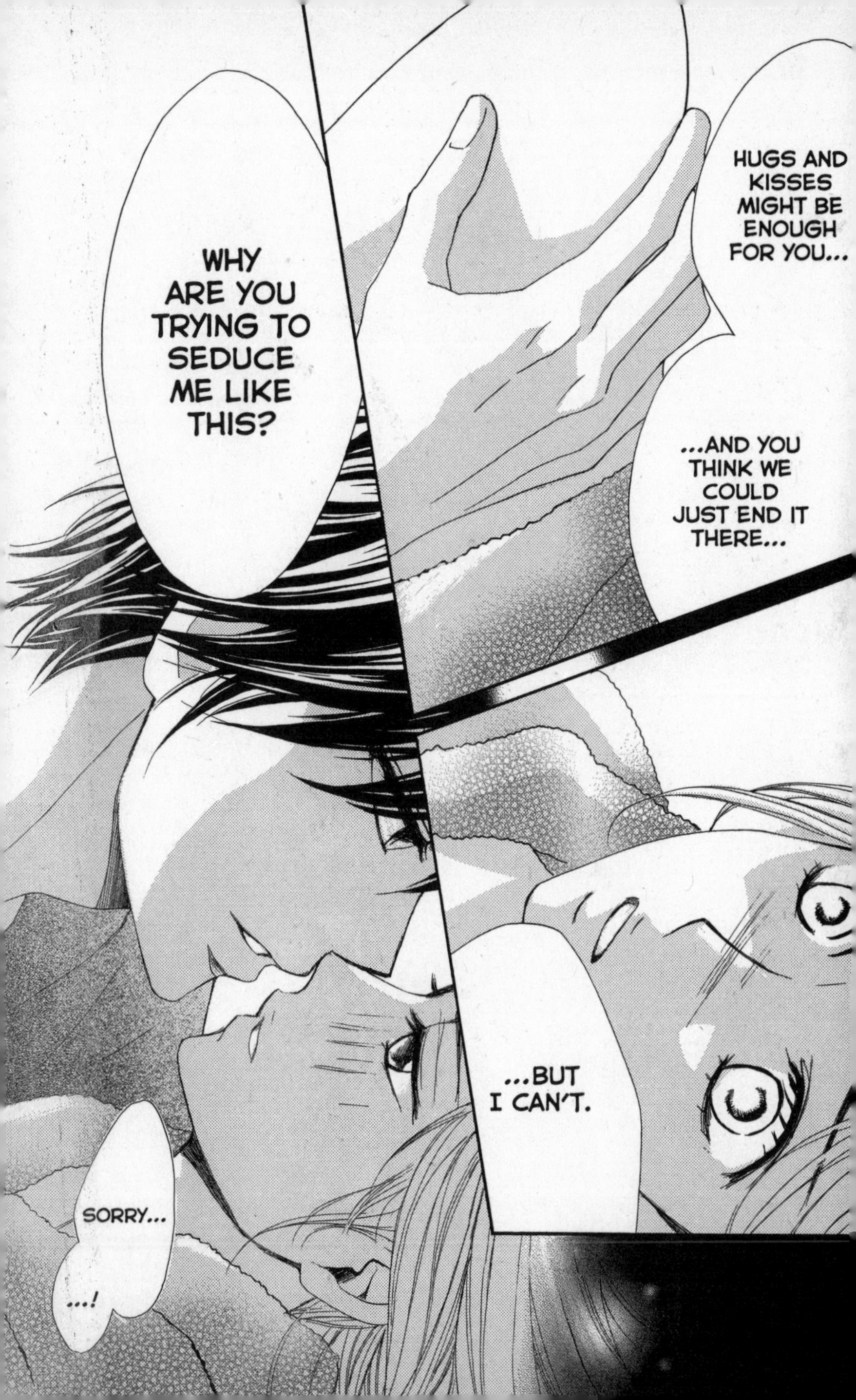
HUGS AND KISSES MIGHT BE ENOUGH FOR YOU...
...AND YOU THINK WE COULD JUST END IT THERE...
...BUT I CAN'T.
WHY ARE YOU TRYING TO SEDUCE ME LIKE THIS?
SORRY...
...!

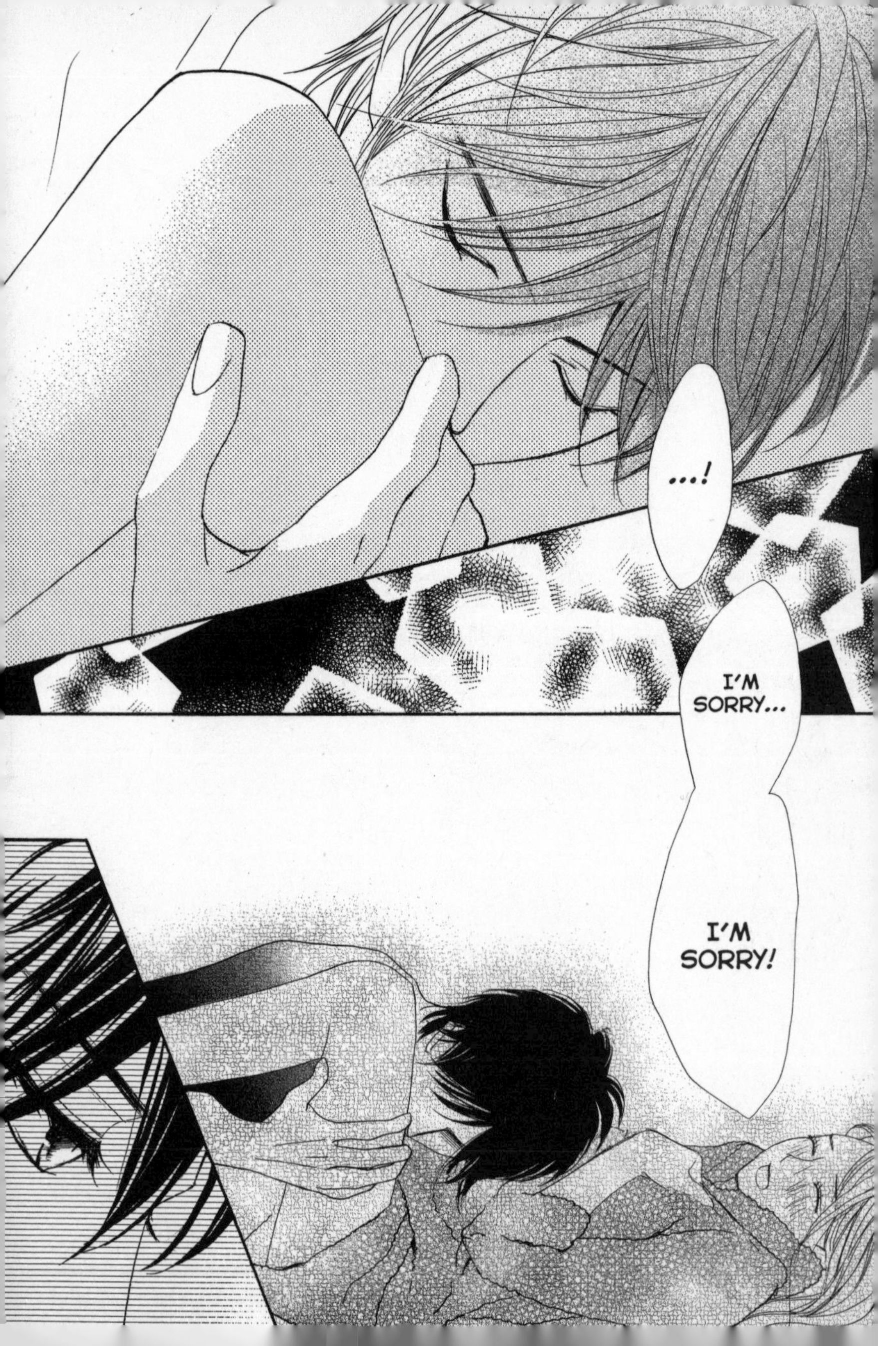
...!
I'M SORRY...
I'M SORRY!

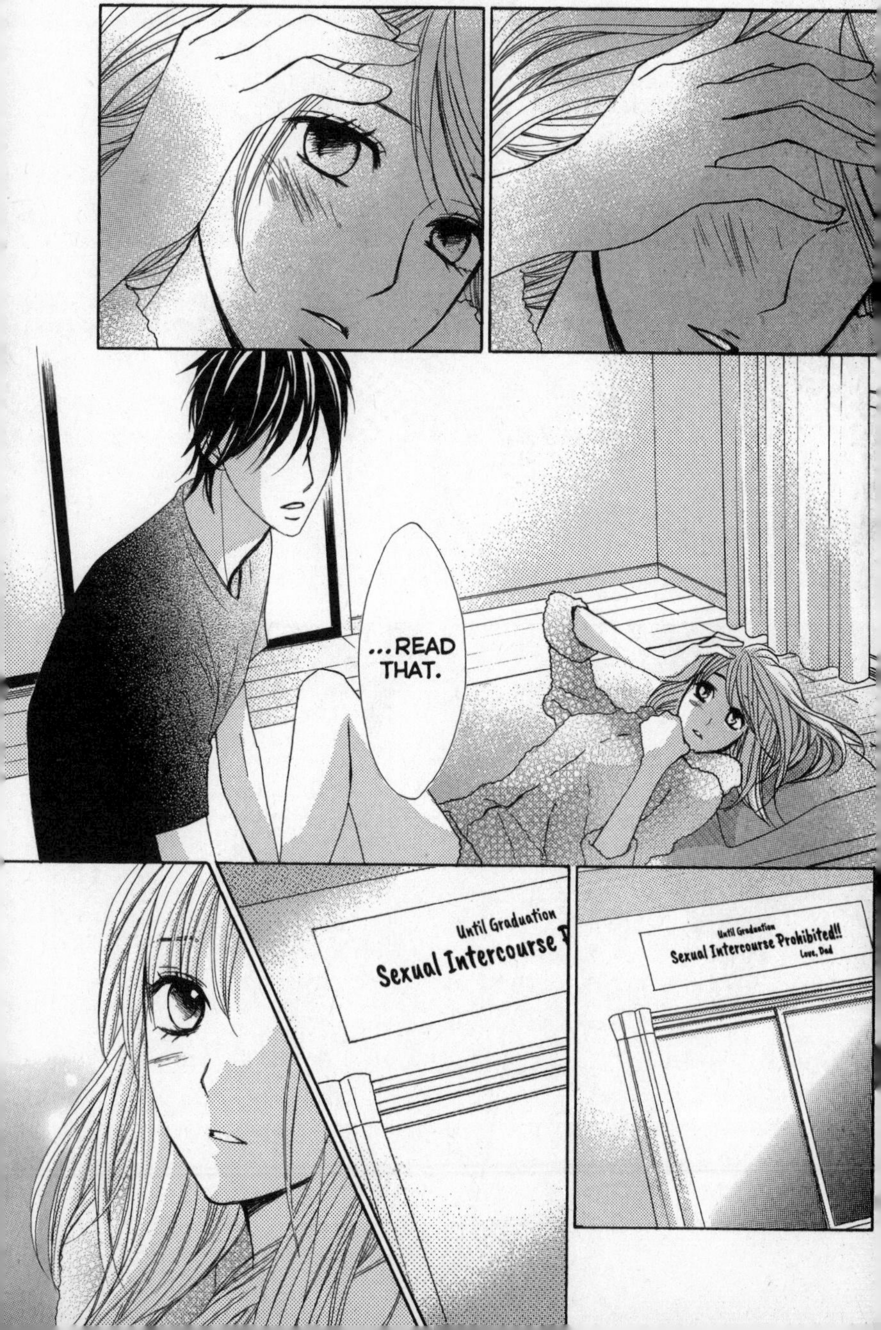
...READ THAT.
Until Graduation
Sexual Intercourse Prohibited!!
Love, Dad
Until Graduation
Sexual Intercourse

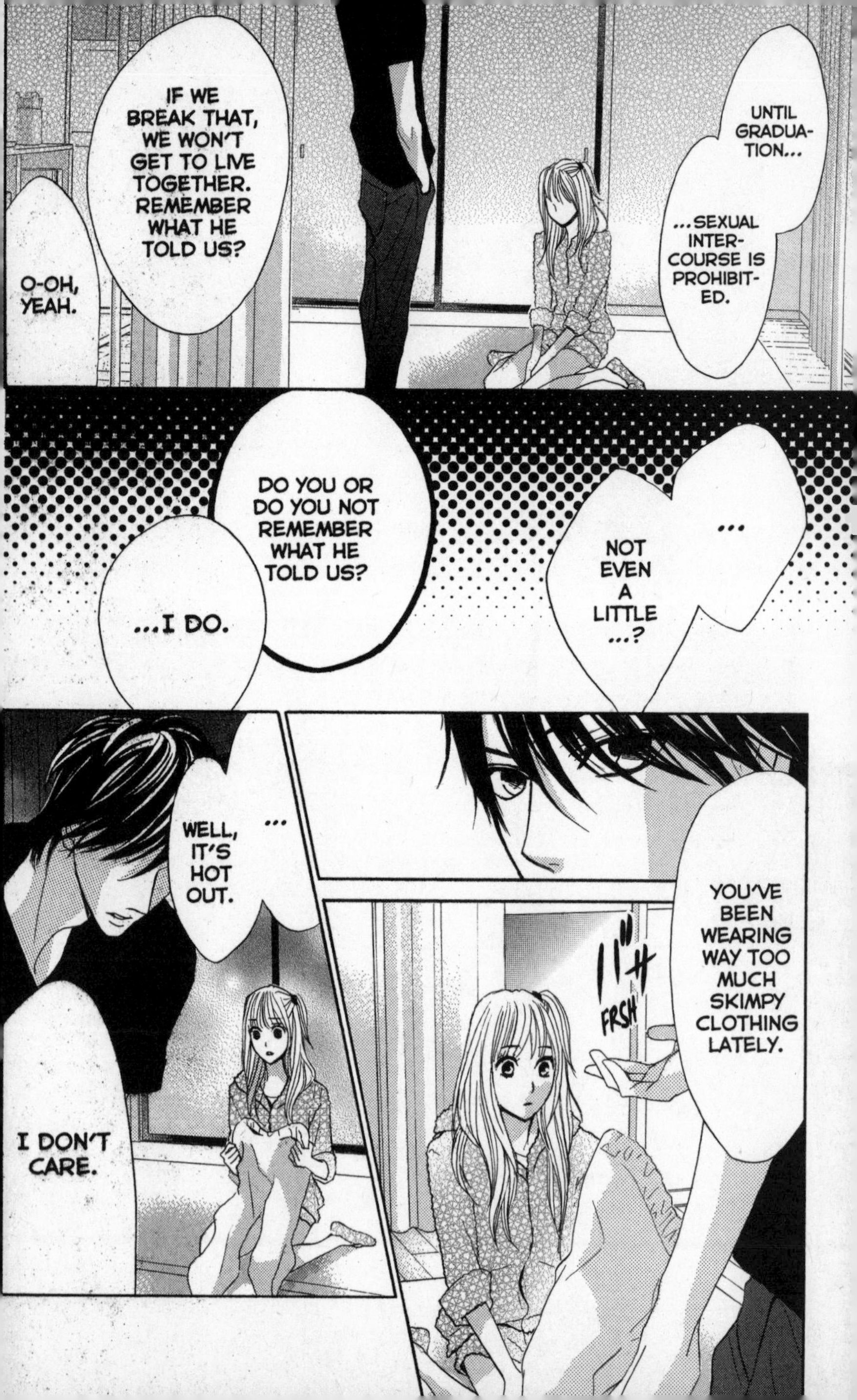
UNTIL GRADUATION...
...SEXUAL INTERCOURSE IS PROHIBITED.
IF WE BREAK THAT, WE WON'T GET TO LIVE TOGETHER. REMEMBER WHAT HE TOLD US?
O-OH, YEAH.
...
NOT EVEN A LITTLE ...?
DO YOU OR DO YOU NOT REMEMBER WHAT HE TOLD US?
...I DO.
YOU'VE BEEN WEARING WAY TOO MUCH SKIMPY CLOTHING LATELY.
FRSH
...
WELL, IT'S HOT OUT.
I DON'T CARE.

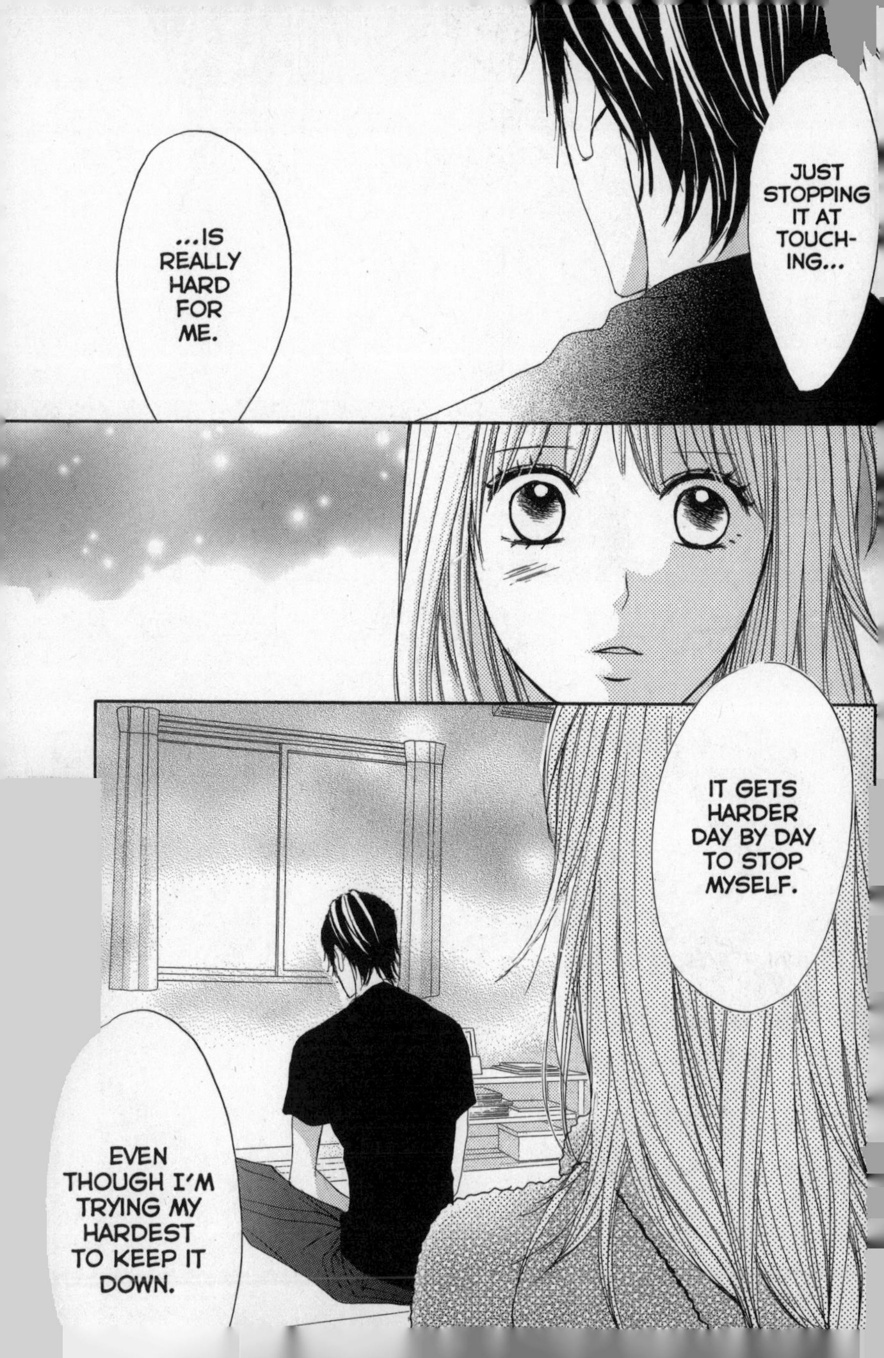
JUST STOPPING IT AT TOUCH-ING...
...IS REALLY HARD FOR ME.
IT GETS HARDER DAY BY DAY TO STOP MYSELF.
EVEN THOUGH I'M TRYING MY HARDEST TO KEEP IT DOWN.

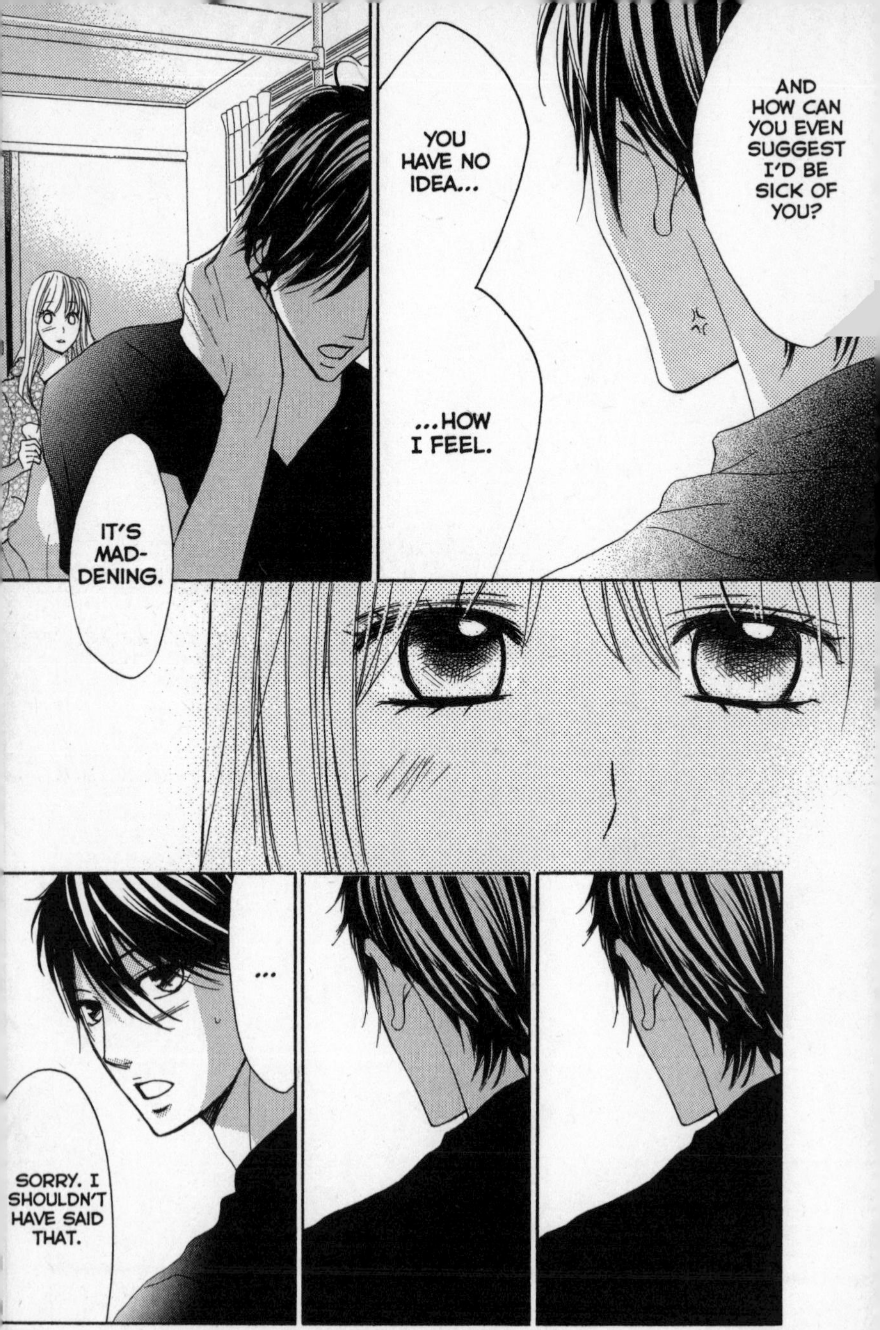
AND HOW CAN YOU EVEN SUGGEST I'D BE SICK OF YOU?
YOU HAVE NO IDEA...
...HOW I FEEL.
IT'S MAD-DENING.
...
SORRY. I SHOULDN'T HAVE SAID THAT.

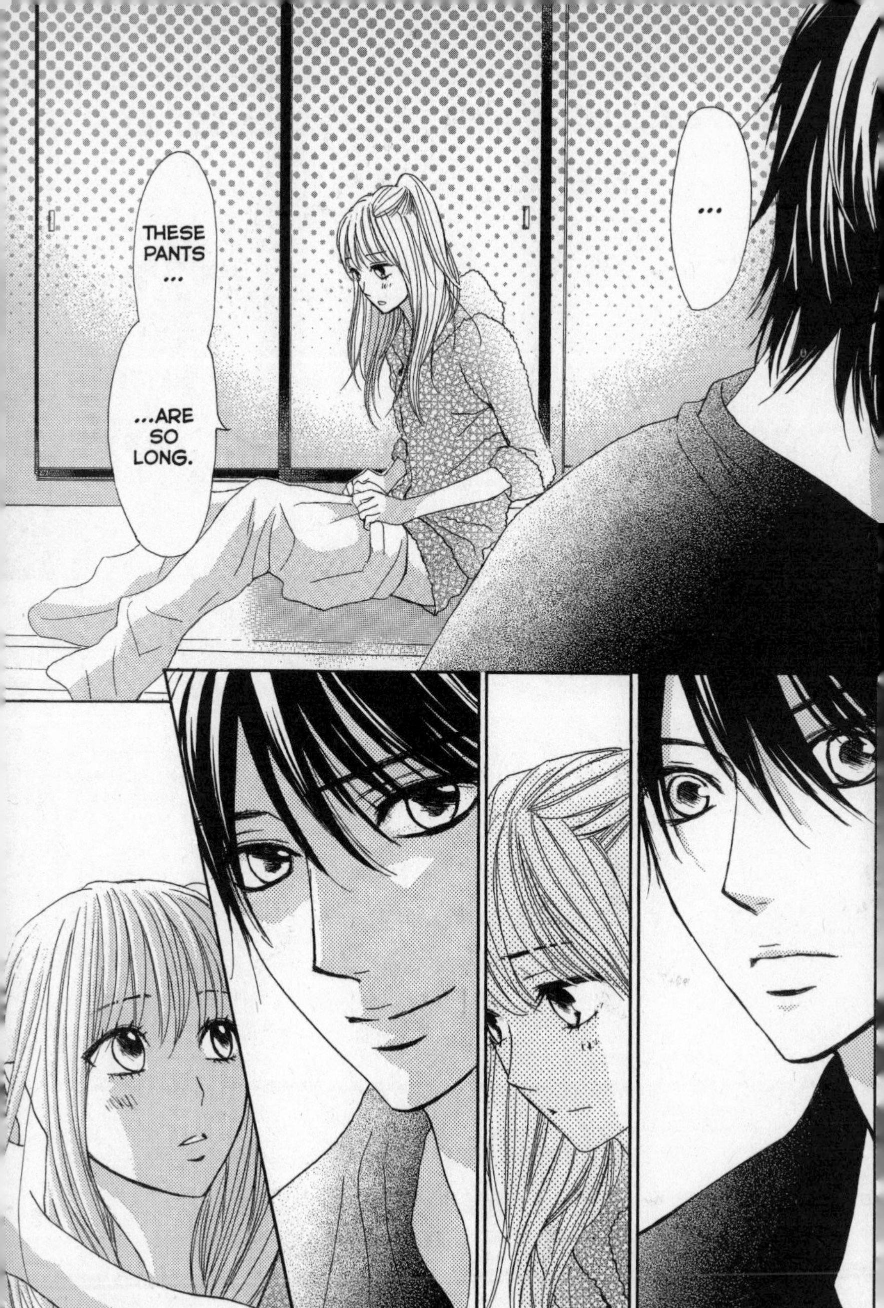
...
THESE PANTS ...
...ARE SO LONG.

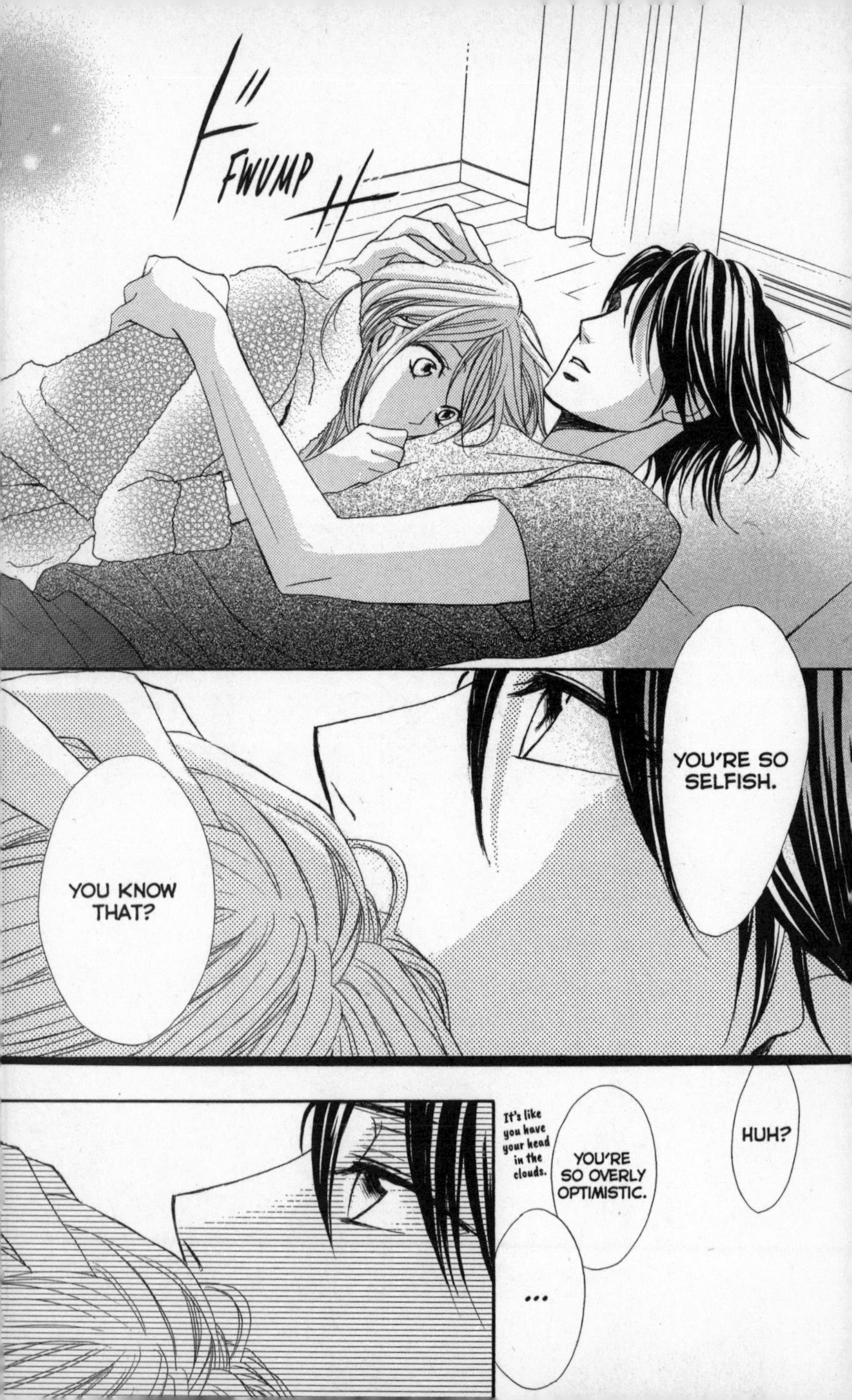
ド
FWUMP
YOU'RE SO SELFISH.
YOU KNOW THAT?
HUH?
YOU'RE SO OVERLY OPTIMISTIC.
It's like you have your head in the clouds.
...

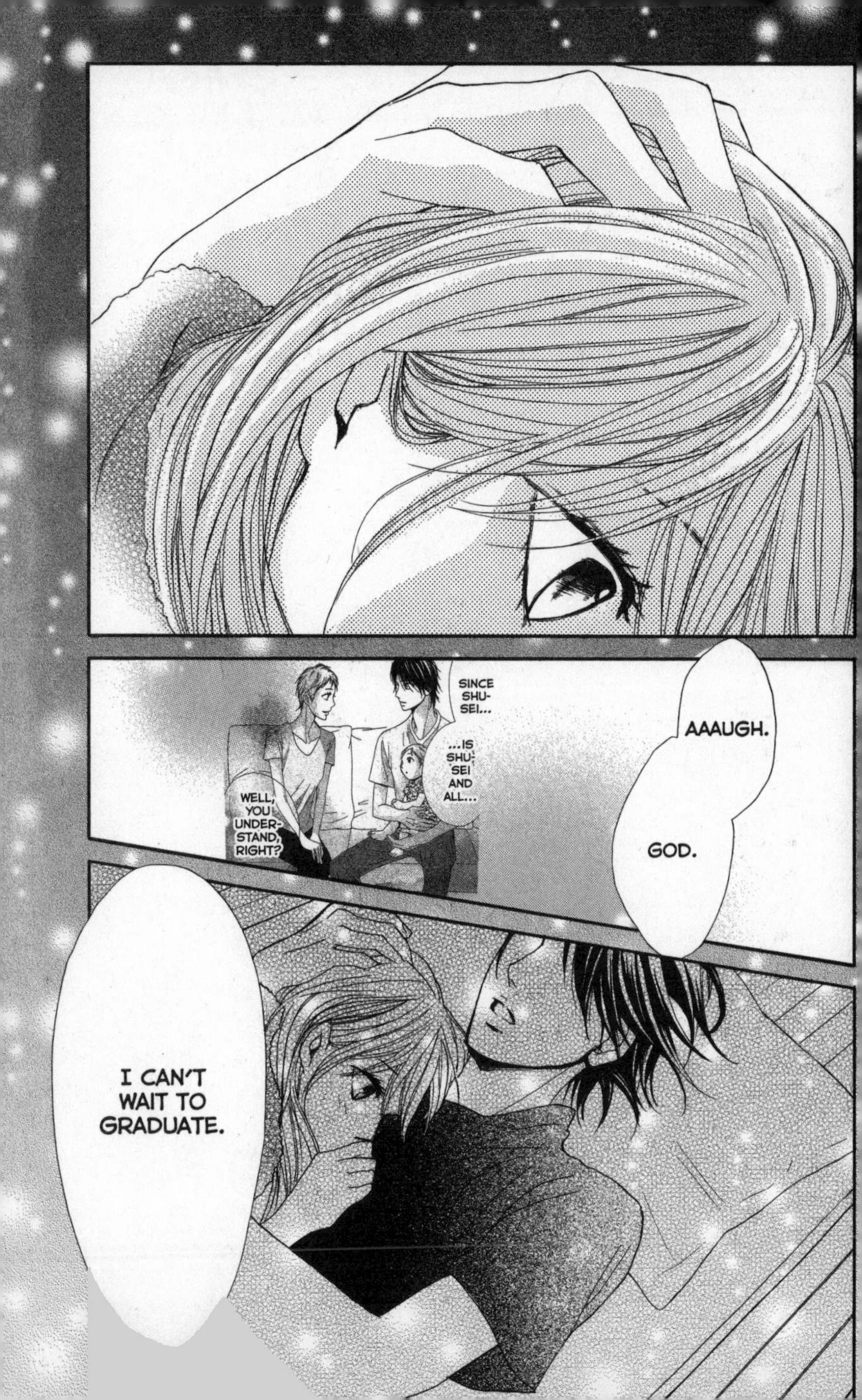
AAAUGH.
GOD.
SINCE SHU-SEI...
...IS SHU-SEI AND ALL...
WELL, YOU UNDERSTAND, RIGHT?
I CAN'T WAIT TO GRADUATE.

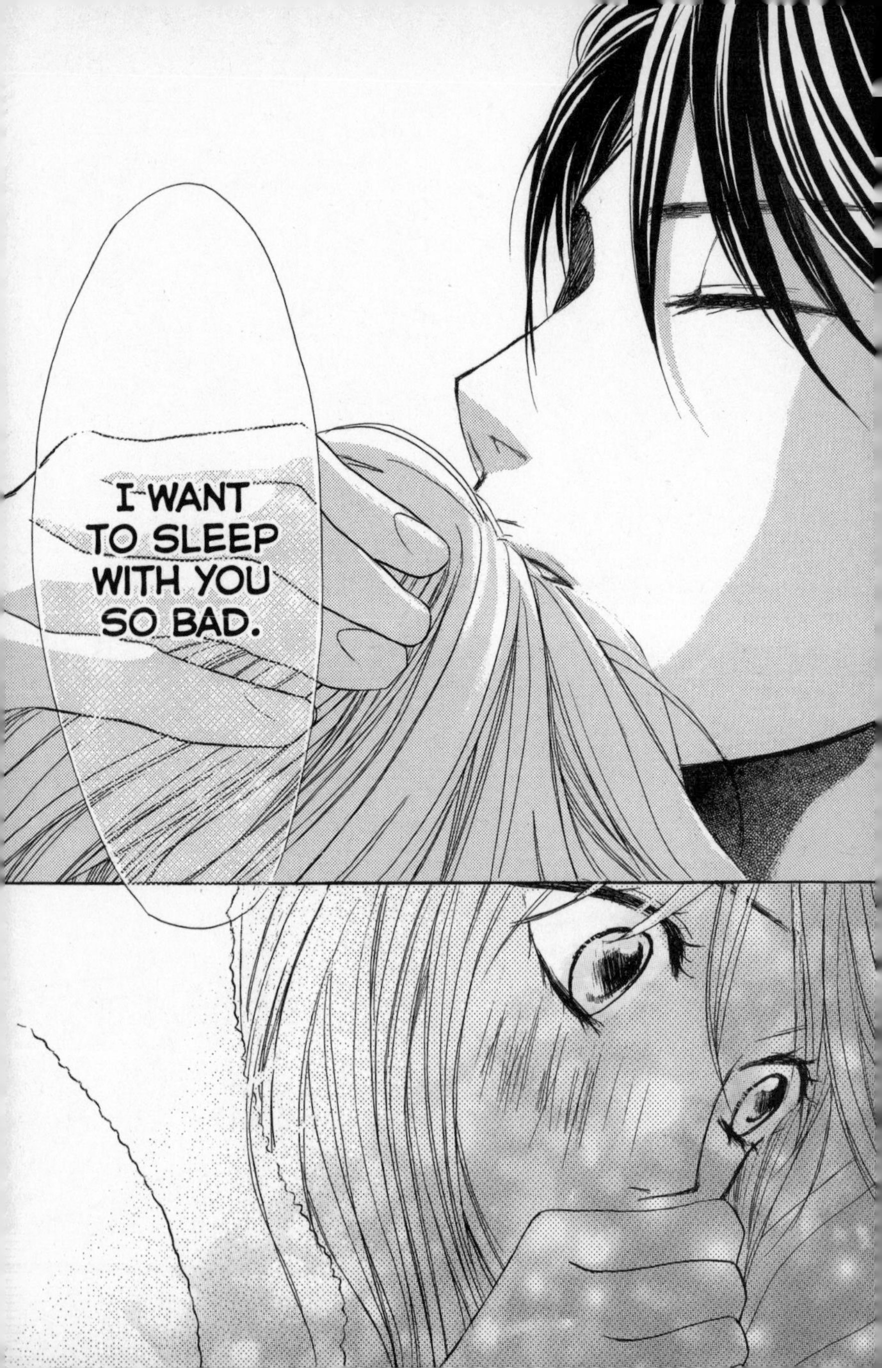
I WANT TO SLEEP WITH YOU SO BAD.

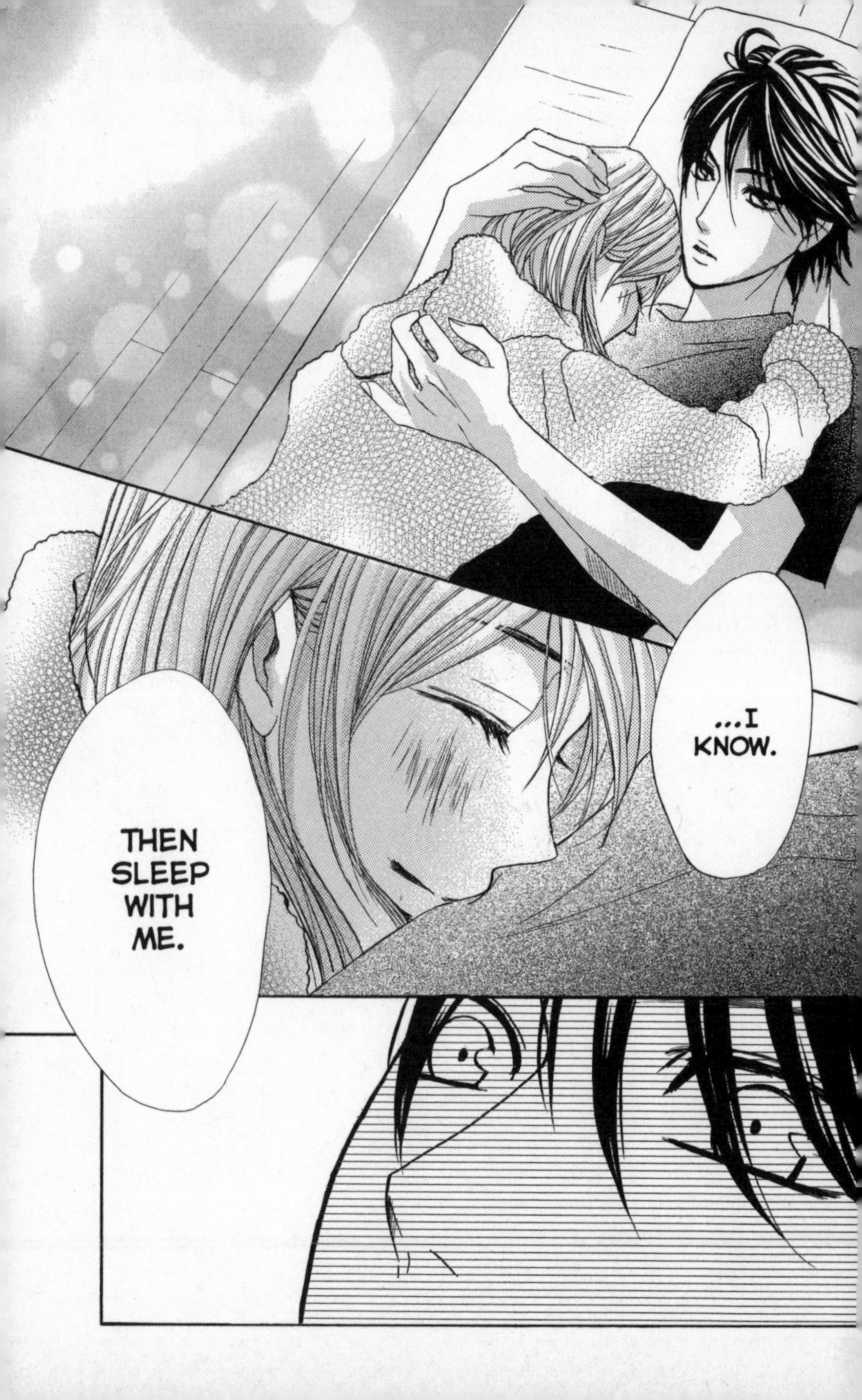
...I KNOW.
THEN SLEEP WITH ME.

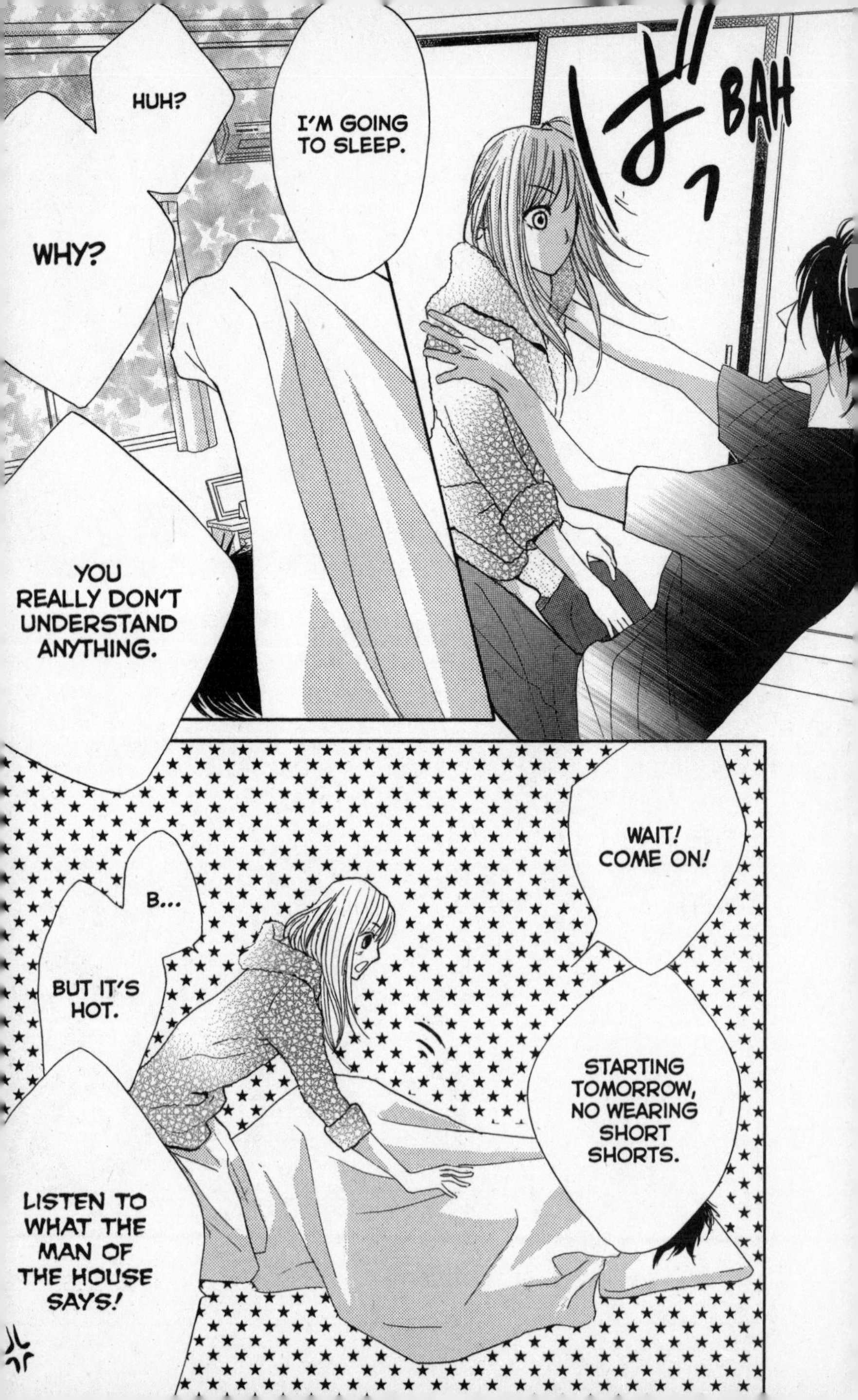
ば BAH
I'M GOING TO SLEEP.
HUH?
WHY?
YOU REALLY DON'T UNDERSTAND ANYTHING.
WAIT! COME ON!
STARTING TOMORROW, NO WEARING SHORT SHORTS.
B...
BUT IT'S HOT.
LISTEN TO WHAT THE MAN OF THE HOUSE SAYS!

L♥DK

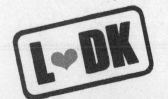

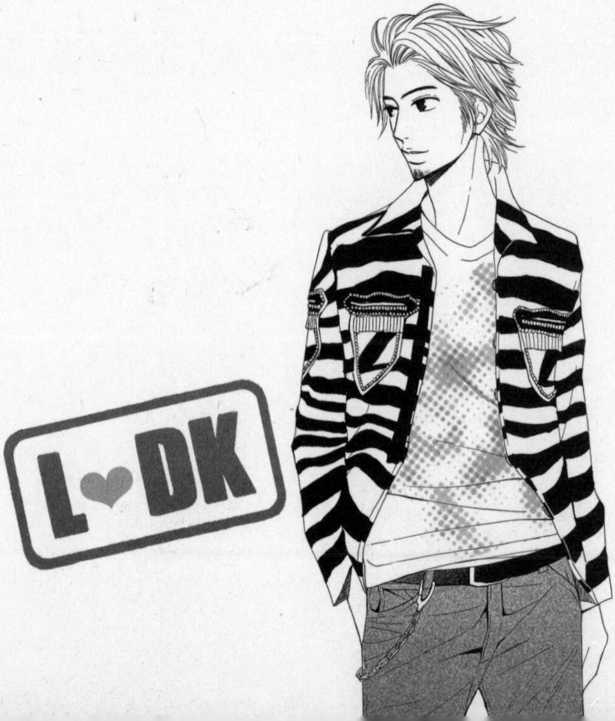
L♥DK

#60 And Then You're a Dad

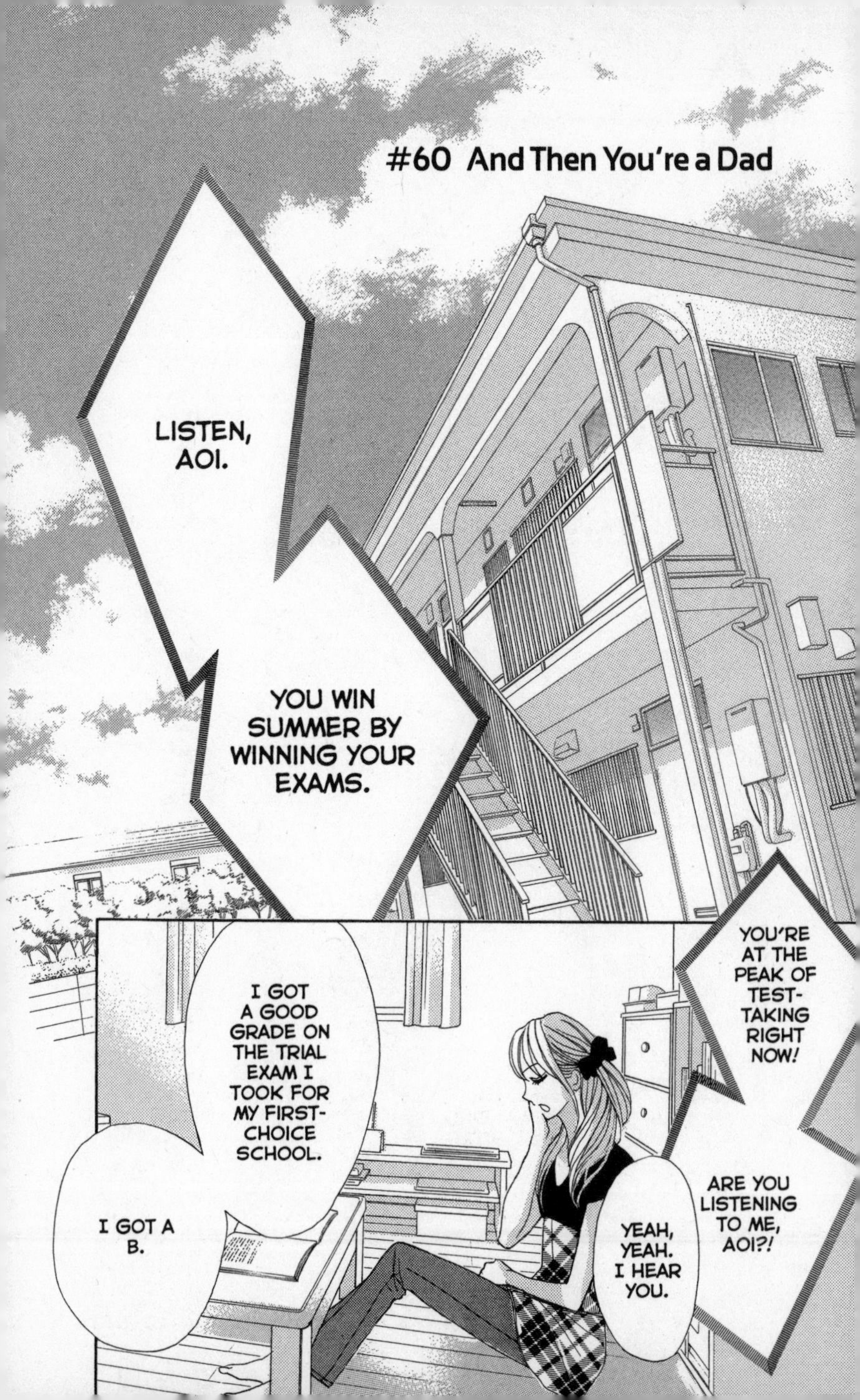
LISTEN, AOI.
YOU WIN SUMMER BY WINNING YOUR EXAMS.
YOU'RE AT THE PEAK OF TEST-TAKING RIGHT NOW!
ARE YOU LISTENING TO ME, AOI?!
YEAH, YEAH. I HEAR YOU.
I GOT A GOOD GRADE ON THE TRIAL EXAM I TOOK FOR MY FIRST-CHOICE SCHOOL.
I GOT A B.

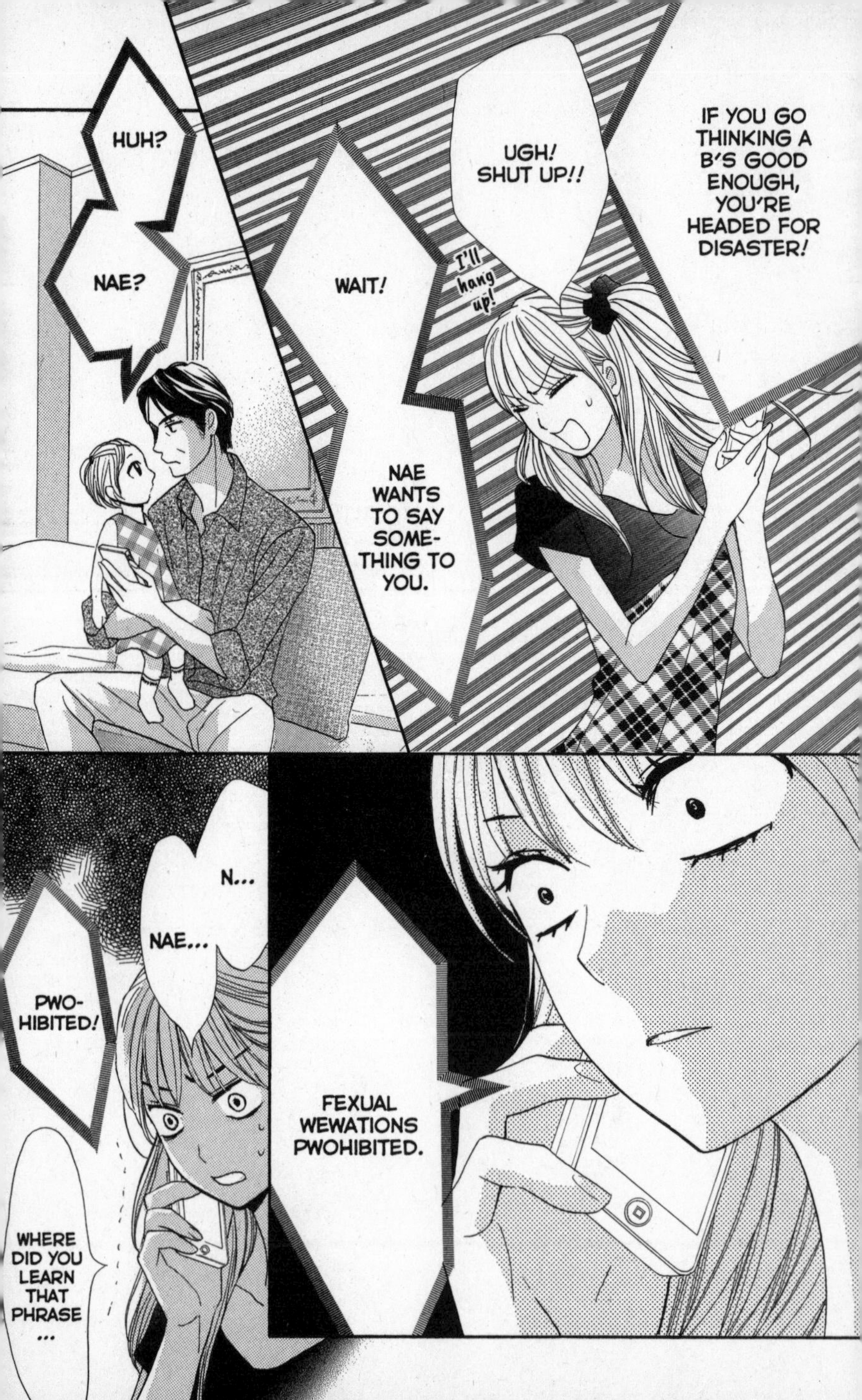
IF YOU GO THINKING A B'S GOOD ENOUGH, YOU'RE HEADED FOR DISASTER!
UGH! SHUT UP!!
I'll hang up!
WAIT!
NAE WANTS TO SAY SOME-THING TO YOU.
HUH?
NAE?
FEXUAL WEWATIONS PWOHIBITED.
N...
NAE...
PWO-HIBITED!
WHERE DID YOU LEARN THAT PHRASE ...

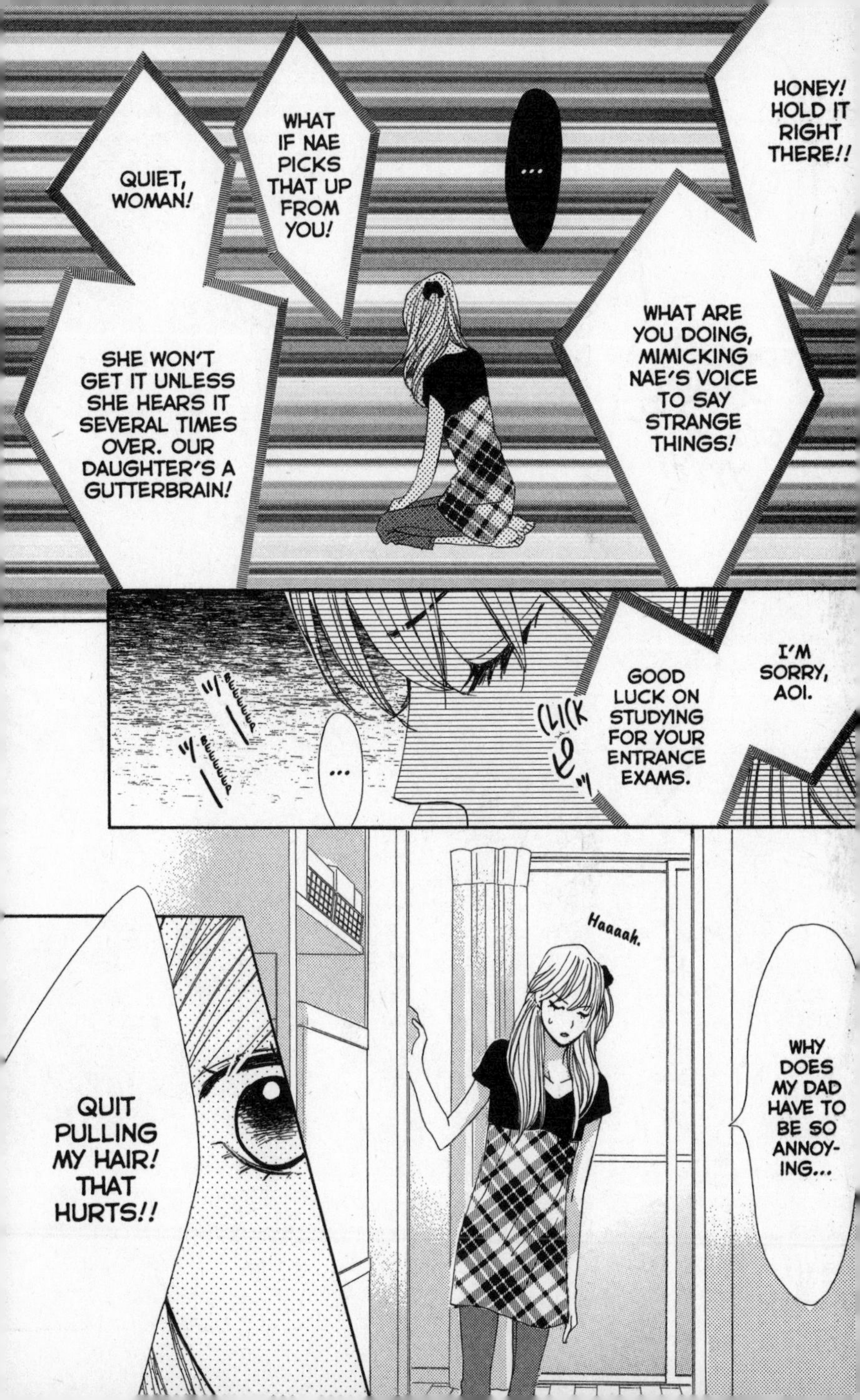
HONEY! HOLD IT RIGHT THERE!!
...
WHAT IF NAE PICKS THAT UP FROM YOU!
QUIET, WOMAN!
WHAT ARE YOU DOING, MIMICKING NAE'S VOICE TO SAY STRANGE THINGS!
SHE WON'T GET IT UNLESS SHE HEARS IT SEVERAL TIMES OVER. OUR DAUGHTER'S A GUTTERBRAIN!
I'M SORRY, AOI.
GOOD LUCK ON STUDYING FOR YOUR ENTRANCE EXAMS.
CLICK
...
WHY DOES MY DAD HAVE TO BE SO ANNOY-ING...
Haaaah.
QUIT PULLING MY HAIR! THAT HURTS!!

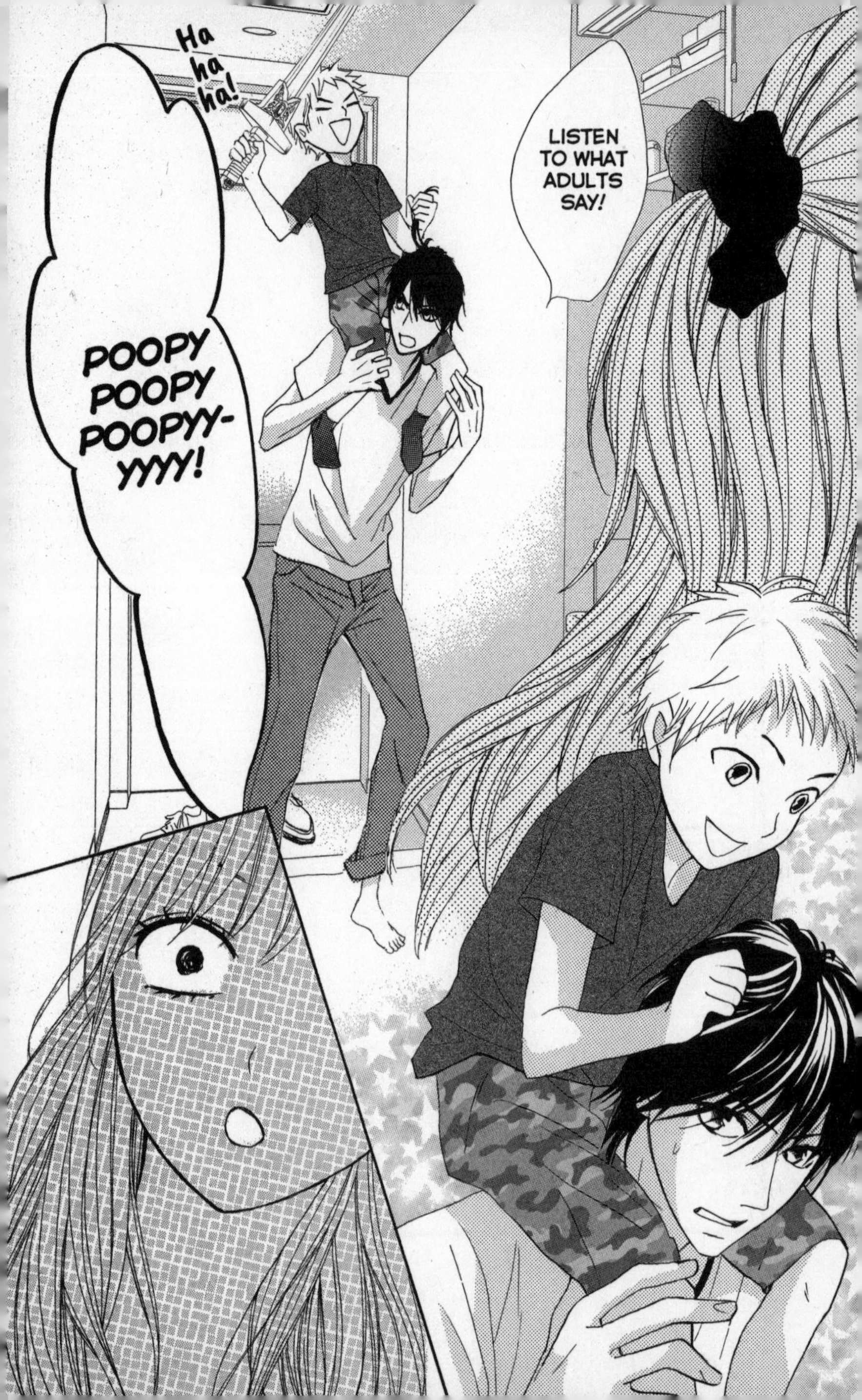
LISTEN TO WHAT ADULTS SAY!
Ha ha ha!
POOPY POOPY POOPYY-YYYY!

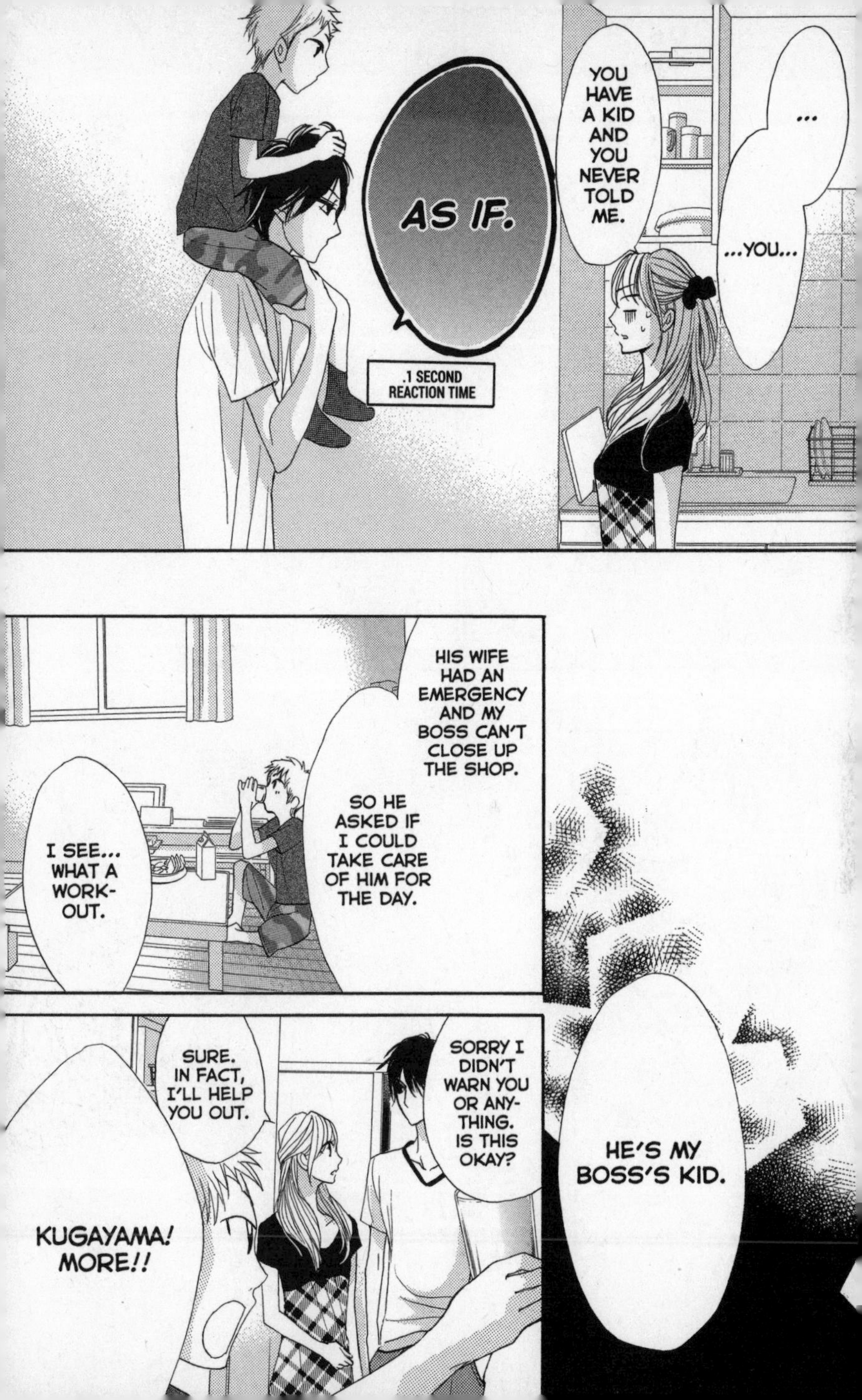
...
...YOU...
YOU HAVE A KID AND YOU NEVER TOLD ME.
AS IF.
.1 SECOND REACTION TIME
HE'S MY BOSS'S KID.
HIS WIFE HAD AN EMERGENCY AND MY BOSS CAN'T CLOSE UP THE SHOP.
SO HE ASKED IF I COULD TAKE CARE OF HIM FOR THE DAY.
I SEE... WHAT A WORK-OUT.
SORRY I DIDN'T WARN YOU OR ANY-THING. IS THIS OKAY?
SURE. IN FACT, I'LL HELP YOU OUT.
KUGAYAMA! MORE!!

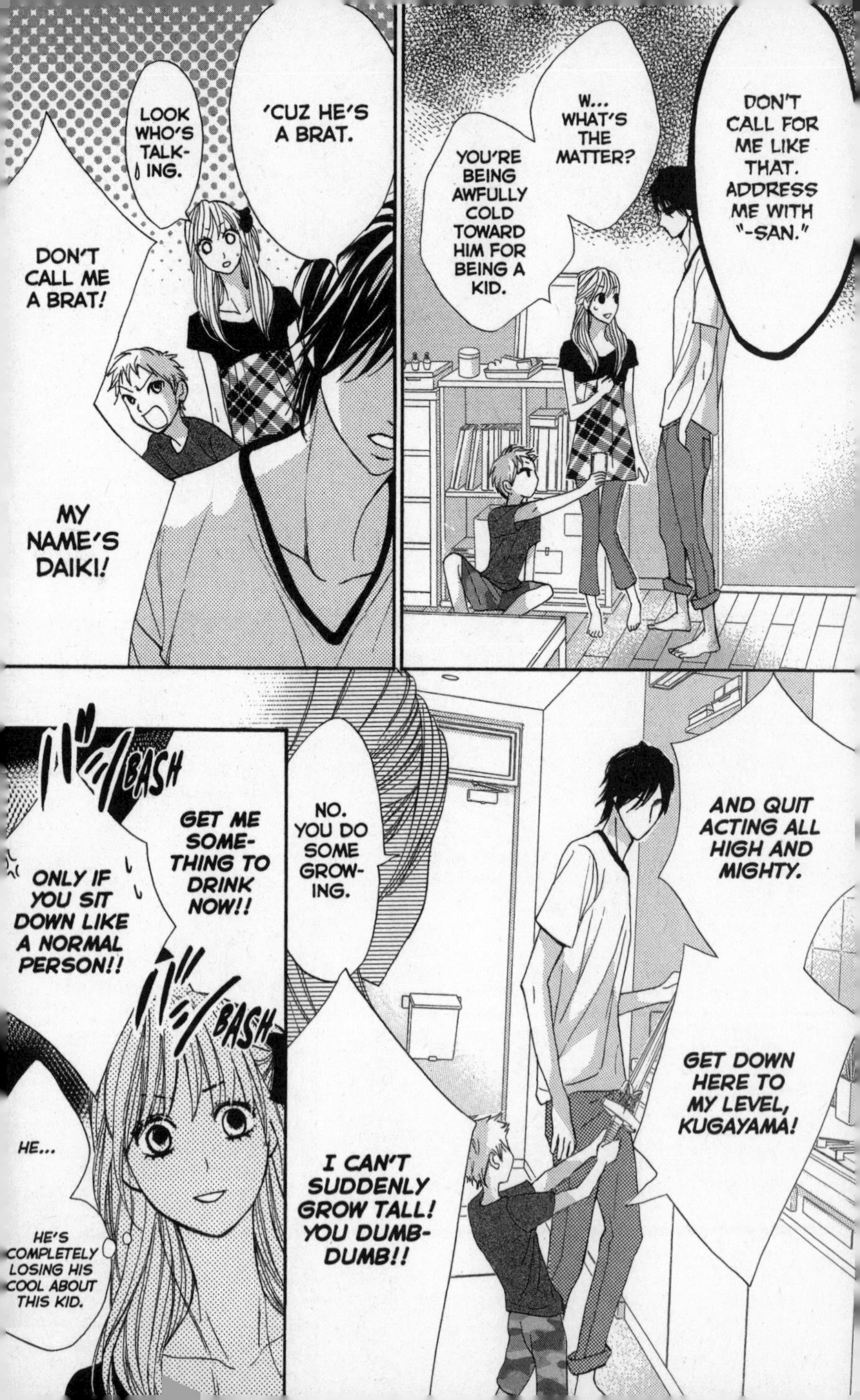
DON'T CALL FOR ME LIKE THAT. ADDRESS ME WITH "-SAN."
W... WHAT'S THE MATTER?
YOU'RE BEING AWFULLY COLD TOWARD HIM FOR BEING A KID.
'CUZ HE'S A BRAT.
LOOK WHO'S TALK-ING.
DON'T CALL ME A BRAT!
MY NAME'S DAIKI!
AND QUIT ACTING ALL HIGH AND MIGHTY.
GET DOWN HERE TO MY LEVEL, KUGAYAMA!
NO. YOU DO SOME GROW-ING.
I CAN'T SUDDENLY GROW TALL! YOU DUMB-DUMB!!
BASH
GET ME SOME-THING TO DRINK NOW!!
ONLY IF YOU SIT DOWN LIKE A NORMAL PERSON!!
BASH
HE...
HE'S COMPLETELY LOSING HIS COOL ABOUT THIS KID.

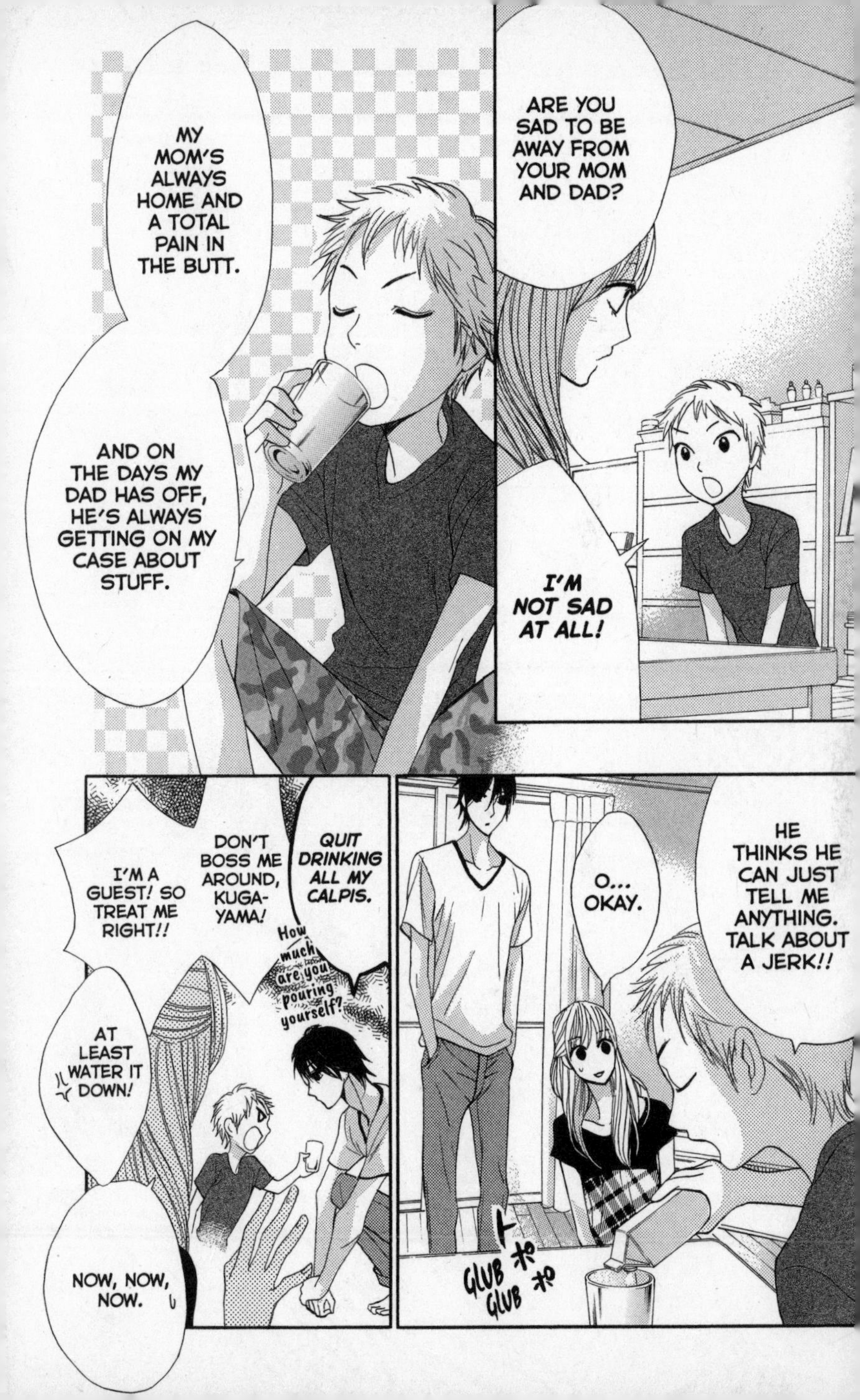
ARE YOU SAD TO BE AWAY FROM YOUR MOM AND DAD?
I'M NOT SAD AT ALL!
MY MOM'S ALWAYS HOME AND A TOTAL PAIN IN THE BUTT.
AND ON THE DAYS MY DAD HAS OFF, HE'S ALWAYS GETTING ON MY CASE ABOUT STUFF.
HE THINKS HE CAN JUST TELL ME ANYTHING. TALK ABOUT A JERK!!
O... OKAY.
GLUB GLUB
QUIT DRINKING ALL MY CALPIS.
DON'T BOSS ME AROUND, KUGA-YAMA!
I'M A GUEST! SO TREAT ME RIGHT!!
How much are you pouring yourself?
AT LEAST WATER IT DOWN!
NOW, NOW, NOW.

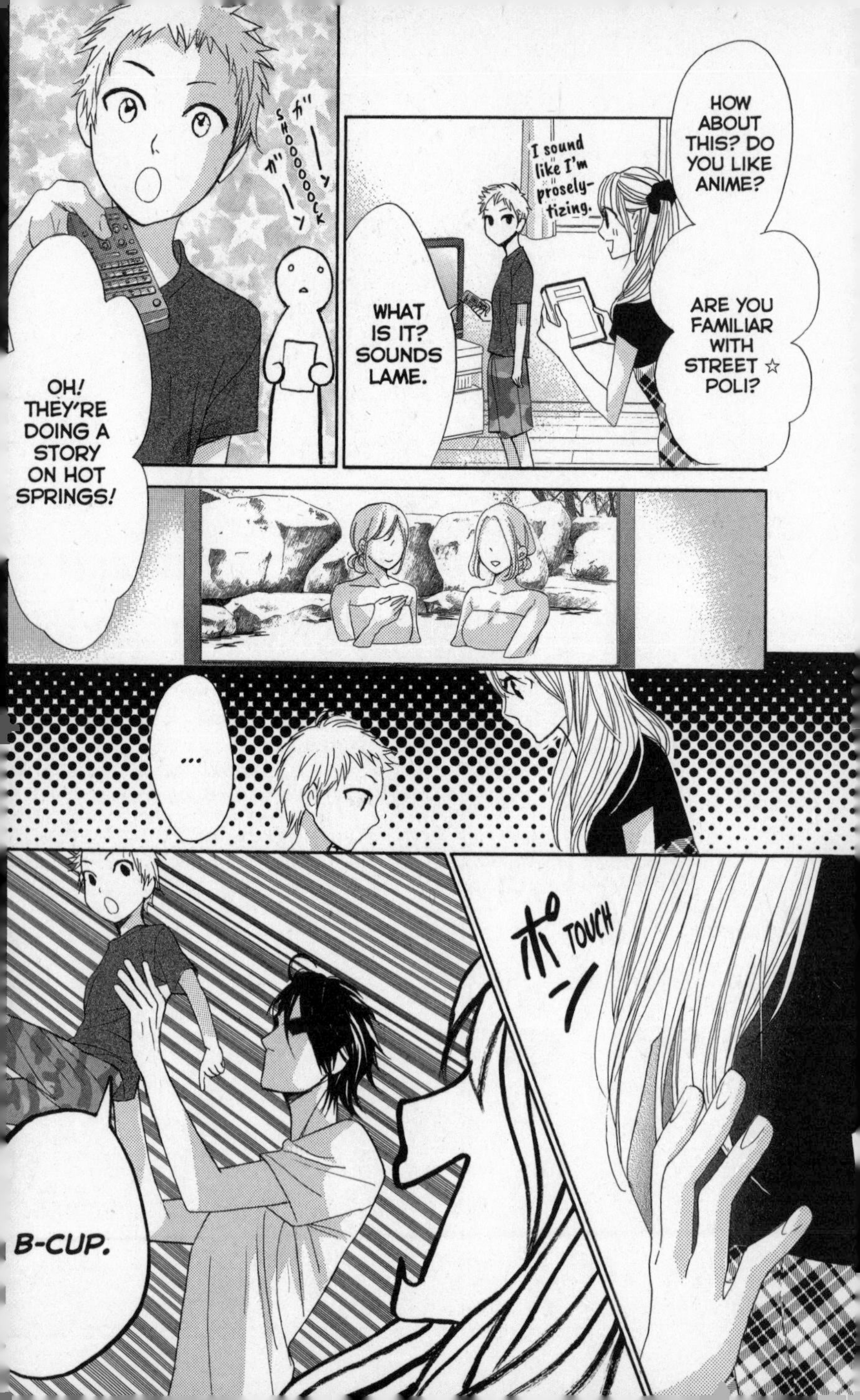
HOW ABOUT THIS? DO YOU LIKE ANIME?
I sound like I'm proselytizing.
ARE YOU FAMILIAR WITH STREET ☆ POLI?
WHAT IS IT? SOUNDS LAME.
SHOOOOOOOCK
OH! THEY'RE DOING A STORY ON HOT SPRINGS!
...
TOUCH
B-CUP.

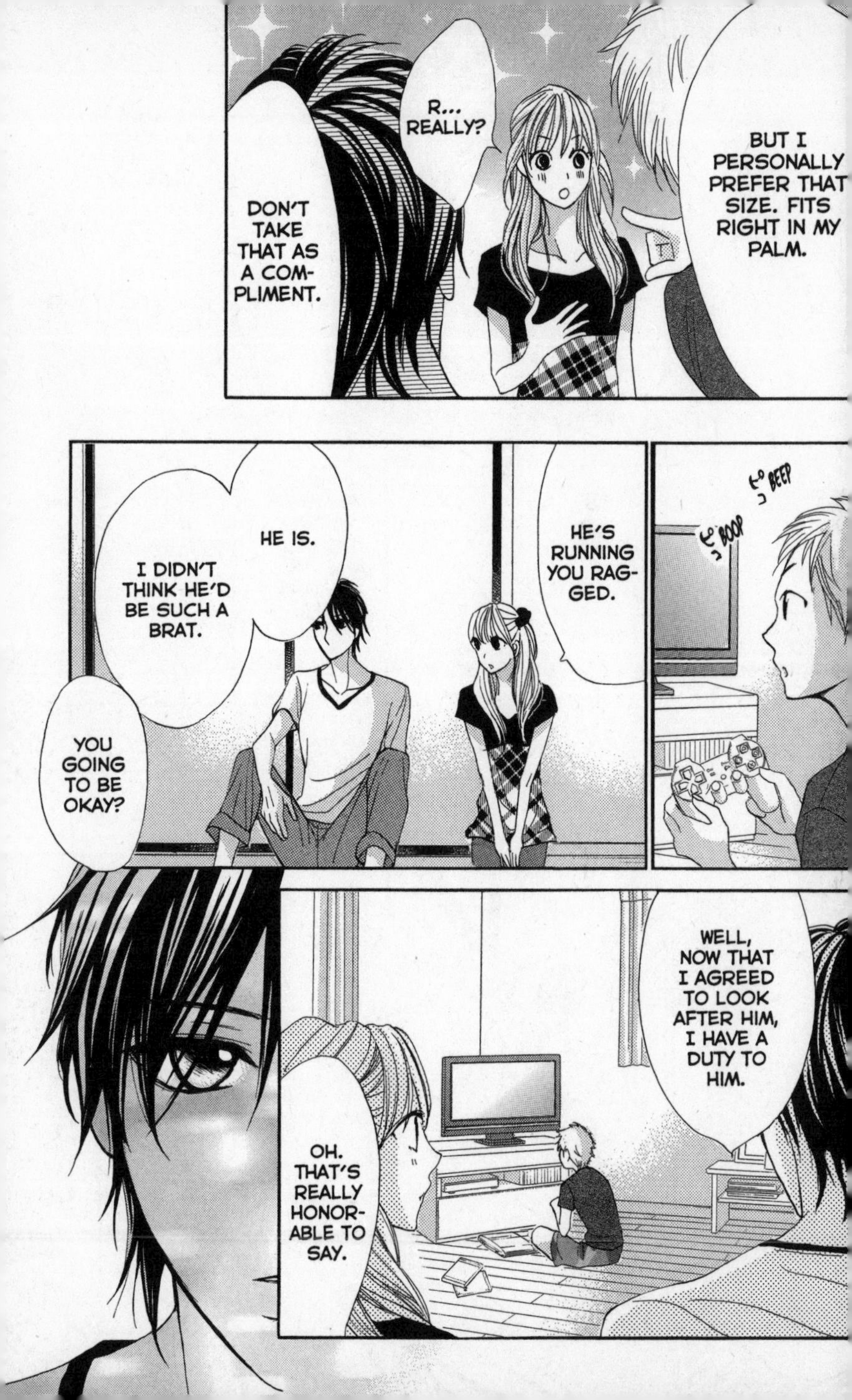
BUT I PERSONALLY PREFER THAT SIZE. FITS RIGHT IN MY PALM.
R... REALLY?
DON'T TAKE THAT AS A COMPLIMENT.
BEEP
BOOP
HE'S RUNNING YOU RAGGED.
HE IS.
I DIDN'T THINK HE'D BE SUCH A BRAT.
YOU GOING TO BE OKAY?
WELL, NOW THAT I AGREED TO LOOK AFTER HIM, I HAVE A DUTY TO HIM.
OH. THAT'S REALLY HONORABLE TO SAY.

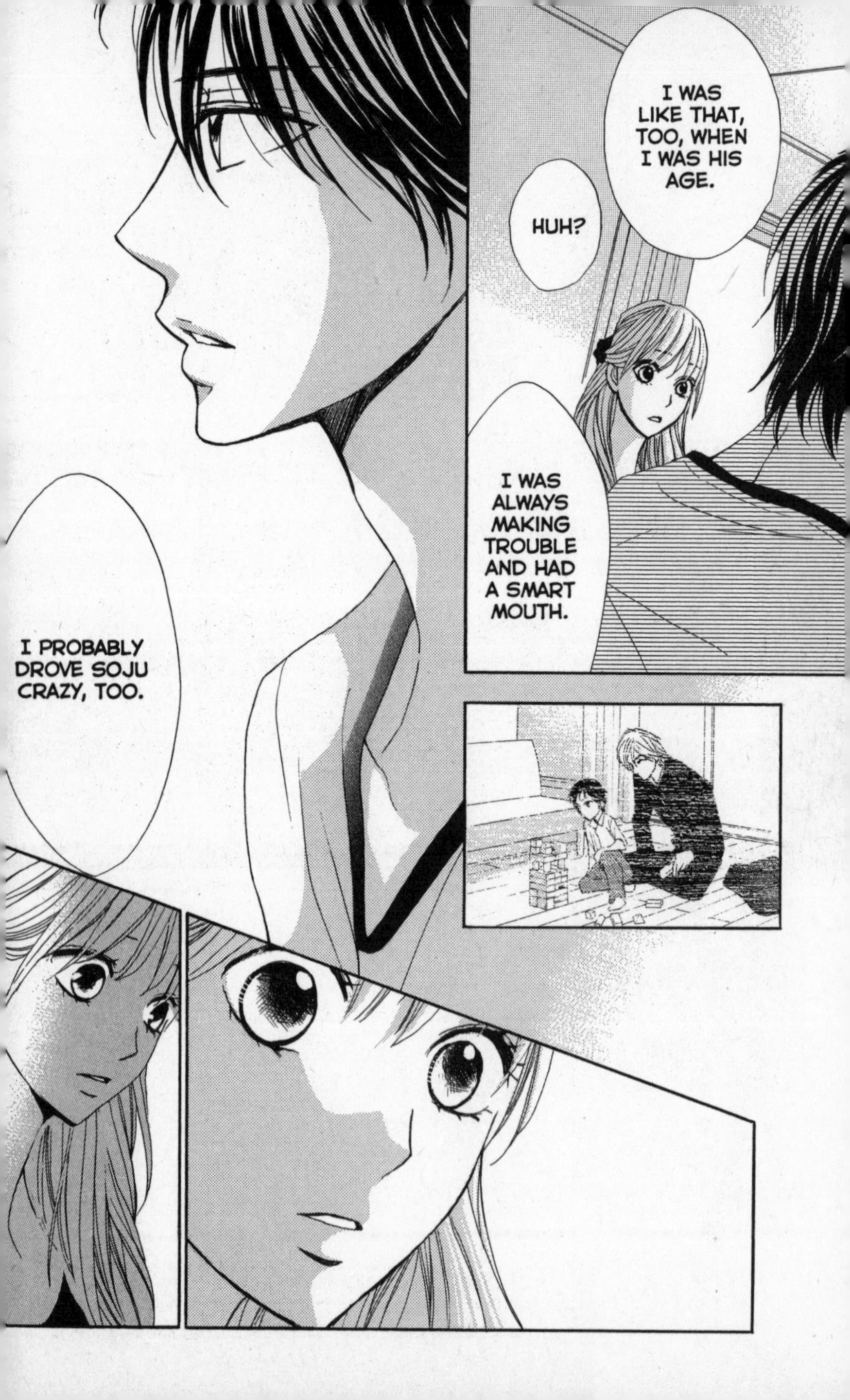
I WAS LIKE THAT, TOO, WHEN I WAS HIS AGE.
HUH?
I WAS ALWAYS MAKING TROUBLE AND HAD A SMART MOUTH.
I PROBABLY DROVE SOJU CRAZY, TOO.

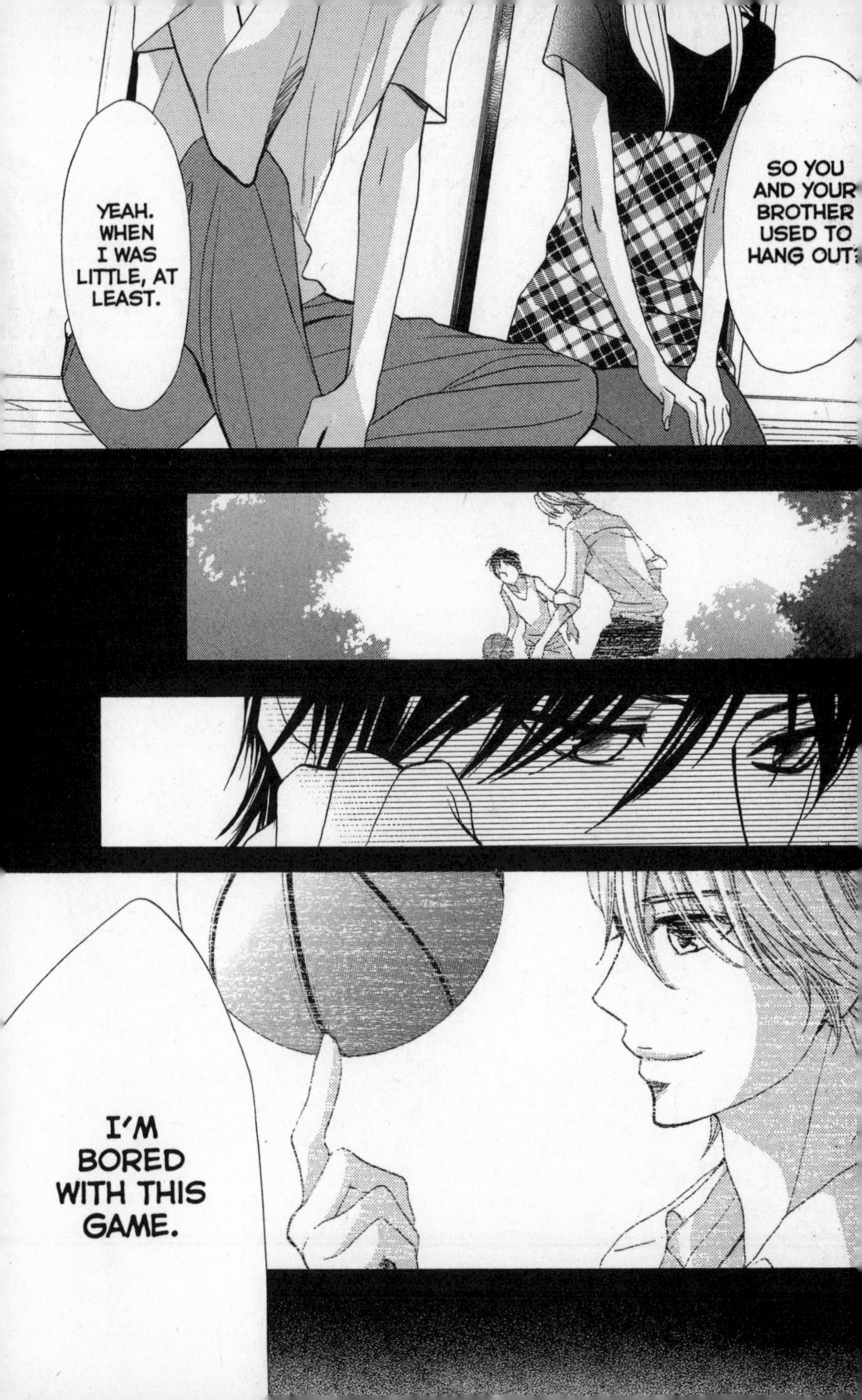
SO YOU AND YOUR BROTHER USED TO HANG OUT?
YEAH. WHEN I WAS LITTLE, AT LEAST.
I'M BORED WITH THIS GAME.

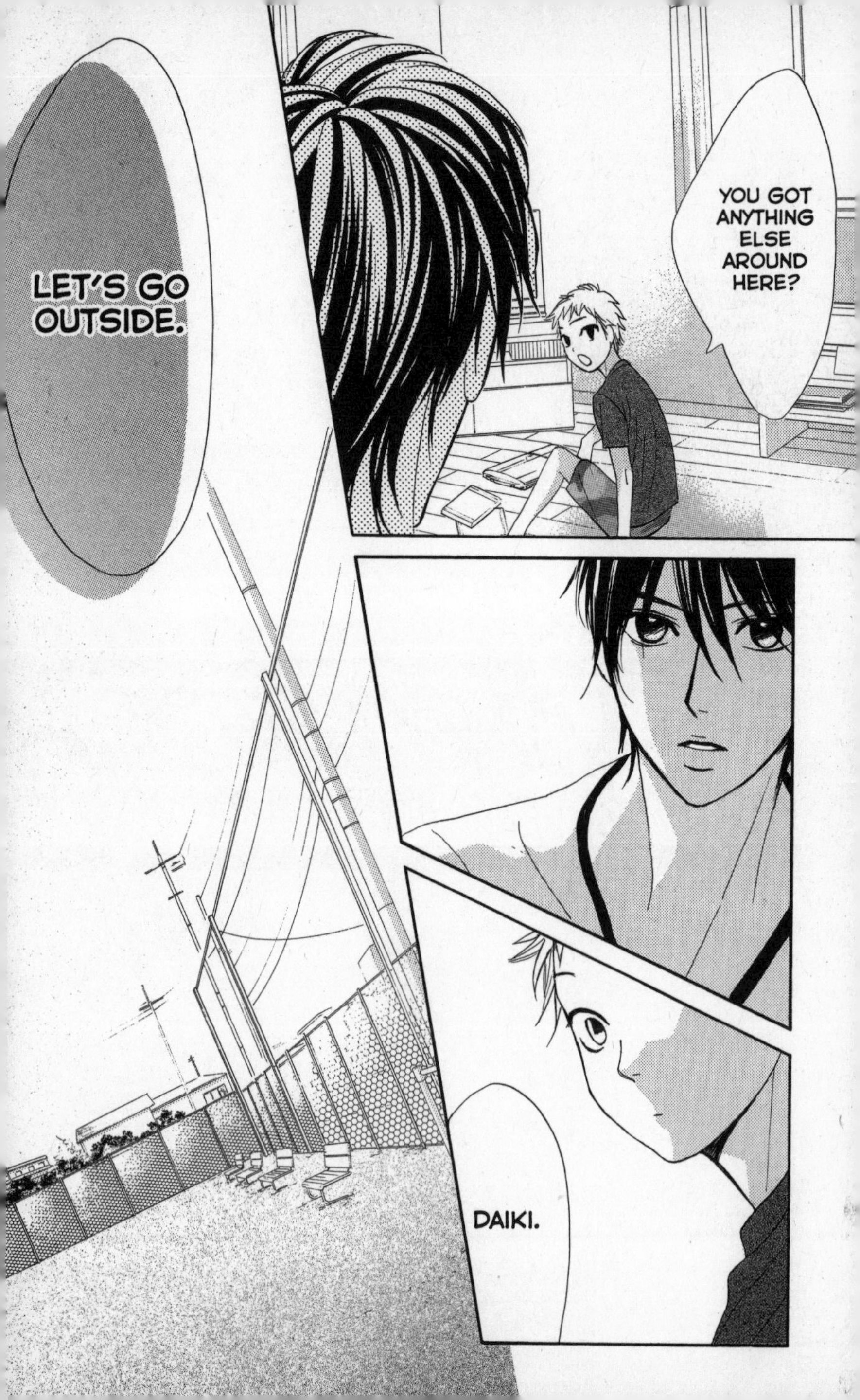
YOU GOT ANYTHING ELSE AROUND HERE?
DAIKI.
LET'S GO OUTSIDE.

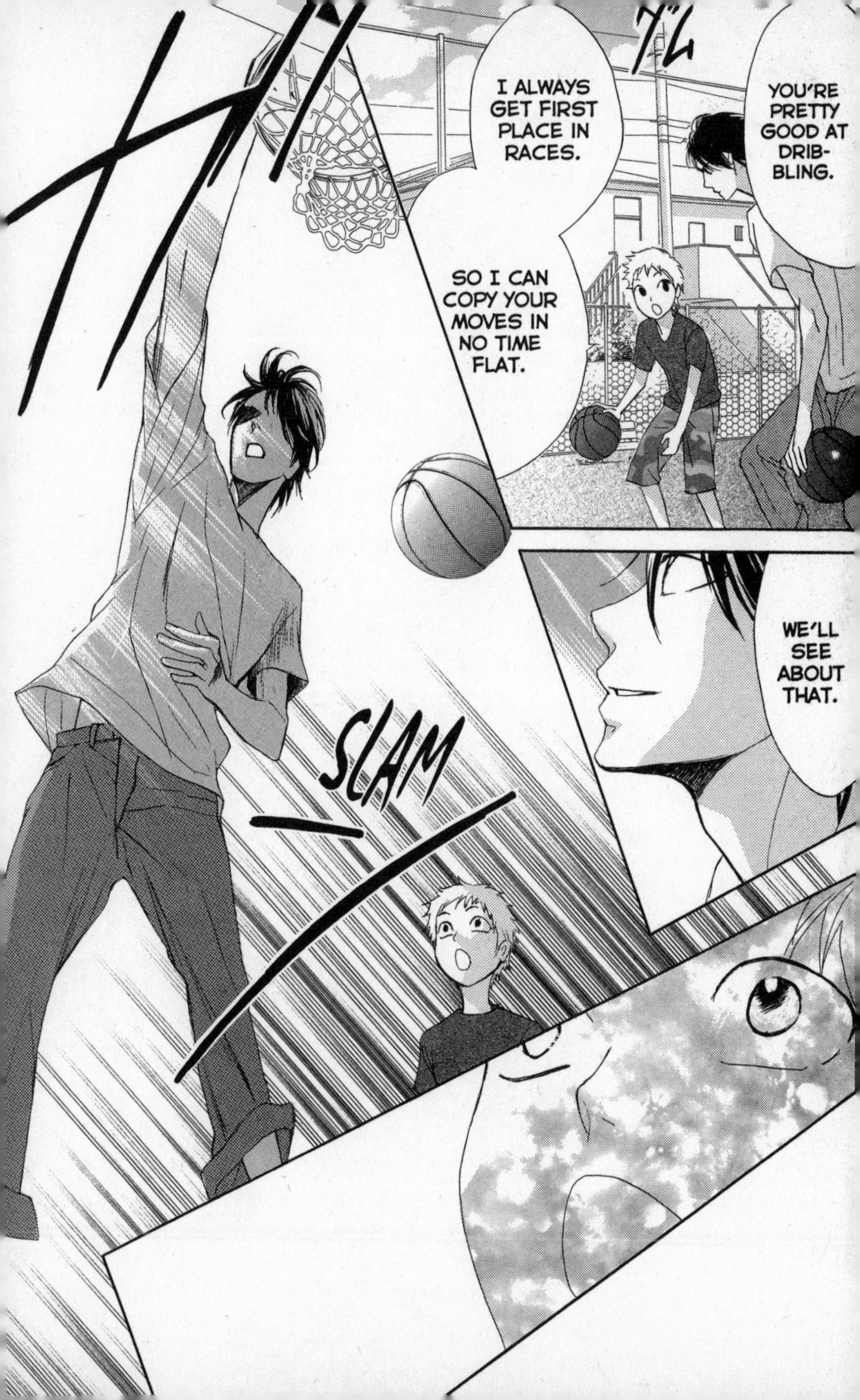
YOU'RE PRETTY GOOD AT DRIB-BLING.
I ALWAYS GET FIRST PLACE IN RACES.
SO I CAN COPY YOUR MOVES IN NO TIME FLAT.
WE'LL SEE ABOUT THAT.
SLAM

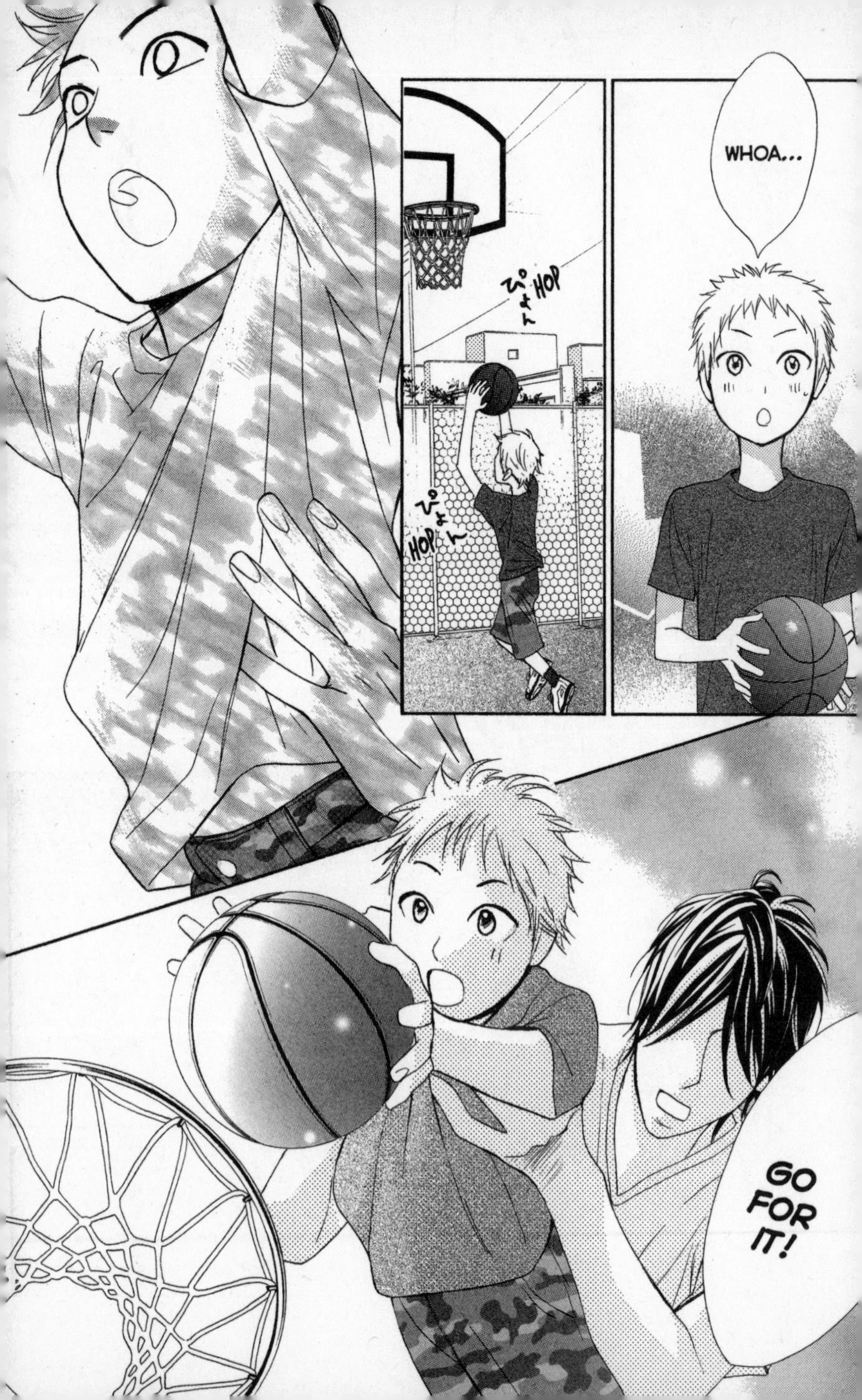
WHOA...
ぴょん HOP
ぴょん HOP
GO FOR IT!

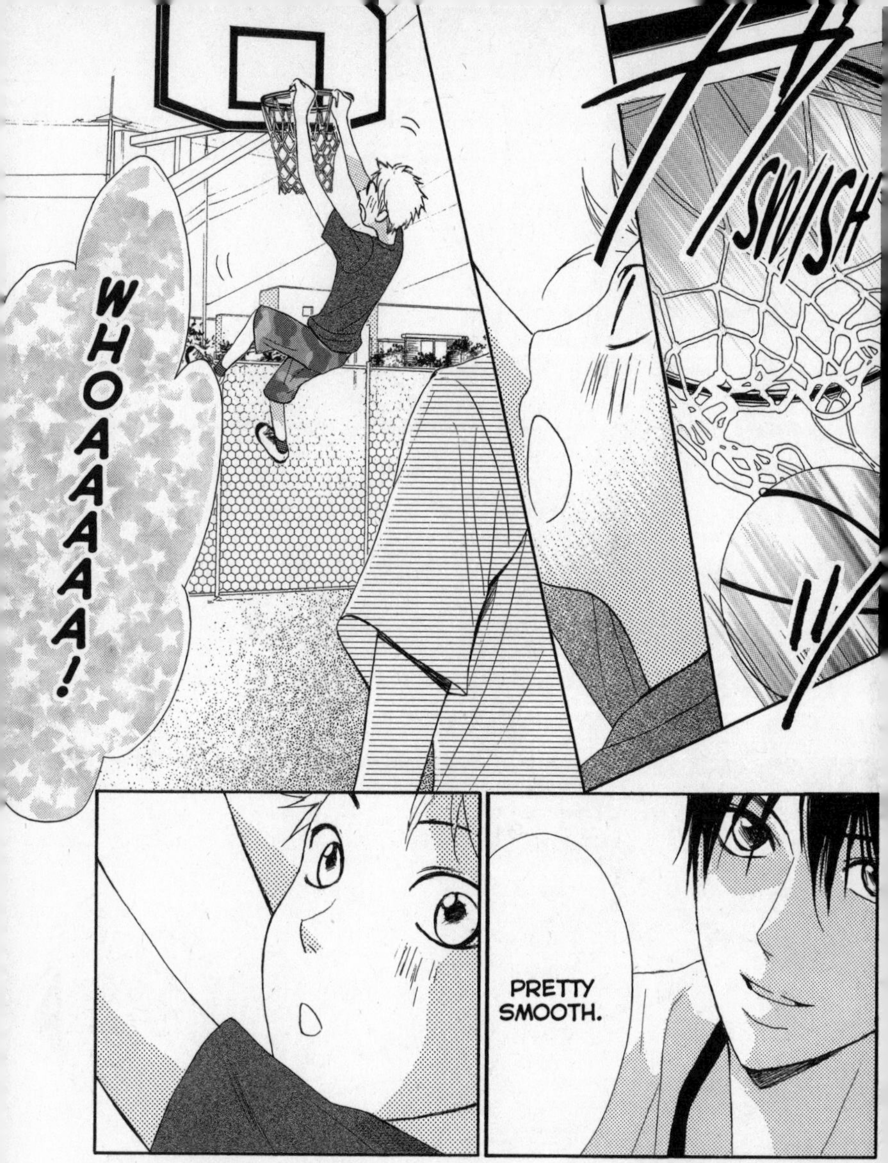
SWISH
WHOAAAAAA!
PRETTY SMOOTH.

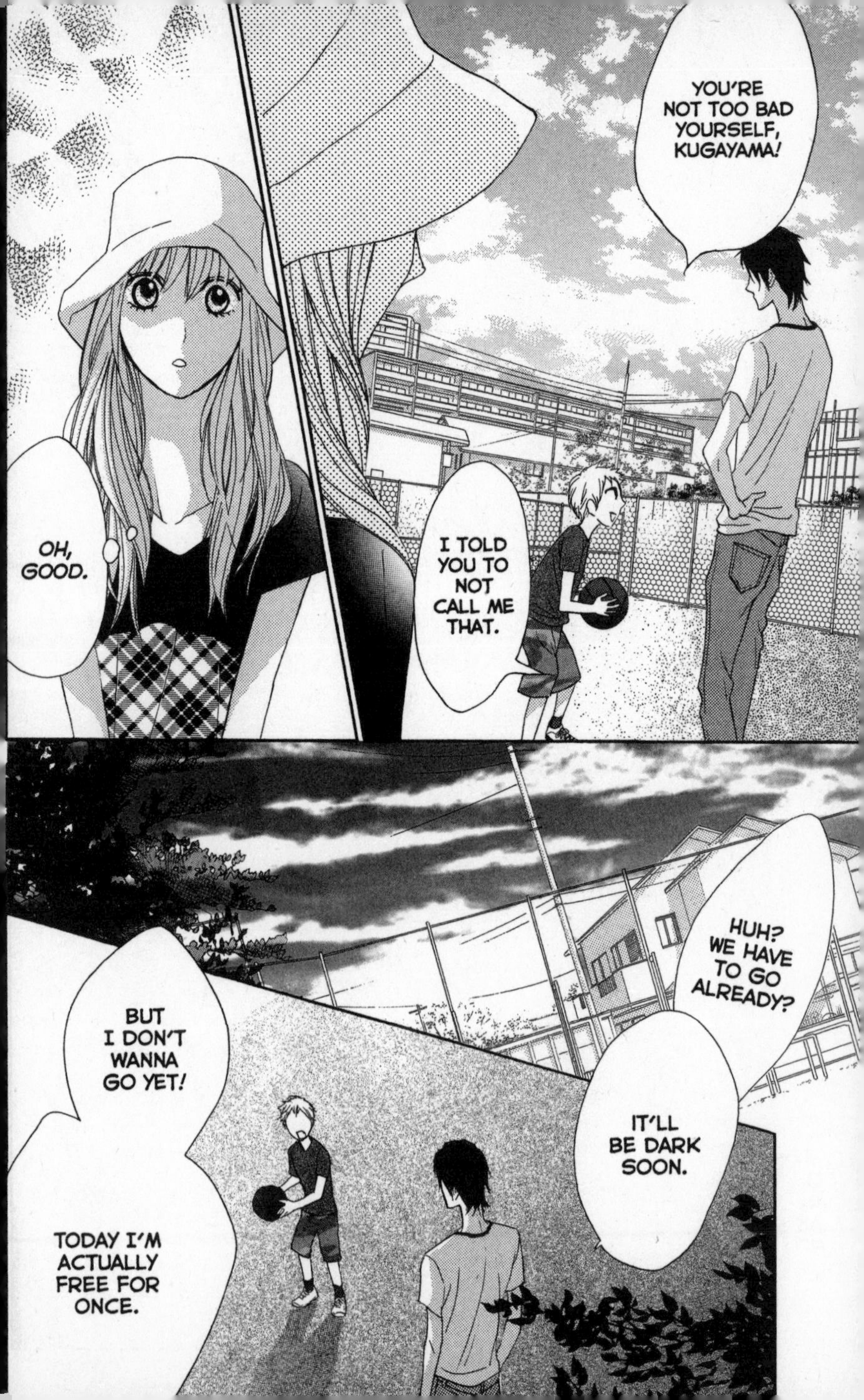
YOU'RE NOT TOO BAD YOURSELF, KUGAYAMA!
I TOLD YOU TO NOT CALL ME THAT.
OH, GOOD.
HUH? WE HAVE TO GO ALREADY?
IT'LL BE DARK SOON.
BUT I DON'T WANNA GO YET!
TODAY I'M ACTUALLY FREE FOR ONCE.

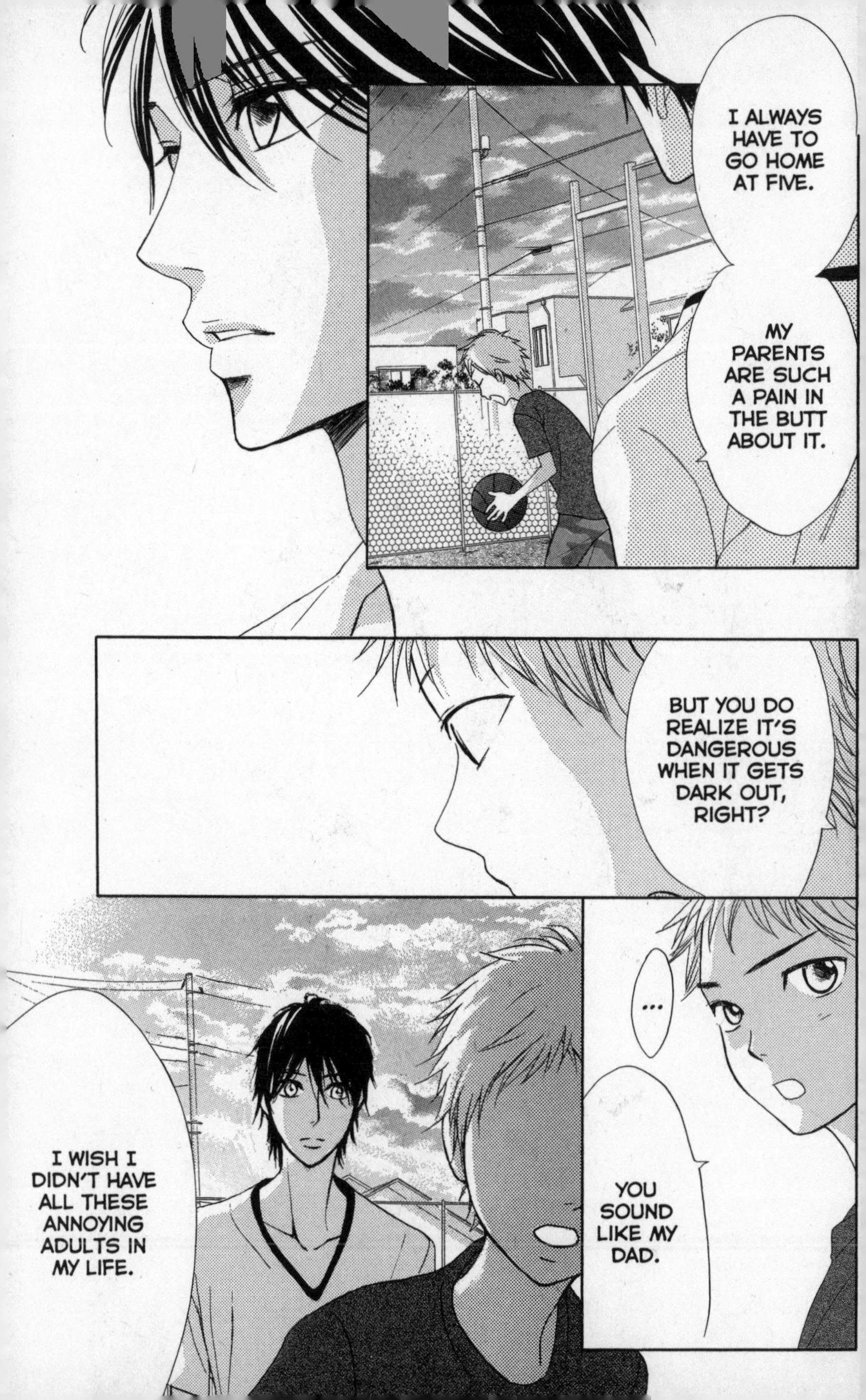
I ALWAYS HAVE TO GO HOME AT FIVE.
MY PARENTS ARE SUCH A PAIN IN THE BUTT ABOUT IT.
BUT YOU DO REALIZE IT'S DANGEROUS WHEN IT GETS DARK OUT, RIGHT?
...
YOU SOUND LIKE MY DAD.
I WISH I DIDN'T HAVE ALL THESE ANNOYING ADULTS IN MY LIFE.

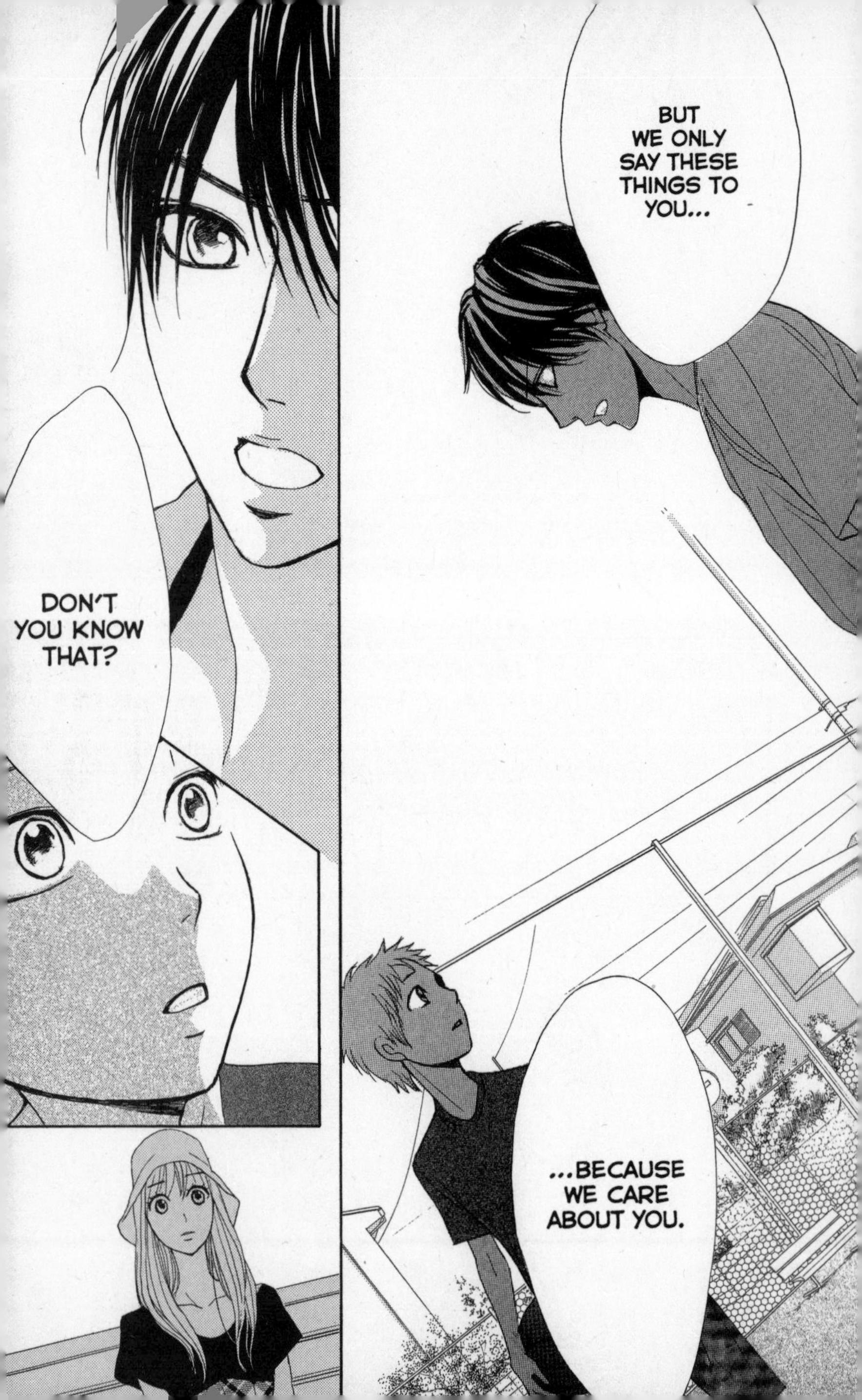
BUT WE ONLY SAY THESE THINGS TO YOU...
...BECAUSE WE CARE ABOUT YOU.
DON'T YOU KNOW THAT?

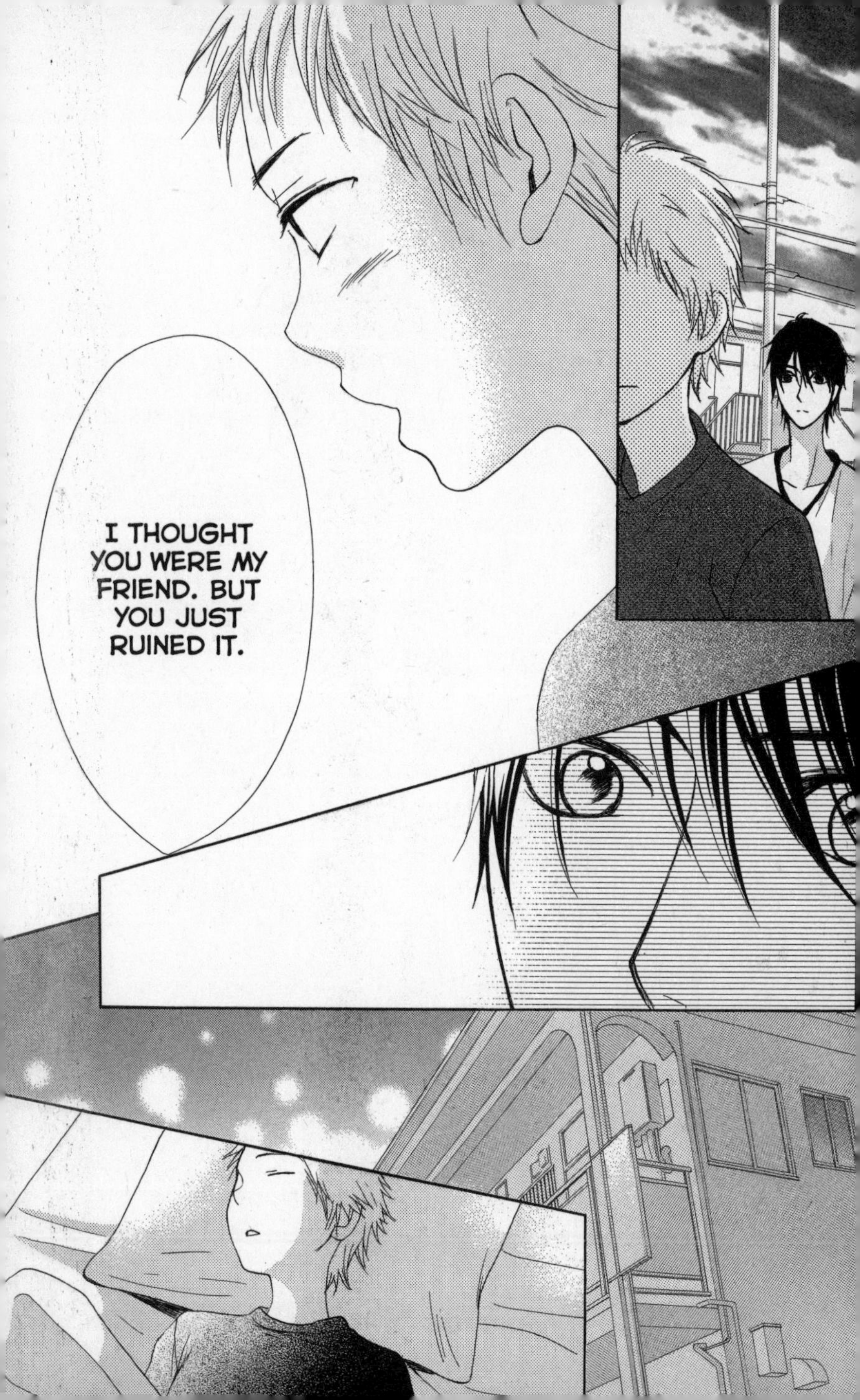
I THOUGHT YOU WERE MY FRIEND. BUT YOU JUST RUINED IT.

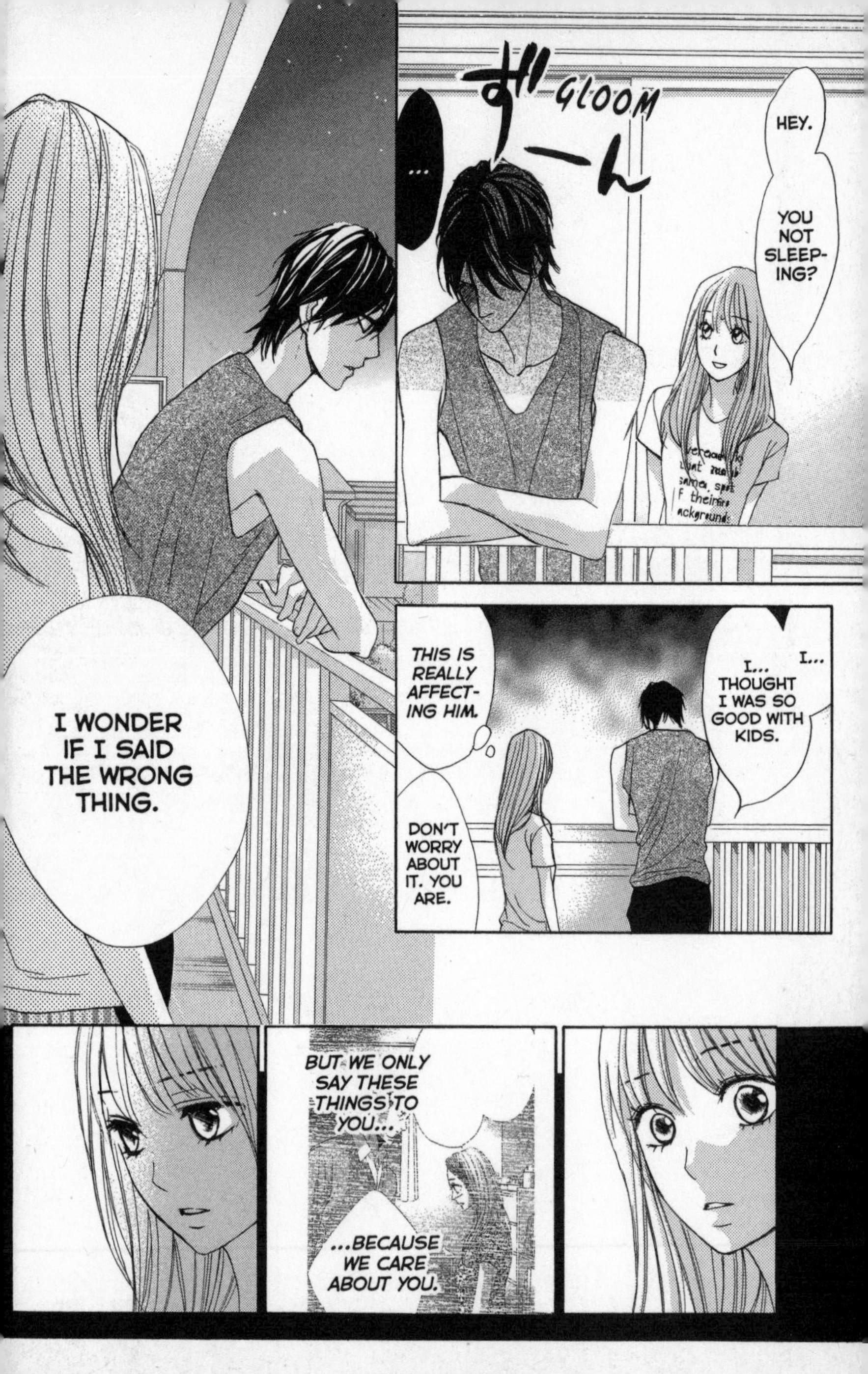
HEY.
YOU NOT SLEEPING?
ずーん GLOOM
...
I... I... THOUGHT I WAS SO GOOD WITH KIDS.
THIS IS REALLY AFFECTING HIM.
DON'T WORRY ABOUT IT. YOU ARE.
I WONDER IF I SAID THE WRONG THING.
BUT WE ONLY SAY THESE THINGS TO YOU...
...BECAUSE WE CARE ABOUT YOU.

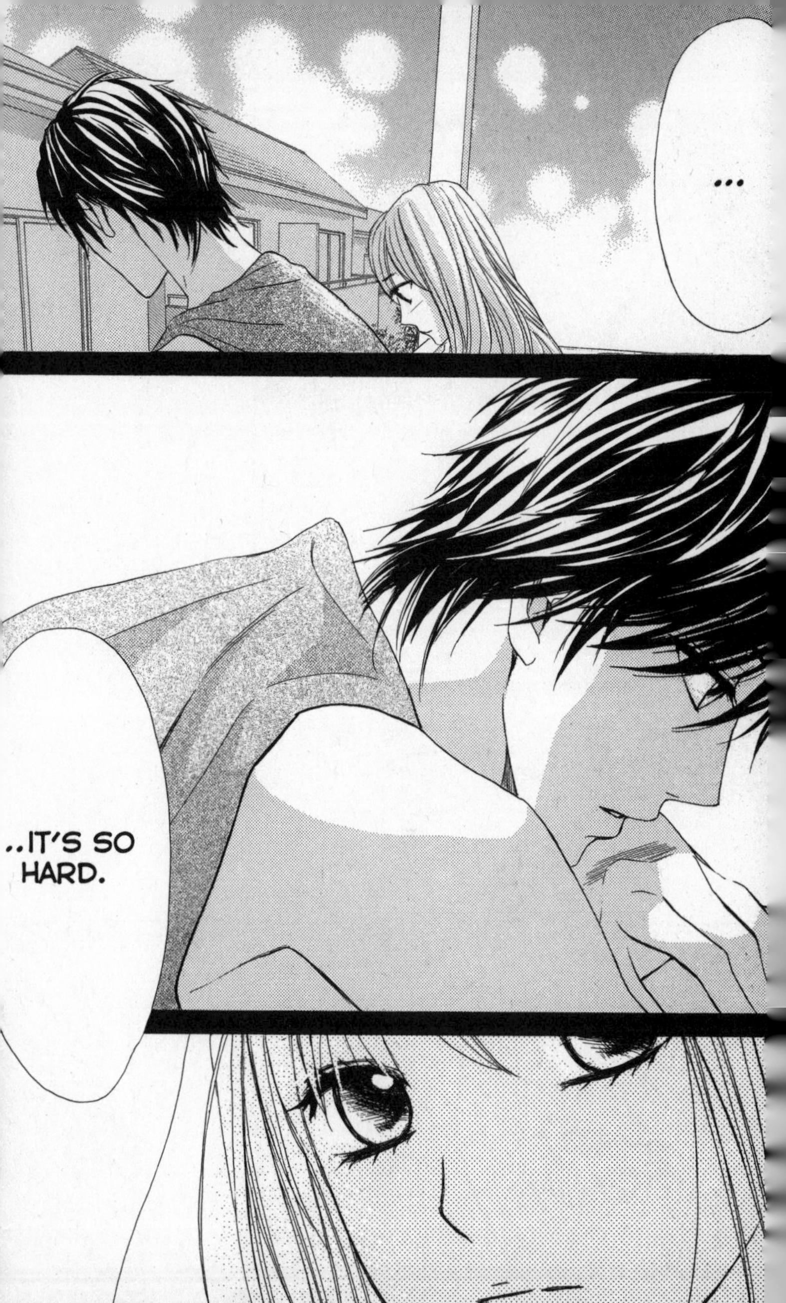
...
..IT'S SO HARD.

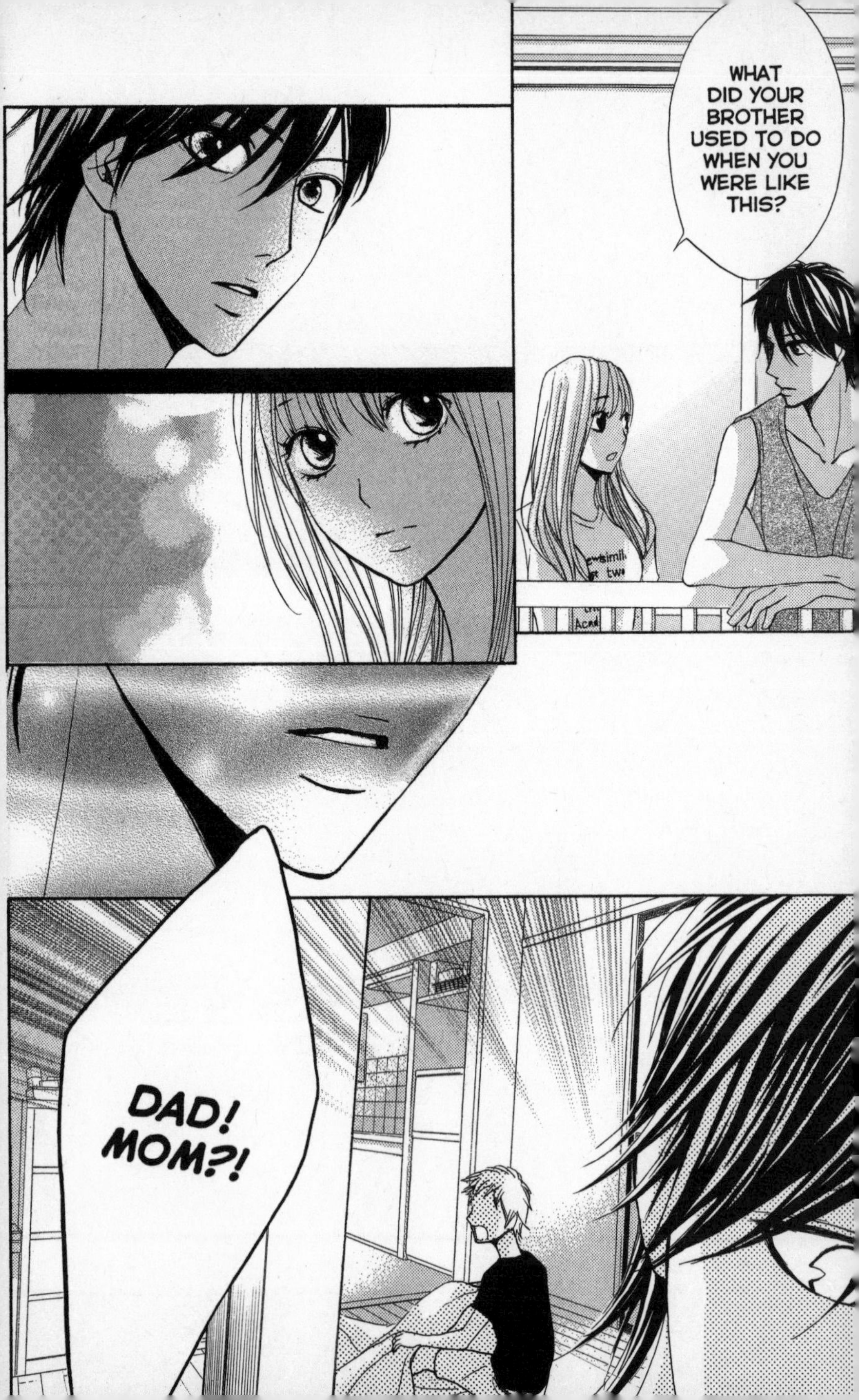
WHAT DID YOUR BROTHER USED TO DO WHEN YOU WERE LIKE THIS?
DAD! MOM?!

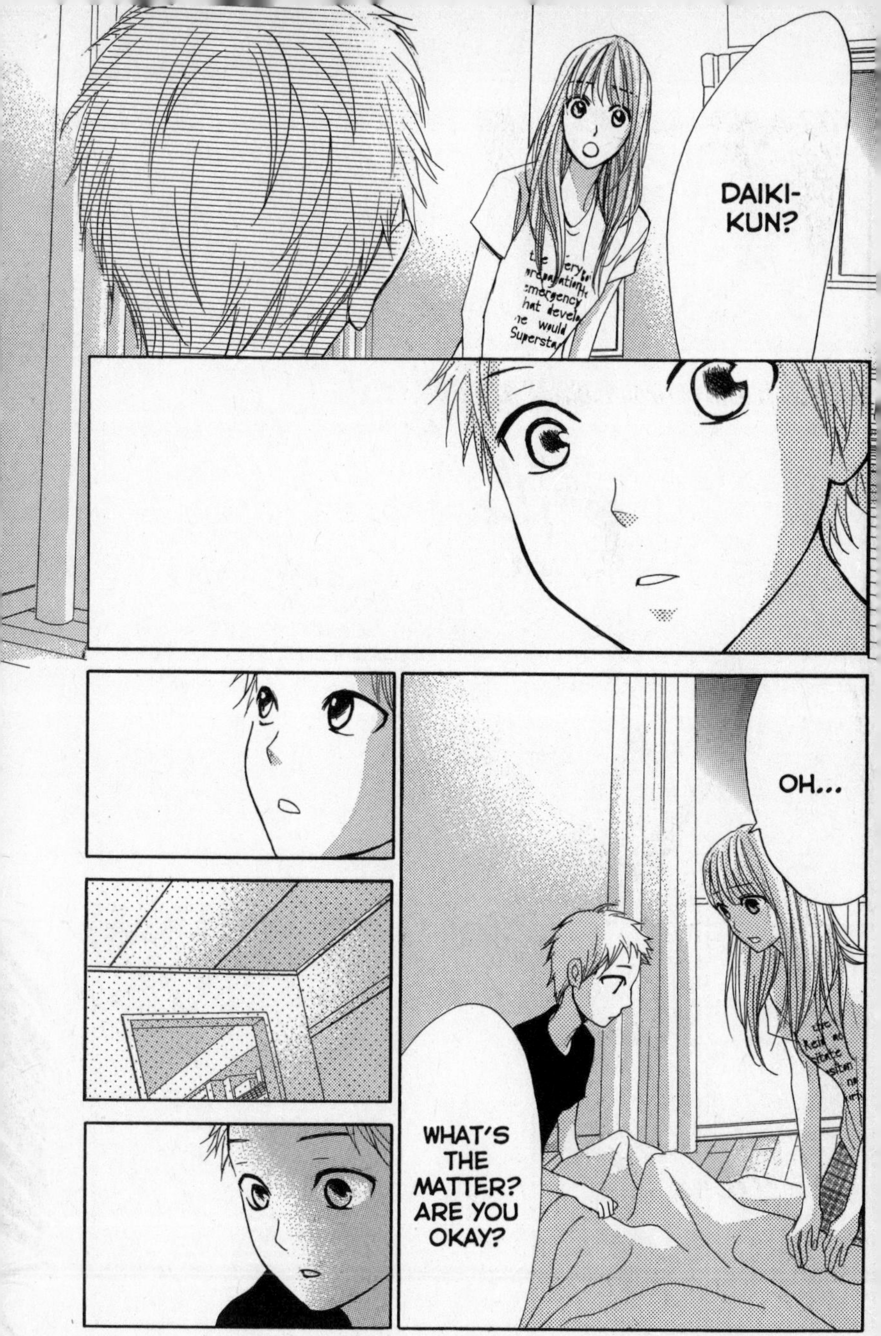
DAIKI-KUN?
OH...
WHAT'S THE MATTER? ARE YOU OKAY?

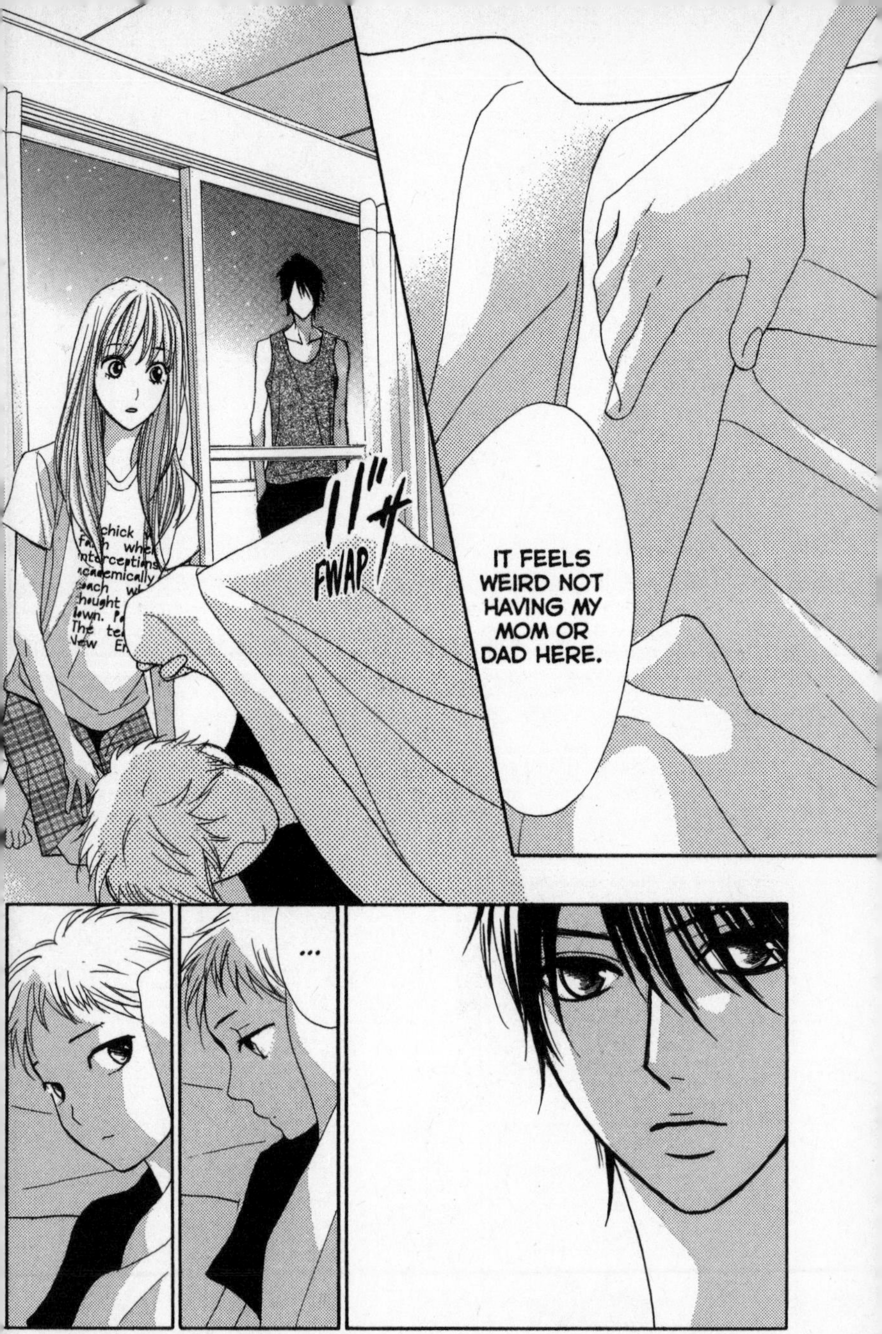
IT FEELS WEIRD NOT HAVING MY MOM OR DAD HERE.
FWAP
...

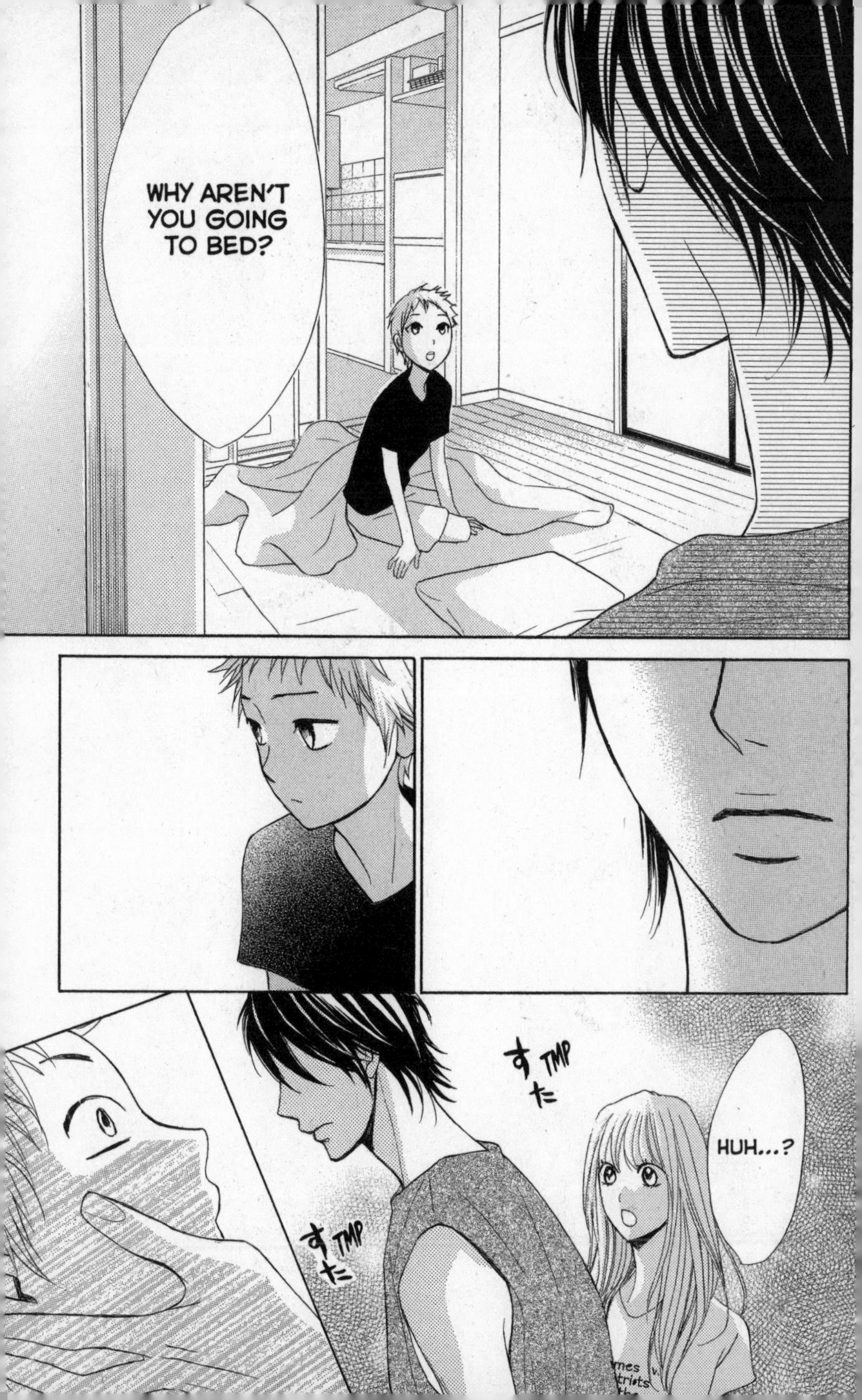
WHY AREN'T YOU GOING TO BED?
HUH...?
すた TMP
すた TMP

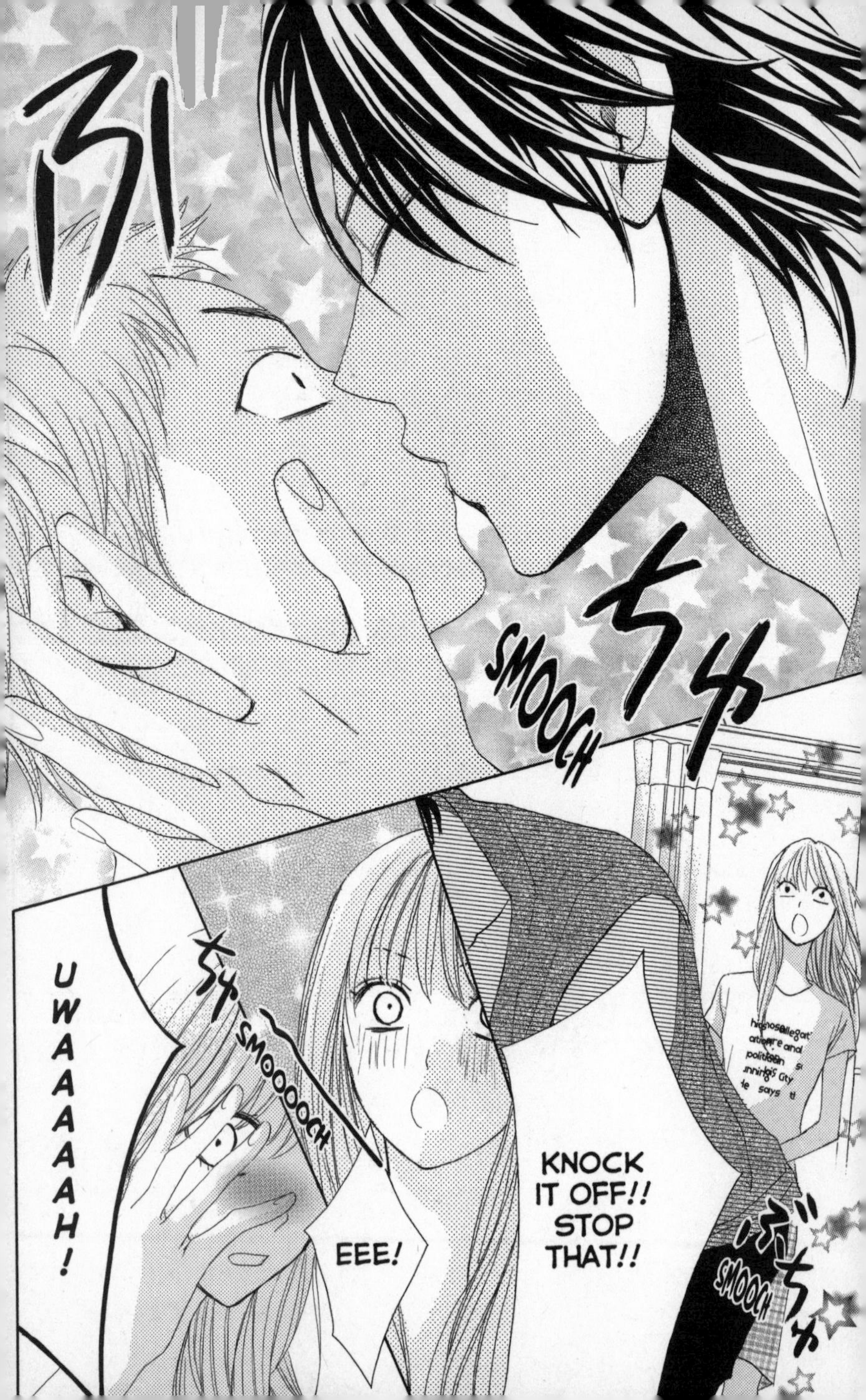

ちゅ
SMOOCH
KNOCK IT OFF!! STOP THAT!!
ぶちゅ
SMOOCH
EEE!
SMOOOOOCH
UWAAAAAAAH!

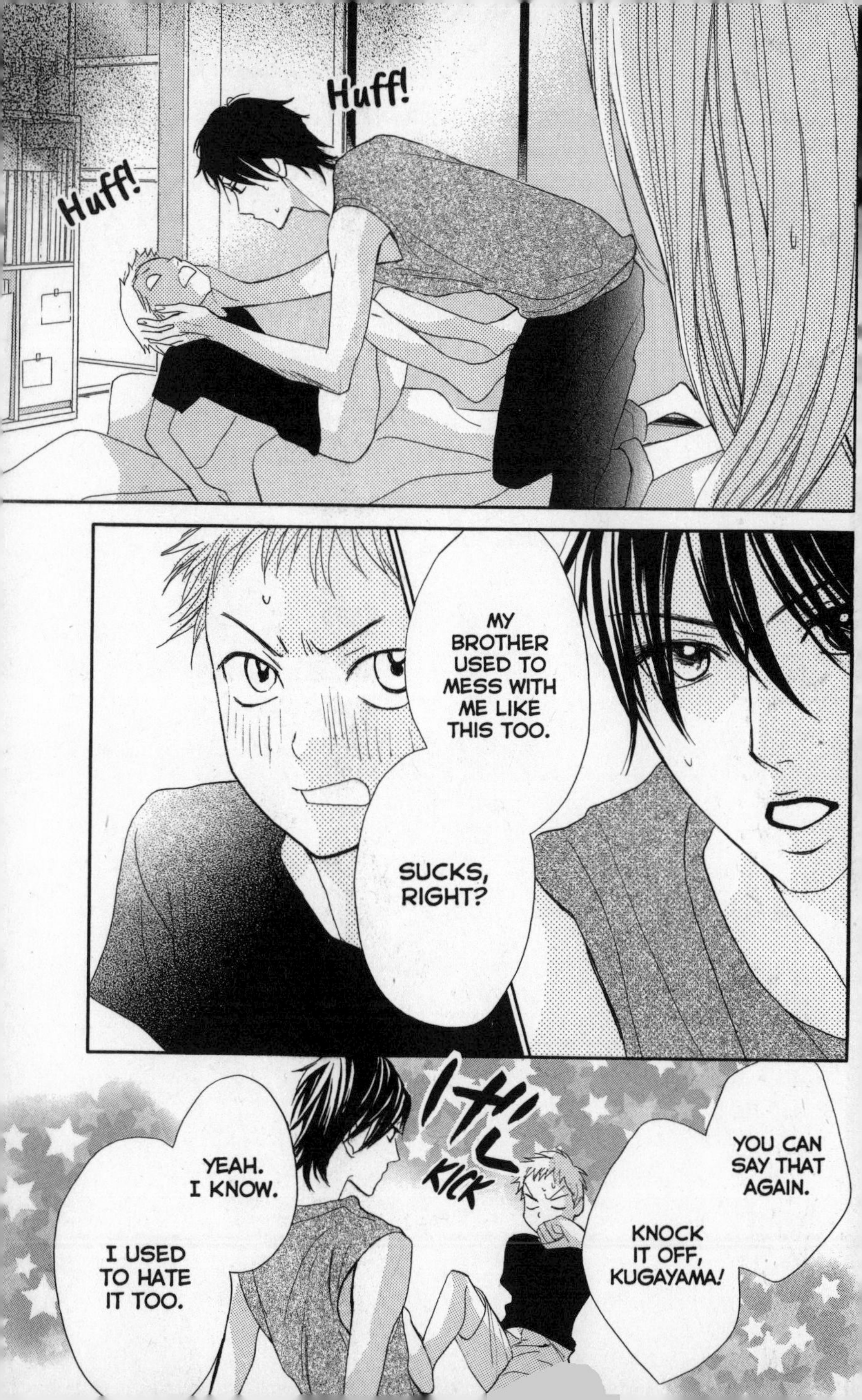
Huff!
Huff!
MY BROTHER USED TO MESS WITH ME LIKE THIS TOO.
SUCKS, RIGHT?
YOU CAN SAY THAT AGAIN.
KNOCK IT OFF, KUGAYAMA!
KICK
YEAH. I KNOW.
I USED TO HATE IT TOO.

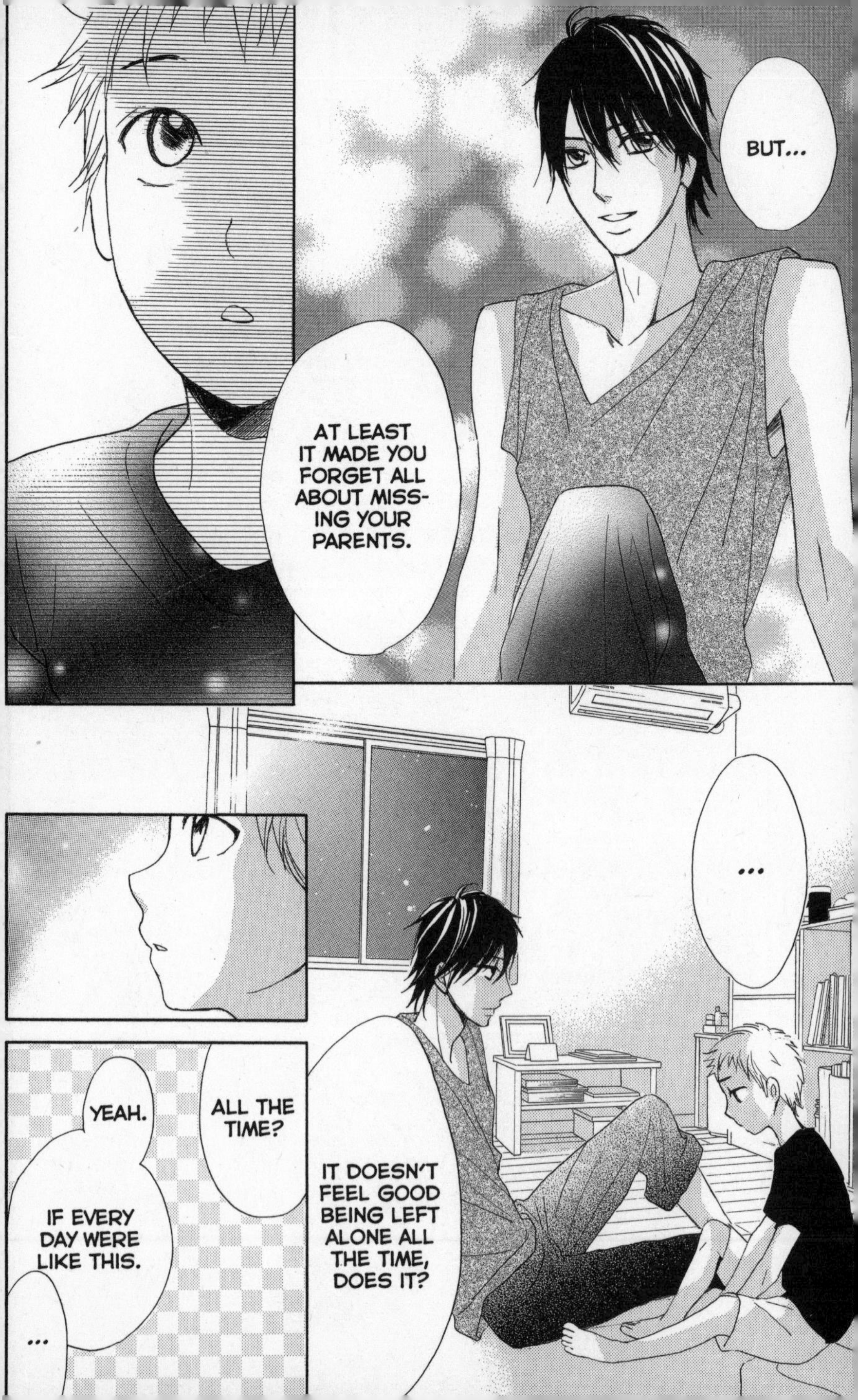
BUT...
AT LEAST IT MADE YOU FORGET ALL ABOUT MISSING YOUR PARENTS.
...
IT DOESN'T FEEL GOOD BEING LEFT ALONE ALL THE TIME, DOES IT?
ALL THE TIME?
YEAH.
IF EVERY DAY WERE LIKE THIS.
...

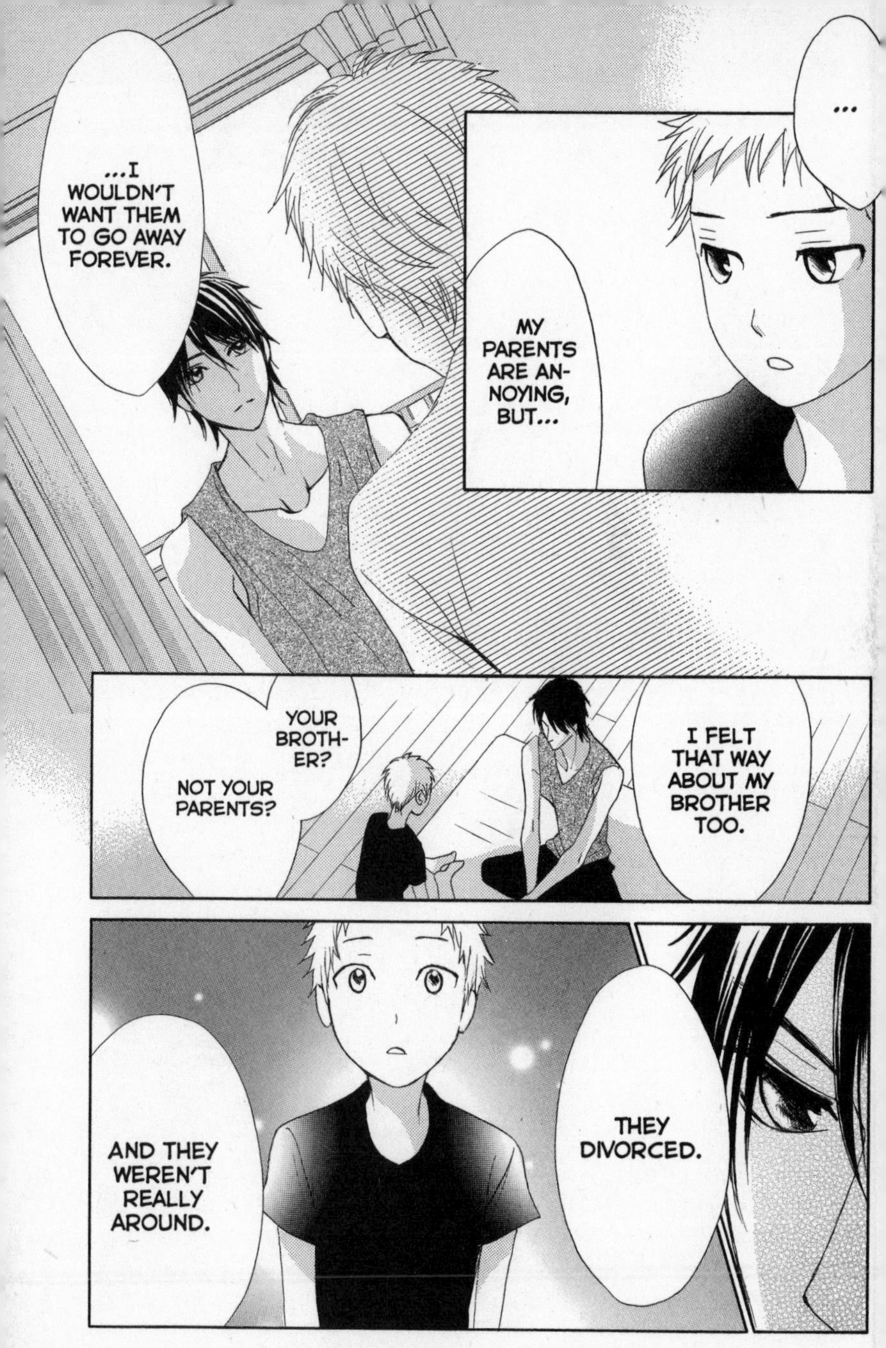
...
MY PARENTS ARE AN- NOYING, BUT...
...I WOULDN'T WANT THEM TO GO AWAY FOREVER.
I FELT THAT WAY ABOUT MY BROTHER TOO.
YOUR BROTH- ER?
NOT YOUR PARENTS?
THEY DIVORCED.
AND THEY WEREN'T REALLY AROUND.

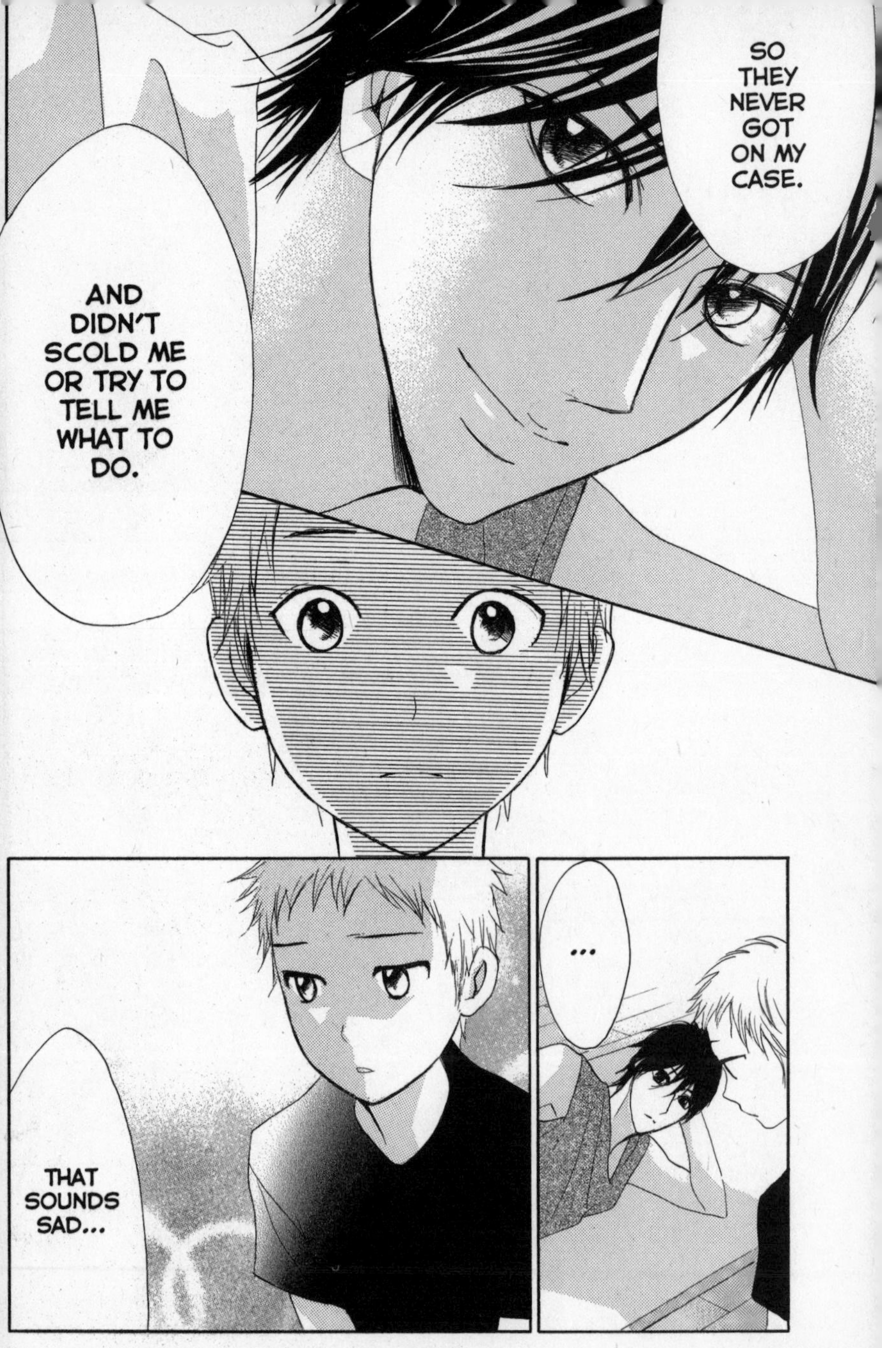
SO THEY NEVER GOT ON MY CASE.
AND DIDN'T SCOLD ME OR TRY TO TELL ME WHAT TO DO.
...
THAT SOUNDS SAD...

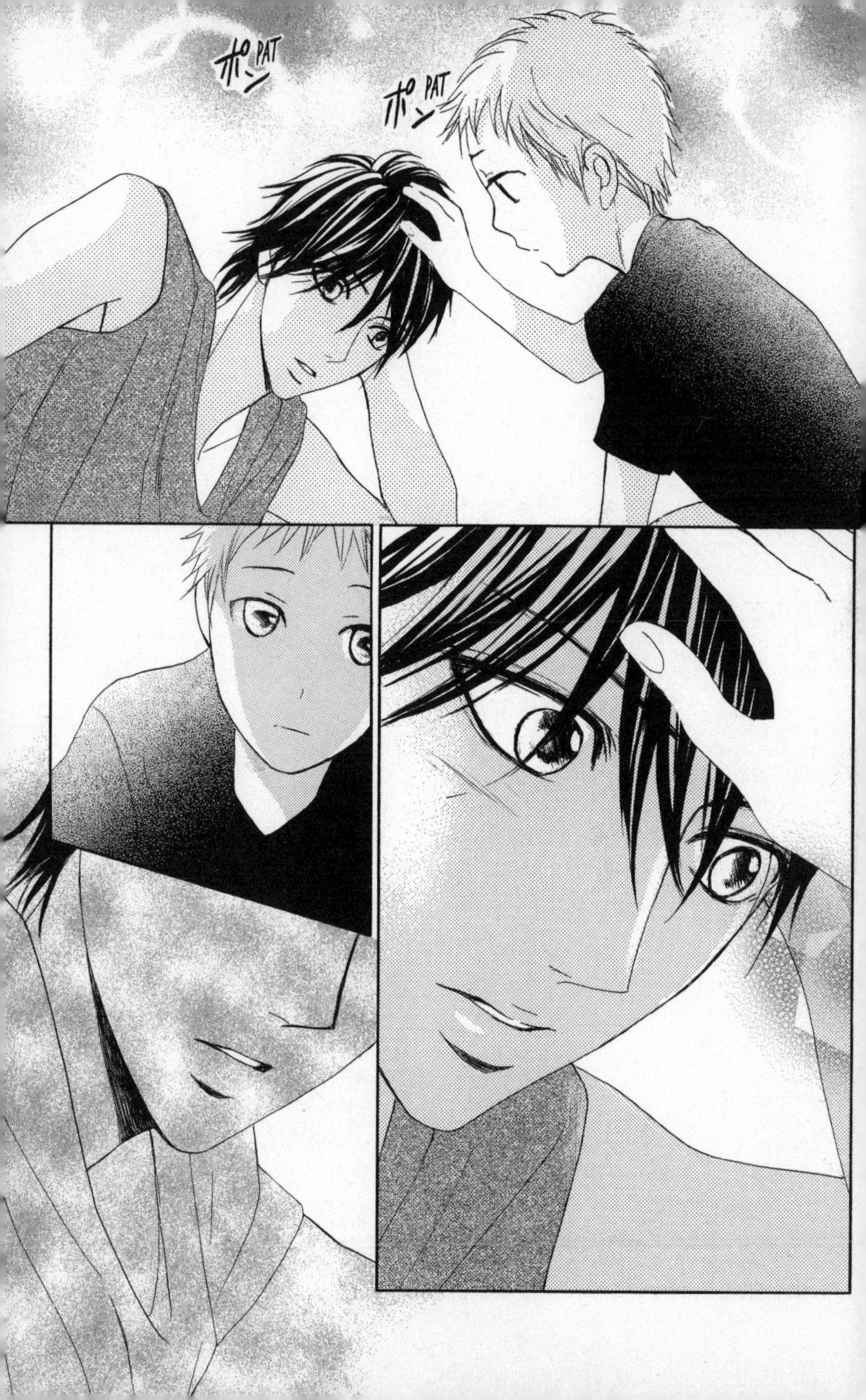
ポン PAT
ポン PAT

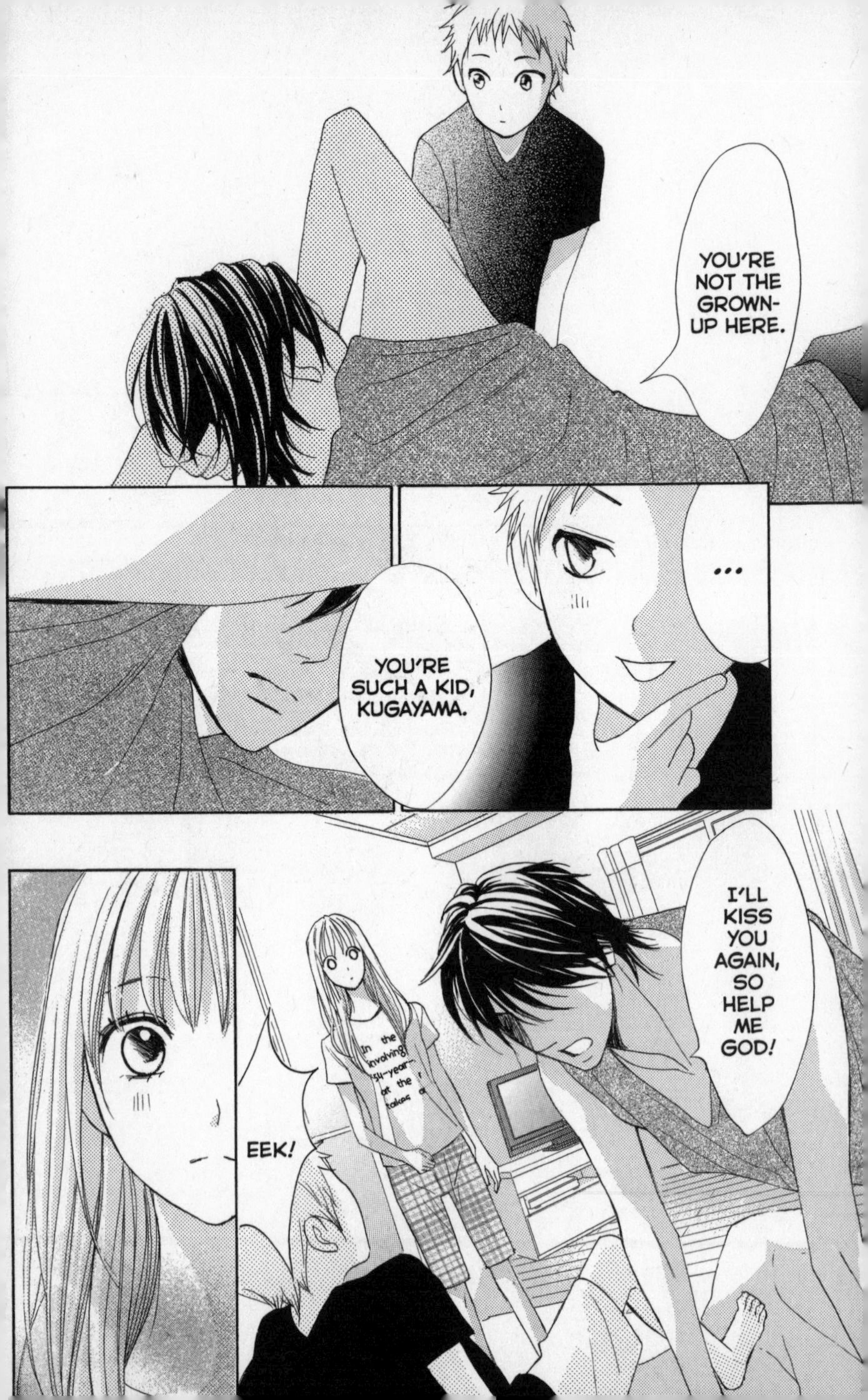
YOU'RE NOT THE GROWN-UP HERE.
...
YOU'RE SUCH A KID, KUGAYAMA.
I'LL KISS YOU AGAIN, SO HELP ME GOD!
EEK!

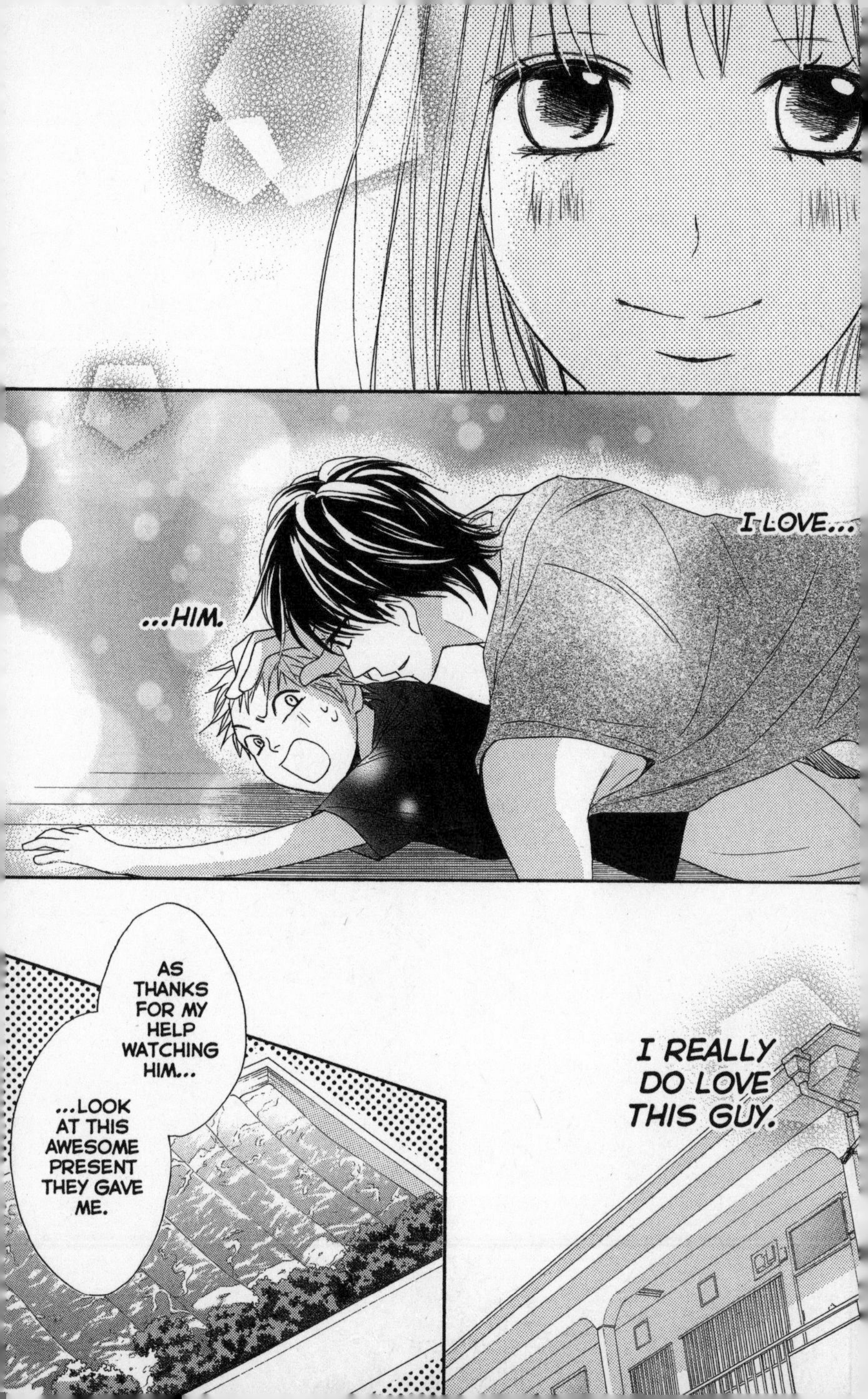
I LOVE...
...HIM.
I REALLY DO LOVE THIS GUY.
AS THANKS FOR MY HELP WATCHING HIM...
...LOOK AT THIS AWESOME PRESENT THEY GAVE ME.

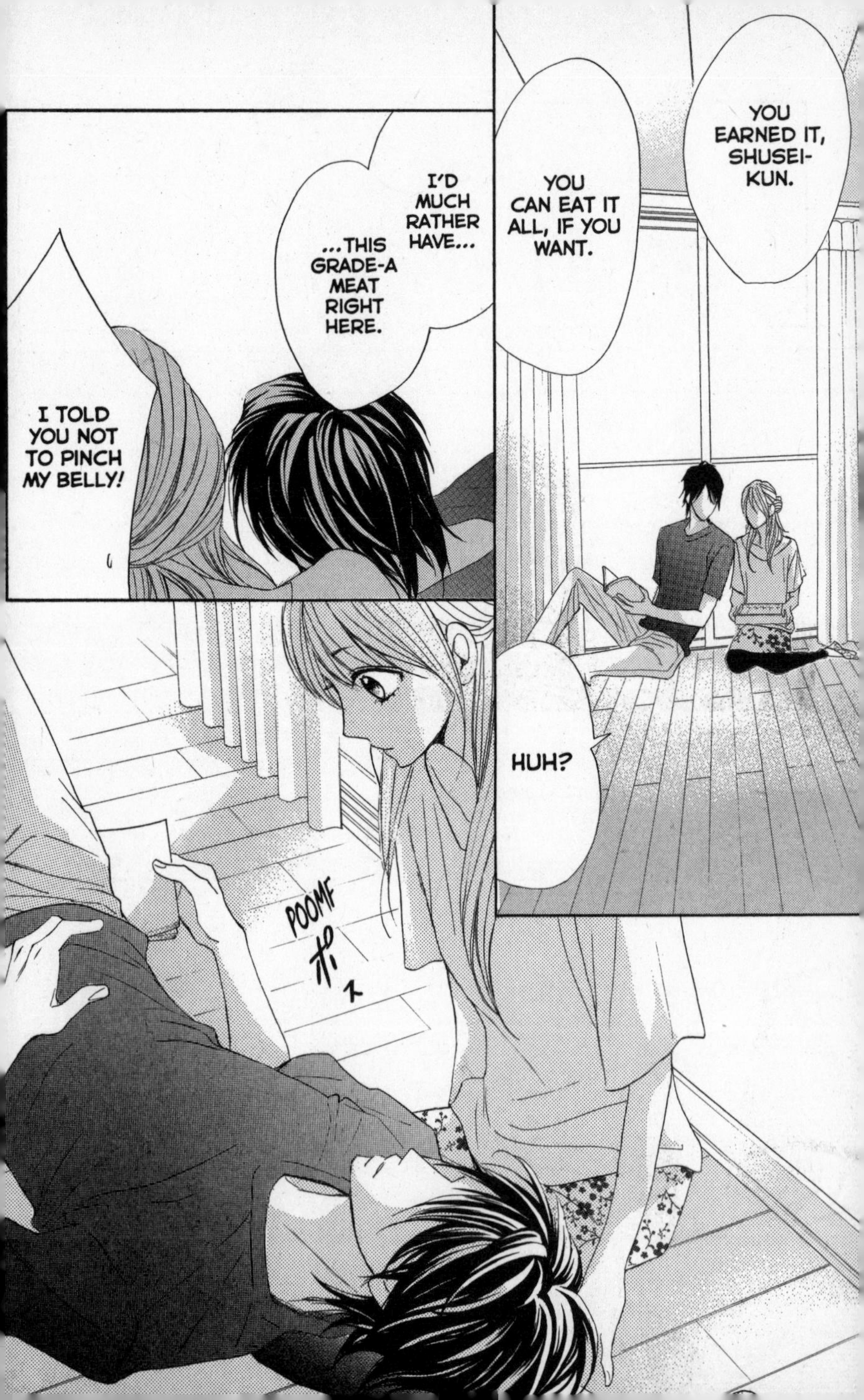
YOU EARNED IT, SHUSEI-KUN.
YOU CAN EAT IT ALL, IF YOU WANT.
HUH?
I'D MUCH RATHER HAVE...
...THIS GRADE-A MEAT RIGHT HERE.
I TOLD YOU NOT TO PINCH MY BELLY!
POOMF
ポス

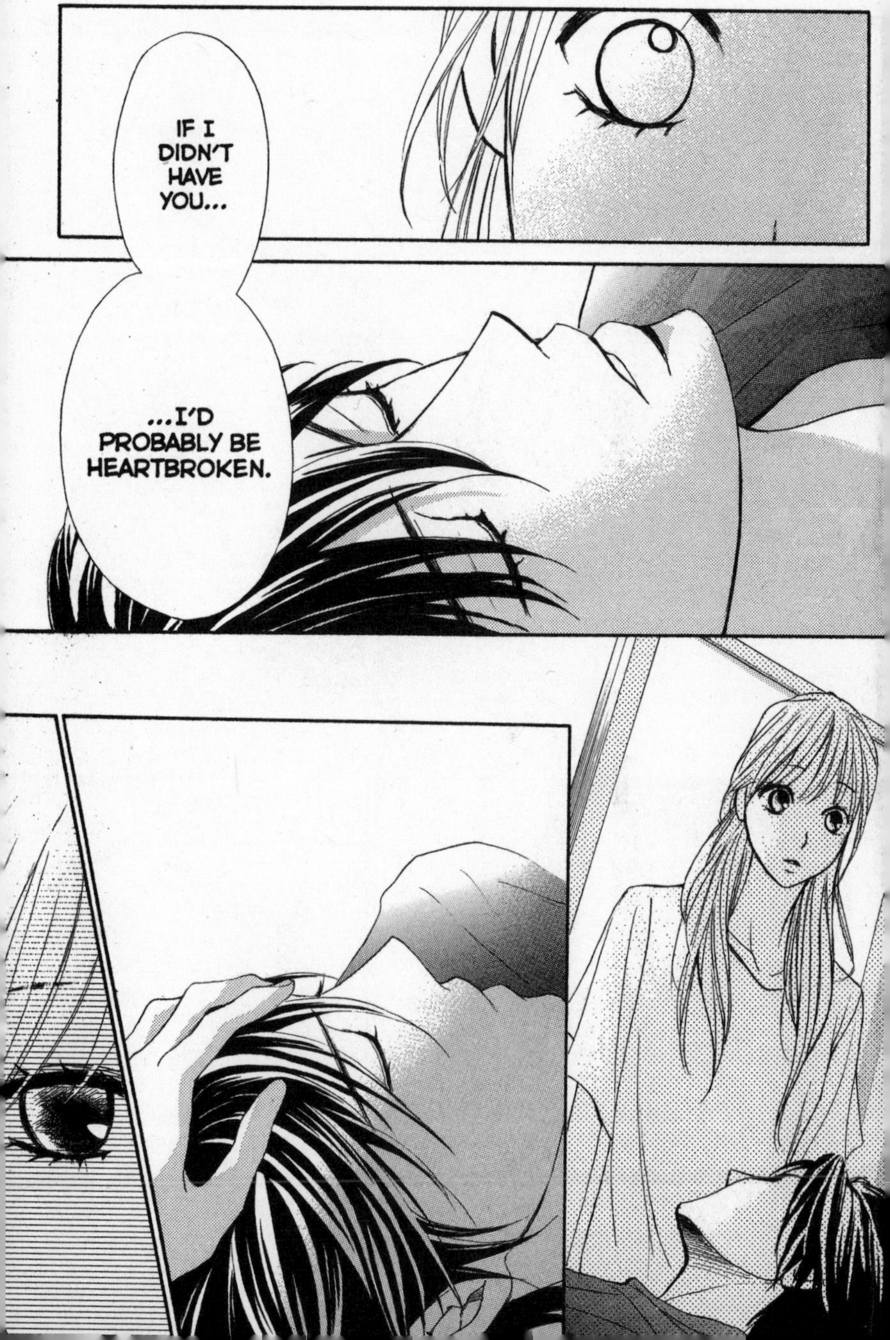
IF I DIDN'T HAVE YOU...
...I'D PROBABLY BE HEARTBROKEN.

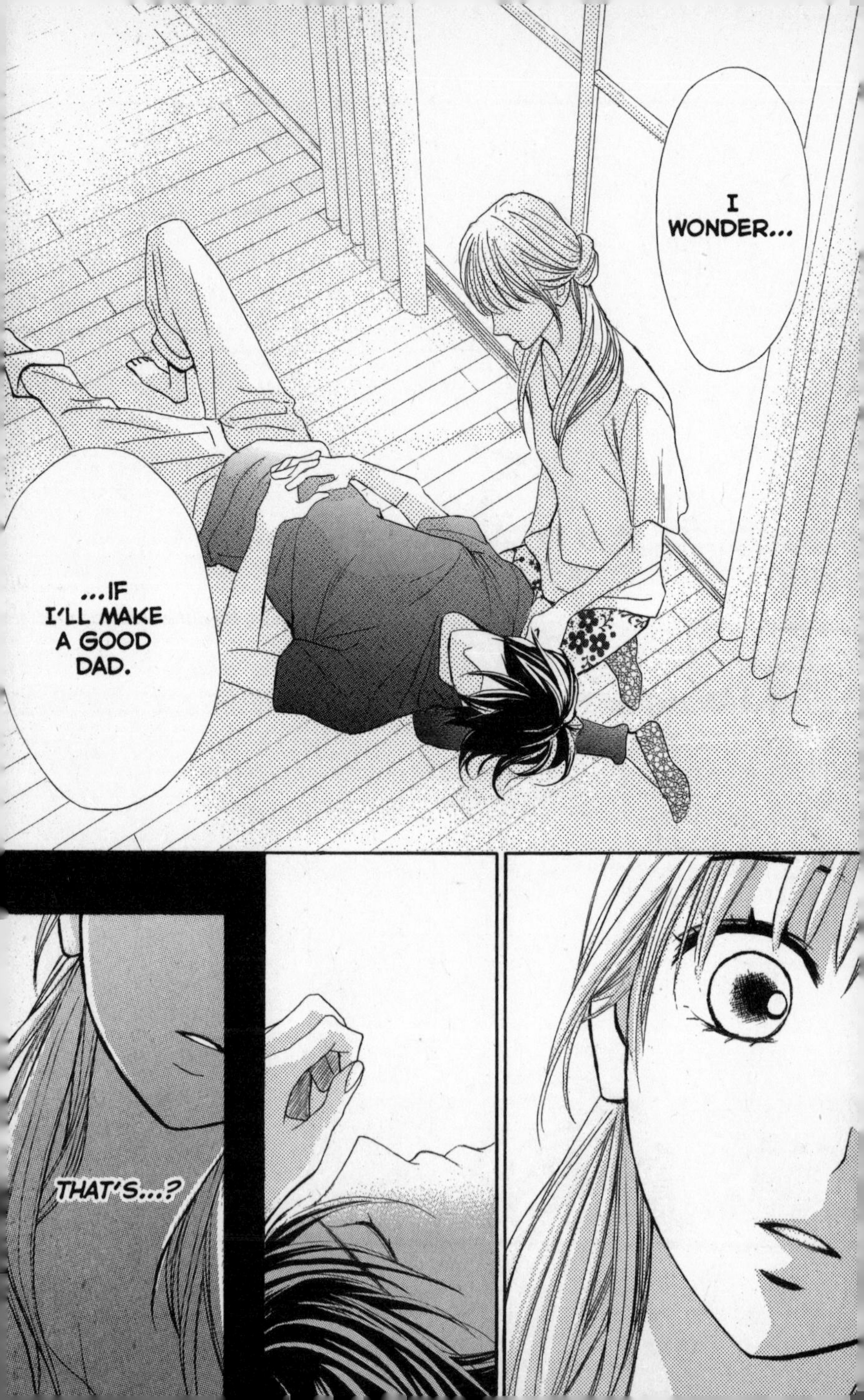
I WONDER...
...IF I'LL MAKE A GOOD DAD.
THAT'S...?

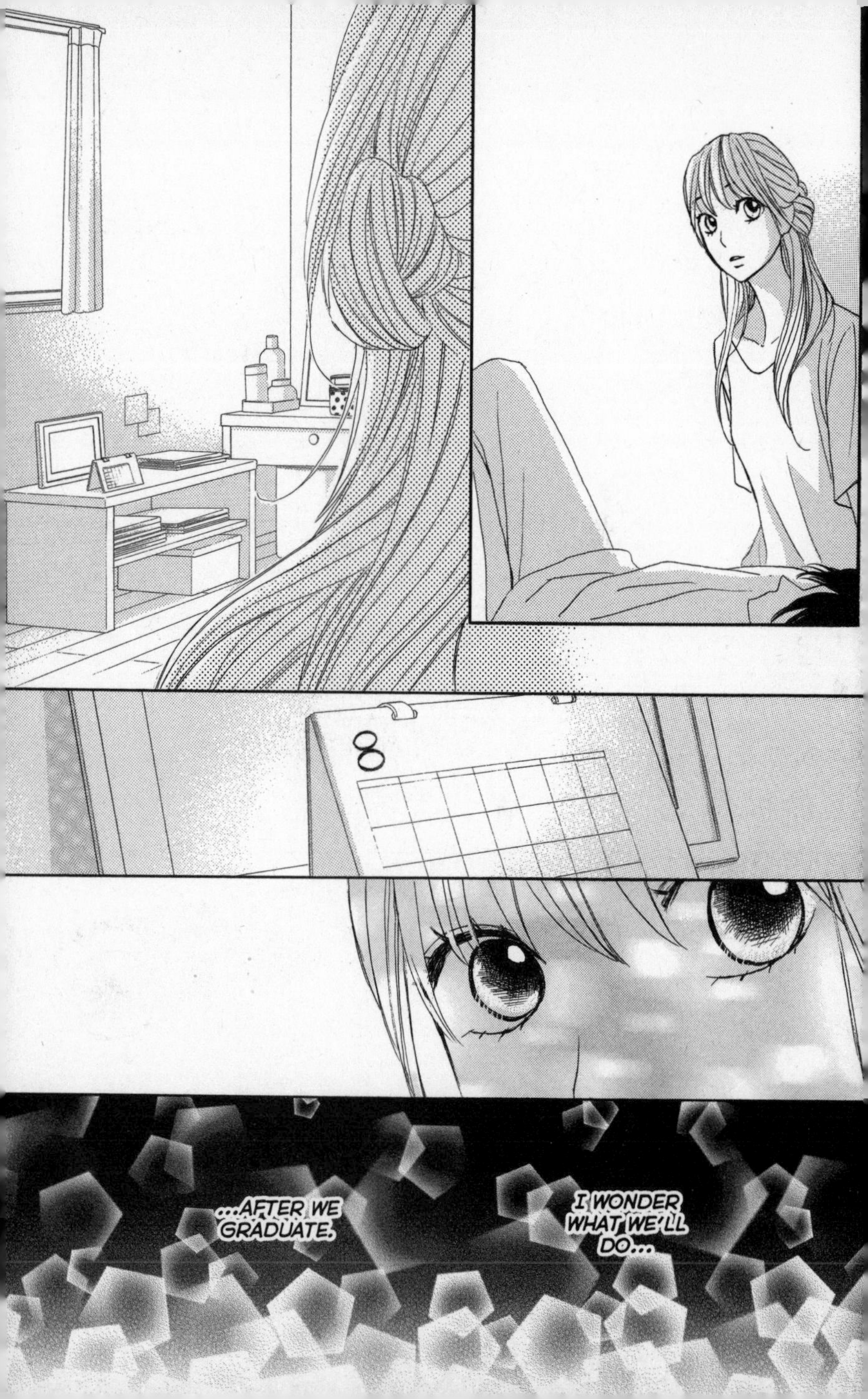
I WONDER WHAT WE'LL DO...
...AFTER WE GRADUATE.

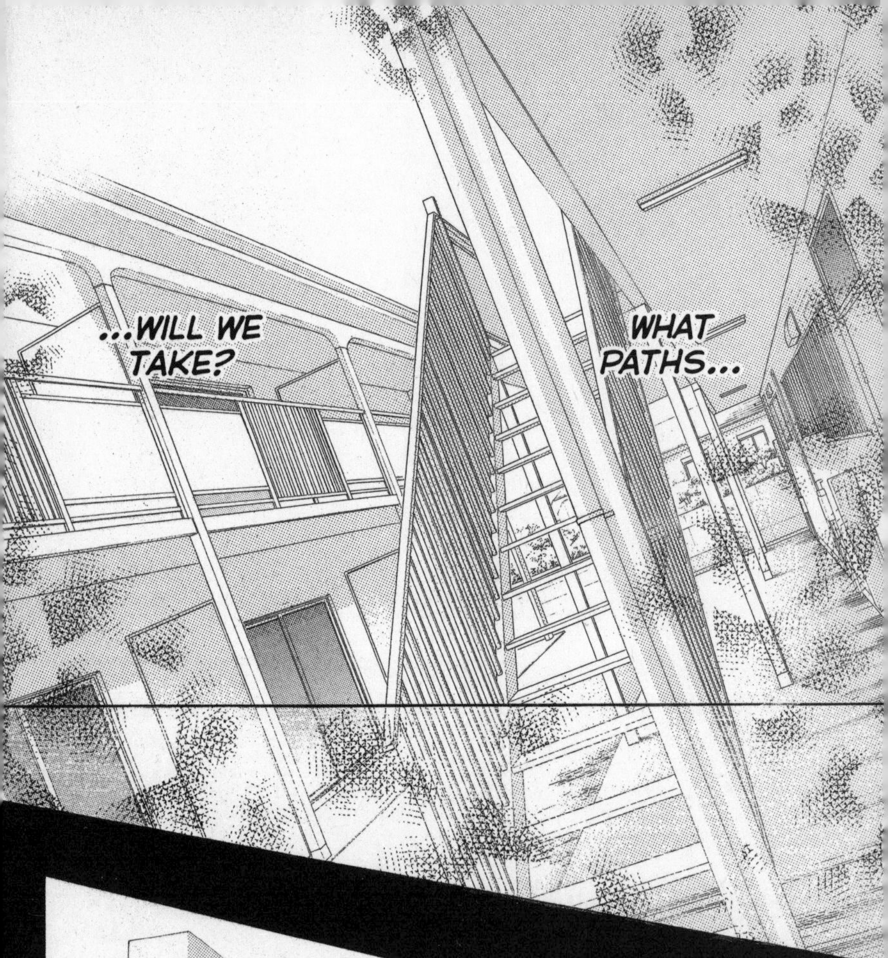
WHAT PATHS...
...WILL WE TAKE?
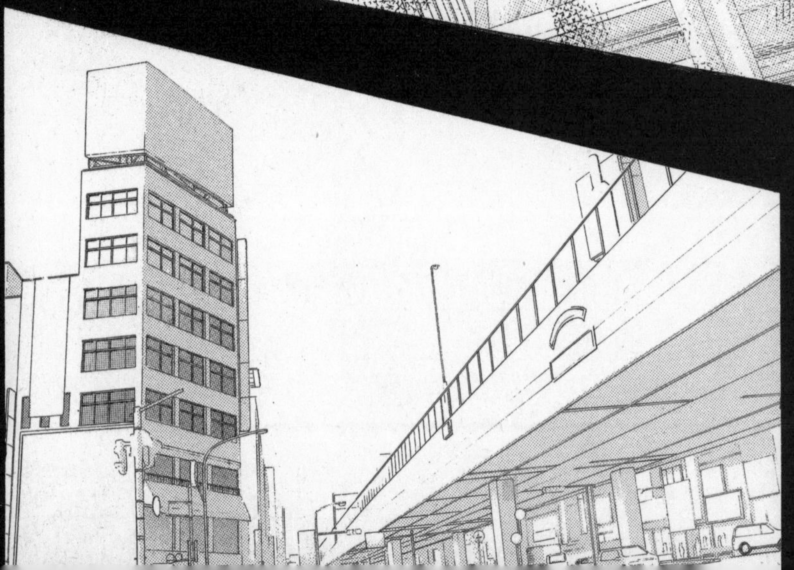

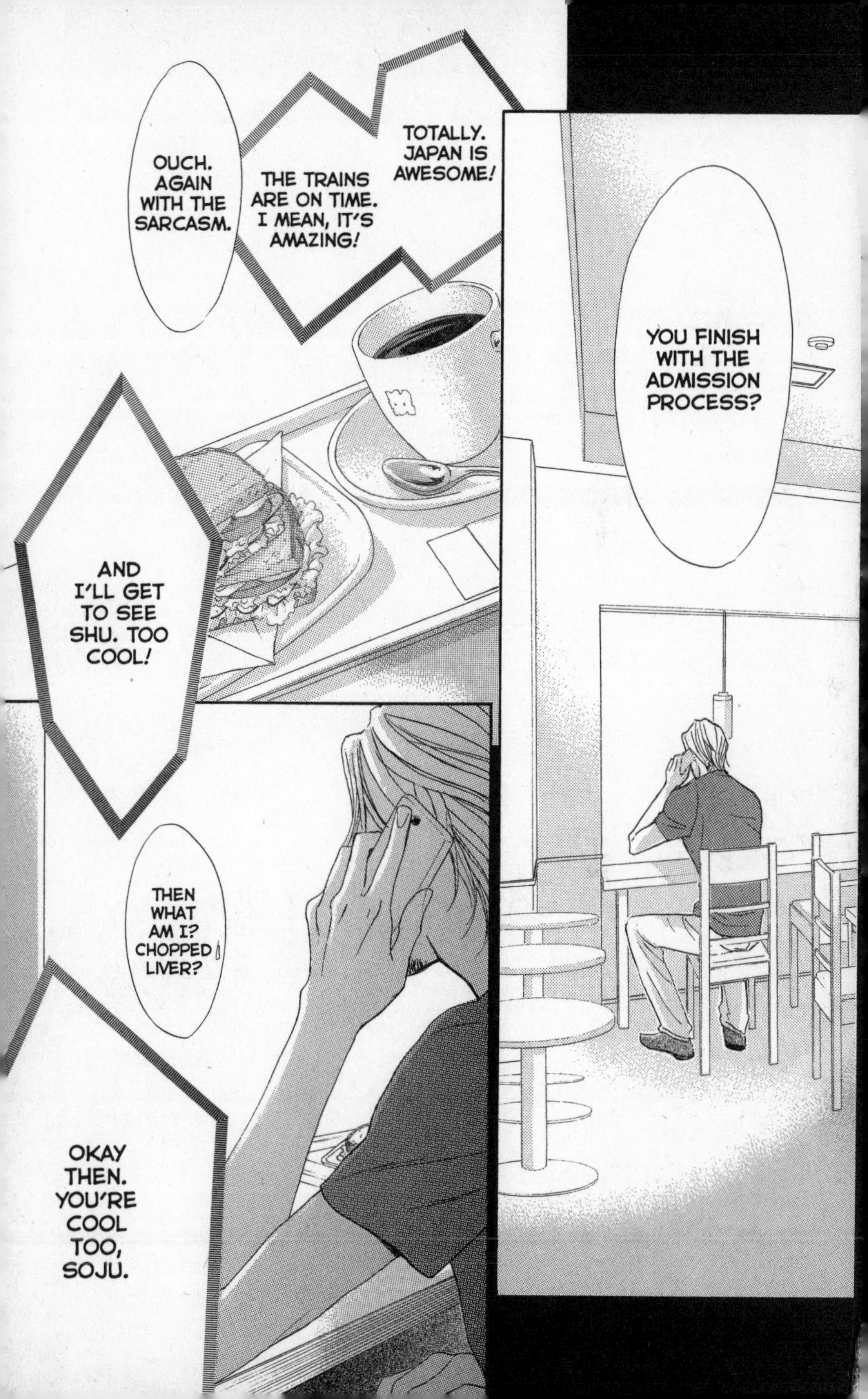
YOU FINISH WITH THE ADMISSION PROCESS?
TOTALLY. JAPAN IS AWESOME!
THE TRAINS ARE ON TIME. I MEAN, IT'S AMAZING!
OUCH. AGAIN WITH THE SARCASM.
AND I'LL GET TO SEE SHU. TOO COOL!
THEN WHAT AM I? CHOPPED LIVER?
OKAY THEN. YOU'RE COOL TOO, SOJU.

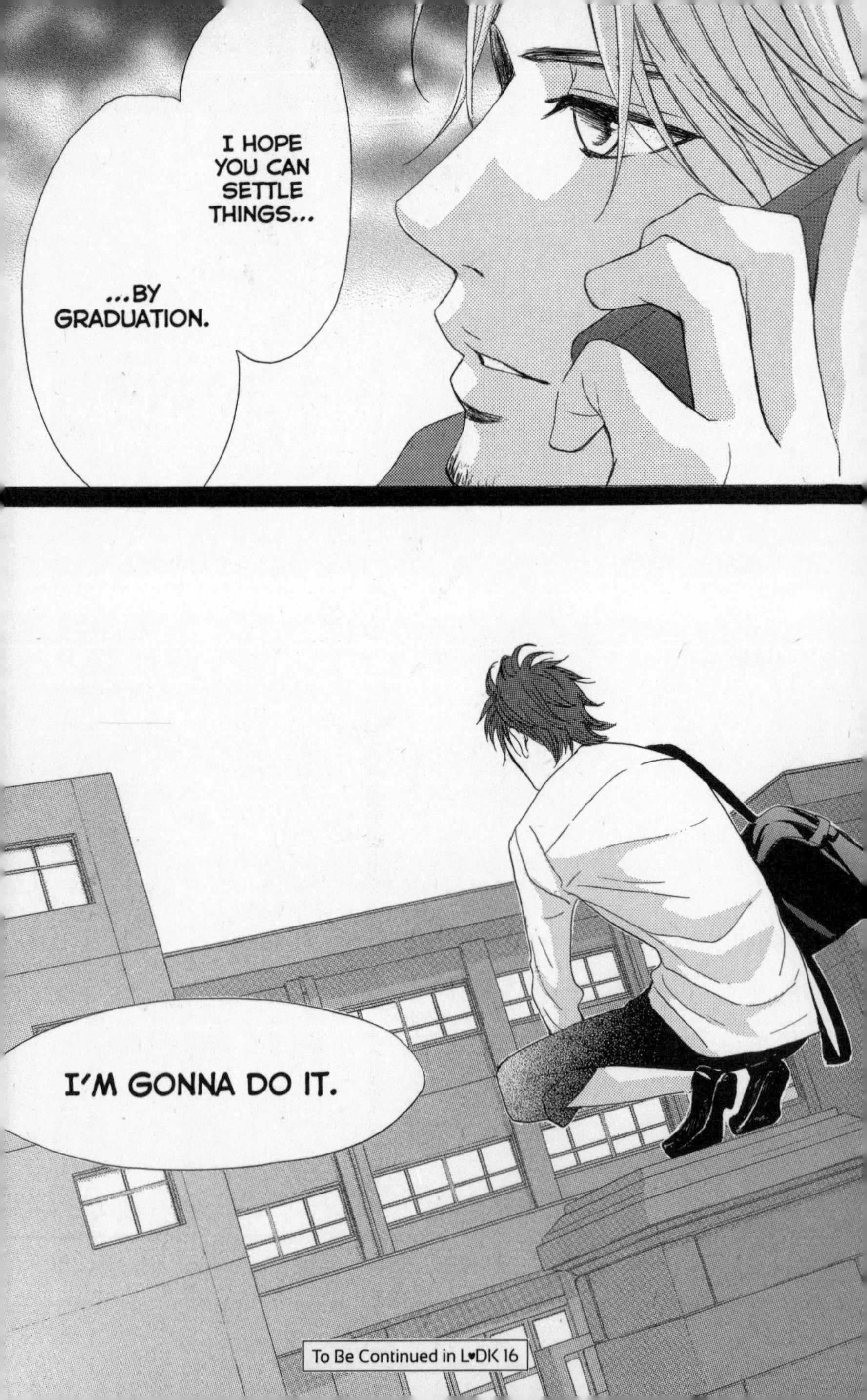
I HOPE YOU CAN SETTLE THINGS...
...BY GRADUATION.
I'M GONNA DO IT.
To Be Continued in L♥DK 16

L♥DK

Hello, everyone. Thank you for picking up volume 15 of L♡DK. And!! Thank you to everyone who took the time to go see the live-action release of L♡DK in theaters!! I was so happy to hear how many people turned out to see it. Since they had time restraints on it, there are some parts of the story that they had to change, but I personally really enjoyed seeing the original scenes they made as well as reenactments of scenes from the story, and every time I saw it, I came away with some new discovery or other. The director, Kawamura-san, screenwriter Matsuda-san, and the entire cast really did a good job portraying the characters. I also really appreciate all the readers who always felt so passionately for the characters. By the way, the title L♡DK stands for "living room, dining room, kitchen" as well as "lovey dovey kiss," "last danshi koukousei," and others. And when I asked readers what they thought of when they saw L♡DK I got a huge response!!
 - LDK (**L**ord, **d**o I **k**now how to love?)
 - LDK (**l**azy, **d**elinquent **k**id)
 - LDK (**l**ove, **d**ang it's **k**ool!)
 - LDK (**L**otte **D**aae **K**intetsu) ← my personal favorite
I like how everyone really pulled out all the stops for this one (LOL). I'm still accepting more, if you have them (LOL)! And with that, I hope to see you in the next volume.

special thanks

K. Hamano   my family   M. Morita

N. Imai   my friends   S. Ryu

Mosuko   Y. Ikumi

A. Hioki   M. Horiuchi

S. Naka

AND YOU

Ayu Watanabe

May 2014